RECOVERING
the WAY

How Ancient Discoveries Help Us
Follow the Footsteps of Jesus Today

BOB ROGNLIEN

Cover Design: Timothy J. Bergren
Book Design: C. J. Darlington
Editor: Robert Neely
ISBN: 978-0-9815247-5-7
Published by GX Books

PRAISE FOR RECOVERING THE WAY

"Bob's life as an archaeologist and teacher of the Bible has uniquely equipped him to help us understand the life of Jesus. His work has significantly helped my understanding of the background and setting of Christ's ministry and mission—something that is so important if we are to be effective as his disciples. And so, I'm sure *Recovering the Way* will help you see things you've seen before with greater depth and intensity, and things you've never seen before with amazing clarity."

Mike Breen, author of *Building a Discipling Culture* and *Family on Mission*

"My faith has been influenced by the scholarship and wisdom of my friend, Bob Rognlien. He is a rare biblical scholar, commanding a wealth of wisdom *and* the ability to convey it in a digestible way. For readers serious about understanding the life of Christ, *Recovering the Way* will be an invaluable resource."

Brian Tome, Senior Pastor of Crossroads Church-Cincinnati and author of *The Five Marks of a Man*

"*Recovering the Way* is an enjoyable and fascinating read, combining historical insights from the time of Jesus with practical encouragement for our lives today. All that Bob has learned and experienced in three decades of leading pilgrims through the land of Israel provide the reader with a rich treasure of biblical instruction, wise application, captivating stories, along with over a hundred beautiful illustrations which help the reader to see the world where Jesus ministered."

Todd Bolen, Professor at The Master's University and Founder of BiblePlaces.com

*I dedicate this book to all the pilgrims who have journeyed with us
in the Footsteps of Jesus over these past three decades.
Thank you for helping me recover the Way.*

ACKNOWLEDGEMENTS

Thanks to my New Testament professors from Princeton Theological Seminary, Dr. Joel Marcus and Dr. James Charlesworth, who first showed me the power of understanding Jesus in his original context. My deepest gratitude goes to the late Dr. Kenneth Bailey and the late Fr. Jerome Murphy-O'Connor who lived and taught New Testament in the Middle East for a combined tenure of nearly a century. I was honored to study under them in Jerusalem and gained so much from their profound insights into the Way of Jesus.

Thanks to the friends and colleagues who helped make this book better: to Matt Switzer and Eric Laverentz for reading and giving feedback on the entire manuscript; to Lisa Bergren for consulting on the format of the book; to Tim Bergren for designing a fantastic cover; to Bobby Rognlien for creating compelling graphics; to Robert Neely for once again making my writing flow more smoothly; to C. J. Darlington for putting all the pieces together in a lovely layout; and to Pam Rognlien for meticulously finding my many mistakes. Special thanks to Leen Ritmeyer for enriching my words with incredible pictures that bring the places to life.

Thanks to the many hundreds of Footsteps of Jesus pilgrims who have hiked with me up the hills, down the wadis, climbed on walls, clambered into cisterns, and picked up potsherds; who have read Scripture in the blazing sun and prayed prayers with sweat and tears in all the places where Jesus did the same. You have taught me more than any book and have truly become family to me and Pam.

Thanks to my kids and grandkids who have patiently endured my long absences while walking the dusty hills of the Holy Land and to my beloved Pamela who has taken so many of those unnumbered steps with me. I could never have hoped for a more faithful partner than you.

And above all, thanks to Jesus for being my Way, Truth, and Life. Following you is the greatest adventure of all!

CONTENTS

INTRODUCTION
JESUS' FOOTSTEPS: FINDING JESUS' WAY

"He is not here, for he has risen, as he said. Come, see the place where he lay." (Matthew 28:6)

STORY: THE FIRST DAY OF THE WEEK

Hurrying through the darkened streets of Jerusalem, Mary of Magdala looked back and could just make out the forms of the other women disciples following her. She sensed the dawning day before she could see it, as a dim light began to emerge as they exited the city walls through the Garden Gate. Mary paused to let the others catch up, calling, "Hurry, we need to be there when the sun comes up!" As they approached the old quarry, long since converted into a garden cemetery, they saw the hulking outline of the rock of Golgotha, the place where the Romans carried out their most gruesome executions. The women shuddered as they hurried past the bloody rock. Mary blinked back the tears pooling in her eyes.

Even in the gray light of the dawning day, there was no mistaking the nearby tomb in which Jesus' body had been laid. It was newly cut in the rock wall of the quarry and fitted with an expensive rolling stone. On Friday afternoon the women had watched carefully as Joseph and Nicodemus pried loose a wedge holding the massive stone back, allowing it to roll down in its carved slot and seal Jesus inside with a dull thud. "Do you still have the spices?" Mary asked Joanna. Joanna held up the expensive package to show Mary that nothing was missing. The men had done their best to anoint Jesus' body for burial, but they were rushed by the setting of the Sabbath sun. Now the female followers of Jesus were determined to honor their Rabbi by finishing the job, regardless of the risks. Mary's eyes strained in the early morning gloom, as she looked for the squad of Roman soldiers who had been dispatched to guard the tomb. She had no idea how they would convince these hardened men to break the seal and roll back the stone, but if there was one thing she had learned from Jesus, it was to trust God for what seemed impossible.

"Where are they?" whispered Salome, her voice betraying the fear she felt at the thought of confronting the soldiers. None of the women answered because the Romans were nowhere to be found. But that was far from the biggest surprise. The women were soon dumbfounded to discover the tomb's stone had already been rolled back.

"Who did this?" gasped Mary the mother of James. Mary Magdalene bent over and looked inside the low doorway. In the growing light of dawn, she could just make out the shelf carved into the wall of the tomb where Jesus' body had been laid. A jolt of shock ran through her body as she realized the shelf was empty, save for a linen burial shroud. Mary let out a cry of horror as she came to the obvious conclusion. "Someone has stolen his body!"

Who was it? Why would they take him? What have they done with his body? These haunting questions swirled as Mary quickly retraced her steps to the home of Mary the mother of John Mark, in order to tell the other disciples what they had seen. The rest of the disciples rubbed sleep from their eyes and tried to comprehend what Mary was saying. "It's a trap," said Thomas, "I'm not going out there!" Finally, John and Peter decided to see for themselves. After running to the tomb, they arrived, crouched down, and went inside. They stared at the empty shelf and the strangely arranged grave cloths. Leaving the tomb (while arguing as usual), Peter and John made their way back to the house, confirming the women's report to the rest of the disciples.

All the women could do now was wait outside the empty tomb and pray. They didn't even have a body to anoint. Mary's head pounded as she leaned against the cool limestone wall of the ancient quarry-turned-cemetery. As the early morning sun started spreading its light in this dark place, she began to weep, great sobs welling up from deep within. *Lord God, who would do such a terrible thing?*

Horrible images flashed through her mind like flickering flames from the watchman's fire: Judas' kiss in Gethsemane. Torches and soldiers. Swords and shouts. Caiaphas tearing his robes. The crowd shouting "crucify him!" Pilate washing his hands. It was like a bad dream that wouldn't end. Mary fought back the sick feeling creeping up from the pit in her stomach. She desperately tried to blot out the excruciating memories of Jesus nailed to that bloody cross, crying out to his Father. It was as if those old familiar demons were trying to claw their way back in.

But something began to stir in Mary. Wiping away her tears, she bent over once again to look inside the rock-cut tomb. And there, on either end of the burial shelf, sat two angelic messengers. Mary fell to her knees in terror, then heard the divine messengers: "Do not be afraid, for I know that you seek Jesus who was crucified. He is not here, for he has risen, as he said. Come, see the place where he lay." In her shock, these angelic words were simply too much for her to comprehend.

Stumbling out of the tomb, overwhelmed and confused, Mary found the cemetery caretaker standing there and pleaded, "Sir, if you have carried him away, tell me where you have laid him, and I will take him away." But in response, Jesus' voice cut through the jumbled maze in her heart and mind, suddenly making sense of it all. "Mary." She blinked, hardly able to believe what she heard. *Could it really be him? It is him!* She turned and said to him in Aramaic, "Rabboni!" (which means Teacher). Suddenly an unspeakable tidal wave of joy washed over her, filling the bottomless pit of despair in her soul!

Falling at Jesus' feet she clung to him, as did the other women, weeping still but now for joy. *I will never let go of him. I will never let go!* Jesus said to her, "Do not cling to me, for I have not yet ascended to the Father; but go to my brothers and say to them, 'I am ascending to my Father and your Father, to my God and your God.'" And then he was gone! Talking excitedly among themselves, the women hurried back arm in arm into the walled city and through the streets to the upper room. Mary Magdalene burst through the outer door into the courtyard and announced to the disciples, "I have seen the Lord!"[1]

THE POWER OF PILGRIMAGE

What drew Mary and the other women back to the tomb where Jesus had been buried? Ostensibly it was to finish the job of anointing his body for burial, but something deeper was happening. It is a powerful experience to return to the places where transforming events have transpired. It can renew or deepen the impact of those transformational moments in our lives. The women went to the tomb that morning because they needed to see the place where Jesus had died and been buried. They needed to

1 The Introduction and Epilogue of this book open with a dramatized account of a biblical passage, with details added to fill out the story and illustrate the historical and cultural context. While some of these details are speculative, most are taken directly from archaeological data, historical sources, and cultural insights.

touch the stones and anoint his body. They needed to convince themselves it was not just a bad dream. And there they received the angel's invitation to "Come, see the place where he lay." They wanted closure, but they got so much more.

I remember the first time I visited Jerusalem in January 1986. As a twenty-one-year-old, I was meeting my best friend Stephen to spend a month doing research in the Holy Land for my history thesis. I arrived at night and somehow managed to find my way through the narrow, winding streets of the walled Old City to the guest house where I was staying. Like the women followers of Jesus, I was awake before dawn, so I decided to take a short hike across the Kidron Valley to the top of the Mount of Olives. From an ancient Jewish cemetery, I watched the first light illuminate Jerusalem's skyline as it gradually spread out before me. It took my breath away. The City of David! The Temple of Solomon! The place of Jesus' crucifixion and resurrection! Jesus' ascension and the outpouring of the Holy Spirit! I had come for historical research but had no idea the personal impact this journey would have on me.

A pilgrimage is a journey to places where people have encountered God in order to share in that encounter once again. When the women went to the tomb, they expected an opportunity to anoint Jesus' body and mourn, but the angels told them to look at that empty burial shelf and encounter the risen Jesus. That is exactly what happened, and they were forever changed! Ever since the women made that first pilgrimage, followers of Jesus have returned to the places where he lived and carried out his mission in order to encounter him in new ways. For over thirty years now I have been drawn back again and again to visit and study the places of Jesus' life, death, and resurrection in order to understand and experience more fully the significance of Jesus and the singular life he lived.

My wife Pam and I and our newborn son lived in the Old City of Jerusalem for an academic year while I studied New Testament archaeology there. Since then I have led over thirty trips to the Holy Land to follow in the footsteps of Jesus. We are very clear that our trips are not "tours," because we are not tourists and are not sightseeing. We are Christian pilgrims practicing the ancient spiritual discipline of pilgrimage by visiting, praying, and worshiping in historically verifiable places where Jesus carried out his mission. This rare privilege has certainly brought us greater historical and cultural understanding of Jesus, and it has also provided countless opportunities to encounter the living Jesus in fresh and powerful ways. That is why we keep going back and taking people with us. Although we lead five or six of these two-week trips every year, we never tire of it because it is such a privilege to help people experience life-changing encounters in these historical places!

Let me be clear; as enlightening and transforming as a pilgrimage in the footsteps of Jesus can be, it would be heresy and idolatry to suggest you must travel to Israel to encounter God. Jesus told the disciples he would make his home inside of those who trust and follow him. When Jesus died the curtain enclosing the Holy of Holies in the Temple was torn in two. God made it clear he is not confined to a building in Jerusalem but will inhabit the lives

AUTHOR AND SON ON THE TEMPLE MOUNT

of his people wherever they live. Jesus' resurrection from the dead made the way for the Holy Spirit to be poured out on all his followers. Jesus is not confined to one place on planet earth; he is always everywhere through the power of the Spirit. Jesus is just as real and present in your home, family, and neighborhood right now as he is in Jerusalem or Galilee! Jesus told Thomas, who believed because he saw, *"Blessed are those who have not seen and yet have believed."* (John 20:29) Encountering him is not dependent on your ability to travel to the places where he carried out his mission; it is determined by your willingness to open yourself to his presence and respond in faith to his Word and the prompting of his Spirit.

Having said that, I will also say great value is found in pilgrimage that illuminates the Gospel accounts as we thoughtfully and prayerfully visit the significant sites of Jesus' life. I am writing to share those insights with you. This book is an invitation to come with me on a virtual pilgrimage in the footsteps of Jesus in order to encounter him afresh and learn more fully the Way and the Truth and the Life he embodied here on earth. Whether you have ever been to the Holy Land or ever plan to go, as you open yourself to the Jesus who is real and present to you wherever you are and respond to him in faith, I am confident you will encounter him on the pilgrimage laid out in these pages.

OUR PILGRIM GUIDE

A very adventurous friend of mine was traveling in Europe and on a whim decided to take a three-day side trip to Israel. He arrived with no specific knowledge of the country. After three days of exploration, he came away with some wonderful stories to tell, but because he had no guide he missed much of what a more informed pilgrimage could have offered. I don't recommend this approach.

Starting in the fourth century, when followers of Jesus from other parts of the world began to make pilgrimages to the land of Jesus, pilgrims have recorded their experiences in journals that became guides for those who followed. It helps to have a trustworthy guide! Although we will be drawing on rich historical, cultural, archaeological, and geographical sources as well as my own experience, our primary guide on this pilgrimage will be the four eyewitness accounts of Jesus' life, death, and resurrection which have been preserved for us in the biblical books of Matthew, Mark, Luke, and John.

My elder son Robert works as a producer and director, designing and broadcasting professional gaming tournaments around the world. They record these events and stream them online using numerous cameras shooting from multiple angles in order to capture a more complete picture of the complex scene of teams, screens, and spectators in the arena. Their job is to mix the various shots into a seamless whole that invites the online viewers into the excitement of the tournament as if they were there in person.

It is no accident that the Bible contains four separate accounts of Jesus' life, each one with its own distinct perspective, to give us a more complete view of Jesus' remarkable life. There is great value in reading and studying each Gospel on its own and understanding that particular account of Jesus in the historical and cultural context of its author. However, on our pilgrimage the various "camera angles" of the four Gospels will be our guide. We will bring these perspectives together in order to enter more fully into the sweep of Jesus' life as if we were actually there.

As we read the four Gospels and seek to form an accurate chronology of Jesus' life, we quickly come face to face with the fact that the authors were not necessarily concerned with putting together a strictly linear account of the events and his teachings. In many ways they read more like the script of a postmodern film with flashbacks and flash forwards that can make the timeline difficult to discern. Initially the teaching and events of Jesus' life were recounted from memory by those who were with Jesus, as part of the regular gatherings of the earliest generations of his followers. This made perfect sense in a primarily oral culture where writing was a specialized skill and written accounts were very laborious and expensive to copy.

Even today Middle Eastern people love to recount long and complex stories from memory. I remember years ago sitting on a rooftop in Jerusalem one night with a group of young Palestinian Christians and being amazed that they could recite epic poems that were ten or fifteen minutes long from memory! This was the storytelling culture of the earliest followers of Jesus. However, as the years went by, it became apparent that these oral accounts of the eyewitnesses needed to be written down while they were still alive to ensure these records would continue to be transmitted accurately to future generations.

Naturally each Gospel writer presented the events and teachings of Jesus in a way that would be most helpful for their community. Papias, Bishop of Hierapolis in the early second century, explains the writing of Mark's Gospel this way, "Mark, having become the interpreter of Peter, wrote down accurately whatsoever he remembered. It was not, however, in exact order that he related the sayings or deeds of Christ. For he neither heard the Lord nor accompanied Him. But afterwards, as I said, he accompanied Peter, who accommodated his instructions to the necessities of his hearers, but with no intention of giving a regular narrative of the Lord's sayings."[2] As we read each Gospel carefully we begin to notice similarly unique approaches of each writer.

The Gospel of Mark, the shortest of the four biblical accounts of Jesus' life, focuses for the first eight chapters on Jesus' identity and the second eight chapters on Jesus' ultimate destiny. John Mark's writing has an immediacy that reads like a mystery novel building to a climactic revelation. On the other hand, Matthew groups Jesus' teachings

[2] *Ante-Nicene Fathers*, Vol. 1., ed. A. Roberts, J. Donaldson, and A. Cleveland Coxe, (Buffalo, NY, Christian Literature Publishing, 1885), Fragments of Papias, Chapter VI, Digital.

into five major discourses, like the five books of the Jewish Law, framing Jesus as the Prophet like Moses who was foretold in the book of Deuteronomy. The Gospel of Matthew seems to be aimed at the Jewish community as it highlights the many ways Jesus fulfills Old Testament prophecy. John's Gospel begins with a carefully crafted prologue modeled after the creation story in Genesis 1, brilliantly blending this with key phrases from Greek philosophers, reflecting his context as a church leader in Ephesus, one of the leading cities of the Greco-Roman world. Written later than the other Gospels, John's account is more theologically developed and offers commentary on the meaning of Jesus' teachings and actions.

Luke, a Gentile physician who was part of Paul's team on his second and third missional journeys as well as his journey to Rome, is the only Gospel writer who demonstrates a deliberate concern for chronology. He explained his research methodology among the eyewitnesses in this dedication to his literary patron: *Inasmuch as many have undertaken to compile a narrative of the things that have been accomplished among us, just as those who from the beginning were eyewitnesses and ministers of the word have delivered them to us, it seemed good to me also, having followed all things closely for some time past, to write an orderly account for you, most excellent Theophilus, that you may have certainty concerning the things you have been taught.* (Luke 1:1-4) As we combine the different Gospel accounts into our pilgrimage guide, we will look to Luke's *"orderly account"* to help us discern a chronological framework of Jesus' life and mission as it unfolds.

LEARNING TO FOLLOW THE WAY OF JESUS

Everyone seems to be interested in Jesus; Jews, Muslims, Buddhists, Hindus, agnostics, and atheists. This is not only because Jesus is considered by so many the greatest spiritual and ethical teacher of all time, but also because his way of life embodied that amazing teaching so completely. The integrity of Jesus' life is such that, whether they believe the claims Jesus made or the claims made about him in the Gospels, people of integrity are compelled to respect and admire the life he lived.

Mahatma Gandhi, the great Hindu leader of India, described him this way, "Jesus Christ … was certainly the highest example of one who wished to give everything, asking nothing in return, and not caring what creed might happen to be professed by the recipient. I am sure that if he were living here now among men, he would bless the lives of many who perhaps have never even heard his name, if only their lives embodied the virtues of which he was a living example on earth; the virtues of loving one's neighbour as oneself and of doing good and charitable works among one's fellowmen. What, then, does Jesus mean to me? To me, he was one of the greatest teachers humanity has ever had. To his believers, he was God's only begotten Son. Could the fact that I do or do not accept this belief make Jesus have any more or less influence in my life? Is all the grandeur of his teaching and of his doctrine to be forbidden to me? I cannot believe so."[3]

In keeping with this perspective, many assume Christianity is a religion that calls its adherents to strive to live up to the moral teachings of Jesus and so gain God's acceptance, much as Muslims strive to live up to the teachings of Muhammad to enter paradise or Buddhists strive to live up to the teachings of Buddha to attain nirvana. While in various times and places throughout history the movement of Jesus has devolved into this kind of moralistic religion, this is a fundamental misunderstanding of what he came to establish.

The reason the accounts of Jesus' life are called "Gospels" is that Jesus' teaching and example convey the Good News that we are loved and accepted by God first, before we have done anything to earn or deserve his favor. This gracious acceptance by God is what Jesus referred to as the "New Covenant," which he ultimately established through his own death and resurrection. As we accept this gift of grace by faith and begin to live in a Covenantal relationship with God through Jesus, then comes the call to participate in what Jesus called the "Kingdom of God." In his model prayer, Jesus defined the Kingdom as God's will being done on earth as it is in heaven. The Kingdom of God is nothing less than heaven breaking into earth! This Kingdom life is not something we accomplish through our own moral effort but is the supernatural outcome of living in Covenant with God—something the Holy Spirit accomplishes through us, much like good fruit is the natural outcome of a branch that is deeply connected to a grapevine.

Once we see both the Covenantal and the Kingdom aspects of Jesus' teaching and life, we begin to understand what Jesus' call to discipleship entails.[4] Jesus invites us to live by grace in a Covenantal relationship with him through faith that will produce in us

3 Mahatma Gandhi, "What Jesus Means to Me," *The Modern Review*, Ramananda Chatterjee, ed. (Calcutta, India, Prabasi Press Limited, 1941), 406, Digital.

4 See Mike Breen, *Covenant and Kingdom* (Pawleys Island, SC, 3DM Publishing, 2010).

more of the Kingdom life he lived here on earth. Jesus told his followers that he came that they might *"have life and have it abundantly."* (John 10:10) Jesus defined that abundant life when he said, *"I am the way, and the truth, and the life."* (John 14:6) Many of us have focused almost exclusively on the *Truth* of Jesus, but simply studying the teaching of Jesus and understanding the person of Jesus is not discipleship. We are also called to actually *do* the things Jesus did in his *Life* here on earth. However, when we try to go from the *Truth* of Jesus directly to the *Life* of Jesus we tend to fall into one of these fatal mistakes:

The Truth of Jesus + Trying to Live the Life of Jesus = Legalism

When we study the *Truth* of Jesus and then apply self-discipline to try and live the *Life* of Jesus by our own moral effort, we fall into the age-old trap of legalism. Saul of Tarsus, Martin Luther, and countless others have pursued this path only to discover it is a crushing dead end. This is the way of the Pharisees who received Jesus' most stinging rebuke. Another approach is:

The Truth of Jesus + Falling Short of the Life of Jesus = Condemnation

When we study the *Truth* of Jesus, but then through trial and error find that the *Life* of Jesus seems impossibly out of our reach, we can slip into self-condemnation. Those who are painfully aware how far short they fall in living up to Jesus' example often end up living in constant guilt or get caught in a cycle of confession and forgiveness that does not move them forward. This was the experience of those branded "sinners" by the Pharisees. Perhaps the most common approach is:

The Truth of Jesus + Giving Up on the Life of Jesus = Apathy

Some of us comfort ourselves with theological interpretations that eliminate the challenge of measuring our life by Jesus' *Life*. We attribute the things Jesus did that seem out of our reach to his divinity and conclude we were never meant to do those things. The result is the apathy of accepting that being nice and fulfilling reasonable religious expectations is enough. This was the self-justification of the Sadducees.

To avoid these timeless traps, it is critical for us to recognize that proclamation of the *Truth* Jesus taught also came with an invitation to learn a *Way* of life with him. This is what Jesus meant when he gave the invitation, *"Follow me."* Learning to follow the *Way* of Jesus, combined with understanding and trusting the *Truth* of Jesus, is what ultimately empowered his followers to live the *Life* he modeled for them. The existential theologian Soren Kierkegaard expressed this connection between Jesus' *Way* and *Truth* when he wrote, "Christ is the truth inasmuch as he is the way. He who does not follow in the way also abandons the truth. We possess Christ's truth only by imitating him, not by speculating about him."[5] There was a distinct pattern and rhythm to the *Life* Jesus lived. This is the *Way* of Jesus we are called to imitate. When we trust the *Truth* of God's grace and accept Jesus' invitation to imitate his *Way*, the *Life* of Jesus supernaturally begins to grow in us and spread to others. We can express this as a simple spiritual equation:

The Way of Jesus + The Truth of Jesus = The Life of Jesus

This simple insight has literally transformed my life as a Christian. Being a disciple of Jesus is coming to trust the *Truth* of Jesus and learning to follow the *Way* of Jesus, so the *Life* of Jesus grows in us and flows through us to others. We can't do this by trying harder or working at it more diligently in our own strength. Trusting the *Truth* of Jesus' grace sets us free from condemnation and fuels a genuine desire to learn his *Way* and live his *Life*. The *Life* of Jesus only grows in us as we surrender to him and exercise the faith he gives us one step at a time. A year after I wrote this, I discovered that my hero Eugene Peterson had the very same thought over a decade earlier! He wrote, "We can't suppress the Jesus way in order to sell the Jesus truth. The Jesus way and the Jesus truth must be congruent. Only when the Jesus way is organically joined with the Jesus truth do we get the Jesus life."[6]

However, the problem that often confronts us in connecting Jesus' *Way* to his *Truth* is the fact that we are separated from that *Way* by twenty centuries of history and live in vastly different cultural contexts. Our vision of the *Truth* and the *Way* of Jesus is often clouded by our own cultural presuppositions that keep us from living and passing on that *Life*. This book seeks to peel off those presuppositions and gain a more accurate,

[5] Soren Kierkegaard, *Training in Christianity*, trans. Walter Lowrie, ed. J. Thornton and S. Varenne (Princeton, NJ, Princeton Univ. Press, 1944).

[6] Eugene H. Peterson, *The Jesus Way: A Conversation on the Ways That Jesus Is the Way* (Grand Rapids, MI, Eerdmans Publishing, 2017). Digital, Kindle Locations 103-104.

first-century view of the Jesus we meet in the Gospels. We will follow Jesus' life from birth to resurrection as presented to us in the four Gospels. Each chapter is comprised of three different sections:

The Way: Digs into biblical sites, ancient texts, archaeological finds, cultural analysis, and historical perspectives that illuminate the way Jesus actually lived.

The Truth: Explores several Gospel texts in the light of these insights to bring greater clarity on the meaning of Jesus' life.

The Life: Reflects on what all this might mean for our way of life today.

I invite you to join me on a spiritual pilgrimage as we go with Mary Magdalene, the other disciples of Jesus, and all the witnesses of the resurrection to answer the angel's invitation to "come and see." As we learn a more accurate understanding of the *Way* of Jesus which illuminates the *Truth* of Jesus, we will be empowered to live out more of the extraordinary *Life* of Jesus. Let's begin this adventure!

PART I

JESUS' WORLD:
THE FIFTH GOSPEL

Jesus prayed: "They are not of the world, just as I am not of the world. Sanctify them in the truth; your word is truth. As you sent me into the world, so I have sent them into the world."
(John 17:16-18)

HEROD'S PALACE IN JERICHO

CHAPTER ONE

ROMANS AND HERODIANS: THE POWER BROKERS

Jesus said to them, "Render to Caesar the things that are Caesar's, and to God the things that are God's."
(Mark 12:17)

TEXT AND CONTEXT

Every text has a context. If we read the text separate from its context, we are liable to misunderstand its meaning. It is like the child who prays, "Our Father, who does art in Heaven, how didja know my name? Give us this steak and jelly bread and forgive us our mattresses. Lead a snot into temptation and deliver us from email. Amen!" Too often when we read the Gospels, we recognize the words but miss much of their meaning because we don't understand the context.

Sometimes the context is *geographical*. When you have walked up the Kidron Valley into the Old City of Jerusalem, you understand why the Bible always describes the pilgrim's journey as *"going up to Jerusalem."* (Matthew 20:17)

Sometimes context is *archeological*. When you have stood on the excavated Herodian street and looked up at the massive stones that form the retaining walls of the Temple Mount, you understand why the disciples stood there and said to Jesus, *"Look, Teacher, what wonderful stones and what wonderful buildings!"* (Mark 13:1)

Sometimes context is *historical*. When you read about the political tightrope the Jewish religious leaders constantly had to navigate between the Romans, the Herodians, and the people of the land, you understand why the High Priest Caiaphas said, *"it is better for you that one man should die for the people, not that the whole nation should perish."* (John 11:50)

Sometimes context is *cultural*. When you walk the narrow streets of Jerusalem and see that in Middle Eastern culture people of prominence don't hurry in public, you understand what a lavish act of grace it was in Jesus' parable when the father disregarded his neighbors' disdain and ran through the village to embrace the returning prodigal son (Luke 15:20).

But understanding the cultural context of the Bible can be elusive when you are formed by a different culture. I remember when we were living in Jerusalem when our son Bobby was just a toddler. We were walking from Bethany up the eastern slope of the Mount of Olives back toward our small apartment in the Old City. As we passed by a simple home, a little boy of similar age played on the front step. His parents stood in the doorway behind him and invited us in for a cup of coffee.

Knowing it would be rude to refuse, we accepted the unexpected invitation and sat down on their couch. Assuming a natural posture for my culture, I crossed my legs as our generous hosts served us coffee. To my chagrin I later learned that the typical Western habit of crossing your legs is considered very rude in Middle Eastern culture, because feet are considered the most unclean part of your body. Extending your foot toward someone is taken as an insult. Thankfully our hosts overlooked my cultural faux pas, but I nonetheless learned a lesson in how subtle cultural differences can be.

When we read biblical texts without the benefit of historical and cultural insights, we can easily misunderstand their intended meaning. The longer this misinterpretation continues, the harder it is to read the text as it was originally intended. Dr. Ken Bailey, who lived and taught the New Testament in the Middle East for over forty years, said it this way: "The more familiar we are with a biblical story, the more difficult it is to view it outside of the way it has always been understood. And the longer imprecision in the tradition remains unchallenged, the deeper it comes embedded in Christian consciousness."[7]

---

[7] Kenneth Bailey, *Jesus Through Mediterranean Eyes* (Downers Grove, IL, 2008), 25, Digital. I am deeply indebted to the work of Dr. Bailey, with whom I was privileged to become friends when we lived in Jerusalem. Dr. Bailey taught New Testament in Egypt, Beirut, Jerusalem, and Cyprus for over 40 years and has taught me much of what I know about the cultural context of the Gospels. I am also grateful for the privilege of studying for a year under Jerome-Murphy O'Connor at the *École biblique et archéologique française de Jérusalem*. Dr. Murphy-O'Connor lived in Jerusalem and taught New Testament from a cultural and archaeological perspective for over 45 years. Both have recently passed away, leaving a great legacy of learning and insight behind them.

READING THE FIFTH GOSPEL

It is an incredible gift that we have four eyewitness accounts of Jesus' incomparable life! If we are going to gain all that is offered to us in this gift, we must learn to read these powerful texts in their own contexts and then bring them together into a comprehensible account. If the four Gospels are like four camera angles that need to be edited together to get the most accurate and complete view of Jesus' story, then the land of Israel, the history of the time, the cultures of those who lived there, and the discoveries that have been made since that time are like the sound stage, the backdrops, the sets, and the minor characters surrounding these cameras.

Those who visit the land of the Bible sometimes refer to this background information as "the fifth gospel" and learn to read it along with the four biblical Gospels. This term does not indicate that we are trying to add anything to the revelation of Scripture, but instead that we are seeking a fuller and more accurate understanding of what has already been revealed to us.

In Part I of this book, we are going to start reading the fifth gospel by examining six key groups from Jesus' World in three pairs: the Romans and Herodians, the Sadducees and Pharisees, and the Essenes and Zealots. As we meet them, I want to encourage you to put yourself into the world we describe. Although this world is separated from ours by twenty centuries and great cultural differences, it is inhabited by people who are remarkably like us, with the same kind of hopes, dreams, fears, and longings. The more we get to know the world Jesus inhabited and enter into that world, the more closely we will learn to follow the *Way* of Jesus, and the more clearly we will understand the *Truth* of Jesus, which in turn will lead us to live the *Life* of Jesus more fully.

 # THE WAY

THE ROMANS: REIGNING CONQUERORS

Since ancient times the world has been dominated by superpowers. The history of the Bible is intertwined with powerful kings and nations who attacked, invaded, and occupied the land of Canaan, a tiny strip of land connecting Egypt and North Africa to the Tigris and Euphrates valleys to the northeast, and the Anatolian Plateau to the northwest.

This is the strip of land God promised to Abraham, that Joshua invaded, and that the tribes of Israel settled. Because of its strategic significance as the bridge between Africa, Asia, and Europe, the ancient superpowers of these regions have fought over this land for millennia. Sadly, it continues today.

The biblical people of Israel suffered under the oppression of a succession of neighboring superpowers: the Egyptians, the Assyrians, the Babylonians, the Persians, and the Greeks, among others. In 63 BC the Romans became the next to invade the land of Israel, as General Pompey wrested control from the Jewish Hasmoneans. Jesus was born, and the entire New Testament was written, under the occupation of the Roman army in the provinces that Rome referred to as Judea and Galilee, later combined into Syrian Palestine.

Under Julius Caesar in the first century BC, the democratic ideals of the Roman Republic gave way to the imperialism of the Roman Empire. With this imperialism came astonishing territorial conquest and wealth. Caesar's adopted son Octavian continued that aggressive expansion and firmly established his rule across the Empire, eventually taking the name Caesar Augustus and the title *divi filius,* or "son of a God." By the time of Jesus' birth, the Romans had built a far-flung empire knit together by carefully developed networks of roads, bridges, shipping lanes, and ports. The primary strategy of this rapidly expanding Empire was to conquer a territory, colonize it, improve the infrastructure, promote the economy, and tax the people, ultimately directing revenues and commerce back to Rome.

In the conquered lands closer to Rome, they tended to rule the population directly with Roman Governors supported by occupying troops. As the Empire grew larger, the distances became impractical for direct control, so Rome established client rulers who pledged their allegiance to Caesar, promising to enforce Roman policy and deliver large annual tax payments to Rome. By this strategy Roman Emperors and their vassal rulers amassed great wealth, which financed the construction of massive palaces, temples, and various public works, the ruins of which we still find scattered from Egypt to England.

ARTIFICIAL HARBOR OF CAESAREA MARITIMA

In 40 BC the Roman Senate appointed Herod the Great as their vassal king to rule Judea, Samaria, and Galilee on behalf of Rome. After Herod's death Augustus divided the territory between three of Herod's sons. However, one of them was so incompetent that the Romans decided to take direct control over Judea and Samaria through a Roman governor. These governors established their headquarters at the Herodian port city of Caesarea and took up residence in Herod's beautiful seaside palace. This was the primary residence of Pontius Pilate, the Roman governor during the time of Jesus.

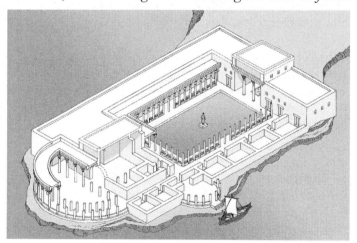

It is also where the Apostle Paul was brought in protective custody from Jerusalem by the Roman army and imprisoned by the governors Festus and Felix for two years before appealing his case to Caesar in Rome (Acts 24-26).

By the end of Augustus' reign in AD 14, twenty-five legions were spread across the Empire, comprised of about 150,000 Roman soldiers. Four

HEROD'S SEASIDE PALACE AT CAESAREA

of these legions were stationed in Syria and occupied Palestine. When Jesus began his mission, garrisons of Roman soldiers were found in all the principal cities of Judea, including a large contingent stationed at the Antonia Fortress, built into the northwest corner of the Temple Mount in Jerusalem. A smaller garrison of Roman soldiers commanded by a centurion was based just east of Capernaum on the Sea of Galilee, where Jesus centered his mission.

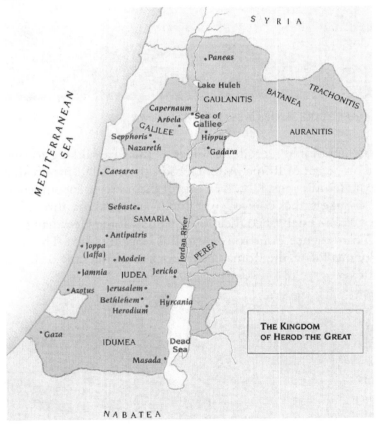

Roman soldiers were a regular part of the daily life of Jews in the first century and would have been both feared and hated by many in the local population who felt deeply humiliated and oppressed by the Romans. Roman soldiers could force anyone to carry their armor and gear for one mile, enforced the collection of taxes for Rome, supported the Temple police, and brutally put down any signs of rebellion.

However, there were also positive relationships between Romans and Jews. The centurion of Capernaum paid for the construction of the large synagogue there and turned to Jesus for help when his servant was dying (Luke 7:1-10). The Roman centurion Cornelius, stationed in Caesarea on the coast, and his extended family were some of the first Gentiles to put their faith in Jesus after the day of Pentecost (Acts 10:1-48).

THE HERODIANS: VASSAL RULERS

After the Roman general Pompey conquered Palestine in 63 BC, Antipater the Idumean rose to prominence as the governor of Judea under the Romans. Born in Idumea, the biblical Kingdom of Edom south of Jerusalem between the Dead Sea and the Gulf of Aqaba, Antipater's family had been forcibly converted to Judaism under the Hasmoneans, who were the Jewish rulers of Palestine after they threw off the Syrian Greeks during the famous Maccabean Revolt in the second century BC. Antipater, a ruthless warrior and cunning politician, managed to establish himself as a close advisor to the Hasmonean kings and an ally of the Roman General Pompey.

When Pompey was killed in 47 BC, Antipater quickly switched his allegiance to Julius Caesar and so was appointed Procurator of Judea. Antipater in turn appointed his two sons, Phasael and Herod, to be Prefects of Jerusalem and Galilee. After his father was poisoned and his brother was killed in a Hasmonean uprising, Herod fled to Rome, made his case before the Senate, and was unexpectedly appointed ruler on behalf of Rome and given the title "King of the Jews." I love Ken Bailey's tongue in cheek understatement when he says, "Being racially Arab, religiously Jewish, culturally Greek and politically Roman, Herod was a complex man."[8]

Herod returned to Palestine from Rome with the Senate's backing and spent the next three years securing his rule by 37 BC through political alliances, guerilla warfare, and the brutal execution of those who challenged him, even members of his own family. Although

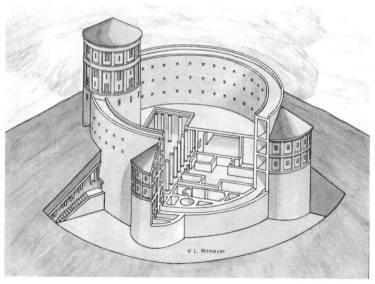

THE PALACE-FORTRESS OF HERODIUM

8 Bailey, *Mediterranean Eyes*, 56.

Herod claimed to follow the religion of the Jews, his Idumean ancestry, decadent life-style, and loyalty to Rome left him under consistent criticism from the Jewish religious leaders, both the Sadducees and the Pharisees. We can see evidence of Herod's deeply flawed character, and perhaps even compromised sanity, in his slaughter of the baby boys of Bethlehem at the time of Jesus' birth and the paranoid execution of his own sons in the final months of his life.

Despite these profound moral flaws and the opposition of religious Jews, Herod built the most extensive system of fortress-palaces the ancient world had ever seen. These monuments to architectural achievement combined impenetrable defenses with the royal comforts befitting Herod's lavish lifestyle and served to guard the eastern frontier of his territory. One of the most unique of these fortresses was the self-named Herodium located about nine miles south of Jerusalem. Herod hollowed out an entire mountain, built a circular fortress protruding from the top, and adorned the base of the mountain with a sprawling pleasure palace, complete with massive swimming pool. Archaeologists recently discovered a theater built into the side of the mountain and Herod's own mausoleum where he was buried.

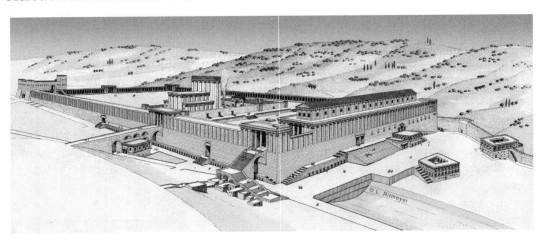

HEROD'S TEMPLE MOUNT

Even though he was not particularly pious, the greatest of all Herod's construction projects, the one which brought him the greatest recognition, was his expansion of the gigantic courts surrounding the Jewish Temple in Jerusalem. While it did not accomplish

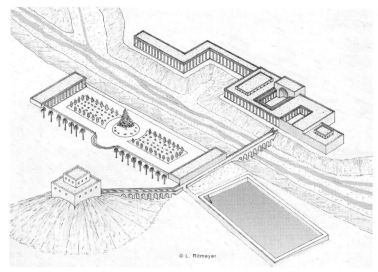

© L. Ritmeyer

HEROD'S PALACE IN JERICHO

his goal of winning the support of the religious leaders and the Jewish people, it did secure his place in history as one of the greatest builders of all time.

In the final months of his life, Herod languished in his favorite palace just outside of Jericho, suffering terribly from a disease which seemed to magnify his lifelong paranoia that those closest to him were constantly plotting to steal his power. This was where Herod had his young Hasmonean nephew drowned in the swimming pool one evening early in his reign because he was perceived as a threat. Perhaps Herod was remembering that heinous act in his final days when he ordered two of his sons executed for imagined treason. In this same period, he changed his will seven times, finally appointing his son Archelaus as ruler of Judea and Samaria, giving the elder Antipas the less strategic territory of Galilee and Perea, and Philip the least significant area northeast of Galilee. Upon Herod's death in 4 BC, all three sons sailed back to Rome to appeal to Caesar, just as their father had done 36 year earlier. Antipas argued he should rightfully take his father's place as King of the Jews, while the other two petitioned for the will to be honored as written.

Some 30 years later, Jesus was traveling with his disciples along the Roman road from Jericho to Jerusalem when he passed by that palace where Herod had suffered in his final months, ordered the execution of his son Antipater, changed his will, and died. Luke tells us that it was in this very spot that Jesus told a parable that begins, *"A nobleman went into a far country to receive for himself a kingdom and then return."* (Luke 19:12) This reference would not be lost on any of the disciples, who certainly knew these dramatic events from their childhood.

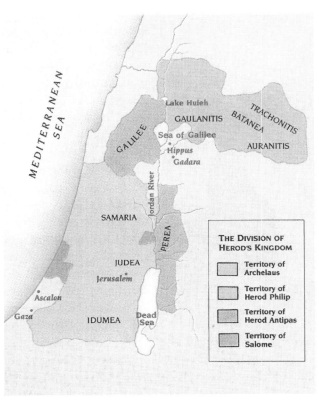

THE DIVISION OF
HEROD'S KINGDOM

Territory of
Archelaus

Territory of
Herod Philip

Territory of
Herod Antipas

Territory of
Salome

In the end, Caesar Augustus decided not to give any of Herod's sons their father's title King of the Jews, instead affirming Herod's division of his territory between the three and conferring on them the lesser title of "Tetrarch." Philip embraced Greek culture and built his capital in the far north at the pagan shrine to Pan, naming it Caesarea Philippi after his Roman patron and himself. In AD 6 Archelaus, who ruled from Jerusalem, was deposed by Caesar for incompetence, and a Roman Governor was appointed to rule Judea and Samaria in his place. Meanwhile, Herod Antipas had begun lavish improvements to his capital city of Sepphoris, just a few miles north of the village of Nazareth. Eventually he changed course and decided to build a new capital on the western shore of the Sea of Galilee, naming it Tiberias after Augustus' successor as emperor.

Like his father, Antipas' moral failings brought him under the criticism of religious leaders such as the charismatic and popular John the Baptist, whom Antipas subsequently imprisoned in the fortress of Macherus on the eastern shore of the Dead Sea. This is where, at a lavish banquet, Antipas beheaded John at the request of Salome, the daughter of his lover Herodias, who had been married to his brother (Mark 6:17-29). Flavius Josephus, the first-century Jewish historian writing for the Romans, described it this way: "Now when many others came in crowds about [John the Baptist], for they were very greatly moved by hearing his words, Herod [Antipas], who feared lest the great influence John had over the people might put it into his power and inclination to raise a rebellion, for they seemed ready to do anything he should advise, thought it best, by putting him to death, to prevent any mischief he might cause, and not bring himself into difficulties… Accordingly he was sent a prisoner, out of Herod's suspicious temper, to Macherus, the castle I before mentioned, and was there put to death."[9]

Following this tragic incident, Jesus referred to Anitpas derisively as "that fox" and refused to perform miracles for him when he was on trial in Jerusalem (Luke 13:31-32; 23:6-12). After 43 years as ruler of Galilee, the political tide turned against Antipas, and he was deposed and exiled to Gaul.

 # THE TRUTH

A KINGDOM LOST

When Jesus began his public ministry, he returned from his baptism by John in the Jordan River and his time of testing in the Judean wilderness to his home region of Galilee, teaching in synagogues along the way. It is clear from the Gospel accounts that the central theme of Jesus' teaching was a visionary message he summed up with the loaded term, "the kingdom of God." When the people of Capernaum wanted him to stay in their town, Jesus said, *"I must preach the good news of the kingdom of God to the other towns as well; for I was sent for this purpose."* (Luke 4:43)

Why was the kingdom of God that Jesus proclaimed such good news?

A kingdom is literally the region where the king's will is being enacted. Jesus taught his disciples to pray, *"Your kingdom come, your will be done, on earth as it is in heaven"* (Matthew 6:10). The kingdom of God is very simply the way things are when God's will is being done. Because God is such a good Father and such a powerful King, it is very good news when his will is being done!

When God created the heavens and the earth and all its creatures, with man and

---

9 Flavius Josephus, *Antiquities of the Jews,* trans. William Whiston, (Delmarva, 2016), Book 18, Chapter 5, Section 1, Digital.

woman in his own image, it was profoundly good because it was a reflection of the Creator's infinite goodness. God's will is the ultimate good, and why life is always the most abundant when his will is being done. But as soon as Adam and Eve chose to believe and act on the lie of the serpent that they should be their own judge of good and evil rather than their Father the King, the creation has not functioned according to God's will.

With their rejection of God's Kingship, sin entered into the good creation and with it came shame. Shame cut off Adam and Eve from their intimate relationship with the Creator. Isolated from the source of all goodness and life, things quickly went from bad to worse. They had forfeited their role of representing the King and ruling creation on his behalf. Adam's efforts produced thorns rather than good fruit. Eve experienced pain in childbirth. The man began to rule over the woman rather than rule beside her. Cain lifted his hand against Abel. Broken relationships resulted from Adam and Eve's attempt to replace the true King. With this rebellion came universal fruitlessness, pain, suffering, oppression, injustice, and ultimately death.

The Jewish people in Jesus' time were reminded on a daily basis that God's good rule was not being enacted in their lives. Every time they saw a Roman soldier humiliating one of their neighbors, they knew God's Kingdom had still not come. Every time the local tax collector came to shake them down in order to fund the latest Herodian building project, they knew God's Kingdom had not yet come. Every time they saw Pontius Pilate deploy extra troops in Jerusalem to prevent rebellion at the time of the Passover, they knew that God's Kingdom had not yet come.

The kingdoms of this world, no matter how good we try to make them, always fall woefully short of the reign of our true King. Those who put their hopes in an earthly king are inevitably disappointed. History offers endless testimony of how the kingdoms of this world are co-opted by the kingdom of darkness to steal, kill, and destroy the goodness of God's intention for his creation and his children. The Jews of Roman Palestine recognized a demonic stronghold in the iron fist of their pagan overlords and the decadence of their supposedly "Jewish" proxy rulers.

A KINGDOM RESTORED

The Hebrew prophets proclaimed a vision of a coming reality in stark contrast to the kingdoms of this world and the kingdom of darkness. They proclaimed a coming

Kingdom where justice is done, where there is peace and harmony between nations, where lambs and lions lie down together, where God is once more reunited with his children, and where everyone is invited to gather around the King's table for a feast that never ends. They give us a vision of God once again reigning on earth as he does in heaven. "Heaven" is a biblical way of talking about the realm where God's will is being carried out perfectly. In heaven there is no pain, disease, suffering, injustice, isolation, or death because God reigns as the King of heaven.

It is interesting that Matthew, reflecting Jewish sensitivity to the use of God's name, consistently translates Jesus' key declaration as "the Kingdom of Heaven." He is telling us that Jesus' proclamation of the Kingdom of God is nothing less than an announcement that heaven is coming to earth. We can see God's initial pronouncement of his Kingdom at Jesus' baptism in the tearing open of the heavens, the outpouring of the Spirit, and the declaration of the Father's affirmation of Jesus as his beloved Son. John's Gospel tells us that, unlike the Old Testament kings and prophets who were temporarily filled with the Spirit, the Holy Spirit would remain on Jesus (John 1:33). Jesus has become the permanent portal between heaven and earth, and the Kingdom of God is coming to earth through him.

No wonder Andrew, a disciple of John the Baptist, identified Jesus as the Messiah after spending just one afternoon with him beside the Jordan River (John 1:41). The prophets foretold the coming of a descendant of David who would be "the anointed one" (Hebrew: "Messiah," Greek: "Christ"). This Messiah would come as the true King to restore God's rule over his creation and set every wrong right again. Although in the beginning, Jesus did not explicitly claim to be the Messiah, those who interacted with him consistently came to that conclusion, either in faith to follow him or in outrage to stone him.

People identified Jesus as the Messiah because he not only declared the coming reign of God, but also demonstrated that reign by doing God's will on earth as it is done in heaven. When Jesus announced his vision in the synagogue of his hometown Nazareth, he quoted the passage from Isaiah 61 that describes the Messiah offering *"good news to the poor... liberty to the captives... recovering of sight to the blind... liberty to those who are oppressed..."* He then stated the obvious but shocking truth, *"Today this Scripture has been fulfilled in your hearing."* (Luke 4:18-21) Jesus' actions demonstrated the immediacy of the Kingdom his words described.

When John the Baptist sent his disciples to Jesus to inquire if he was the anointed King they were anticipating, Jesus answered them, *"Go and tell John what you have seen and heard: the blind receive their sight, the lame walk, lepers are cleansed, and the deaf hear, the dead are raised up, the poor have good news preached to them. And blessed is the one who is not offended by me."* (Luke 7:22-23) When the hungry are fed, the unclean are cleansed, outcasts are welcomed, demons are bested, and the dead are raised, it is hard to reach any other conclusion except that God's Kingdom is coming and Jesus is the King!

A KINGDOM EXPLAINED

Jesus not only announced this coming kingdom and demonstrated it, he also explained it. Jesus began his most-famous sermon by sitting down on a hill overlooking the Sea of Galilee and describing the unexpected values of God's Kingdom:

"Blessed are the poor in spirit, for theirs is the kingdom of heaven.
"Blessed are those who mourn, for they shall be comforted.
"Blessed are the meek, for they shall inherit the earth.
"Blessed are those who hunger and thirst for righteousness, for they shall be satisfied.
"Blessed are the merciful, for they shall receive mercy.
"Blessed are the pure in heart, for they shall see God.
"Blessed are the peacemakers, for they shall be called sons of God.
"Blessed are those who are persecuted for righteousness' sake, for theirs is the kingdom of heaven."
(Matthew 5:3-10)

Notice the first and last statements both refer to the Kingdom of Heaven. In Middle Eastern thought, this bookending of ideas applies the statements at the ends to everything in between. Imagine the kingdom of Rome lauding the value of the meek and the mournful. Imagine the Herodians promoting the poor and the hungry. It would never happen! But in the Kingdom of Heaven, value is found in these experiences. In the kingdoms of this world the merciful, the pure, the peacemakers, and the persecuted are downtrodden, but in the Kingdom of Heaven they triumph.

Jesus loved to tell stories about the Kingdom of God. He said, *"The kingdom of heaven is like a grain of mustard seed... the kingdom of heaven is like leaven... the kingdom of heaven is like treasure hidden in a field... the kingdom of heaven is like a merchant in search of fine pearls... the kingdom of heaven is like a net that was thrown into the sea... the kingdom of heaven is like a master of a house who went out early in the morning to hire laborers for his vineyard..."* Jesus used these simple but surprising stories to paint pictures illustrating what life looks like when we live in the Kingdom of God.

In the Kingdom of God, running fathers lavish gifts on returning prodigals who have squandered the family farm. In the Kingdom of God, workers hired at the end of the day are paid the full day's wage. In the Kingdom of God, things as tiny as a mustard seed become as big as a mustard tree. In the Kingdom of God, fields that cost all you have contain priceless treasures you could never afford. In the Kingdom of God, shrewd stewards who use their master's money to make indebted friends are praised by their masters. In the Kingdom of God, servants who take risks to increase their master's capital receive ten times as much to manage. In the Kingdom of God, hated Samaritans stop to help their Jewish enemies in need. In the Kingdom of God, powerful kings invite outcasts to their wedding banquets.

Jesus' teaching and demonstration of God's Kingdom evoked a powerful response from the Jewish people who lived under the oppression of the Romans and the corruption of the Herodians, because they heard from him and saw in him a completely different kind of Kingdom than the kingdoms to which they were subject. Jesus embodied and promised the kind of world for which they longed and prayed every day. However, the majority of those who followed Jesus failed to comprehend just how different the Kingdom of God is from the kingdoms of this world. When the crowds thought Jesus' Kingdom was meant to provide them with endless supplies of free bread, Jesus explained to them that God's Kingdom operates on a far deeper level: *"Do not work for the food that perishes, but for the food that endures to eternal life, which the Son of Man will give to you."* (John 6:27)

When Jesus came over the Mount of Olives and into Jerusalem on a donkey for his final Passover, the crowds understood he was making a Messianic declaration. But most assumed Jesus would later take over the seat of Pontius Pilate in Herod's former palace. They failed to understand what Jesus would later explain to Pilate five days later in that very palace when the Roman governor asked if he really was a king, *"My kingdom is not of this world. If my kingdom were of this world, my servants would have been fighting, that I might not be delivered over to the Jews. But my kingdom is not from the world."* (John 18:36)

Although the majority failed to understand the true nature of the Kingdom Jesus proclaimed, at the end 120 disciples in an upper room in Jerusalem finally got it. Through the crushing disappointment of Jesus' crucifixion, the dizzying glory of his resurrection, and the transformational outpouring of his Holy Spirit, this family of followers learned to live as a part of this new and coming Kingdom by faith in Jesus and the power of his presence within them. They came to understand that the Kingdom of God is not a better version of the kingdoms of this world, but something completely different. As they learned to follow the *Way* of Jesus, they came to trust the *Truth* of his powerful rule, and so they began to live the extraordinary *Life* of Jesus, demonstrating the transforming reality that Heaven is invading earth and restoring creation to its one true King.

 # THE LIFE

LIVING MY WAY

I have always been a bit of a dreamer. As a kid I dreamed of climbing mountains and exploring jungles. I never followed the directions in the Lego kit, instead creating my own castles and spaceships. By my early teens, I was already designing the equine vet center I was going to build once I had my degree in veterinary medicine. I had a plan, and it was mainly about me.

God, of course, had a different plan. A better plan. Like Jacob at Peniel, it took a lot of wrestling with God before I could let go of my plans and receive his better way. I met Jesus in my later teens with an overwhelming experience of his grace and love. I began to read his Word and open myself to his Spirit. I had a pastor and a youth pastor who showed me a different way to live. I went to college with a growing realization God had a plan and a purpose for my life. During my freshman year I finally came to accept God's calling for my life.

I switched my major from biology to theology and started down a different path. But I was still looking for a way to enact my plans. As a young pastor, I had a clear vision and a passion to accomplish that vision. I still believe it was God's vision, to reach the lost with the Father's love, help them become disciples of Jesus, and send them out to change the world in the power of the Spirit. The only problem was I assumed it was up to me to find a way to fulfill that vision. I didn't understand that Jesus had already laid out a Way for me to follow. I spent many years trying to fulfill God's vision *my* way.

Pam and I have been married over thirty years now, and it has been an amazing journey. God has used her to bless me beyond description and shape me more into Jesus' image every day. It has happened through a step-by-step process of learning to let go of my way and seek Jesus' way with her. But every day part of me still rebels and wants to bend her to my will. I remember our initial trip to the grocery store to stock the shelves of our very first kitchen. It was an hour-long tug of war. I wanted my brand of ketchup, my favorite cereal, my kind of lunchmeat. And she wanted hers. We were getting our first lesson in finding a better way together. Thirty years later we continue to learn that lesson!

The problem all started when Adam and Eve believed the lie that their way would be better than God's way. Ever since a war has waged in the heart of every man and woman. Will I let God be King, or will I try to control my own life? The answer to that question determines the world in which you live. Will you live in a kingdom of your own design or the Kingdom of God? The kingdoms of this world or the Kingdom of Heaven? The kingdom of darkness or the Kingdom of light?

Jesus led the disciples to Jerusalem for his final Passover. He told them repeatedly the difficult destiny that awaited him there. But, in spite of all that Jesus had taught them and shown them, James and John were still working on their own plan and vying for a good seat in the kingdoms of this world. They eyed the massive palace of Herod and wondered which room theirs would be. They asked Jesus, *"Grant us to sit, one at your right hand and one at your left, in your glory." Jesus said to them, "You do not know what you are asking."* (Mark 10:37-38) It wouldn't be long before the kingdom of darkness had coopted the kingdoms of Caiaphas and Pilate to enact its dark purpose, and the sons of Zebedee would have to learn the hard way that God's Kingdom is something completely different than their kingdom. They learned what we will have to learn as well; the only way into God's Kingdom is by dying to self.

LIVING IN THE KINGDOM

Roman citizens lived in the Roman Empire by obeying the laws of Rome. Jews in first-century Palestine lived as subjects of the Herodians by obeying their royal decrees. But Jesus shows us that the way to live in the Kingdom of God is not by legalistic obedience, but by faith in and submission to our true King. Jesus did not wake up every day and resolve to try harder to do God's will on earth. Rather he entrusted himself fully to the Father and so submitted completely to his Father's will. Jesus said, *"Truly, truly, I say to you, the Son can do nothing of his own accord, but only what he sees the Father doing. For whatever the Father does, that the Son does likewise."* (John 5:19) Jesus told his disciples, *"The words that I say to you I do not speak on my own authority, but the Father who dwells in me does his works."* (John 14:10) The secret of Jesus' extraordinary life was his relationship with the Father whom he trusted and to whom he submitted as his King.

Not that this was easy or automatic. Jesus is fully God but is also fully human. In fact, when Jesus was facing his final destiny in the Garden of Gethsemane, the pressure to follow his own plan was so great he began to sweat blood. He prayed, *"Father, if you are willing, remove this cup from me. Nevertheless, not my will, but yours, be done."* (Luke 22:42) In the end Jesus trusted his Father enough to submit to him, even to the point of death on a cross. Jesus says this is the same journey we are called to walk if we are going to live in his Kingdom, *"If anyone would come after me, let him deny himself and take up his cross and follow me. For whoever would save his life will lose it, but whoever loses his life for my sake and the gospel's will save it."* (Mark 8:34-35)

So how are we to learn to live this Kingdom way of life? I used to assume it was something I could learn on my own by reading the Bible, praying, reading books, watching videos, and practicing spiritual disciplines. I discovered that, while all these are good and helpful things, they are not the primary way we learn to live in the Kingdom of God. The way people like Peter and Andrew, James and John, Joanna and Suzanna learned to do God's will on earth as it is in heaven was through a relationship--the relationship of disciples to their Rabbi. They were close enough to Jesus and spent enough time with him that they not only got to *know* what he knew, but they learned how to *do* what he did.

Discipleship is learning to live in the Kingdom of God by trusting and submitting to Jesus by the power of his Spirit. Our Covenant relationship with Jesus is the starting point for learning to live in the Kingdom of God rather than living in the kingdoms of this world. As we take up our cross and follow Jesus, our way begins to die and the Spirit brings us to new life so we can live in a whole new way. When Peter was faced with the sacrifice of dying to his own way of life, he asked Jesus what they would have left when it was all said and done. Jesus answered, *"Truly, I say to you, there is no one who has left house or wife or brothers or parents or children, for the sake of the kingdom of God, who will not receive many times more in this time, and in the age to come eternal life."* (Luke 18:28-30) Following Jesus into a life of faith and submission in God's Kingdom will cost us everything, but it is where we will find the abundant life we were created to live, both in this age and in the age to come.

Several years ago, Pam and I sensed God was leading us to give up the financial security of our full-time jobs, leave the support of a community we had come to love over 16 years, and invest ourselves full-time in the wider mission we had been doing on the side for many years. After weighing and confirming this leading, we decided to trust and submit. We gave up our good salary and benefits for no guaranteed income. We went on the road for over seven months of the year. We sold our home and lived with friends for a year and a half before buying a house in a less desirable neighborhood. From some people's point of view this all seemed crazy! We are at a stage of life when financial stability, medical benefits, and saving for retirement are considered crucial. But we were convinced this was God's calling, and decided to seek his kingdom above financial stability and retirement security. Looking back five years later we can see what God was up to. Taking a big step of faith and submitting to Jesus in this way has opened up all kinds of new opportunities, relationships, experiences, and fruitfulness in our lives by the power of the Spirit. Our faith is stronger, our marriage is richer, our impact is greater, our hearts are fuller, and we are having the time of our lives. I would not trade this kingdom journey for anything, and could not be more blessed than I am right now!

Jesus said it this way, *"But seek first the kingdom of God and his righteousness, and all these things will be added to you."* (Matthew 6:33) The irony is that we spend most of our lives seeking after "all these things" and miss the real treasure God has for us. What are you seeking after? Is it your kingdom or God's Kingdom? Are you living according to the kingdoms of this world or the Kingdom of Heaven? Are you submitting to a Roman Caesar or the King of Heaven? Are you following Herod or Jesus? Is the Kingdom of Light shining in you, or does the kingdom of darkness have a hold on you?

Jesus shows us what God's Kingdom looks like, explains how things work when God is King, and calls us to take up our cross and follow him into that Kingdom today. There is no shortcut. There is no easy way. There is only the Way of the cross. Jesus said, *"Enter by the narrow gate. For the gate is wide and the way is easy that leads to destruction, and those who enter by it are many. For the gate is narrow and the way is hard that leads to life, and those who find it are few."* (Matthew 7:13-14) Will you trust Jesus enough to submit to him, take up your cross, and let his Spirit show you the Way?

CHAPTER TWO

SADDUCEES AND PHARISEES:
THE RELIGIOUS ESTABLISHMENT

Jesus said to them, "Watch and beware of the leaven of the Pharisees and Sadducees."
(Matthew 16:6)

 THE WAY

THE SADDUCEES: MEDIATORS OF HOLINESS

Josephus described the key groups within first-century Jewish society as follows, "At this time there were three sects among the Jews, who had different opinions concerning human actions; the one was called the sect of the Pharisees, another the sect of the Sadducees, and the other the sect of the Essenes. Now for the Pharisees, they say that some actions, but not all, are the work of fate, and some of them are in our own power, and that they are liable to fate, but are not caused by fate. But the sect of the Essenes affirm, that fate governs all things, and that nothing befalls men but what is according to its determination. And for the Sadducees, they take away fate, and say there is no such thing, and that the events of human affairs are not at its disposal; but they suppose that all our actions are in our own power, so that we are ourselves the causes of what is good, and receive what is evil from our own folly." [10]

Now we turn our attention first to the official religious leaders of Jesus' world, the

---

10 Flavius Josephus, *Antiquities of the Jews,* trans. William Whiston, (Delmarva, 2016), Book 13, Chapter 5, Section 9, Digital.

Sadducees and the Pharisees. When God established the Twelve Tribes of Israel, he decreed that the Tribe of Levi would be the priests of Israel serving in Israel's sacred tent, the Tabernacle. The descendants of Moses' brother Aaron actually performed the priestly functions of offering and sacrifice, while the rest of the Levites took on supportive roles such as singing, playing instruments, providing security, taking care of the priestly vessels and garments, and supplying the water, wood, and animals for sacrifices.

This was the place of worship for Israel up to the days of King David. After he built his own palace at the north end of his new capital Jerusalem, David bought the threshing floor of Aruna, a huge flat rock on the top of Mount Zion, the ridge that ran north from the city. In the 10th century BC, David's son Solomon built the First Temple there, with the large rock forming the floor of the inner sanctum called the Holy of Holies. The Temple was destroyed by the Babylonians in 587 BC and rebuilt by the returned exiles under Zerubbabel after 538 BC. This rebuilt Temple never lived up to the memory of Solomon's Temple, although later rulers expanded the surrounding courts.

When Herod the Great came to power, he tried to win over the religious population he ruled by expanding the Temple courts to nearly twice their size and rebuilding the Temple itself in white marble and gold. In order to prevent any interruption in the sacrificial system, Herod had 1000 Priests and Levites trained as stonemasons, so they could rebuild the Temple while maintaining its sanctity. The Royal Stoa, a huge columned building spanning the southern end of this courtyard, was where the Sanhedrin met.

The enormous Temple Mount dominates Jerusalem still today, measuring the size of 25 American football fields. This was Herod's greatest architectural achievement among many impressive projects and was the preeminent symbol of the often-hyper-critical religious establishment.

Since the Tribe of Levi was non-geographical, the Priests and Levites were dispersed throughout Israel. Once Solomon built the Temple and the sacrificial system was restricted to worship in Jerusalem, each Priest and Levite traveled from his hometown twice a year to serve at the Temple for one week at a time. Sacrificial offerings were made every morning and afternoon at the open-air altar of sacrifice in front of the

Temple building, with an additional two sacrifices offered on the Sabbath. Incense was offered inside the Sanctuary of the Temple twice a day. Private sacrifices brought by individuals were offered throughout the day. On the eve of the Sabbath, the new course of Priests and Levites arrived to serve their week and overlapped with the previous course until the end of the Sabbath. The new priests began their week of service by replacing the showbread inside the Temple sanctuary and then taking up the sacrificial rituals.

While serving their one week of service at the Temple, the priests drew lots to determine who would actually perform the various sacrifices and rituals. Because of the numbers, a typical priest might only have his lot drawn once in a lifetime to actually enter the Temple itself and make an offering there. Luke tells us that Elizabeth's husband Zechariah was a priest serving his rotation at the Temple when his lot was drawn to offer incense inside the Temple. While Zechariah was alone inside the Temple, the angel Gabriel appeared to him and announced the conception of his son John (Luke 1:8-17).

Ever since Aaron was called to assist his brother Moses in representing God to his people, the leadership of Israel included a priestly role. The first kings of Israel appointed one priest to be preeminent among all the Priests and Levites, and this role came to be called the "High Priest." David's High Priest Zadok became the predecessor of the High Priests after his time. By the time of Jesus, the Roman Governor exercised the power to appoint High Priests, and so it is no surprise that they were closely aligned with the purposes of Rome.

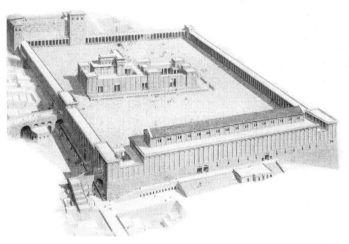

HEROD'S TEMPLE MOUNT

The High Priest served as the leader of the Sanhedrin, the Council of Seventy which ruled in religious and legal matters for the Jewish people under Roman rule. While the Herodians ruled over the political system of Jesus' time, the Sanhedrin was entrusted with oversight of the religious life of Jerusalem and the wider Jewish population. The Romans ceded authority to the Sanhedrin over matters relating directly to Jewish Law but reserved the right of execution for themselves. Made up of the widely divergent camps of the Sadducees and Pharisees, this Council of 70 was often stirred by controversy and divided along party lines. They normally met in the Chamber of Hewn Stone on the Temple Mount in Jerusalem, and they commanded their own militia to enforce their policies and preside over the huge Temple complex.

The High Priest also functioned in special ceremonial roles at the Temple, including entering into the Holy of Holies, the inner sanctum, once a year on Yom Kippur, the Day of Atonement, to make the sin offering on behalf of the people. In the years before Jesus' time, there had been a string of High Priests who were quickly deposed after being appointed, a reflection of the power struggles between the Jewish and Roman rulers of Jerusalem. Annas and his son-in-law Caiaphas, High Priests during the time of Jesus, were some of the longest serving in that position, indicating how careful they were to protect the interests of Rome.

Over the centuries descendants of the High Priest Zadok rose to the upper ranks of priestly leadership and became what the New Testament refers to as the "chief priests." These leaders came from four prominent families of chief priests who dominated Jewish affairs in Jerusalem at the time of Jesus up to AD 70, and from their ranks were chosen the priestly officers of the Temple: the High Priest, the Captain of the Temple, and Treasurer of the Temple. Their control of the Temple's sacrificial system and its presumed access to God's presence afforded this group tremendous power among the Jewish people at the time of Jesus. The chief priests were drawn primarily from the wealthy aristocratic families of Jerusalem, and they held onto power by aligning themselves closely with the occupying Romans.

The leading party of these aristocratic Chief Priests was the Sadducees, who comprised a large segment of the Sanhedrin. The Sadducees only accepted the Torah, the first five books of the Old Testament Law, as authoritative Scripture, and as such did not believe in the resurrection of the dead or the final judgement foretold by the Prophets. These views put them into direct conflict with the Pharisees, the rabbinical party that made up the other power bloc of the Sanhedrin. Because of the Sadducees' political alignment with the Romans, these aristocratic priestly families seemingly took on many of the cultural styles of Rome, except they strictly avoided any representations of people or animals in their art and demonstrated a scrupulous attention to maintaining ritual purity.

According to the Mosaic Law, before any priest could carry out his duties it was imperative that he be considered ritually clean. Ritual purity in ancient Judaism was not a matter of ethical acts or the moral condition of a person's soul, it was a strictly symbolic status. A person could be considered unclean from things such as menstruation, childbirth, nocturnal emissions, eating non-kosher foods, wearing clothes with mixed fibers, touching a dead body, or touching anyone who is in a state of impurity. Likewise, a person could attain a state of ritual purity simply by immersing themselves in a ritual bath (Hebrew: *mikveh*).

It was believed that if a priest was ritually unclean and tried to offer a sacrifice, that sacrifice would be ineffective. If the person bringing the sacrifice was impure, his or her offering would also be considered null and void. In fact, if someone was to enter the inner courts of the Temple in an unclean state, the Levites were to take them out of the Temple and kill them! No wonder that archaeologists have uncovered hundreds of ancient ritual baths (Hebrew plural: *mikvot*) around the entrances of the Temple courts.

On the southwest hill of Jerusalem, archaeologists have discovered a number of large, extended family homes dating to the first century, reflecting a wealthy segment of Jerusalem's population at the time of Jesus. Many of these homes had very elaborate ritual baths and expensive dishes carved from limestone. It was believed that pottery dishes could not be purified, while stone dishes were impervious to impurity. Based on the wealth of these homes and their exaggerated concern for ritual purity, they have been interpreted to be homes of the Temple's chief priests.

In 1990 in the Talpiot neighborhood of Jerusalem, construction workers accidentally discovered a first-century family tomb filled with 12 stone ossuaries (bone boxes) designed to contain a secondary burial of the bones of those placed in a tomb. One of the most ornately decorated ossuaries was inscribed "Yehosef bar Qayafa" on the long side, and "Yehosef bar Qafa" on the narrow side. This has been interpreted with

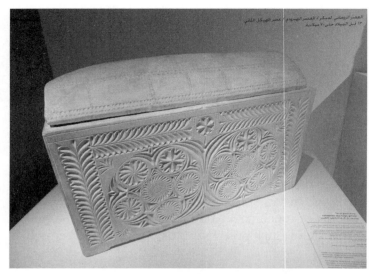

a high degree of confidence as the family tomb and ossuary of Joseph Caiaphas, the very High Priest who condemned Jesus.

BONE BOX FROM THE TOMB OF CAIAPHAS

THE PHARISEES: TEACHERS OF THE LAW

Ever since Moses led the children of Israel through the wilderness to the foot of Mount Sinai where God revealed his particular will for them, the Law (Hebrew: *Torah*) became the normative basis for their Covenant relationship with Yahweh. Teaching and observance of the Law stood alongside the sacrificial rituals of Temple worship as the defining elements of Israelite life.

When the Babylonians destroyed the Temple in 587 BC and took many Jerusalemites as captives to Babylon, the study and teaching of the *Torah* took central stage in Jewish life. This is when synagogues began to develop and the role of rabbi, teacher of the Law, was established. After the return from exile and the rebuilding of the Temple in Jerusalem, the priests resumed their sacrificial role in the life of the Jewish people, and this set up the political rivalry that grew between the Sadducees and the Pharisees at the time of Jesus.

According to Jewish tradition, any ten Jews who gather together for prayer and worship can form a synagogue (Hebrew: *beth knesset*, lit: "house of assembly"). Although this could take place in an extended family home or a building built for other purposes, by the time of Jesus most Jewish towns had at least one building especially designed for

Sabbath and other community gatherings. Men and women attended the Sabbath prayer services there along with God-fearing Gentiles who believed in the God of Israel but had not fully converted to Judaism through circumcision and observance of ceremonial laws. The synagogue not only functioned as a place of prayer and study but housed the elementary school and other kinds of community gatherings too large for an extended family home.

Although many 3rd to 6th-century AD synagogues have been discovered in Israel, until recently only a handful of first-century AD synagogues had been found, and none in Galilee. In 2009 during the building of a pilgrim guesthouse, a first-century synagogue was discovered just a few feet underground at the site of ancient Magdala on the northwest shore of the Sea of Galilee. This extraordinary discovery features pillars to support a raised central roof, built-in stone benches around the perimeter, geometrically-patterned mosaic floors, and fragments of brightly colored frescoes on the walls.

FIRST-CENTURY SYNAGOGUE IN MAGDALA

The most remarkable artifact was a large limestone block carved on all five visible sides with images taken from the Temple in Jerusalem. This was used a table to support the biblical scrolls when they were unrolled and read. Magdala is the hometown of Mary Magdalene, Jesus' leading female disciple. Since Jesus *"went throughout all*

Galilee, teaching in their synagogues" (Matthew 4:23) and this is the nearest synagogue to Capernaum where Jesus made his home in Galilee, we can be quite confident that Jesus taught in this synagogue.

First-century synagogues in Israel are typically rectangular, have one main entrance, and feature built-in stepped seats around the perimeter and two rows of pillars to support a higher central roof, allowing light into the center of the main room. Each synagogue was overseen by a group of synagogue rulers responsible for organizing worship services and inviting rabbis to teach. Jairus was a synagogue ruler from Capernaum who came to Jesus asking healing for his twelve-year old daughter (Mark 5:21). Synagogues also had attendants whose responsibility was protecting the Torah scrolls

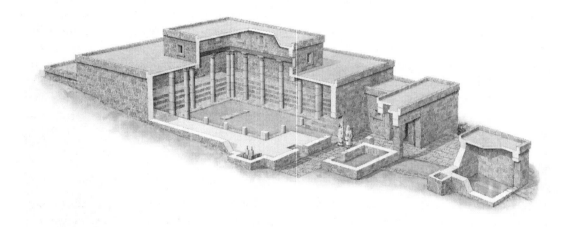

FIRST-CENTURY SYNAGOGUE IN GAMLA

and maintaining the other furnishings of the synagogue. Such an attendant at the synagogue in Nazareth handed Jesus the Isaiah scroll and then took it back from him when he finished reading from it (Luke 4:17, 20).

The rabbis were the teachers of the Law and functioned as the grass-roots religious leaders of Jesus' day. While the chief priests exercised power because of their control over the sacrificial system in the Temple, the rabbis' influence was rooted in the rhythms of their local synagogues. Whereas most people hated the Romans and Herodians for their oppression and were cynical toward the chief priests for their collusion with Rome, they tended to respect the rabbis because of their knowledge of the *Torah*.

The New Testament refers to the rabbis as "teachers of the law," "scribes," "sages," and "lawyers." These teachers interpreted God's Law for their community in the weekly Sabbath prayer services and applied these legal principles to the local disputes brought to them for mediation. They taught the children of the community to read and write and acted as scribes, drawing up legal documents such as wedding covenants and business contracts. Often rabbis carried out these functions in their spare time, in addition to their primary vocation which was part of their extended family business.

The Pharisees were the leading party of the rabbis in the first century and held to a strict interpretation of the *Torah*, which they scrupulously memorized. As the other major party in the Sanhedrin council of 70 in Jerusalem, the Pharisees were often in conflict with the Sadducees over theology and politics. Unlike the Sadducees, the Pharisees believed in the entire Hebrew Scriptures, including the Law, the Writings, and the Prophets. However, much of their teaching was based on the extensive Oral Law, which was comprised of various rabbinical interpretations of the written Law that would be written down in the Mishnah some 170 years after Jesus. They believed in prophecy, God's supernatural power, angels, demons, life after death, and the bodily resurrection of the dead.

But the Pharisees didn't disagree with the Sadducees about everything. Like the Sadducees they were concerned about ritual purity, but for different reasons. For priests ritual purity was important to ensure the sacrifices they offered were effective. For the Pharisees it was about carefully following the letter of the ritual laws in the *Torah* and the various interpretations of those rules in the Oral Law.

The Pharisees' theology was the closest to Jesus' teaching of any Jewish group at that time, but they were also the target of Jesus' harshest criticism because of their persistent legalism, externalism, spiritual pride, and hypocrisy (cf. Matthew 23:1-36). However, some Pharisees seemed to support Jesus' mission and respond to his teaching. Pharisees who tried to warn Jesus that Herod Antipas was plotting to kill him (Luke 13:31). The Pharisee Nicodemus was a member of the Sanhedrin and came to Jesus for spiritual counsel (John 3:1). By the time of Jesus' death, Nicodemus' commitment to Jesus was strong enough for him to join Joseph of Arimathea at the tomb with spices to anoint Jesus' body (John 19:39).

About thirty years after Jesus' death, the Zealots led an uprising against Rome that was brutally crushed by the Tenth Legion, who burned Jerusalem and destroyed the Temple. Another uprising about sixty years later was similarly put down by the Romans, and Emperor Hadrian expelled all the Jews from Jerusalem. The Jewish Temple was never rebuilt and the sacrificial system has never been reestablished. In the absence of a Temple, the need for a priesthood soon disappeared, allowing the rabbinical party to fill the vacuum and become the dominant religious leaders of Judaism, as they are to this day.

 # THE TRUTH

FIGHT OR FLIGHT?

How do you respond when threatened? Some animals automatically react with flight mode, and others with fight mode. Still others will freeze or play dead. I come from Montana where we have plenty of both fight and flight animals. I am writing this at our family cabin on Flathead Lake, and nearly every day a white-tailed deer will wander past our deck, munching away calmly, until it sees or hears me. At first, it freezes, assessing the threat. If I move or make a sound, it then explodes in a frenzy of legs and leaps, disappearing in an instant into the underbrush.

When we visit nearby Glacier National Park, we often see grizzly bears foraging for huckleberries on the mountainsides, bulking up for their long winter nap. All hikers in Glacier know that surprising a grizzly can be a fatal mistake, and so they often affix bells to their equipment and carry loud air horns. Although bears will typically run from loud noises, if a grizzly is surprised and feels cornered, it will almost always attack. Researchers tells us that human beings are also wired for flight or fight. When we feel threatened, our body's sympathetic nervous system stimulates our adrenal glands, which supercharge our other systems to prepare us for either battle or escape.

When Jesus emerged from his time of testing in the wilderness, the consistent reaction of people to what he said and did was awe and amazement: the twelve disciples, the people in Simon and Andrew's home, those in the synagogue of Capernaum, the people of Nazareth, Talitha's parents, the crowds in Galilee, Pontius Pilate, and even the Roman soldiers who crucified Jesus! The Gospel writers explain this was a response to the authority of Jesus' words and the power of his deeds. For example, after Jesus taught in the synagogue of Capernaum and delivered a man from unclean spirits: *And they were all amazed, so that they questioned among themselves, saying, "What is this? A new teaching with authority! He commands even the unclean spirits, and they obey him."* (Mark 1:27) But this authority and power evoked one of two very different reactions from people in the various political and religious parties.

For some, amazement drew them to Jesus; fishermen dropped their nets, tax collectors left their booths, morally questionable women broke open their alabaster jars, and wealthy women donated their silver. Huge crowds in the countryside of Galilee and in the Temple courts of Jerusalem gathered around Jesus, the people of Capernaum squeezed into the home of his newly adopted family, and twelve men quit their jobs to follow him. While many flocked to Jesus and some followed him, others felt threatened and resorted to flight or fight responses. When Jesus encountered demons oppressing a person who was open to him, he only had to command them, and they fled like a scared deer! But the response of the religious leaders was strikingly different. Threatened by Jesus' authority and power, they attacked him with an increasing determination to fight.

RELIGIOUS TRADITIONS THREATENED

One of the first negative reactions to Jesus was criticism from the rabbinical leaders of Galilee about the company he kept. Because of their concern for all the additional religious rules of the Oral Law, the Pharisees had very strict rules stipulating with whom they could and couldn't eat. Jesus, on the other hand, seemed eager to spend time with anyone who was open and responsive to the way of life he taught and modeled. Shockingly, Jesus even went so far as to invite a tax collector named Levi (also called Matthew) into his spiritual family. Tax collectors were the most hated members of the Jewish community because they were considered traitors for working with the Herodians to collect taxes destined for the coffers of Rome, and because they overcharged to line their own pockets.

Not only did Jesus invite Levi to be his disciple, but then he took his other disciples to Levi's home to spend time with him and share a meal with his tax collector friends. Mark describes the outrage of the Pharisees: *as he reclined at table in his* [Levi's] *house, many tax collectors and sinners were reclining with Jesus and his disciples, for there were many who followed him. And the scribes of the Pharisees, when they saw that he was eating with sinners and tax collectors, said to his disciples, "Why does he eat with tax collectors and sinners?" And when Jesus heard it, he said to them, "Those who are well have no need of a physician, but those who are sick. I came not to call the righteous, but sinners."* (Mark 2:15-17)

It wasn't that Jesus rejected the teaching of the Old Testament Law or the gathering on the Sabbath in the synagogue for worship. On the contrary, Luke tells us he attended the synagogue on the Sabbath and regularly taught from the Law *as was his custom* (Luke 4:16). It was the nature of their teaching and the hypocrisy of the synagogue leaders that Jesus criticized so harshly. Jesus was very clear that he was not bound by the extra-biblical religious rules that were such an obsession for the Pharisees. For instance, the Day of Atonement is the only fast day prescribed in the Hebrew Bible, but many other fast days developed as religious traditions. Jesus and his disciples did not follow those extra-biblical traditions, as he explained it, because his Way calls for celebrating not fasting. It is a way of life that calls for a new approach, new expressions.

Jesus was often criticized by the Pharisees for doing things on the Sabbath that they considered forbidden. They had developed many complex rules about keeping the Sabbath: how many steps you could take, how many letters you could write, what could and could not be carried, and so on. Even touching a tool on the Sabbath was considered breaking the Law. One Sabbath Jesus and the disciples plucked some heads of grain as they were walking through a grain field, and the Pharisees said to him, *"Look, why are they doing what is not lawful on the Sabbath?"* Jesus responded to their made-up rules by pointing to an example from the life of David and then summed up the biblical purpose of Sabbath rest by saying, *"The Sabbath was made for man, not man for the Sabbath. So the Son of Man is lord even of the Sabbath."* (Mark 2:24-28)

On another Sabbath Jesus came to the synagogue for the prayer service. A man with a deformed hand was present, and the Pharisees were specifically watching to see if Jesus would heal him. When Jesus realized what they were doing, he called the man over and said to the leaders, *"Is it lawful on the Sabbath to do good or to do harm, to save life or to kill?" But they were silent. And he looked around at them with anger, grieved at their hardness of heart, and said to the man, "Stretch out your hand." He stretched it out, and his hand was restored. The Pharisees went out and immediately held counsel with the Herodians against him, how to destroy him.* (Mark 3:1-6) They were so threatened by Jesus' power and his refusal to submit to their religious rules that the Galilean Pharisees decided to join forces with their political enemies to figure out a way to remove the threat that Jesus posed to their religious systems.

In addition to directly challenging the Pharisees, Jesus sometimes used them as a negative example in teaching his way of life: *He also told this parable to some who trusted in themselves that they were righteous, and treated others with contempt: "Two men went up into the temple to pray, one a Pharisee and the other a tax collector. The Pharisee, standing by himself, prayed thus: 'God, I thank you that I am not like other men, extortioners, unjust, adulterers, or even like this tax collector. I fast twice a week; I give tithes of all that I get.' But the tax collector, standing far off, would not even lift up his eyes to heaven, but beat his breast, saying, 'God, be merciful to me, a sinner!' I tell you, this man went down to his house justified, rather than the other. For everyone who exalts himself will be humbled, but the one who humbles himself will be exalted."* (Luke 18:9-14)

As Jesus' influence spread from Galilee to Jerusalem, the instinctive fight response of the rabbinical leaders only grew stronger. Some Pharisees came from Jerusalem to Galilee to investigate Jesus and his disciples and saw that they did not follow the elaborate hand-washing rituals the rabbis had established. They confronted Jesus saying, *"Why do your disciples not walk according to the tradition of the elders, but eat with defiled hands?" And he said to them, "Well did Isaiah prophesy of you hypocrites, as it is written, 'This people honors me with their lips, but their heart is far from me; in vain do they worship me, teaching as doctrines the commandments of men.' You leave the commandment of God and hold to the tradition of men."* Jesus went on to point out specific ways their religious traditions actually contradicted the clear commands of Scripture (Mark 7:5-13). Jesus was pointing out the sad irony of the Pharisees becoming so obsessed with their own religious traditions that they violated the revealed will of God!

Jesus was careful not to undermine the principle of genuine spiritual leadership that the Pharisees were meant to represent, but he was fiercely critical of the hypocrisy he saw in their failure to practice what they preached. *Then Jesus said to the crowds and to his disciples, "The scribes and the Pharisees sit on Moses' seat, so do and observe whatever they tell you, but not the works they do. For they preach, but do not practice."* (Matthew 23:1-3) Since teachers typically sat down to teach in the synagogue, Moses' seat functioned as the seat of authority in the synagogue from which both Jesus and the Pharisees taught. An elaborately carved stone Moses' seat was discovered in the third-century synagogue of

Chorazin, built over the synagogue where Jesus often taught and ministered. Jesus was pointing out that it is healthy to submit to appropriate authority, but the mere position of authority does not automatically condone the way that authority is being exercised.

Not only did Jesus criticize the Pharisees for their hypocrisy and for preferring their own religious traditions to the written Law, but also because their legalistic externalism completely missed the intention of the Law. Jesus said their focus on merely meeting the external requirements of the Law was like eating from a bowl that was only washed on the outside or whitewashing the outside of a tomb and ignoring the rotting corpses within. By focusing exclusively on the letter of the Law, these would-be experts were oblivious to the spirit of the Law (Matthew 23:25-28).

RELIGIOUS RITUALS THREATENED

When Jesus began to turn his face toward Jerusalem, the tension between him and the Jewish religious leaders continued to grow. Not only were the Pharisees threatened by Jesus' authority, but also the Chief Priests of the Temple and their leader, the High Priest Caiaphas, who began to see Jesus as a direct threat to their power. Jesus was not as overtly critical of the Sadducees as he was of the Pharisees. But as with his participation in the synagogue, Jesus did not avoid the worship and rituals of the Temple. In fact, Jesus seemed to center his Jerusalem mission in the courts of the Temple Mount where he gathered huge crowds, but while he did, he pointed out the hypocrisy of those who put ritual concerns at a higher priority than doing God's will.

Jesus said, *if you are offering your gift at the altar and there remember that your brother has something against you, leave your gift there before the altar and go. First be reconciled to your brother, and then come and offer your gift.* (Matt. 5:23-24) In his famous parable of the Good Samaritan, Jesus described a priest and a Levite who pass by a badly injured person on their way to serve at the Temple in Jerusalem rather than helping a man in dire need (Luke 10:29-37). Jesus decried the practice of declaring property *"corban,"* meaning dedicated as an offering for the Temple, in order to avoid using that property to support elderly parents (Mark 7:10-13). In these teachings Jesus was continuing the great prophetic tradition of criticizing the ritualization of a relationship with God by making external religious acts more important than internal attitudes and moral responsibilities.

Perhaps Jesus' most radical challenge to the power base of the Sadducees was his statement, *"Hear me, all of you, and understand: There is nothing outside a person that by going into him can defile him, but the things that come out of a person are what defile him."* (Mark 7:14, 15) This directly contradicted the external ritualism exemplified in the elaborate rituals that took place at the Temple, which could only be considered effective if those performing them were ritually pure. While the Sadducees were obsessed with not touching or eating anything that would make them ritually impure, Jesus challenged them to consider what had the power to affect their thoughts and intentions and therefore corrupt their words and actions that resulted. Jesus was calling them to shift their attention from external religious rituals to the internal state of their hearts and minds.

Rather than embracing this shift toward internal holiness, the Chief Priests and Sadducees began to collude with the Pharisees, considering how to fight the growing influence of Jesus' teaching and his popularity with the people. In the end, the raising of Lazarus from the dead proved to be the final straw for these religious leaders. Not long before his final Passover, Jesus and his disciples came to Bethany, the village located on the opposite slope of the Mount of Olives from Jerusalem, in response to the news of his close friend's death. When he dramatically called the rotting corpse of Lazarus out of the tomb and back into life, it evoked powerful positive and negative reactions.

John writes, *many of the Jews therefore, who had come with Mary and had seen what he did, believed in him, but some of them went to the Pharisees and told them what Jesus had done. So the chief priests and the Pharisees gathered the council and said, "What are we to do? For this man performs many signs. If we let him go on like this, everyone will believe in him, and the Romans will come and take away both our place and our nation." But one of them, Caiaphas, who was high priest that year, said to them, "You know nothing at all. Nor do you understand that it is better for you that one man should die for the people, not that the whole nation should perish." He did not say this of his own accord, but being high priest that year he prophesied that Jesus would die for the nation, and not for the nation only, but also to gather into one the children of God who are scattered abroad. So from that day on they made plans to put him to death.* (John 11:45-53)

Jesus was so aware of this impending threat that he withdrew from the region of Jerusalem and hid out for a while in the rural village of Ephraim. The Chief Priests had notified their informants to let them know if they saw Jesus entering Jerusalem for Passover. As the crowds began to gather for the festival, they wondered if Jesus would show up (John 11:55-57). When he and his disciples did finally enter Jerusalem,

Jesus was riding a donkey, just as was prophesied of the Messiah in Zechariah 9:9, and the crowds were shouting out "hosanna" from the Messianic Psalm 118:25. We begin to understand why the Pharisees and Sadducees were freaking out! Now the problem for these increasingly desperate religious leaders was how to arrest Jesus without triggering a riot from the crowds.

Rather than try to calm the frayed nerves of the Sadducees and Pharisees, Jesus did the opposite by entering into the courts of the Temple and turning over the tables of the moneychangers and those selling doves. We will consider the purpose of this provocative act more closely later, but for now we can note what a direct challenge this was to the Temple hierarchy and the base of their power. In the days that followed, Jesus and his disciples spent the nights with their close friends Mary, Martha, and Lazarus in Bethany, drawing attention to the fact that Lazarus was still alive, and spent their days in the courts of the Temple where Jesus taught the crowds and told parables.

One of those parables was about a master who planted a vineyard and leased it out to tenants. When the master sent servants to collect the rent, the tenants refused to pay, beating and killing a succession of servants. When the master decided to send his own son, the tenants threw him outside the walls of the vineyard and killed him, hoping to have the vineyard for themselves. We know that Jesus was pointing to his impending death outside the walls of Jerusalem, but the religious leaders noticed that he was pointing to them as the scheming tenants. Matthew sums up Jesus' interaction with them by saying, *When the chief priests and the Pharisees heard his parables, they perceived that he was speaking about them. And although they were seeking to arrest him, they feared the crowds, because they held him to be a prophet.* (Matthew 21:33-46)

In the midst of this explosive tension strange bedfellows became even stranger. The Sadducees and the Pharisees decided to team up with the Herodians and hatched a plot to justify Jesus' arrest and eventual execution without causing riots. The first-century rabbinical method of teaching was called "midrash." This was a dialogical approach in which the rabbi posed questions for the people listening, and they in turn asked questions of the rabbi. The religious leaders decided to formulate tricky questions that would paint Jesus into a corner and force him into self-incrimination. This would give them the basis for arresting Jesus and quietly getting rid of him.

While Jesus was teaching the crowds who gathered in the Temple courts, the Pharisees and Herodians took the first shot at him by asking, *"Is it lawful to pay taxes to Caesar, or not?"* They knew if Jesus affirmed paying Roman taxes they could discredit him with the people by branding him as a collaborator. Likewise, if Jesus rejected Rome's right to exact taxes they could bring him before Pilate as a revolutionary. Jesus subverted their attempt to trap him by pointing to a coin bearing the image of Augustus, asking about the image on it, and offering the brilliant response, *"Therefore render to Caesar the things that are Caesar's, and to God the things that are God's."* (Matthew 22:17-21) Jesus, of course, was referring back to Genesis 1:27 which says we were created in God's image, and therefore is calling us to offer all of who we are back to God!

The Sadducees took another shot at Jesus by posing a question about how to implement the law of Levirate marriage in Deuteronomy 25:5-6 which requires the brother of a man who dies childless to marry their deceased brother's wife in order to produce children to carry on his line. Since the Sadducees did not believe in the resurrection, they surmised a situation in which a series of seven brothers died after having been married to the same woman and then asked, *"In the resurrection, therefore, of the seven, whose wife will she be? For they all had her."*

They assumed Jesus would either have to deny the validity of the Law, which would undermine his status as a rabbi, or support the unlikely scenario that seven men could be married to one woman in the afterlife. Either way Jesus' teaching would come into question and his followers would be divided. Again, Jesus took the debate to a whole new level when he answered, *"You are wrong, because you know neither the Scriptures nor the power of God. For in the resurrection they neither marry nor are given in marriage, but are like angels in heaven."* He then went on to quote Exodus 3:6 in defense of the reality of the resurrection (Matthew 22:23-33). In the end, Jesus knew that the power base of the Sadducees was soon coming to an end. When one of his disciples expressed amazement at the huge stones and soaring architecture of Herod's Temple Mount, Jesus said to him, *"Do you see these great buildings? There will not be left here one stone upon another that will not be thrown down."* (Mark 13:2) Forty years later the Roman legions fulfilled this prophecy quite literally.

If we put ourselves in the place of the crowds who first witnessed these theological duels between Jesus and the religious leaders, we will be amazed at Jesus' incredible insight and authority. But we will also understand that this same authority terrified and confounded the religious leaders who eventually resorted to the bribery of one of Jesus' own disciples, a snatch-and-grab in a darkened garden, and a sham trial in the middle of the night to enact their ill-fated plan aimed at silencing Jesus. The authority and power of Jesus as exemplified in the lives of his followers continues to threaten our humanistic religious systems and impulses today.

 # THE LIFE

LOSING SIGHT

A friend of mine tells the story of of the woman who was preparing a Christmas ham for an upcoming family feast. Her young daughter was watching as she carefully cut off the ends of the ham and placed it in a large roasting pan. The little girl asked, "Mommy, why do you cut the ends off the ham?" Her mother replied, "I am not sure darling, I think it is to allow the juices to flow more freely. It is the way my mother always did it." That night the extended family was seated at the table enjoying the meal, and everyone complemented the cook for the delicious ham. Her daughter piped up, "Grandma, why do you cut the ends off the ham?" The cook's mother replied, "I don't know dear, I think it makes the ham taste better. That is the way my mother always did it." At the end of the table her mother, the elderly matriarch of the family, began to chuckle. "Have you both been cutting off the ends of your ham all these years? I did it because it was the only way I could fit it into my small roasting pan!"

It is easy to lose sight of the reasons we do the things we do. When legal observances and religious rituals become an end in themselves, we slip into the core mistake of the Pharisees and the Sadducees. Although Jesus spent time in synagogues and at the Temple, he was not interested in the minutiae of religious traditions or the proper execution of complex religious rituals. Instead, Jesus focused on seeing and hearing the will of his Father in heaven and celebrating the good fruit that naturally flows from the lives of those who respond in faith to the rule of their true King here on earth. Jesus explained one of his most famous parables by saying, *"As for that* [seed] *in the good soil, they are those who, hearing the word, hold it fast in an honest and good heart, and bear fruit with patience."* (Luke 8:15)

The Pharisees rightly recognized that God had revealed himself in the Mosaic Law, but they made the fatal mistake of thinking they could legislate a right relationship with God by working harder to obey both those Laws and also the myriad rules they constructed to implement that Law in every area of their lives. They lost sight of the purpose of the Law, which was to connect them more closely to their heavenly Father so they could do his will in their daily lives.

The Sadducees rightly recognized the transcendent holiness of God but made the fatal mistake of thinking that correctly practicing religious rituals could make them holy as well. They lost sight of the purpose of the Temple rituals, which was to connect them more closely to the King of kings so they could extend his reign on earth. These misguided leaders twisted their rules and rituals into a toxic religion they could use to control others and enrich themselves. The Way of Jesus threatened all this.

REGAINING SIGHT

Jesus was clear that the goal of his life was not observing the Law, but rather knowing and doing his Father's will on earth as it is done in heaven. He said, *"Truly, truly, I say to you, the Son can do nothing of his own accord, but only what he sees the Father doing. For whatever the Father does, that the Son does likewise."* (John 5:19) Jesus didn't call people to follow the Law, he called them to follow him, so they could learn to hear the Father's voice and so do the Father's will. Jesus was not a lawbreaker as some claimed, but rather was going to the heart of the Law by inviting his followers into a world where God's will is done on earth as it is in heaven. This kingdom can't be imposed from the outside with laws and rules; it has to start within by the transformation of our hearts and the renewing of our minds.

When the blind man whom Jesus healed at the Pool of Siloam was interrogated by the Pharisees, the blind man asked them, *"Do you also want to become his disciples?"* And they reviled him, saying, *"You are his disciple, but we are disciples of Moses."* (John 9:27-28) Being a disciple of Jesus is very different than being a disciple of Moses. Following Jesus means entering into a new kind of relationship which God promised through the Prophet Jeremiah: *For this is the covenant that I will make with the house of Israel after those days, declares the Lord: I will put my law within them, and I will write it on their hearts. And I will be their God, and they shall be my people. And no longer shall each one teach his neighbor and each his brother, saying, 'Know the Lord,' for they shall all know me, from the least of them to the greatest, declares the Lord.* (Jeremiah 31:33-34)

Jesus was clear that external rituals cannot make us clean and pure before God. Instead, he invited people into a new kind of covenant relationship that would transform them from the inside out. This relationship is not defined by following religious rituals, but by receiving the cleansing presence of the Holy Spirit who empowers us to love God with all of our heart, soul, mind, and strength. Jesus was fulfilling God's promise through Ezekiel: *"I will take you from the nations and gather you from all the countries and bring you into your own land. I will sprinkle clean water on you, and you shall be clean from all your uncleannesses, and from all your idols I will cleanse you. And I will give you a new heart, and a new spirit I will put within you. And I will remove the heart of stone from your flesh and give you a heart of flesh. And I will put my Spirit within you, and cause you to walk in my statutes and be careful to obey my rules."* (Ezekiel 36:24-27)

Jesus radically challenged the entire system of ritual purity that led some to reject those they considered unclean and left others ostracized by circumstances that had nothing to do with their moral condition. This is why Jesus didn't seem to care about elaborate hand-washing rituals or making sure he did not touch anyone considered unclean. In fact, he scandalously reached out and touched lepers and commended a hemorrhaging woman who touched him because he understood that unclean people don't make clean people unclean. In the Kingdom of God, quite the opposite is true—those who have been made clean by Jesus have the power to make the unclean clean!

If we are going to learn the *Way* of Jesus in order to embody more fully the *Life* of Jesus, we will need to reconsider our entire orientation toward religion as a whole. Those of us who are church leaders, church members, or consider ourselves religious would do well to remember that Jesus was most critical of the most religious people of his time. Religion is simply how we seek to relate to God, but it becomes toxic when it is used to serve human rather than divine purposes. A religion that is defined by external observance and elaborate ritual puts us in control and allows us to put ourselves above others. We are all susceptible to the Pharisees' obsessive legalism or the Sadducees' cynical apathy.

Those who follow the Way of Jesus will inevitably come into conflict with the religious establishment, because the Kingdom of God is intrinsically opposed to the human control that religious systems are designed to establish. On the last night he was with them, Jesus told his disciples, *"They will put you out of the synagogues. Indeed, the hour is coming when whoever kills you will think he is offering service to God. And they will do these things because they have not known the Father, nor me."* (John 16:2-3) Those who seek to gain position and power through their religious systems will always be threatened by people who are following the Way of Jesus.

Dietrich Bonhoeffer, a pastor in Germany during World War II who was arrested by the Nazis for his involvement in a plot to assassinate Hitler, came face to face with the evil of religious systems that get co-opted by human agendas. He wrote these prophetic reflections to his brother-in-law from a prison cell in Berlin: "What keeps gnawing at me is the question, what is Christianity, or who is Christ actually for us today? The age when we could tell people that with words—whether with theological or with pious words—is past, as is the age of inwardness and of conscience, and that means the age of religion altogether. We are approaching a completely religionless age; people as they are now simply cannot be religious anymore. Even those who honestly describe themselves as 'religious' aren't really practicing that at all; they presumably mean something quite different by 'religious.'"[11]

The more we come to understand the way of the Pharisees and Sadducees and the reasons they were in such violent conflict with Jesus, the more deeply each of us will have to search our own soul to ask difficult questions. How do I use religious rules to keep God at arm's length and justify my self-righteous pride? How do I use religious systems to control others and guard my own sense of security and privilege? Am I hiding behind rituals that keep me from giving the Holy Spirit access and freedom to transform me from the inside out? Do my religious convictions actually keep me from the life that Jesus modeled and calls me to imitate?

As a pastor who has spent most of my adult life seeking to reform entrenched religious cultures into more Jesus-shaped cultures, I have often experienced first-hand the fight or flight reaction of both leaders and members in my churches. As it was with the rich young ruler who walked away from Jesus' invitation, it is sad when we see people leaving a faith community because they choose the familiar security of a religious system over a dynamic relationship with Jesus. It can also be very painful when church leaders respond to Jesus' criticism of externalized or ritualized religion with accusations and personal attacks, as the Sadducees and Pharisees did. I have

11 Dietrich Bonhoeffer, *Letters and Papers from Prison*, (New York, Touchstone, 1971), 279.

been repeatedly accused of self-serving motives and attacked as a heretic for trying to lead churches into a way of life that looks more like Jesus. Some have even claimed I was demon-possessed for such pursuits! Jesus shows us that challenging an established religious culture is not for the faint of heart.

Those of us who receive Jesus' invitation *"follow me"* have to decide if we are going to be disciples of Moses or disciples of Jesus (see John 9:28). It is a choice between outward conformity and inward transformation. We ultimately have to choose either religious systems that put us in control and allow us to see ourselves as better than those who are not like us, or a way of life that leads us to let go of control, take up our cross, and die. The way of humanistic religion offers status, position, power, and control. The Way of Jesus offers an indestructible Life which produces good fruit that lasts and even more carries the seeds of multiplication to produce an overflowing abundance that will never run out.

CHAPTER THREE

ESSENES AND ZEALOTS: THE RADICAL REBELS

They said, "Lord, shall we strike with the sword?" And one of them struck the servant of the high priest and cut off his right ear. But Jesus said, "No more of this!" And he touched his ear and healed him. (Luke 22:49-51)

 ## THE WAY

THE ESSENES: PRIESTLY SEPARATISTS

Now we come to the Essenes and Zealots, the other two influential groups in Jesus' world. These groups represent a more radical expression that contrasted the Sadducees and the Pharisees. In the middle of the second century BC, one of the Chief Priests at the Temple in Jerusalem came into serious conflict with the High Priest over the proper administration of the sacrificial rituals and rites. He became known to his followers as "The Teacher of Righteousness" and his nemesis the High Priest was called "The Wicked Priest." The disagreement between these two priestly leaders was probably over the correct dating of festivals and holy days. Because the Jewish people use a lunar calendar, based on the rotation of the moon around the earth, their months continually migrate earlier in the solar year, which is based on the earth's rotation around the sun. To keep the Jewish months in roughly the same solar seasons, they add a leap month every other year. You can imagine how easily the specific date of a festival could get confused.

The dating of festivals might not seem like a big deal to us, but for the Chief Priests this was important because the efficacy of the Temple sacrifices could be questioned if they were carried out on the wrong days. The Teacher of Righteousness brought such harsh criticism against the Temple hierarchy that the High Priest expelled him from the Temple and from Jerusalem. In response the Teacher of Righteousness took about 50 of his priestly followers into the desert and settled in an abandoned Israelite fortress on the northwest shore of the Dead Sea at a site called Qumran. There they formed a highly structured community who saw their mission as living a uniquely pure lifestyle to prepare the way for the coming of the Messiahs. This community grew in numbers, was decimated by an earthquake in 31 BC, and then flourished again until AD 68 when the Roman Tenth Legion expelled them and destroyed the site, which was never inhabited again. Nearly 1900 years later, three young Bedouin shepherds stumbled across a discovery at Qumran that would revolutionize our understanding of Jesus' world.

CAVE FOUR AT QUMRAN

In the winter of 1946-47, these three young men were wintering their flocks along the northwest shore of the Dead Sea when they accidently discovered a cave containing leather scrolls in clay jars. Disappointed the jars did not contain gold, they consoled themselves by trying to sell the rolls of leather to a shoemaker in Bethlehem. Thankfully an antiquities dealer recognized they were something special and smuggled them into the Old City of Jerusalem to the Monastery of St. Mark, where they were identified as rare ancient scrolls. So began the greatest discovery of ancient texts in modern history!

This discovery prompted the excavation of nearby Qumran and extensive study of the people who lived there at the time of Jesus. Eventually ancient scrolls were discovered in eleven different caves located in the limestone cliffs just west of the settlement. These caves yielded over 900 different manuscripts, comprised primarily of copies of books of the Hebrew Scriptures, but also included previously-known intertestamental books, devotional books, books written to guide the life of the community, and even a copper treasure map!

When we compare the description of the community life outlined in the scrolls to the settlement at Qumran, it appears that the people who lived there produced this unique scroll library. They lived a rigorously ascetic lifestyle preparing for the Messianic age by pursuing their vision of holiness. One of their disciplines was continually copying biblical and other scrolls. The result was a massive library that they carefully sealed in tall clay jars and hid in caves in the cliffs to protect them from the Roman army, which had come to put down the Jewish revolt in AD 66-70.

When we compare the writings and the settlement to ancient accounts of Jewish groups from that period, it appears that the community at Qumran

ESSENE SCRIBES AT QUMRAN

was made up of Essenes. Ancient historians Philo, Josephus, and Pliny the Elder all describe the unique lifestyle of the Essenes, and many of those details align with the excavated remains and the way of life described in the scrolls. For that reason, most scholars believe that an Essene community at Qumran produced the Dead Sea Scrolls.

These Essenes took as their mission statement the passage from Isaiah that reads, *A voice cries: "In the wilderness prepare the way of the Lord; make straight in the desert a highway for our God."* (Isaiah 40:3) They believed that two Messiahs were coming: a royal Messiah and a priestly Messiah. To prepare the way for the coming of these Messiahs, they sought to establish a completely pure and righteous community in the desert. To that end they followed an extraordinary regimen of ritual purity and held to a very strict interpretation of the Mosaic Law.

The Essenes at Qumran were even stricter about Sabbath observance than the Pharisees, going so far as to restrict defecation on the Sabbath. When it came to ritual purity, they were even more obsessed than the Sadducees. For instance, they seemed to throw away their pottery dishes after every meal, since pottery couldn't be ritually purified. Despite the scarcity of water in their bone-dry desert environment, they took full immersion baths for ritual purification twice a day. They built an elaborate water system designed to capture and store water from the flash floods that pour down from the cliffs above during the occasional winter thunderstorms. These aqueducts supplied water to as many as ten *mikvot* (ritual baths) that excavators have discovered in Qumran.

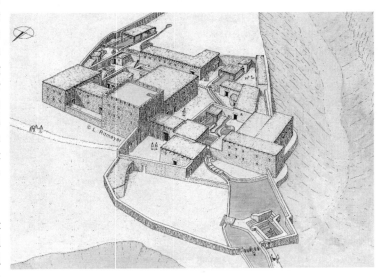

ESSENE COMMUNITY AT QUMRAN

This community at Qumran was organized on a democratic model where each member was given a vote in decisions affecting the community. Those who wished to join the community underwent a two-to-three-year probationary period before being accepted as full members. Those who broke one of the many rules of Qumran were marked down in a book. After two infractions a member could be expelled. The Qumran community was self-sufficient, growing dates, grain, and grapes, and raising livestock. They ate their meals together in silence seated in a specific order based on their rank in the community. They took an ascetic approach to life, eschewing comforts and pleasures. Most of the Essenes seemed to live a celibate life, but even those who were married were to engage in sexual intercourse only to procreate and otherwise to abstain.

The theology expressed in the writings composed at Qumran was decidedly fatalistic and apocalyptic, describing God as exercising his omnipotence by predetermining everything that would happen in creation and bringing history to a violent climactic conclusion. This predetermined plan reflected a profoundly dualistic worldview with only two ways for people to follow: the way of good or the way of evil. People could only belong to one of two groups: the Sons of Light or the Sons of Darkness. God and his angels move all things toward the final triumph of the Sons of Light over the Sons and Angels of Darkness in a great final battle led by the two coming Messiahs.

In the end there was a final battle at Qumran, but it was the Roman Tenth Legion who brought the community to an end in AD 68 during the first Jewish revolt. Some of these Essenes fled from Qumran south to Masada where they sought refuge with the Zealots who had taken control of the massive rock fortress.

THE ZEALOTS: POLITICAL REBELS

Now we turn to the sixth group from Jesus' world, which Josephus describes in great detail because he was formerly one himself.

In the year AD 6 the Roman Governor of Syria, Quirinius, carried out a census of Judea because that region had come under direct Roman rule following the deposition of Herod's son Archelaus. A Roman census had powerful political ramifications because it was the basis on which the Romans set the tax rates, and thus it was deeply resented by the conquered people who suffered under this burden. It was this deep resentment that sparked a tax revolt led by a resident of Gamla known as Judas the Galilean. Judas proclaimed that "taxation was no better than an introduction to slavery"[12] and admonished his fellow Jews not to register for the census. Judas began

---

12 Flavius Josephus, *Antiquities of the Jews*, trans. William Whiston, (Delmarva, 2016), Book 18, Chapter 1, Section 1, Digital.

gathering a following of rebels who intimidated the less revolutionary by burning the houses and stealing the cattle of those who did register.

GAMLA, ZEALOT STRONGHOLD

Although the tax revolt of Judas was quickly crushed by the Romans and in the subsequent decades was not thought to have amounted to anything (see the comment by Gamaliel in Acts 5:37), it became the beginning of a revolutionary movement dedicated to throwing off Roman rule by any means necessary. Josephus referred to this movement as the "Zealots" and identified them as the "fourth sect" of Judaism along with the Pharisees, Sadducees, and Essenes. He writes, "But of the fourth sect of Jewish philosophy, Judas the Galilean was the author. These men agree in all other things with the Pharisaic notions; but they have an inviolable attachment to liberty, and say that God is to be their only Ruler and Lord. They also do not value dying any kinds of death, nor indeed do they heed the deaths of their relations and friends, nor can any such fear make them call any man lord… And it was in Gessius Florus's time that the nation began to grow mad with this distemper, who was our procurator, and who occasioned the Jews to go wild with it by the abuse of his authority, and to make them revolt from the Romans."[13]

The Zealots were not a unified or well-organized movement, but were comprised of various groups of outlaws, rebels, and bandits of varying moral character. They were primarily religious nationalists who proclaimed God as their only true King and sought to overthrow Roman rule by covert violent action. Their theology and practice were closest to the Pharisees, from whom they drew a number of their leaders. They were absolutely opposed to the Herodians and deeply critical of the Sadducees, branding both as traitors and collaborators. Their military actions were aimed primarily at

13 Josephus, *War of the Jews,* trans. William Whiston, (Delmarva, 2016), Book 1, Chapter 6, Section 2.

ZEALOT BANDITS

Romans and Greeks, and they employed guerrilla tactics due to the fact that they were hopelessly outnumbered by the Roman legions.

A subset of the Zealots were the even more radical Sicarii, named after the curved daggers they carried. They aimed their fury not only at Romans and Greeks, but also at Jews they perceived as collaborators. At Passover they waded into the crowds in Jerusalem with their daggers hidden under their robes and began stabbing people at close quarters before melting back into the crowd. They also carried out targeted assassinations of high-ranking Jewish leaders such as Jonathan the High Priest. The most well-known leader of the Sicarii was a messianic figure named Menachem ben Yehuda, son of Judas the Galilean. When the First Jewish Revolt broke out in AD 66, Menachem claimed kingship of Jerusalem but was quickly killed by other Jewish factions.

As the Jewish revolt was just breaking out, Zealot commandos managed to sneak into most of the Herodian fortresses and take control of these imposing strongholds through surprise attack. The greatest of all these fortresses that fell under Zealot control stood on the southwest shore of the Dead Sea and was named *Masada* (Hebrew for "fortress"). Built by Herod the Great as his place of last refuge, Masada was the most impressive and impregnable of all the great Herodian strongholds guarding the eastern border of Israel.

THE FORTRESS OF MASADA

The Hasmonean rulers of Israel were the first to fortify this imposing site in the second century BC, but Herod was the one who turned it into one of the most luxurious yet defensible structures in the ancient world. Conceiving of it as a place of final refuge should he and his family need it, Herod stocked its massive storerooms and cisterns with enough provisions to supply an army under attack for years. In addition to these utilitarian storerooms and military barracks, there were ultra-luxurious residential buildings, Roman baths, a three-level palace carved into the northern end of the mountain, and even a huge swimming pool. It was here that the Essenes and Zealots fled the conquering Romans who came to quell the Jewish Revolt and attempted to make their ill-fated last stand against the Tenth Legion in AD 73.

THE TRUTH

DIFFERENT KINDS OF RADICAL

Whereas the Pharisees and Sadducees represented the Jewish religious and political *establishment*, the Essenes and the Zealots represented the Jewish religious and political *radicals*. This is the fabric of the world into which Jesus came. Jesus threatened the leaders of the establishment because he too was a radical, calling for the overthrow of the present order with a revolutionary new way of life. But he was a profoundly different kind of radical from either the Essenes or the Zealots.

The Essenes worked for a supernatural revolution in which the angels of heaven

NORTHERN PALACE AT THE FORTRESS OF MASADA

would wage war against the Romans and Herodians under the leadership of the two Messiahs to establish a new golden era of righteous Messianic rule. The Zealots worked for a flesh and blood revolution in which their armed forces would lead the Jewish people to throw off the shackles of Rome, replacing them with a restored Jewish monarchy. Jesus proclaimed a new era in which heaven is breaking into earth and God begins to rule on earth as he does in heaven. This vision is not so far from the vision of the Essenes and Zealots, but the means by which Jesus seeks to fulfill this vision is completely different.

Jesus rejected the Zealots' use of violence and coercion to accomplish political ends and fulfill their vision. After Jesus miraculously fed the crowds at the Sea of Galilee, John tells us, *Perceiving then that they were about to come and take him by force to make him king, Jesus withdrew again to the mountain by himself.* (John 6:15) The Kingdom that Jesus proclaimed is not one that can be established through political systems or by military force, but by the opposite. In his way of life, his parables, and his actions, Jesus demonstrated that the kingdom of God comes first through inner transformation which ultimately expresses itself in a community marked by outward actions of love and justice, self-sacrifice, and power.

In his famous Sermon on the Mount, Jesus explained the nature of his kingdom this way, *"You have heard that it was said, 'An eye for an eye and a tooth for a tooth.' But I say to you, Do not resist the one who is evil. But if anyone slaps you on the right cheek, turn to him the other also. And if anyone would sue you and take your tunic, let him have your cloak as well. And if anyone forces you to go one mile, go with him two miles. Give to the one who begs from you, and do not refuse the one who would borrow from you".* (Matthew 5:38-42) Not exactly the Zealot manifesto! Jesus was clear that this is not just an individualistic moral code, but a communal way of life that we learn together. Luke tells us, *Being asked by the Pharisees when the kingdom of God would come, he answered them, "The kingdom of God is not coming in ways that can be observed, nor will they say, 'Look, here it is!' or 'There!' for behold, the kingdom of God is in the midst of you."* (Luke 17:20-21)

FIRST-CENTURY GROUPS	BASIS OF POWER	SPHERE OF INFLUENCE	VIEW OF GOD	PRIMARY GOAL	PRIMARY STRATEGY
ROMANS	Brute Military Might	Conquered Territory	Many Capricious gods	Maximize Taxation Revenues	Control the People, Keep the Peace
HERODIANS	Authorization by Rome	Judea, Samaria, Galilee	Nominal Jewish Monotheism	Demonstrate Power and Status	Tax More, Build Bigger Monuments
SADDUCEES	The Sacrificial System of the Temple	The Temple Mount in Jerusalem	Holy and Unapproachable	Mediate God's Presence	Correctly Perform Rituals
PHARISEES	Knowledge of the Written and Oral Law	The Local Synagogue	A Just and Demanding Judge	Lead Others to Do God's Will	Teach in the Synagogues
ESSENES	A Common Rule of Life	A Separatist Community	A Conquering Priestly King	Prepare for the Messiahs	Establish a Perfectly Holy Community
ZEALOTS	Terrorism and Guerrilla Warfare	Public Places and Military Outposts	A Victorious Warrior King	Replace Rome with Jewish Rule	Attack Soldiers and Terrorize the People
JESUS	*Demonstrated Love and Power*	*Hearts and Minds of People*	*A Loving Father and Reigning King*	*Establish God's Kingdom by a New Covenant*	*Train Disciples to Multiply Families on Mission*

It is interesting to note that one of Jesus' twelve closest disciples was known as "Simon the Zealot" (Matthew 10:4). Some have interpreted this as a description of his enthusiastic nature, but it is more likely that Simon is one of the many "used-to-be's" of Jesus' inner circle. Some used to be fishermen, some used to be tax collectors, some used to be prostitutes, and perhaps Simon used to be a member of the Zealot party. If so, this Simon had realized that Jesus' Way was far better than the bloody and doomed path of his fellow Zealots.

Perhaps Simon or the wider influence of the Zealot movement had an impact on other disciples as well. Many have pointed out that Judas' remorse after betraying Jesus indicates he was seeking very different outcome than the arrest and execution of Jesus. Perhaps Judas was trying to force Jesus' hand to impose his rule by force. Even Peter had to be reminded that violent force is not the Way of Jesus. In the Garden of Gethsemane, when the Sanhedrin's soldiers were about to arrest Jesus, Peter grabbed a sword and cut off the ear of Malchus, the high priest's servant. Jesus said to Peter, *"Put your sword back into its place. For all who take the sword will perish by the sword. Do you think that I cannot appeal to my Father, and he will at once send me more than twelve legions of angels? But how then should the Scriptures be fulfilled, that it must be so?"* (Matthew 26:52-54)

Jesus rejected violence, but that doesn't mean he denied his identity as a King. While on trial before Pontius Pilate, Jesus had a private conversation with the Roman governor that John recounted: *So Pilate entered his headquarters again and called Jesus and said to him, "Are you the King of the Jews?" Jesus answered, "Do you say this of your own accord, or did others say it to you about me?" Pilate answered, "Am I a Jew? Your own nation and the chief priests have delivered you over to me. What have you done?" Jesus answered, "My kingdom is not of this world. If my kingdom were of this world, my servants would have been fighting, that I might not be delivered over to the Jews. But my kingdom is not from the world." Then Pilate said to him, "So you are a king?" Jesus answered, "You say that I am a king. For this purpose I was born and for this purpose I have come into the world—to bear witness to the truth. Everyone who is of the truth listens to my voice." Pilate said to him, "What is truth?"* (John 18:33-38)

Jesus was a radical who challenged the status quo and claimed to be the King who would reestablish God's rule on earth, but his revolution was not the fiery conflagration of the Zealots whose dream ultimately died in the rubble of the Temple and on the ramparts of Masada. Instead, Jesus' revolution began by welcoming the outcasts, healing the broken, feeding the hungry, delivering the oppressed, and declaring good news. His coronation took place on a rock outside of Jerusalem, where he wore a crown of thorns and allowed himself to be nailed to a cross. His reign began in an empty tomb and an upper room, where his Spirit was enthroned in the hearts of his followers. Those who follow Jesus are called to serve their King by continuing this revolution today.

PREPARING THE WAY FOR WHAT?

The Essenes took the opposite path of the Zealots. Instead of trying to take control of their society, they retreated from it. Abstaining from the comforts and pleasures of the world, they diligently pursued a life of strict discipline and ritual observance in the isolation of the desert—a stark contrast to the perceived corruption of their leaders in Jerusalem. Anticipating a coming cosmic conflict, they sought to align themselves with God's will in order to participate in his triumphant victory over the evil forces of darkness that hold captive God's people. At Qumran they built a community that reflected their radical ideals of purity and obedience, believing this would pave the way for the coming of the Messiahs who in turn would accomplish this great victory.

As we reflect on the unique setting, lifestyle, and teaching of the Essenes at Qumran, our thoughts are naturally drawn to John the Baptist who baptized people in the Jordan River just eleven miles north of Qumran. Like these Essenes John came from a priestly background. He retreated into the desert and pursed an ascetic lifestyle as did they. His diet of wild locusts and date honey matched the diet allowed by the rules of the Qumran community who vowed not to receive food or clothing from those outside their circle. John proclaimed a similarly apocalyptic message of God's coming judgment and used the same term, "brood of vipers," to describe their corrupt religious leaders. The outward mark of John's ministry was ritual immersion, much like the exaggerated number of *mikvot* at Qumran.

By far the most striking similarity between John and the Essenes at Qumran was their stated purpose in the desert. As with the writings of the Qumran community, the key Scripture verse the Gospel writers associated with John's mission was Isaiah 40:3. When the religious leaders from Jerusalem asked John who he was and why he baptized, he quoted this very passage, *"I am the voice of one crying out in the wilderness, 'Make straight the way of the Lord,' as the prophet Isaiah said."* (John 1:22-23) Both John and the members of the Qumran community understood their mission was to make messianic preparations in the desert. Later, after John had been imprisoned by Herod Antipas, Jesus described John by quoting from Malachi 3:1, *"This is he of whom it is written, 'Behold, I send my messenger before your face, who will prepare your way before you.'"* (Matthew 11:10)

What was the relationship between John the Baptist and the Essenes at Qumran? Was John influenced by their teaching and practice? Was John a member of their community? These are questions for which we do not have definitive answers. However, the proximity and similarities are so strong that it seems nearly impossible John had no connection with Qumran. Given the age of John's parents when he was born and the Essene practice of adopting orphaned children, some have surmised that John may have been adopted into the community at Qumran. This possibility seems more likely in light of the cryptic comment Luke makes about John after his birth: *The child grew and became strong in spirit, and he was in the wilderness until the day of his public appearance to Israel.* (Luke 1:80)

The Gospel writers make no mention of Essenes coming to hear John preach or submitting to his baptism, but they do describe the extremely broad scope of those who came to John. Mark describes the response to John this way: *All the country of Judea and all Jerusalem were going out to him and were being baptized by him in the river Jordan, confessing their sins.* (Mark 1:5) Again, we can't say with certainty, but it would be hard to imagine that the Essenes living so nearby did not at least send some representatives to investigate John's message.

If John were a part of the Qumran community at some point, it is easy to see why he would have left or been expelled given the differences between their theology and methodology. While the Essenes withdrew into the desert as an elite band to remove themselves from a corrupt world, John called people of all walks of life to join him in the desert. While writers of the scrolls anticipated two Messiahs, John was preparing the way for just one. While those at Qumran practiced constant ritual bathing to sustain an external purity, John invited people into a one-time immersion as a sign of an internal reorientation he described with the admonition "repent." While the Essenes believed that God had long ago determined who would be the Sons of Light and the Sons of Darkness, John earnestly called everyone to prepare their hearts to recognize and receive the Messiah and so become part of God's coming kingdom.

Perhaps the most striking difference between the Qumran Essenes and John the Baptist was the nature of the messianic age for which they were preparing. While the Qumran community was preparing for a military battle between the forces of light and the forces of darkness, led by a royal Messiah and a priestly Messiah, John looked at Jesus and declared, *"Behold, the Lamb of God, who takes away the sin of the world!"* (John 1:29) Not only was John prophetically recognizing that Jesus would conquer by laying down his life as a sacrificial offering, but he was also proclaiming that this transformational victory would be available to all people, not just a predetermined select few.

If Thursday evening were the official start of Passover, then the High Priest and Chief

Priests violated the Law on Friday morning when they petitioned Pilate to crucify Jesus, because the first day of Passover is to be a day of rest (Leviticus 23:7). However, if Jesus celebrated Passover a day earlier than the Temple officials, it does not necessarily mean that Jesus was following the Essene calendar. There was also a discrepancy in calendars between the Pharisees in Galilee and the Sadducees in Jerusalem. Most likely, Jesus was following the Galilean calendar and celebrated the Passover a day earlier than the Temple officials.

While we might try to point out a few parallels between Jesus and the Essenes, in almost every way they are diametrically opposed in their way of life. The community at Qumran represented an even more extreme form of the Sadducees' obsession with ritual purity and the Pharisees' obsession with legalistic minutiae, and so the Way of Jesus diverges that much more from the way of the Essenes. While the Essenes separated themselves in an attempt to be pure, Jesus engaged the unclean in order to make them clean. Where the Essenes created even more rules and rituals to try and manufacture holiness, Jesus hung out with tax collectors and said, *"Go and learn what this means, 'I desire mercy, and not sacrifice.' For I came not to call the righteous, but sinners."* (Matthew 9:13) Where the Essenes prepared to fight a battle to establish God's rule for a predetermined few, Jesus prepared to lay down his life to bring God's kingdom to all people. In the end we see the stark contrast of outcomes. The Way of Jesus became a movement that changed the world, while the way of the Essenes melted into the mists of time.

 # THE LIFE

IN THE WORLD BUT NOT OF THE WORLD

Those who have answered Jesus' call to discipleship need to understand the world in which Jesus lived, so we can relate to our world the way he related to his. On the last night Jesus was with his disciples, they walked in the light of a full moon from the large house in the southwest part of Jerusalem, where they had celebrated the Passover, across the Kidron Valley, and up to the Garden of Gethsemane on the western slope of the Mount of Olives. While they walked, Jesus continued to teach them and then concluded with an extensive prayer for them. In that petition he said to the Father, *"I have given them your word, and the world has hated them because they are not of the world, just as I am not of the world. I do not ask that you take them out of the world, but that you keep them from the evil one. They are not of the world, just as I am not of the world. Sanctify them in the truth; your word is truth. As you sent me into the world, so I have sent them into the world."* (John 17:14-18)

Jesus was praying for our Heavenly Father to save us from two fatal mistakes: the error of the Essenes and the error of the Zealots. The Zealots wanted to change their world, but by employing the worldly means of coercive power, they ended up becoming thoroughly like the world they were trying to change. Although they set out to establish God's righteous rule, anytime they gained control of a city or fortress, their rule looked more like the Romans they hated than the God they claimed to serve. They imposed their will through violent terror. They plundered defenseless peasants. They lined their own pockets. They killed each other when they disagreed. In the end the Romans systematically wiped them from the face of the earth. When Jesus' disciples felt the temptation to use coercive force to establish his rule, Jesus warned them, *"For all who take the sword will perish by the sword."* (Matthew 26:52) To use the language of Jesus' prayer, the Zealots had become "of the world" rather than those who were changing the world.

The Essenes also wanted to change the world. They knew only God could bring about the changes that were needed, so they withdrew from the world to wait for God to come and do the work. As powerful as prayer and contemplation of Scripture can be, the problem for the Qumran community was that they isolated themselves so completely that they no longer had any impact on the world around them. While they obsessed over their religious rituals and rules, the world continued on its self-destructive path unchanged. After the Romans came and destroyed their settlement at Qumran, the Essenes simply faded into obscurity, mostly unknown for the next 1900 years. If it were not for the library of scrolls they hid in the cliffs, we would know almost nothing about them today. To use the language of Jesus' prayer, they had gone "out of the world."

Like the Essenes and Zealots, Jesus came to change the world, but by his clear example and teaching Jesus offered a fundamentally different Way. Jesus refused to impose his will on anyone and utterly rejected violence as a means to God's ends. He not only taught his followers to turn the other cheek and go the extra mile, but he did it himself, all the way to Golgotha. Jesus refused to separate himself from people on the basis of religious rules and categories. He embraced the unclean, welcomed the outcasts, and broke bread with sinners. In so doing, Jesus was the one who impacted the world, not the other way around.

Jesus was clear that those who follow him will do the same. He said, *"You are the salt of the earth, but if salt has lost its taste, how shall its saltiness be restored? It is no longer good for anything except to be thrown out and trampled under people's feet. You are the light of the world. A city set on a hill cannot be hidden. Nor do people light a lamp and put it under a basket, but on a stand, and it gives light to all in the house. In the same way, let your light shine before others, so that they may see your good works and give glory to your Father who is in heaven."* (Matthew 5:13-16) The Zealots had lost their saltiness and became just like the Romans they were trying to overthrow. The Essenes claimed to be the Sons of Light, but any light in them was completely covered up by the basket of their religious separatism. Jesus calls us to a different Way by which we will learn how to live in the world, but not of the world.

CHANGING OUR WORLD

Do you want to change your world? The first followers of Jesus believed this was their calling, and they fulfilled their mission in the most remarkable way. From Philip baptizing the Ethiopian eunuch, to Peter stepping over the threshold of Cornelius' house, to Paul establishing the pagan center of Ephesus as the hub of a missional movement that lasted for centuries, these early followers of Jesus lived in the world in order to transform lives, but certainly did not compromise their integrity and become of the world. Incredibly, in less than 300 years, more than half the people in the Roman Empire had come to embrace Jesus! Gradually, however, the errors of the Zealots and the Essenes began to creep into the movement of Jesus.

When Constantine issued the Edict of Milan in AD 313, officially recognizing Christianity as an accepted religion in the Roman Empire, it seemed like a victory for the followers of Jesus. But this edict also marked a deadly shift toward the error of the Zealots, as the Roman emperors wedded their political ambitions to their Christian faith. Within 80 years the acceptance of Christianity turned into the imposition of Christianity. In AD 392 Emperor Theodosias I issued a decree threatening sanctions and violence against those who did not adhere to the official doctrines and practices of the church. He declared, "It is Our will that all the peoples who are ruled by the administration of Our Clemency shall practice that religion which the divine Peter the Apostle transmitted to the Romans... The rest, whom We adjudge demented and insane, shall sustain the infamy of heretical dogmas, their meeting places shall not receive the name of churches, and they shall be smitten first by divine vengeance and secondly by the retribution of Our own initiative."[14] Like the Zealots before them, these leaders believed they could change the world by imposing their understanding of God's will on others by force. This mindset eventually led to atrocities such as the Crusades and the Spanish Inquisition. It is hard to imagine how anyone who claims to follow Jesus could justify the evil of trying to convert others at the tip of a sword, but this is what can happen when we allow our culture to form us into people who are not just in the world but have become of the world.

Ironically, in the early church the ultimate test of faith was faithfulness to Jesus at the tip of a sword. The martyrs who gave up their lives for their faith became the spiritual ideal of early Christianity. After the Edict of Milan, the heroism of martyrdom gave way to the rise of monasticism as a spiritual ideal. Monks and nuns who forsook worldly comforts, pleasures, and possessions were seen as those who refused to compromise their complete devotion to Jesus. It is true that many monks did devote themselves to a life of worship, teaching, and service, even preserving a form of the discipling and missional spiritual family that Jesus built in Capernaum (see Chapter 7). But over time the monastic movement began to look more like the Essenes than the first followers of Jesus. Some of these medieval monks became obsessed with the minutiae of their elaborate rituals and ascetic rules, completely separating themselves from the world around them. In order to avoid becoming of the world, they ended up no longer being in the world.

In his classic book *Christ and Culture*, H. Richard Niebuhr describes three ways the followers of Jesus have related to the world around them: 1. "Christ against culture" 2. "Christ of culture" 3. "Christ over culture."[15] Christ against culture is the Pharisees' and Essenes' mistake of distancing ourselves from an evil world. Christ of culture is the Sadducees' and Zealots' mistake of becoming like the world we are seeking to change. Christ over culture is the recognition that Jesus transcends all cultures in order to transform this broken world into the Kingdom of God. Rejecting options 1 and 2 as aberrations of the Way of Jesus, Niebuhr unpacks Christ over culture by describing three complementary ways we can engage with the world around us: by bringing Christ and our culture together (synthesis), by holding Christ and our culture in tension (paradox), and by shaping our

---

14 Codex Theodosianus XVI 1.2, Henry Bettenson, ed., Documents of the Christian Church, (London: Oxford University Press, 1943), p. 31, Digital.

15 H. Richard Niebuhr, *Christ and Culture* (New York, Harper and Row, 1951)

culture by Christ (transformation). Learning how to embody the Good News of Jesus for those in the world around us without compromising the vision and values of his Kingdom is the great mission of Jesus' disciples in every age.

When I first came to know Jesus as a teenager, I was zealous for God and veered dangerously close to the mistake of the Pharisees and Essenes. I felt I had come to a very clear understanding of God's will and wasn't too shy to share it with those around me. I remember being surprised by the reaction of the girls in my youth group when I declared that wearing makeup was a sin. I remember the hurt on the face of my friend's mother when I declared at his birthday party that the fortune cookies she was serving us were influenced by the devil. I wanted to set up rules that would keep us untainted by the world. I still needed to learn what Jesus meant when he said, *"Hear me, all of you, and understand: There is nothing outside a person that by going into him can defile him, but the things that come out of a person are what defile him."* (Mark 7:14-15)

Others in my youth group made the opposite mistake of the Sadducees and Zealots, losing their distinctiveness by fully embracing the vision and values of the world around them rather than those of God's Kingdom. It was hard to distinguish them and their way of life from the unbelieving students in our high school. As Jesus put it, *"if salt has lost its taste, how shall its saltiness be restored? It is no longer good for anything except to be thrown out and trampled under people's feet."* (Matthew 5:13)

How do you respond to the world around you? Do you find yourself being influenced by the seductive values of the prevailing culture so that you begin to lose your saltiness? Or do you find yourself withdrawing from the repulsive values of the prevailing culture so much that you begin to lose touch with those who are far from God? How do you respond to the person and example of Jesus? Are you willing to trust him and follow his example? Like him, are you reaching out to touch the unclean, opening your spiritual family to welcome the outcasts, showing compassion on the sheep who are without a shepherd, and yet inviting them all to follow you as you follow Jesus in a far better Way?

It all comes down to how we respond to Jesus. The Romans killed Jesus because they could not abide his claim to be a King. The Herodians, Pharisees, and Sadducees plotted against Jesus because they were terrified that their authority was threatened by his. The Essenes ignored Jesus because they did not realize he was the Messiah for whom they were preparing. The Zealots sought to co-opt the revolutionary message of Jesus because they misunderstood the nature of God's Kingdom. Crowds flocked to Jesus, demons fled from Jesus, leaders fought with Jesus, and disciples followed Jesus.

Jesus came into a world very different than ours in some ways, but very much like ours in other ways. If we look closely, we can see the Romans, Herodians, Sadducees, Pharisees, Essenes, and Zealots at work all around us today. We all face forces like Rome that simply want to dominate us. We face forces like the Herodians who claim to have our best interests at heart but do not. We can either collaborate with these forces like the Sadducees, legislate against them like the Pharisees, try to fight them like the Zealots, or simply withdraw like the Essenes. Jesus chose to engage all these forces in the authority of his Father and by the power of the Spirit, pointing people to a better Way. In the end Jesus laid down his life and rose from the dead in order to transform culture and create a whole new world—the Kingdom of God.

Following Jesus is not disengaging from the world around us nor forcing our way upon the world, but instead being the agents of Jesus' love and power to transform this broken world by laying down our lives as he did. If we are going to be salt and light in our world today, we will intentionally reject the way of the Zealots and the way of the Essenes, embracing instead the Way of Jesus. How can we live in this world, but not end up being of this world? How can we become the conduits of God's love and power that alone can transform the kingdoms of this world into the Kingdom of God? Only by trusting the Truth of Jesus and learning to follow the Way of Jesus will the Life of Jesus be increasingly manifested and multiplied through our lives. It is to the extraordinary and unparalleled Way of Jesus that we now turn.

PART II

JESUS' PREPARATION:
NO WINE BEFORE ITS TIME

"But new wine must be put into fresh wineskins." (Luke 5:38)

JOHN BAPTIZING IN THE JORDAN RIVER

CHAPTER FOUR

JESUS' BIRTH: THIS CHANGES EVERYTHING

And the Word became flesh and dwelt among us, and we have seen his glory, glory as of the only Son from the Father, full of grace and truth. (John 1:14)

TIME TO PREPARE

I am not a patient person by nature. A product of my culture and my personality, I like things to happen quickly. I hate to wait. But over the years I have learned the value of taking time to prepare. Some things, you just can't rush. For example, stew cooked in the Crock-Pot tastes so much better than a microwave dinner.

We regularly lead people on spiritual journeys in the Footsteps of Jesus and Paul. Our Jesus trips pose a physical challenge for most people because we do so much walking around the Old City of Jerusalem and hiking in the desert. We coach people to prepare for our trips with a specific training regimen and course of study. We can always tell the difference between those who have taken the time to prepare properly, and they get so much more out of the experience because of this preparation.

Jesus understood the importance of preparation. Even though God could have incarnated himself as a grown man, he chose to be born as a baby and grow into manhood. Even though he was already smart enough as a teenager to confound the greatest teachers of Israel, the boy Jesus chose to submit to his parents and live an apparently unremarkable life in Nazareth until he turned thirty. Even though he could have gone directly from his extended family home to the local synagogue to announce his messianic vision, instead he first traveled south to the Judean wilderness where he submitted to baptism and a time of testing in the desert.

In doing all this, Jesus knew the Father was preparing him for his unique mission. He was rooting Jesus in the life of an extended family and community. He was planting his Word deep in Jesus' heart and mind. He was growing Jesus in his identity as the Son of the Father. He was preparing Jesus to exercise the authority of the King of kings and to live in his power. It did not happen overnight. It took time.

Creating something that is new and good quality takes time, like fine wine. And like new wine, it needs new containers. New wine was kept in leather bags because the leather could stretch to accommodate the expansion of the fermenting wine. Old wineskins are already stretched out and would burst as the new wine ferments. Jesus pointed this out: *"no one puts new wine into old wineskins. If he does, the new wine will burst the skins and it will be spilled, and the skins will be destroyed. But new wine must be put into fresh wineskins."* (Luke 5:37-38) As a member of the Jewish people and a descendant of David, Jesus fulfilled the prophetic promise of the expected Messiah. He represents the continuation of God's unchanging purpose since the creation of the world. And yet Jesus came to fulfill those promises and that purpose in such an unexpected way that he had to demonstrate radically new wineskins for this amazing new wine! That new wine had to be carefully prepared in the new wineskin of Jesus, and it took thirty years to ferment.

Those of us who seek to follow Jesus would do well to note the significance of this season of preparation. In our enthusiasm to learn the Way of Jesus more fully, it would be tempting to jump directly into his Galilean mission, because it is so significant for us. However, doing so could easily cause us to misunderstand the meaning of that mission for us. If Jesus had to be prepared for the new wine of his mission, how much more do we need to submit to seasons of preparation? Understanding Jesus' season of preparation will help us to prepare for the new things God wants to do in and through our lives. So, we begin at the beginning, in the little town of Bethlehem.

 # THE WAY

CITY OF THE KING

The city of Bethlehem, meaning "house of bread," is located about seven miles south of Jerusalem. It is first identified in the time of Jacob and Rachel (Genesis 35:19) but is hardly mentioned in the Bible until the rise of David, who was born there to an Ephrathite family. The prophet Samuel visited Bethlehem and unexpectedly anointed David, the eighth and youngest son of Jesse, to replace Saul as King of Israel. We know that ancient Bethlehem was a walled city with a well, as reflected in David's homesick cry from the cave of Adullam, *"Oh, that someone would give me water to drink from the well of Bethlehem that is by the gate!"* a wish quickly fulfilled by three of his mighty men (2 Samuel 23:15-17). Beyond this we have no other biblical descriptions of David's hometown.

CHURCH OF THE NATIVITY IN BETHLEHEM

Perhaps that is because, when he was publicly anointed as King of Israel, David made the strategic decision not to make his hometown the capital of his new kingdom. Instead, he captured the Jebusite city of Jebus near the border between Judah and Benjamin, in order to unify the tribes of Israel under a neutral capital renamed Jerusalem. Bethlehem began to slip into obscurity, until the Prophet Micah proclaimed some 200 years later, *"But you, O Bethlehem Ephrathah, who are too little to be among the clans of Judah, from you shall come forth for me one who is to be ruler in Israel, whose coming forth is from of old, from ancient days."* (Micah 5:2) From that point on "the City of David" became a source of messianic inspiration.

The Gospel of Luke tells us that Joseph and Mary were compelled to travel south from Nazareth in Galilee to Bethlehem in Judea because of an injunction issued by Caesar Augustus during *the first registration when Quirinius was governor of Syria* (Luke 2:2). As we discussed in Chapter 3, the Romans periodically conducted population counts to establish their tax quotas. Josephus tells us about a local census conducted by Quirinius some ten years later, in AD 6, which sparked the revolt led by Judas the Galilean. No record of an earlier census has yet been discovered, but it certainly would not have been an unusual occurrence for those living under Roman domination.

For those in modern western cultures, our picture of Jesus' birth has been massively shaped by the popular representations of these events at Christmastime. However, much of what we picture is not true to Middle Eastern culture and traditions. Let's look more closely at some of the cultural factors that form the backdrop of Jesus' birth in Bethlehem.

ALL IN THE FAMILY

One of the biggest cultural differences between modern western cultures and biblical culture is the nature and role of the family. In most North American and European cultures today, the family is assumed to be parents and children—the nuclear family. The home is assumed to be the place where a single nuclear family lives—a single-family dwelling. Work is assumed to be something that takes place in an office or a workplace, separate from the home and family.[16] I grew up in a single-family home with my dad, mom, and sister, and my parents left the house to do their work. That's how my parents grew up, and that is how we raised our sons.

In biblical times no one would ever willingly choose to live that way, because it was too dangerous and difficult. Unless they were destitute or an outcast, people lived as part of an extended family comprised of at least three generations of both blood and non-blood relations, including grandparents, great aunts and uncles, parents, aunts and uncles, brothers and sisters, cousins, business partners, close family friends, and slaves. Multiple nuclear families lived together in a house designed with multiple rooms built around an open-air central courtyard.

This extended family was built around a common family business and generally carried out that business in the courtyard of the house where they also shared life and meals together. This extended family and the home they shared is called the *beth* in Hebrew Scriptures and the *oikos* in the Greek New Testament. There is no word in English exactly corresponding to these terms, so we usually translate them "household," "house," or "family," but none of those words accurately convey the way that

---

16 Although the internet is rapidly changing this assumption.

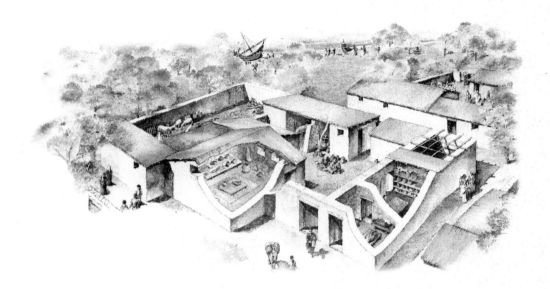

EXTENDED FAMILY HOME

biblical people actually lived and the way many Middle Eastern people still live today.

The two primary reasons nearly everyone in Jesus' time lived as part of an *oikos* was protection and provision. If you were living with just a nuclear family and bandits attacked your home, you were on your own. There was no 911 to call. No police cars patrolled the neighborhood. One dad alone might not be able to protect his family, but an extended family could band together and protect the extended family home. Likewise, if you were living as only a nuclear family and mom and dad fell sick, who would bring in the crops and care for the kids? In the biblical *oikos* everyone worked together to make the family business a success and provide for everyone in the family no matter what challenges came along.

We have found this largely true in the Middle East today. Our closest friends in the Old City of Jerusalem belong to two extended families of Palestinian Christians who have lived there for many centuries. Two brothers from one family married two sisters from another family, and now the two extended families are deeply interconnected. Anytime we are invited to their homes, at least three generations are represented there. We have been honored to attend baptisms, confirmations, and graduations, and they always celebrate with their extended families. They opened a lovely new restaurant in Jerusalem, and every time we go there, multiple members of both families work together to make the family business a success. We see this same pattern lived out time and time again in our travels across Israel, Egypt, Turkey, and Greece.

Supporting your extended family is one of the highest values in biblical culture. One of the other highest values is hospitality. From Abraham's welcome of the three strangers (Genesis 18:1-8) to Zacchaeus' welcome of Jesus (Luke 19:1-10), we see countless examples of the importance of hospitality throughout the Bible. Again, we have experienced this many times on our travels in biblical lands over the past 30 years. Failing to offer hospitality implies that your family is not able to provide it, which brings shame upon the whole extended family. Failing to provide hospitality for a visiting relative is unthinkable!

THE GUEST ROOM

The extended family homes from the time of Jesus that we have described were normally comprised of three to eight rooms, each connecting to an open courtyard. Sometimes these homes were built onto the front of a natural cave or man-made room cut into a stone face or slope. We can see first-century examples of this in the house of Mary's family and the house of Joseph's family in Nazareth. We can also see current examples of this in the village of Silwan, just outside of Jerusalem, where numerous homes are built as extensions of ancient rock-cut tombs and caves in the hillside. Because hospitality was such a high value, one of the rooms in the house was often designated a guest room. This room might be used for other purposes when no guests were present but would always be available to house visiting family and friends. Sometimes this room served the dual purpose of guest room and dining room when the family needed to eat inside due to the weather. Sometimes this was an upstairs room in larger homes or a lightweight structure built on the roof of smaller homes.

In addition to the rooms built around the courtyard, there was often a section of the extended family home reserved for the family's animals. Ancient people did not typically keep pets, but even families who were not shepherds by trade would own some livestock to provide wool, milk, butter, cheese, eggs, and meat for the family. During the day these livestock would be taken outside the village to graze in the fields or were tethered outside the house, but at night they were brought inside for safe keeping. Sometimes the area set aside for the animals was a lower level of the main room in the house or a separate walled section connected to the house. We can see a first-century example of this in the house of Simon and Andrew in Capernaum, where one end of the house had an attached pen for the animals.

SHEPHERDS AND WISE MEN

Since their beginning, the people of Israel have herded flocks of sheep and goats. When Abram and Sarai came to Canaan, they brought with them such extensive livestock that overgrazing was a source of conflict (Genesis 13:2-7). Moses was herding his flocks when God revealed himself and called him (Exodus 3:1-12). King David grew up keeping his family's sheep and goats, and the most famous of all his psalms describes the God of Israel as the ultimate Good Shepherd (Psalm 23). In contrast to these idealized examples of Hebrew shepherds, Ezekiel prophesied against the corrupt leaders of Israel, describing them as bad shepherds (Ezekiel 34).

BEDOUIN SHEPHERD AND FLOCK

Keeping flocks was very time-consuming and difficult work. The shepherd rose early in the morning, led his sheep and goats from their pen in the village out into the surrounding hillsides where their flocks could graze and find water. There were no fenced pastures, so the shepherd had to work vigilantly to keep the sheep and goats from straying into danger. Aside from the winter months, green grass is hard to find in the Middle East, and it was the shepherd's job to lead the flock down into the desert valleys (wadis) where water collects, and the flock could graze. But in these wadis, the danger of predators and flash floods threaten the flock, so the shepherd would use his rod to protect the sheep and his staff to guide the sheep.

At the end of the day, the shepherd led the flock back into the village and carefully counted as each passed back into the pen. As spring turned into summer, the shepherd had to lead their flocks further and further to find green pasture, necessitating sleeping out in the open or in a nearby cave with their flocks for weeks or months on end. They fashioned a temporary pen out of stones and brush and slept in the opening of the pen to prevent thieves and predators from entering or livestock from wandering off. We still see this same pattern being lived out today by the traditional Bedouin shepherds we meet when we are hiking the valleys of the Judean desert. Jesus referred to this practice when he said, *"Truly, truly, I say to you, he who does not enter the sheepfold by the door but climbs in by another way, that man is a thief and a robber. But he who enters by the door is the shepherd of the sheep. To him the gatekeeper opens... Truly, truly, I say to you, I am the door of the sheep."* (John 10:1-3, 7)

The constant demands of shepherding flocks kept shepherds from much of the normal social and religious interactions of their community. It is easy to see why shepherding was considered one of the lowest professions on the social ladder and was often delegated to the youngest member of the family or the poorest member of the community. Remember that David, the youngest of eight brothers, was missing from the house of Jesse when the prophet Samuel came to visit because he was out in the fields with their flocks. (1 Samuel 16:11)

Despite the prevalence of positive shepherd images in the Hebrew Scriptures, by the time of Jesus religious leaders generally looked down on real-life shepherds not only as socially deprived, but morally flawed as well. As the oral law of Judaism developed, it became more and more difficult for shepherds to follow its many religious rituals and rules, due to the rigors of their profession. As a result, the Pharisees in Jesus' time considered shepherds and other "people of the land," unclean, assuming they could not keep the minutiae of these many complex rules. These Pharisees and other rabbis refused to eat with shepherds, along with tax collectors and others they considered unredeemed "sinners."[17] That God chose to announce Jesus' birth to lowly shepherds before anyone else gives us a hint as to the kind of Messiah Jesus turns out to be. Not a pampered prince growing up in a palace, but a stone-cutter growing up as part of an ordinary family living in an anonymous village of Galilee. Not a religious elitist limiting himself to the upper crust of society, but a Good Shepherd seeking lost sheep and having compassion on sheep who are without a shepherd.

17 Kenneth Bailey, *The Good Shepherd* (Downers Grove, Il, Intervarsity Press, 2014) 110-116, Digital. This is by far the most in-depth and accurate cultural and historical study of the role of shepherds in the Bible

At the other end of the social ladder, in stark contrast to these shepherds, were the exotic, wealthy, and powerful magi from Persia. Leading figures in the religious court of Persian kings, these priestly scholars combined astrology, wisdom traditions, and magical incantations in an attempt to understand life in the present and predict events in the future. They studied the stars alongside ancient manuscripts and drew conclusions to suggest the best path forward. Many Jews remained in Persia after their liberation from the Babylonian exile, so it is certain that the magi would have been familiar with the prophets of Israel and their promise of a coming Messiah. Although these Magi would have been regarded as pagans by the Jews of Jesus' time, they would also have evoked great awe, curiosity, and wonder in a village like Bethlehem, having come from over 900 miles away and representing such a mysterious and different culture. The visit of the Magi points to the true identity of Jesus. Although clothed in the humble circumstances of an unremarkable and ordinary birth, Jesus is anything but ordinary. We see in his exotic royal visitors a sign of his heavenly origins, divine nature, and royal lineage. In the visit of both shepherds and wise men we begin to see the great paradox of Jesus' true identity: the all-powerful God of the universe who emptied himself, took on human flesh, and walked among us.

 # THE TRUTH

A TRIP TO BETHLEHEM

Unlike some of his medieval portrayals, Jesus did not simply appear on earth as a fully grown thirty-year-old man. Because he was both fully divine and fully human, Jesus had to go through a process of development and preparation like all human beings. The writer of Hebrews puts it this way: *Although he was a son, he learned obedience through what he suffered. And being made perfect, he became the source of eternal salvation to all who obey him...* (Hebrews 5:8-9) The more accurately we understand the events surrounding Jesus' birth, the better starting point we will have for learning to follow the Way of Jesus.

Although Jesus' mother Mary came from Nazareth, it seems that Joseph originally came from Bethlehem. It is likely that Joseph's family, who were builders (Greek: *tekton*), had moved from Bethlehem to Nazareth at the end of the first century BC in order to benefit from the building boom that was taking place there due to Herod Antipas' rebuilding of nearby Sepphoris. During Mary's tumultuous pregnancy, she and Joseph traveled more than one hundred miles from Galilee in the north to Bethlehem, just in time for her son to be born.

Luke tells us it was a Roman census that caused them to take this perilous journey to Joseph's hometown. Although the dating of that census is difficult to corroborate, several decades ago an ancient papyrus was discovered in Egypt which confirms the requirement for people to return to their hometowns to register for a Roman census. It reads, "Gaius Vibius Maximus, Prefect of Egypt, declares: The census by household has begun and it is accordingly necessary that all persons who are not resident at home for one reason or another at this time return to their homeplaces in order to undergo the usual registration formalities and to attend to the cultivation of land which is their concern."[18] It is fascinating that a Roman decree is what brought Joseph and Mary to the ancestral birthplace of David which is where the prophet Micah foretold the Messiah was to be born, *But you, O Bethlehem Ephrathah, who are too little to be among the clans of Judah, from you shall come forth for me one who is to be ruler in Israel, whose coming forth is from of old, from ancient days.* (Micah 5:2)

Most of us are familiar with the amazing accounts of Jesus' birth recorded in Matthew and Luke. However, the familiarity of the story and the traditions that have developed around it can easily cause us to miss the real story of Christmas. Most western Christians picture the very pregnant Mary arriving in Bethlehem on a donkey led by Joseph. As they search the town of Bethlehem, they discover all the hotels are full due to the census, and so they are forced to find shelter in a barn. One of my favorite holiday memories as a kid was setting up our family crèche set, carefully installing the angel hair "snow" on the roof of the wooden stable, and arranging all the ceramic animals, shepherds, and wise men around the Holy Family with the baby Jesus carefully nestled in a wooden manger.

As much as I cherish these memories, my time in the Middle East over the years has taught me that these portrayals of Jesus' birth are shaped more by European culture than by biblical truth. Luke's account of Mary and Joseph's arrival in Bethlehem is very

---

18 Sabine Huebner, *Papyri and the Social World of the New Testament* (Cambridge: Cambridge University Press, 2019) 41-42, Digital.

sparse: *While they were there* [Bethlehem]*, the time came for her to give birth. And she gave birth to her firstborn son and wrapped him in swaddling cloths and laid him in a manger, because there was no place for them in the inn.* (Luke 2:6-7). There are only two phrases in this brief passage that point to something unique about the circumstances of Jesus' birth. The first is that after swaddling him, Mary laid Jesus *in a manger*. That curious detail is then explained by the statement that there was *no place for them in the inn*.

Although those of European descent typically picture the baby Jesus being laid in a wooden manger, like something that might be found in a Bavarian stable, in the Middle East a typical feeding trough is dug out of a block of limestone, almost like a small stone bathtub. Either way it raises the question why the baby Jesus would be laid in an animal's feeding trough. When Luke explains that there was no room for them in the "inn," he uses the Greek word *katalyma*, which has traditionally been translated by the English word "inn." Of course, to the modern western reader this evokes images of a motel with rooms that you can rent for the night. And so, our nativity plays end up featuring a heartless motel manager who turns away this desperate couple because all the rooms are rented.

STONE MANGER

It is interesting that Luke does write about an inn where rooms are rented by an innkeeper when he is recounting Jesus' parable of the Good Samaritan: *"Then he set him on his own animal and brought him to an inn and took care of him. And the next day he took out two denarii and gave them to the innkeeper, saying, 'Take care of him, and whatever more you spend, I will repay you when I come back.'"* (Luke 10:34-35) In this passage the word translated "inn" is *pandochion*, the word translated "innkeeper" is *pandocheus,* and it is clearly a place where you can rent a room for the night. By contrast the word Luke uses in the account of Jesus' birth is *katalyma,* which can mean a public shelter available for use by travelers with their pack animals or it can mean the room in a house reserved for guests.

In considering the meaning of *katalyma,* it is helpful to note that the only other use of this word in Luke's Gospel is when Jesus is giving instructions to his disciples on the eve of the Passover. *He said to them, "Behold, when you have entered the city, a man carrying a jar of water will meet you. Follow him into the house that he enters and tell the master of the house, 'The Teacher says to you, Where is the guest room, where I may eat the Passover with my disciples?' And he will show you a large upper room furnished; prepare it there."* (Luke 22:10-12) Here, the same Greek word *katalyma* is translated *"guest room."* In this case, Luke is clearly referring to the upstairs guest room of a home that can also be used as a dining room.

So, in order to determine the circumstances of Jesus' birth, we need to consider whether it is more likely that Mary and Joseph were turned away from an overfull public shelter for travelers or if there was no space in the guestroom of their relatives' home. It is indisputable that Joseph had relatives in Bethlehem, because it was his ancestral hometown. Given the incredibly high value placed on supporting your extended family and showing hospitality to guests, it is inconceivable that Joseph's relatives would turn him and his pregnant wife away on the eve of Jesus' birth. To do so would bring shame on the entire family. If such an unthinkable event were to occur and no other family in Bethlehem welcomed the desperate young couple into their home, it would have brought shame on the entire community.

It is interesting to compare Matthew's account of Jesus' birth. He gives no details of the birth other than it took place in Bethlehem, but when he describes the visit of the wise men, he says they entered *"the house"* (Matthew 2:11). The Greek word Matthew uses here is *oikos,* meaning the multi-room house of an extended family. When we combine Matthew and Luke's accounts, it is clear that Mary and Joseph were welcomed into an extended family home (*oikos*), but there was no space for them in the guest room of that home.

Now we turn to the question of what the manger tells us about Jesus' birth. Again, the modern western reader assumes the presence of a manger indicates Jesus was born in a separate building dedicated to housing livestock, a stable. However, except for shepherd families who kept large flocks, the vast majority of first-century Jewish families kept their personal livestock in the house where they lived at night. There would typically be two mangers inside that part of the house, one to water the animals and another to feed them. Because Mary laid her newborn son in a manger, it tells us that, since the guestroom was full, she gave birth in that part of the home designated for the livestock.

Now the circumstances of Jesus' birth become clearer. Based on the biblical account and local culture, we can confidently conclude that Mary and Joseph were welcomed into the home of their extended family. However, the room normally reserved for guests was already full due to the requirements of the census, so space was made for Mary and Joseph in the area of the home where the animals were kept. Once Jesus was born, it made perfect sense to lay some straw in one of the nearby stone mangers and place the newly swaddled child there to sleep. Perhaps the questionable circumstances of Mary's pregnancy caused Joseph's relatives to relegate them to the less desirable part of the family home. In this way Joseph's family could fulfill the cultural requirement of providing hospitality, while still expressing their disapproval of Mary's pregnancy before marriage.

I love the way Ken Bailey describes the implications of these insights, "Our Christmas crèche sets remain as they are because 'ox and ass before him bow, for he is in the manger now.' But that manger was in a warm and friendly home, not in a cold and lonely stable. Looking at the story in this light strips away layers of interpretive mythology that have built up around it. Jesus was born in a simple two-room village home such as the Middle East has known for at least three thousand years. Yes, we must rewrite our Christmas plays, but in rewriting them, the story is enriched, not cheapened."[19]

THE FIRST VISITORS

Luke and Matthew each tell us about two very different kinds of visitors who came to recognize the birth of Jesus and show him honor. Luke tells us shepherds were the first to hear the good news of Jesus' birth from the angel Gabriel and a massive angelic choir. They declared the royal lineage and messianic identity of Jesus when

---

19 Bailey, *Jesus Through Middle Eastern Eyes*, 36.

they said, *"Fear not, for behold, I bring you good news of great joy that will be for all the people. For unto you is born this day in the city of David a Savior, who is Christ the Lord."* (Luke 2:10-11)

It must have been late spring or summer because it was warm enough for the shepherds to sleep out in the open fields with their flocks. It wasn't until after the reign of Constantine the Great (AD 306-337) that Christmas came to be celebrated in December at the winter solstice, to coincide with the pagan feast of Saturnalia.

At the angels' direction, these humble shepherds came to see this unique child who had been born to such a heavenly celebration. They recounted what the angel had told them and then returned to their flocks giving praise to God for all they had seen and heard!

Some time later a very different group of visitors arrived at the door of the house where Mary and Joseph and their child were staying in Bethlehem. Based on an astronomical event which they believed marked the birth of a great ruler in Judea, a group of Persian Magi set out on a great journey around the Fertile Crescent to visit and give honor to this newborn king. Perhaps they were familiar with the Israelite prophets who foretold the coming of the Messiah in passages such as Balaam's prophecy that *a star shall come out of Jacob, and a scepter shall rise out of Israel; it shall crush the forehead of Moab and break down all the sons of Sheth.* (Numbers 24:17) They weren't the only non-Jews aware of this messianic expectation; even the Romans were aware of it. The Roman historian Suetonius Tranquillus wrote, "Throughout the whole of the East there had spread an old and persistent belief: destiny had decreed that at that time men coming forth from Judea would seize power and rule the world."[20]

Naturally these wise men assumed a Jewish king would be born in the capital city of Jerusalem, but after conferring with Herod's advisors there they continued their journey to Bethlehem, just south of Jerusalem. It is evident that, unlike the shepherds, these exotic visitors arrived in Bethlehem some months after the birth of Jesus. It would have taken them at least several months to organize a caravan to make the 900-mile journey across the Arabian desert. Since the diabolically paranoid Herod asked the magi about the precise time they first saw the star and then ended up ordering the

---

[20] Suetonius Tranquillus, *The Lives of the Twelve Caesars*, Ed. J. Eugene Reed and Alexander Thomson (Philadelphia: Gebbie & Co., 1889), Vespasian 5, Digital

death of all the boys of Bethlehem two years and under, he was convinced this child had been born more than a year earlier. Matthew's use of the word "child" (Greek: *paidion*) rather than Luke's use of "baby" (Greek: *brephos*) to describe Jesus also indicates the transition from infancy to childhood (Matthew 2:8-10; Luke 2:16).

It is hard to overstate the reaction these visiting magi would have caused in the sleepy town of Bethlehem, coming to offer extravagant gifts and show honor to the son of a young Jewish couple from Nazareth. In the hostile and unpredictable environment caused by the dying Herod's murderous paranoia, the attention this caused was unwelcome, and it was not long before the young family was on their way to Egypt as the magi made their way back to the east, bypassing the palace in Jerusalem.

There could hardly be two more different kinds of visitors to mark Jesus' entry into our world. The lowly Jewish shepherds, stinky and filthy from sleeping in the fields with their sheep, considered unclean by the religious leaders of their time, but testifying to an angelic encounter; contrasted with the wealthy and respected pagan astrologers who had the means and opportunity to travel across the Middle East on a political mission, offering expensive gifts in homage to a powerful new ruler. Jesus was born for all of humanity, both Jew and Gentile, rich and poor, powerful and lowly!

LOCATING THE BIRTHPLACE

Once we have a clearer picture of the cultural setting of Jesus' birth, it naturally gives rise to the question of location. Every Christian pilgrim who travels to biblical lands asks the question, "Where did it happen?" The follower of Jesus does not ask this for superstitious reasons, as if there is something magical about touching the exact spot where a biblical event took place, but to facilitate a more accurate understanding of those events and a more powerful encounter with Jesus in these places. After 30 years of traveling to nearly every known location of Jesus' life and asking that same question, I have become a stickler for historical accuracy who always seeks to determine the degree of certainty we can have about the location of a particular biblical event.

The problem with so-called "holy sites" is that they constantly proliferate. Ever since people began traveling to biblical lands, local guides have been asked that same question, "Where did it happen?" If they don't know the answer, usually they will make it up. The result is the ridiculous identification of places like the cave where Mary used to nurse the baby Jesus, the inn of the Good Samaritan (which was just a story!), the stone Jesus used to mount the donkey on Palm Sunday (crusaders needed a stepping stone to mount their war horses), the stones that would have cried out on the Mount of Olives if the people hadn't, and so on.

When we consider the reliability of an identified holy site, we must first compare it to the biblical account and then to any contemporary historical references we have. Then we refer to the eyewitness descriptions of the earliest pilgrims who first visited these sites. Then we consider this in light of the data produced by modern geographical, archaeological, and cultural studies. Finally, we apply common sense and logic to determine how accurate this identification might be.

When it comes to the birth of Jesus, we know that it took place somewhere in the ancient city of Bethlehem, probably in the extended family home of Joseph's relatives, but beyond that the biblical accounts supply no more geographical details. The earliest descriptions we have of Jesus' birth outside of the New Testament are from the early church father Justin Martyr and the non-canonical Gospel of James. Both date from about 120 years after Jesus, and both describe Jesus' birth in a cave in Bethlehem. When the Roman emperor Hadrian put down the second Jewish Revolt in AD 136, he built pagan shrines over previous places of worship. It is interesting that during the time of Hadrian a grove of trees was planted around the cave as an outdoor pagan worship site dedicated to the pagan god Thammuz. This indicates that some of the local population were worshiping there before the time of Hadrian. In the third century, the church father Origen and church historian Eusebius both describe the birth site as a cave. In the fourth century, Cyril of Jerusalem does the same. When Constantine's mother Queen Helena came to Bethlehem in 326 AD and asked the local Christian community where Jesus was born, they pointed to this cave which was still surrounded by the sacred Thammuz grove.

In the later fourth century, Jerome, who made his home in an adjacent cave for 32 years where he translated the Bible into Latin, pointed out the irony of the building of pagan sites over the rock of Golgotha, the tomb of Jesus, and the cave of his birth. For him this was as a sign of the authenticity of these sites, as he writes, "From the time of Hadrian to the reign of Constantine—a period of about one hundred and eighty years—the spot which had witnessed the resurrection was occupied by a figure of Jupiter, while on the rock where the cross had stood, a marble statue of Venus was set up by the heathen and became an object of worship. The original persecutors, indeed, supposed that by polluting our holy places they would deprive us of our faith in the passion and in the resurrection. Even my own Bethlehem, as it now is, that most venerable spot in the whole world of which the psalmist sings: 'the truth hath sprung out of the earth,' was overshadowed by a grove of Thammuz, that is of Adonis; and in the very cave where the infant Christ had uttered His earliest cry lamentation was made for the paramour of Venus."[21]

When we turn to archaeology to consider the authenticity of the cave as the site of Jesus' birth, we have very little data, because it has been constantly in use as a place of worship for at least 1700 years, and very few artifacts accumulated there. What archaeology can tell us is that the cave is located in the area of biblical Bethlehem and was in use as early as the first century AD. When we combine this with the fact that caves were often incorporated into extended family houses, we can certainly see that this cave could well have been that portion of the home of Joseph's relatives where Mary gave birth to Jesus.

Because of the rise of pilgrimage following the time of Constantine in AD 326, and with it the increase of unsubstantiated holy sites, any identification of sites before the fourth century is likely to be more historically reliable than those after Constantine. Since we have a number of pre-Constantinian sources pointing to the cave as the birthplace, we have to take this location seriously as the potential site of Jesus' birth. However, we must also note that nothing in the biblical text identifies the cave, and little specific archaeological data backs up this identification. While the ancient cave is likely the correct site, we can't be completely confident that this is the place of Jesus' birth.

[21] Jerome, *Letter to Paulinus of Nola,* trans. W.H. Fremantle, G. Lewis and W.G. Martley, in *Nicene and Post-Nicene Fathers, Second Series,* Vol. 6. Edited by Philip Schaff and Henry Wace. (Buffalo, NY: Christian Literature Publishing Co., 1893) Epistle 58.3, Digital.

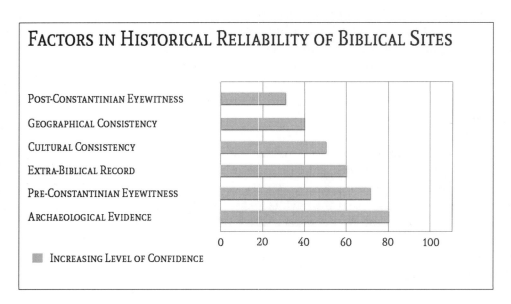

This chart gives us an idea of the various types of evidence we can examine to determine the historical reliability of any identified biblical site. If we only have post-Constantinian references to the site, we must remain cautious about a possible historical identification. If a site also reflects the appropriate geographical and cultural context, it becomes more likely. If the setting fits references to the site outside of the Bible, our confidence in its probable accuracy increases. If we have a pre-Constantinian eyewitness account confirming the site, then our confidence becomes quite high. When archaeological evidence confirms the identification of a site with a biblical event and is consistent with these other forms of evidence, we can become nearly certain of its accuracy.

WORSHIP AT THE CAVE

It is apparent that from the first century on, followers of Jesus gathered at the cave of Jesus' birth to pray and worship the King of kings there. When Queen Helena came to the Holy Land, her mission was to identify what was considered the three most significant sites from the life of Jesus: the place of his birth (incarnation), the place of his death and resurrection (redemption), and the place of his ascension (glorification). Once the cave was identified to her as the place of Jesus' birth, she tasked her engineers to build a great church over the site of the cave. The church was designed with a double-aisled basilica for the main hall with an octagon-shaped transept at one end centered over the cave. In late Roman and early Byzantine architecture, octagonal buildings often mark the site of a significant event. The new Basilica of the Nativity was dedicated on 31 May 339. The altar of the church was placed directly over the cave, and a 12-foot wide opening in the floor surrounded by a railing offered a view of the cave.

Sadly, this Constantinian church was destroyed during the Samaritan uprising of AD 529, after which the Emperor Justinian rebuilt it, retaining the double-aisled basilica, but replacing the hexagonal transept with a triapsidial design (see photo). While nearly all the other churches in the Holy Land from this period have been destroyed, the Justinian Church of the Nativity survived. The mosaic on the façade of the church depicted the Magi offering their gifts in Persian costume, so the Persian invaders passed it by in the seventh century. In the eleventh century the church escaped Hakim the Insane's campaign of church destruction because Muslims were allowed to pray in the south transept of the church. Over time they blocked up the great entrance doors till only a small opening remained, as it is today, preventing attackers from riding their horses into the church!

CHURCH OF THE NATIVITY INTERIOR

Today the Church of the Nativity in Bethlehem stands as one of the oldest and best-preserved churches of the Holy Land, despite an earthquake in 1834 and a fire in 1869. The twin rows of rose limestone monolithic columns support the nave, which is covered in ancient green-glass mosaics depicting a procession of angels, the ancestors of Jesus recorded in Matthew and Luke, and members of various church councils. Two entrances give access to stairways leading down into the cave, above which still stands the ornate altar of the church. Recently an international restoration project has preserved the roof, excavated the floor, and carefully cleaned the interior. This work has revealed large sections of the beautiful fourth-century Constantinian mosaic floors, which have been painstakingly restored. As centuries of soot are removed, the beautiful limestone pillars and the green-gold glass mosaics are coming back to life as the splendor of Justinian's sixth century church is revealed for future generations to enjoy.

 # THE LIFE

ENTERING THE REAL WORLD

Many first-time visitors come to Israel with unrealistic expectations of idyllic settings for biblical stories that match the glowing Sunday school depictions they knew growing up, anticipating they will spend peaceful times of spiritual reflection in these holy places. Sometimes this is the case, but often it is not. When you visit Bethlehem today, it is not the little town with shining streets lying still beneath the starry sky that many of us are used to singing about on Christmas Eve. It is a large, crowded Palestinian city on disputed territory marked by tension, anxiety, injustice, and anger. To visit from Jerusalem, you are forced to clear a security checkpoint manned by heavily armed guards and pass through at a gate in the ugly concrete barrier that runs for over four hundred miles between the State of Israel and the Palestinian Territories, a tragic symbol of the violence and hatred that still divides the people of the Holy Land today. Once inside you are faced with the crushing poverty and simmering resentment that these divisions and injustices inevitably produce.

In some ways this is more like the Bethlehem of Jesus' day than our idealized preconceptions. We so easily forget Jesus was born into a land filled with heavily armed soldiers imposing the will of an occupying army; that tax collectors were exacting a crushing weight of unjust taxation; that resentment and even violent revolt constantly simmered just below the surface. It is important to remember that Jesus was not born at a candlelight Christmas Eve service with a choir singing softly in the background. Yes, there was a choir of the heavenly hosts singing "Glory to God in the highest heaven," but their audience was comprised of stinky shepherds sleeping outside with their sheep and goats. Yes, there was a loving couple experiencing this sacred moment together, but his mother was unwed when she became pregnant and there was shame and even the threat of capital punishment hanging over her head. Yes, a beautiful baby boy was born that night, but he came out crying in a flood of all the blood and mess a normal childbirth entails.

Visiting the Church of the Nativity in Bethlehem is a vivid reminder that we still celebrate this birth two thousand years later because it marks an epochal shift in the history of the world when the infinite and eternal God of heaven chose to enter into the real, broken world in which we live. Visiting the Cave of the Nativity is rarely a serene spiritual experience, at least not for me. If you are able to get in after waiting in line for a break between lengthy religious services, there tends to be a lot of pushing and shoving, a bewildering array of body odor, and an unsympathetic priest brusquely ordering you to "touch it and go, touch it and go!" Not exactly a warm and fuzzy spiritual experience.

When I am experiencing the inevitable contradictory feelings of wonder and offense this all produces, I try to imagine the mix of emotions Mary and Joseph were feeling, the body odor in that crowded house mixed with the mess of the animals sleeping nearby, and the disapproval of judgmental relatives. I try to recall the pain and joy of bringing a child into the world, the wonder and surprise of the shepherds' testimony about the angelic announcement that night, and the shock of wealthy foreign dignitaries bearing gifts for the child months later. This is the whole point of the Incarnation! God chose not to keep our mess at arm's length but entered right into the middle of it by becoming fully human in that tiny baby boy. And still today, in the unholy pushing and the shoving and the body odor of the cave, we touch the stone walls, and it all becomes a little bit more real to us. Not because there is anything magical about touching that stone or the silver star which is supposed to mark the spot where Mary gave birth, but because the feel of that stone beneath our fingertips tells us in a way words can't that God's love, and presence, and power are even more real for us than this rock, because God became human in this place.

INVITING JESUS IN

The insight that Jesus was born in the crowded house of an extended family sets the stage for us to understand more accurately the context of Jesus' entire life and the implications that has for our lives today. Modern western readers of the Gospels tend to picture Jesus primarily as an individual interacting with other individuals because this is the bias of our individualistic culture. Of course, there is some truth to this, but it is not the whole picture. From birth to death and resurrection, Jesus lived his life as part of a nuclear and extended family. We typically picture the baby Jesus lying in the manger with his mother and adoptive father looking on lovingly. What we often miss is the extended family of Joseph's relatives surrounding this nuclear family, which readers from traditionally Middle Eastern cultures instinctively recognize.

Too often we have sought to follow Jesus only as individuals and not in the context of a family. Too often we have sought to live out our faith in the context of a nuclear family, but not with the support of an extended family. It is a helpful corrective to see that Mary and Joseph were invited into an extended family home for Jesus to be born. It raises the question of whether we have done the same thing. I love how Eugene Peterson captures the communal dimension of Jesus' birth in his translation of John's poetic description of the incarnation: *The Word became flesh and blood, and moved into the neighborhood.* (John 1:14) Do we recognize that Jesus has moved into our neighborhood? Have we invited him into our home and into an extended family?

If Jesus is going to be incarnated in our lives today, we will not only open our hearts and minds to him, but our homes and our families as well. The relatives of Joseph had a very full house, but when Joseph knocked on the outer door they invited this couple in and made room for Jesus to be born in their extended family, even though the guest room was already full. Years later, on the barren island of Patmos, Jesus gave the Apostle John a vision of this very invitation he offers to each of us: *Behold, I stand at the door and knock. If anyone hears my voice and opens the door, I will come in to him and eat with him, and he with me.* (Revelation 3:20)

The more we recognize that Jesus has moved into our neighborhood, and the more we make space for him by welcoming him into the daily life of our family, the more our lives will be shaped by his. Pam and I have been learning this lesson over the past ten years, and it has made a huge impact on our marriage, our kids, and those closest to us. This happens best by intentionally inviting Jesus into the regular rhythms of our family life. If you are single, divorced, or have no children, the message is still the same. As we will see in the pages to come, Jesus was a single man who built an amazing extended and nuclear spiritual family, so we can all learn to do the same regardless of our circumstances in life.

Worshiping together at church once a week and praying before meals is a good start, but there are so many other areas of our lives where we can invite Jesus to be incarnate in our regular life with others. Do you have a daily rhythm of reading Scripture and praying with those who are closest to you? Do have a weekly rhythm of intentional rest to abide with Jesus and those close to you? Do you regularly invite others from your neighborhood and networks who might not yet know Jesus to come into your home and family? Do you make it a point as a family to get out of the comfort zone of your home and into your neighborhood, your city, and places where you can connect with new people you might otherwise never meet? Jesus came into the neighborhood to be born in an extended family who welcomed those in need. Jesus is still looking for homes and families where he can be incarnated today.

WHAT KIND OF JESUS?

The starting point of our Christian faith is the recognition that Jesus is more than just a man. I remember vividly when it finally dawned on me as a young teen that Jesus was both fully human and fully God. Suddenly everything he did and said took on a new meaning. Now I understood his death and resurrection had changed everything for me! God made the truth of Jesus' divinity clear from the very beginning through Mary's miraculous conception, Gabriel's angelic proclamation, the testimony of humble shepherds, and the unexpected arrival of exotic scholars bearing expensive gifts. We see Jesus' divine nature demonstrated throughout his life, death, resurrection, and ascension into heaven.

Equally as important as recognizing Jesus' full divinity is recognizing his full humanity. In the first four centuries following Jesus' death and resurrection, his followers hammered out as clear an understanding of his identity as is possible with a divine-human paradox. The early church fathers were clear in articulating the doctrine of the dual nature of Christ that Jesus is 100% God and 100% human at the same time. In the fourth century, Apollinaris of Laodicea taught that there were parts of Jesus that did not become fully human in the incarnation. Gregory of Naziansus (AD 329-390), the great theologian of the early church and archbishop of Constantinople, refuted this heresy with the simple phrase, "what is not assumed is not redeemed."[22] Gregory

22 Jerome, *Letter to Paulinus of Nola,* trans. W.H. Fremantle, G. Lewis and W.G. Martley, in *Nicene and Post-Nicene Fathers, Second Series,* Vol. 6. Edited by Philip Schaff and Henry Wace. (Buffalo, NY: Christian Literature Publishing Co., 1893) Epistle 58.3, Digital.

was pointing out that if Jesus did not become fully human, like us in every way except not choosing to sin, then his death on the cross could not redeem every part of who we are. When we allow the divinity of Jesus to overshadow his humanity, we lose sight of the whole reason God took on humanity in the incarnation.

Since I came to faith in Jesus, I have always believed in both his full humanity and his full divinity, but that belief did not always shape my walk of faith. Somewhere along the way I allowed my belief in Jesus' divinity to impede my view of his humanity. I think this began when I was reading the Gospel accounts of the supernatural things Jesus did. I was vividly aware that Jesus regularly did things I did not feel capable of doing. My fatal mistake came in assuming that these acts of spiritual power were attributable to Jesus' divine nature and therefore impossible for me. I thought to myself, "Of course, Jesus can heal the sick, because *he is God!* Of course, Jesus can know people's unspoken thoughts, because *he is God!* Of course, Jesus can cast out demons, because *he is God!*" The unspoken implication of these thoughts was, "Of course, I can't do these kinds of things because *I am NOT God!*" If I had carefully examined these thoughts I would have seen that they amount to a denial of Jesus' full humanity.

The New Testament is clear that Jesus is not part man and part God, but at the same time fully God and fully human. In his letter to the Philippians, Paul quotes the oldest articulation of Christology we have: *Have this mind among yourselves, which is yours in Christ Jesus, who, though he was in the form of God, did not count equality with God a thing to be grasped, but emptied himself, by taking the form of a servant, being born in the likeness of men.* (Philippians 2:5-7) The Greek word for "emptied" is *kenoo*, which describes how the infinite God squeezed himself into a finite man. When God emptied himself, he chose to temporarily set aside the infinite aspects of his divine nature in order to live as a finite human being and show us the life we are meant to live.

For instance, when Jesus was asked when the end of history would take place, he said, *"But concerning that day or that hour, no one knows, not even the angels in heaven, nor the Son, but only the Father."* (Mark 13:32) When Jesus was in Nazareth, the lack of faith there limited his healing ministry. Mark explains, *And he could do no mighty work there, except that he laid his hands on a few sick people and healed them. And he marveled because of their unbelief.* (Mark 6:5-6) We see here that Jesus temporarily set aside his divine omniscience and omnipotence in order to live fully in this world as a human being.

The writer of Hebrews describes God's temporary self-emptying in Jesus when he says, *We see him who for a little while was made lower than the angels, namely Jesus, crowned with glory and honor… he had to be made like his brothers in every respect…* (Hebrews 2:9, 17). Hebrews goes on to describe Jesus' full humanity this way… *but* [he is] *one who in every respect has been tempted as we are, yet without sin… Although he was a son, he learned obedience through what he suffered.* (Hebrews 4:15, 5:8). This does not mean Jesus forfeited the fullness of his divine nature. It means that, while on earth, Jesus temporarily limited aspects of his divine nature in order to set an example for us to follow. He operated in supernatural authority and power, not on the basis of his divine nature, but in the fullness of his human nature, exercising the divine authority given to every son and daughter of the King. It is after the resurrection that Jesus was glorified in his heavenly body and after the ascension that Jesus was restored to his divine position at the right hand of the Father.

When it comes to understanding the nature of Christ, we are dealing with divine mystery and paradox which we should not try and fit too neatly into our theological boxes. The crucial point the New Testament makes clear is that in his life here on earth, Jesus is, in every way, the perfect example of the life we are meant to live. The whole point of discipleship is that the rabbi sets an example for the disciples to learn from and imitate. When Jesus gave the invitation, *"Follow me,"* he was inviting people to learn how to live the life that he was living. Not just part of that life, but all of it, even the supernatural parts. There is no room for avoiding this challenge with the excuse, "Of course he can because he is God!" Jesus was not demonstrating what only he can do because of his divine nature; he was showing us what we can learn to do in relationship with him.

After all, by the ninth chapter of Luke, we read that the twelve disciples were already learning how to heal and cast out demons. In the next chapter, we read that the seventy-two disciples were learning to do the same. As we read on in the book of Acts, we see that the Spirit-filled followers of Jesus were able to operate in Jesus' supernatural authority and power as an ongoing way of life. Jesus said it very clearly on the last night he was with the disciples before his arrest, *"Truly, truly, I say to you, whoever believes in me will also do the works that I do; and greater works than these will he do, because I am going to the Father."* (John 14:12) If we seek to grow as disciples of Jesus we will learn to follow him in every area of his life here on earth, even the supernatural parts.

How did the followers of Jesus do the things Jesus did? The same way Jesus did, by the authority and power of his heavenly Father. When Jesus sent the disciples out on mission,

Luke says, *And he called the twelve together and gave them power and authority over all demons and to cure diseases, and he sent them out to proclaim the kingdom of God and to heal.* (Luke 9:1) When the risen Jesus gave the Great Commission, he passed on to his followers *"All authority in heaven and on earth"* as the basis for fulfilling that commission (Matthew 28:18). As sons and daughters of our heavenly Father, who is also King of the universe, we have been given Jesus' authority to represent our King, and in the Spirit we have been given divine power that flows from the exercise of that authority. God emptied himself when he became fully human so that Jesus could become like us, show us the life we are meant to live, and offer the perfect sacrifice of atonement on the cross, giving us the authority to live that life by the power of his resurrection and the outpouring of the Spirit.

As I have come to understand Jesus' full humanity in the context of discipleship, I have been learning how to live more consistently in his authority so that the power of God flows through me to do his will on earth as it is in heaven. Through this process I have found greater faith and confidence to live a life that looks more like Jesus' life and produce better and longer-lasting fruit. As a result, now I often receive insights, words, pictures, and messages for people and groups that can be powerfully faith-producing and practically helpful. While I have always prayed to God for healing of the sick and injured, I am learning how to minister to the sick more like Jesus did. As a result, I have seen an increasing number of miraculous healings in our ministry since I have embraced all of Jesus' life as a model for my life. If we really believe the orthodox Christology that God became fully human in Jesus, increasingly we will see that the baby born in Bethlehem came to set an example for us to follow in every way.

Irenaeus, second century Bishop of Lyon, described Jesus' work in us this way: "the Word of God, our Lord Jesus Christ, who did, through his transcendent love, become what we are, that he might bring us to be even what he is himself."[23] It is the ancient heresy of Docetism to believe that Jesus only seemed to be human, but really operated primarily in his divine nature. It is the ancient heresy of Adoptionism to believe that Jesus is merely a perfect human being who was later adopted as the Son of God. Our clearer understanding of Jesus' miraculous birth in a family home in Bethlehem reminds us not to lose sight of the full humanity of Jesus even as we embrace his full divinity. The more we come

---

[23] Irenaeus, *Against Heresies*, from *Ante-Nicene Fathers*, Vol. 1, ed. Alexander Roberts, James Donaldson, and A. Cleveland Coxe (Buffalo, NY: Christian Literature Publishing Co., 1885.) Book 5, Preface, Digital.

to see the child born in Bethlehem as God who has emptied himself, the more we will learn to follow Jesus in every aspect of the life he lived here on earth.

CHAPTER FIVE

JESUS' HOME:
JUST OFF THE BEATEN TRACK

And Jesus increased in wisdom and in stature and in favor with God and man. (Luke 2:52)

 THE WAY

VILLAGE LIFE IN GALILEE

In the middle of lower Galilee, on the northern ridge of the strategic Jezreel Valley, the first-century Jewish village of Nazareth was situated in a fertile hollow surrounded by rocky hilltops. Just to the north of the town, a broad valley, the Nahal Zippori, stretched between Nazareth and the large city of Sepphoris, which Herod Antipas was building as his new capital of Galilee. While there are signs of habitation in this area stretching as far back as the Neolithic period 9,000 years ago, it appears to have been largely unpopulated after the Assyrian destruction of northern Israel in 722 BC until shortly before the time of Jesus.

Although it has become famous by its association with Jesus, the new village of Nazareth was relatively small and insignificant in first-century Galilee. It is not mentioned in the Hebrew Scriptures or in other Jewish writings before the time of Jesus. The location of Nazareth has always been clear, but not until 1962 was a historical reference to this village found on an artifact discovered in the excavations at Caesarea Maritima. This fragmentary inscription from the second century AD lists the twenty-four priestly courses, who served one week twice a year in the Temple, and tells in which towns they resided, including Happizzez, which was identified with Nazareth (see 1 Chronicles 24:15). Archaeologists have estimated the population of first-century Nazareth to be anywhere from 500 to 1500 people, but the modern city built over its ancient ruins makes the first-century population difficult to verify. Recent excavations indicate a larger and more prosperous village than had been earlier assumed.

The economy of Nazareth was comprised primarily of agriculture, livestock, building, handicrafts, and trade. Farmers worked the land surrounding the village, growing

olives, grapes, grains, dates, figs, onions, and garlic. Shepherds kept flocks of sheep and goats, grazing them in the fertile hillsides of the Zippori valley and beyond. Most families kept a few goats or sheep or the occasional cow in their home for milk and some chickens for eggs. Grapes were pressed into juice which was fermented as wine, olives were pressed into oil, grain

FIRST-CENTURY FARM WITH WINEPRESS IN NAZARETH

was ground into flour, milk was made into cheese, dates and figs were turned into honey, onions and garlic were used for flavor.

Archaeologists have discovered an ancient farm on the outskirts of first-century Nazareth. It features stone terraces for olive orchards and vineyards, built to prevent erosion and designed as a natural irrigation system. The farm also includes a watchtower and a rock-cut winepress where grapes were carefully crushed under bare feet and the juice was collected in an adjacent cistern. Equipment used for crushing and pressing olives into oil and grinding grain into wheat were uncovered in the area, in addition to a number of spring-fed wells dating back to the first-century. This farm sounds exactly like the one Jesus described in his parable of the wicked tenants: *"There was a master of a house who planted a vineyard and put a fence around it and dug a winepress in it and built a tower and leased it to tenants, and went into another country."* (Matthew 21:33)

When we read Jesus' parables in Nazareth, we start to realize they were set in the real-life context where he grew up.

Life in first-century Nazareth would have been typical of other Jewish villages from this time. Extended families lived together in homes comprised of several rooms oriented around an open courtyard that opened onto the street. As we have noted, these homes typically housed three generations including grandparents, aunts, uncles, cousins, parents, children, slaves, business partners, and close friends who shared life and carried out a family business together. There were typically two daily meals, a light breakfast before work and a larger dinner after the work day was over. Cooking was done in clay ovens, usually located in the courtyard of the house, where the extended family gathered for meals. Most courtyards also included an underground cistern designed to capture rainwater. These could be filled from one of the local wells with large clay water jars.

Some residents of Nazareth worked as artisans, making pottery vessels, weaving and dying cloth, tanning leather, and forging iron tools. Others were merchants trading in goods like fish, spices, perfume, jewelry, and glassware that were not locally available. The most educated class worked as scribes, copying documents and drawing up official wills, marriage contracts, and business agreements. But by far the fastest growing industry in Nazareth at the time of Jesus was construction because they were in the midst of a building boom.

This is probably the reason Joseph and his family moved from Bethlehem in Judea north to Nazareth in Galilee, because they were builders. The Greek word for "builder," *tekton*, is often translated "carpenter" reflecting the northern European context in which most building was done with wood (Mark 6:3). However, the Greek work tekton could refer to artisans who worked with wood, metal, or stone. Since stone is the primary building material in the Middle East, this word would primarily denote stonemasons who build with stone. The extended family was supported by a family business in which all the members of the family contributed in some way. This business was integrated into the life of the family, and many of the activities of the family business were carried out in the central courtyard of the extended family home. From an early age, the girls would be trained in the managment of the extended family by their mothers, aunts, and grandmothers, while the boys would go during the week to the local synagogue to receive their primary education.

THE WORK OF A TEKTON

Although it has not yet been discovered underneath the modern city, firstcentury Nazareth had a synagogue where the community gathered on the Sabbath for the weekly prayer service. It also served as the community's school. In first-century Jewish communities, children began their formal education around the age of four or five years old in the synagogue school (Hebrew: *Beth Sefer*) where the local rabbi taught them to read and write. The primary curriculum at this stage was the Old Testament Law (*Torah*). *Beth Sefer* concluded around age twelve, and most of the students returned home to focus on learning the family business. The boys began by standing at their father's shoulder and watching him work. Then the father invited his son to learn more by helping with the work, giving him feedback along the way. Then he gave him more and more responsibility until eventually he became fully trained in the family business. The girls stood at their mother's shoulder and watched her manage the extended family. They too began to help, taking on more responsibility and instruction, until they were ready to manage their own family.

The best male students from *Beth Sefer* asked to continue their studies in *Beth Midrash*, where they would not only read and memorize the *Torah*, but also begin to debate the meaning of the Law. Those who were accepted learned the Oral Law, which was comprised of traditional interpretations of the biblical Law passed down from earlier rabbis. When *Beth Midrash* was complete, most of the young men returned to their family business, but the very best of the best students applied to become a disciple of a specific rabbi, which was called *Beth Talmud*. If accepted, the *Talmid* (Hebrew for "disciple") went to live with a rabbi and his extended family. They listened to what the rabbi said, walked where the rabbi walked, ate what the rabbi ate, and slept where the rabbi slept. By imitating the way of their rabbi every day, they not only came to know what their rabbi knew, but also learned how to do what the rabbi did, and so became like their rabbi.

A Village on the Outskirts of the City

To say that Nazareth was a small village at the time of Jesus is not to say that it was isolated. In fact, Nazareth was located near the main Roman road that followed the Via Maris. This ancient trade route called the "Way of the Sea" ran from Egypt in the south, along the Mediterranean coast, around the northern shore of the Sea of Galilee, and then north to Damascus and beyond into the Tigris and Euphrates valleys. Over the millennia every army that ever sought to conquer the Middle East marched up and down this ancient road. In Jesus' time the Via Maris was a key trade route that would have brought a rich variety of commerce and culture into the area, particularly to the walled city of Sepphoris which was located on the Via Maris just four miles from Nazareth in the heart of Nahal Zippori (the Valley of Sepphoris).

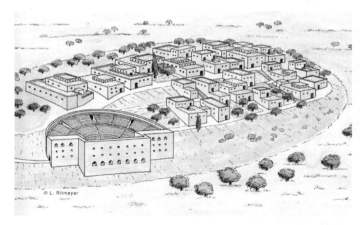

FIRST-CENTURY SEPPHORIS

When Herod the Great died in 4 BC, Judas the son of Hezekiah led a revolt of Galilean bandits and seized control of the city of Sepphoris. Varus, the Roman governor of Syria, promptly sent his legion into Galilee and crushed the revolt, burning the city of Sepphoris and selling the rebels into slavery. As a result, when Herod Antipas inherited control of Galilee, the city of Sepphoris lay in ruins. He decided to make Sepphoris the capital of his territory and rebuild the city in grand Hellenistic style. Josephus describes Antipas' rebuilding of Sepphoris this way, "In the thirty-seventh year of Caesar's victory… Herod [Anit-pas] also built a wall about Sepphoris, which is the ornament of all Galilee, and made it the metropolis of the country."[24] This rebuilding project in the first decades of the first century required a large number of builders and stonemasons.

Massive excavations of Sepphoris have revealed a city deserving of Josephus' title, "the ornament of all Galilee." Beautifully paved, colonnaded streets gave access to large public buildings and wealthy homes. Later in the Roman period, many homes and public buildings in Sepphoris were decorated with the finest ancient mosaics discovered so far in Israel, incorporating various pagan themes taken from Roman mythology and culture. In the lower city (Greek: *polis*) today we can walk on the two major intersecting streets that form the heart of every Roman city, the north-south *Cardo* and the east-west *Decumanus*. The upper city (Greek: *acropolis*) was built on a hilltop and contained many public buildings and grand estates. A beautiful Greek amphitheater, seating about 4500 people, was built into the side of the *acropolis*. Below the *acropolis* archaeologists discovered a fifth-century synagogue which probably lies over the foundations of earlier synagogues.

It is evident from the lack of pork bones and images of humans or animals that first-century Sepphoris was primarily a Jewish city, in spite of its thoroughly Hellenistic design. We see here an example of a Jewish community that enthusiastically embraced Roman culture and commerce while holding on to its Jewish identity and

ANCIENT STREET OF SEPPHORIS

[24] Irenaeus, *Against Heresies*, from *Ante-Nicene Fathers*, Vol. 1, ed. Alexander Roberts, James Donaldson, and A. Cleveland Coxe (Buffalo, NY: Christian Literature Publishing Co., 1885.) Book 5, Preface, Digital.

religion. This reflects an attitude similar to the Sadducees, rather than the more conservative Pharisees. By contrast, the residents of Nazareth, located just four miles away, did not embrace the culture of their occupiers, but held more tightly to their Jewish traditions and way of life.

 ## THE TRUTH

ANYTHING GOOD FROM NAZARETH?

The murderous paranoia of Herod the Great and a prophetic dream led Joseph to take his family into hiding in Egypt. Although Herod's sons were now in power, Joseph felt safe enough after Herod's death to return with his young family to Israel. However, they did not return to the place of Jesus' birth in Bethlehem near Jerusalem, but rather to the little-known village of Nazareth, where Jesus could grow up in relative obscurity. Whereas today Nazareth is one of the largest cities in Galilee, in biblical times it was a small village.

MODERN NAZARETH

Almost thirty years later, when Andrew first invited him to meet Jesus, Nathanael from Cana said, *"Can anything good come out of Nazareth?"* (John 1:46). Rather than a moral judgement, this was a statement about Nazareth's perceived insignificance. Coming from a resident of Cana, another small Galilean town, this was an ironic statement indeed! Perhaps Nathanael's comment reflects the exaggerated rivalry that often grows between nearby small towns. Here, in this small village of Nazareth, on the outskirts of a large cosmopolitan city, the boy Jesus grew into manhood.

While Matthew and Luke give us rich details about the circumstances surrounding Jesus' birth, the story of his boyhood is much more elusive. We know very few details of Jesus' early life from his birth and dedication in the Temple until he came to John at the Jordan River for baptism. Luke sums up the first twelve years of Jesus' life with the brief statement, *And the child grew and became strong, filled with wisdom. And the favor of God was upon him.* (Luke 2:40) The only other event from Jesus' boyhood of which we are aware happened in the Temple courts when Jesus was twelve years old and astounded the rabbis who gathered there to debate the *Torah*. But when we read the Gospels in light of what we have learned about Nazareth, we can begin to see the significance of these "hidden years" of Jesus' life.

Unless we are told otherwise, we can confidently assume that Joseph and Mary, upon their return to Nazareth, moved into the extended family home of Joseph's *oikos*, as this would be the cultural norm. This means they would have shared daily life with several other nuclear families and three generations of relatives. Although the circumstances of Jesus' conception were extraordinary, Joseph and Mary conceived at least six other children naturally and raised them in Nazareth with Jesus. These siblings include four boys named James, Joseph, Judas, and Simon, and at least two sisters whose names are unknown (Matthew 13:55-56).

We don't know the specifics; but we can infer that this nuclear family of nine or more lived as part of a larger extended family in Nazareth. They lived in a home with several rooms built around a central courtyard where meals were cooked and shared together, and where aspects of the family business were carried out. Mary would have joined in running the household and Joseph would have gone to work in the family construction business. Most likely Joseph walked the four miles into Sepphoris and back each day with the rest of the men, because that is where the vast majority of the building trade would have taken place. Meanwhile, once Jesus turned five, he would spend his days with the local rabbis at the synagogue learning to read and write *Torah* in *Beth Sefer*.

Many readers of the Gospels assume Jesus grew up a poor peasant, but this is not an accurate portrayal of his social position. The disparity between the ultra-rich and the rest of the population was so extreme in first-century Palestine that it is not correct to speak of a middle class as we might in our own society. While still part of the lower classes, Jesus' family would have been considered relatively prosperous with a lucrative business, a comfortable house, and a certain amount of security in a time when that could be a rare commodity. When Jesus was about twelve, he would have left *Beth Sefer* to begin his apprenticeship into the family business. By the time he was thirty Jesus was known in Nazareth as a *tekton* (Mark 6:3).

THE FAMILY PILGRIMAGE

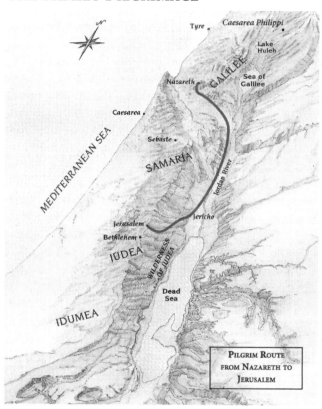

PILGRIM ROUTE FROM NAZARETH TO JERUSALEM

Luke tells us that Jesus and his family *went to Jerusalem every year at the Feast of the Passover.* (Luke 2:41) In Exodus 23 God commanded the people of Israel to make a pilgrimage to the Temple in Jerusalem three times a year for the great festivals of Passover (Hebrew: *Pesach*), Pentecost (Hebrew: *Shavuout*), and Tabernacles (Hebrew: *Sukkot*), but by the first century annual pilgrimages were not considered mandatory. It was quite expensive and time-consuming to make this journey, which normally took more than two weeks to complete. The fact that Jesus' family journeyed five days each way to Jerusalem for the eight-day Passover celebration every year demonstrates their piety and their strong commitment of faith.

Jesus' nuclear family would not have traveled to Jerusalem alone, but with the members of their extended family and perhaps others from Nazareth as well, to protect and support one another. After arriving in Jerusalem, they would have faced the challenge of finding lodging at a time when Jerusalem's population swelled as many as ten times the local residents. Because Mary had relatives who lived in Ein Kerem near Jerusalem—Zechariah and Elizabeth and their son John—it is possible they stayed with them. Another possibility would have been to stay further south with Joseph's relatives back in Bethlehem, where they spent the first year or two of Jesus' life.

After Jesus' twelfth Passover, traditionally considered a Jewish boy's coming of age, when the *oikos* was returning to Nazareth, Joseph and Mary assumed Jesus was with others in their traveling party. When they realized Jesus was not with them, they returned to Jerusalem and frantically searched for their son, only to find him sitting among the rabbis in the expansive courts of Herod's newly rebuilt Temple. As he listened to the rabbinical dialogue, asked questions, and offered his own answers, he amazed the teachers with his understanding. Perhaps it was then that Jesus' unique insights and understanding began to become evident. Jesus explained his actions to his distraught parents who demanded an explanation, *"Did you not know that I had to be in my Father's house?"* This can also be translated, *"Did you not know that I had to be about my Father's business?"* (Luke 2:49)

After experiencing the unique events surrounding Jesus' birth and this incident in the Temple courts, *Mary treasured up all these things, pondering them in her heart.* (Luke 2:19, 51) But Luke also tells us that when Jesus explained why he was in the Temple courts debating with the rabbis, *they did not understand the saying that he spoke to them.* (Luke 2:50). Mary and Joseph loved their twelve-year old son, but they were in *great distress* because they did not understand what Jesus was saying about the Temple being his Father's house and his life being about his Father's business. It must have been very difficult for the young man Jesus to realize that even his own mother did not really understand his unique identity and calling.

At the age of twelve, Jesus already had such wisdom and insight that the leading biblical scholars of his time were amazed! There was so much inside of Jesus waiting to be expressed. And yet Luke tells us something incredible when describing the response of this twelve-year-old boy to his uncomprehending parents: *he went down with them and came to Nazareth and was submissive to them* (Luke 2:51). That means Jesus returned with them to live as part of the extended family and train in the family construction business. And indeed, that is the last we hear of Jesus until 18 years later when he traveled to the Jordan River to be baptized by his cousin John at about the age of 30. The boy Jesus knew that he still had many years of patient submission and preparation ahead of him if he was going to fulfill the calling his Father was giving him.

THREE HOUSES IN ANCIENT NAZARETH

Today Nazareth is a large, bustling city made up of mostly Muslim and Christian Palestinians with a primarily Jewish suburb. The heart of the modern city sits directly over the remains of the ancient village, making archaeological excavation difficult. However, the remains of a few first-century courtyard homes have been discovered. They follow the typical design of a series of rooms built around a central courtyard with a heavily barred gate giving access to the courtyard from the street.

In addition to these first-century homes, the excavators found streets, cisterns, grinding stones, clay pots, and many other artifacts from the first-century village of Nazareth. The remains in these homes indicate the first-century inhabitants were relatively prosperous and held strongly to their Jewish identity through religious practice, in spite of the proximity of Sepphoris and its Roman cultural sympathies. Three first century homes discovered in Nazareth merit our particular attention.

FIRST-CENTURY HOME IN NAZARETH

The first is the most recently discovered, found in the heart of first-century Nazareth during preparations for the building of the Mary of Nazareth Center in 2009. A team of archaeologists, led by Yardenna Alexandre, discovered a house with at least two rooms connected to a central courtyard. It is the only first-century house in Nazareth discovered so far with surviving walls in place that has been excavated using modern archaeological methods. This house was built directly on the sloping bedrock, so the floor of the courtyard consisted of smooth natural rock into which was carved a bell-shaped pit for collecting and storing water. Small channels were cut into the rock to direct rainfall into the cistern, and a depression was cut into the sloping floor, perhaps providing a level spot to place a water jar. The pottery vessels and other remains recovered here date the house to the time of Jesus. Archaeologists discovered vessels carved from chalkstone (rather than pottery), indicating a conservative Jewish religious practice, since stone vessels were considered by Jews to be impervious to ritual impurity.

Remains of a second ancient house were discovered in Nazareth in 1880 when the Sisters of Nazareth Convent was being built just a stone's throw from the modern site of the Mary of Nazareth Center. The nineteenth-century builders discovered ancient remains. They collected the ancient artifacts and then built over the remains, preserving the site. In 1936 Father Henri Senes, a former architect, studied the ancient structures and artifacts previously discovered underneath the convent and recorded his findings in extensive notes and diagrams. In 2006 Ken Dark of the Nazareth Archaeological Project began to study these ancient remains, using modern archaeological methods, and recently published analysis.

Beneath the Sisters of Nazareth Convent lie the foundations of a Crusader church which stood on this spot. Underneath those foundations lie the older foundations of

FIRST-CENTURY HOUSE UNDER SISTERS OF NAZARETH CONVENT

a Byzantine church which was built on a very strong vault constructed of large, finely cut stones. This vault protected an even older Byzantine cave chapel which incorporated a natural spring. Adjacent to this cave are the remains of an early Roman era house cut into the rock hillside. Some of the rooms were constructed out of bedrock, with cut stones completing the walls of the house. One doorway cut into the hillside survives to its full height. The nineteenth-century builders who first uncovered these remains found typical domestic pottery, a stone weaver's spindle whorl, a perfume bottle, and Roman glass vessels, all confirming this as a first-century Jewish home.

Because this house was discovered before the development of modern archaeological methods, we don't have the same level of detailed data as for the first house, but we do have strong historical evidence to identify the occupants of this home. These remains fit well with the account of the seventh-century Abbot Adomnan of Iona, who recorded the reports of a Frankish bishop named Arculf. Arculf had recently visited Nazareth and described two "very large churches, one in the center of the city on the site of the house where Jesus was brought up, the other on the site of the house where Mary received the angel Gabriel." The second sounds like the site of the current Church of the Annunciation, which we discuss below. The first place of worship was called the Church of the Nutrition which stood nearby and was built over a vault covering a spring. Arculf also described two tombs adjacent to the remains identified as the house of Joseph where Jesus was raised. Based on this data we can confidently identify the house underneath the Sisters of Nazareth Convent as a Jewish home inhabited in the early first century which was understood at least by the Byzantine era as the home in which Jesus grew up.

FIRST-CENTURY TOMB UNDERNEATH HOUSE

Unexpectedly, an ancient tomb was incorporated into the base of this home after it was built. The tomb features a large and finely cut rolling stone. One of the unanswered questions about this house is why the tomb was built so close to the house, since Jews generally avoided living too close to tombs for reasons of ritual purity. One interpretation is that the tombs were constructed to venerate an important member of the family who lived in that house. The residents from whom the Sisters of Nazareth purchased this property told them of the tradition that underneath their homes was the ancient "Tomb of the Just Man." It is significant that Matthew describes Joseph as "a just man" (Matthew 1:19). Since Joseph is never mentioned by the Gospel writers during the adult years of Jesus, we can assume that he had died by the time Jesus began his public mission. Was the tomb underneath this first-century house built for Joseph and his extended family? If it is, the presence of such a finely cut rolling-stone tomb is yet more evidence that disproves the common assumption that Jesus grew up in a poor peasant family. This expensive type of tomb shows us that Jesus was part of a financially secure family that was supported by a successful family business. Perhaps Jesus and his brothers, the expert stonemasons, carved this tomb as a final act to honor their father Joseph!

Yet another first-century home is preserved beneath the Basilica of the Annunciation in Nazareth. As with the Sisters of Nazareth Convent, this modern church is built over the ruins of earlier churches dating from the Crusader and Byzantine periods. Beneath the ruins of these churches, a team of archaeologists, led by Bellarmino Bagatti, discovered the foundations of an ancient Jewish home dating to the first century. This home was also built into the rock hillside and presumably included rooms built around an open courtyard. The cisterns and bell-shaped pits cut into the bedrock here are identical to those discovered in the earlier mentioned sites, demonstrating the common design of these three houses. Archaeological discoveries in this home also include typical artifacts reflecting Jewish cooking and domestic use in the first century.

FIRST-CENTURY HOUSE OF MARY'S FAMILY

This house has been identified since ancient times as the home of Mary and her extended family, where the angel Gabriel appeared to her and announced the miraculous conception of Jesus. As early as AD 384, the pilgrim Egeria was shown "a big and very splendid cave" in which Mary had lived. Remarkably, Bagatti discovered that during the first two centuries following Jesus' ministry, this home was converted into a public place of worship. By the early fifth-century, the house was replaced with a Byzantine church, which was replaced by a Crusader church, and now a huge modern church preserves these earlier remains and makes them accessible to visitors today.

We can have a high degree of confidence in the accuracy of the tradition marking this as the home of Mary because ancient records demonstrate that the descendants of Jesus' Jewish relatives continued to live in Nazareth and professed faith in Jesus for several centuries after his death and resurrection. According to Julius Africanus (AD 160-240), the village of Nazareth was a center of Jewish Christian missionary activity at the end of the second century. Conon, martyred in Asia Minor during the reign of Decius (AD 249-51), affirmed in court, "I am of Nazareth in Galilee, I am of the family of Christ to whom I offer a cult from the time of my ancestors."[25]

The archaeological evidence of a Jewish-Christian presence in Nazareth in the centuries following the time of Jesus is consistent with this record of his descendants continuing to profess faith in him as the Messiah, and it means the memory of the exact location of Mary's home underneath the Church of the Annunciation would have been accurately preserved. It also adds to the likelihood that the home of Joseph's extended family where he settled with Mary and Jesus upon their return from Egypt was also accurately identified underneath the Byzantine Church of the Nutrition.

After Jesus was a grown man and had left his extended family home in Nazareth, he told a parable about the relationship between hearing and doing which reflected the exact setting of his boyhood home: *"Everyone then who hears these words of mine and does them will be like a wise man who built his house on the rock. And the rain fell, and the floods came, and the winds blew and beat on that house, but it did not fall, because it had been founded on the rock."* (Matthew 7:24-25) Jesus had grown up in a house with foundations literally cut into the bedrock. As a builder he knew how the foundations of houses were built and had certainly built some himself. The vivid image from this parable was not a hypothetical idea for Jesus and those who were familiar with houses like those on the rock hillside of Nazareth. It was a picture of their way of life.

---

25 As quoted in Jerome Murphy-O'Connor, *The Holy Land* (Oxford, Oxford University Press, 2008) 424, Digital.

 ## THE LIFE

JESUS' NEIGHBORHOOD

Pam and I travel a lot. We love to explore new places and lead people on adventures around the world, but there is something wonderful about coming home and having a neighborhood where you belong, where you know the people who live around you. Recently, Pam and I sold our home of seventeen years and decided to wait before buying a new home. A year and a half later we moved into our new house and began to make a home in our new neighborhood, and we were so excited! It was not easy to go that long without a home and a neighborhood to call our own. It is easy to forget that Jesus had a neighborhood where he was known and where he belonged.

When we look at these three first-century Jewish homes today, it is extraordinary to realize that we can identify with some confidence the house in which Mary grew up, the house in which Jesus grew up, and the house of one of their neighbors. This was the neighborhood, and these were the streets, where the boy Jesus played with his friends and grew into a man who would inaugurate God's plan to save humanity and redeem the whole world. What is most remarkable about this is the normalcy of the environment in which Jesus grew up. His house was just like every other house in Nazareth. His family functioned just like every other family. By all biblical accounts, he lived an ordinary life for his first thirty years. Jesus grew up in a neighborhood just like you and me.

As we have seen, Jesus' birth was extraordinary, and by the age of twelve he had already developed in character and wisdom far beyond his years. Mary treasured the angelic visits and the miraculous events surrounding Jesus' birth and pondered them in her heart. She and Joseph marveled at the prophecies about Jesus spoken by Simeon and Anna in the Temple when he was eight days old, but twelve years later they failed to understand Jesus' explanation of why he stayed back in the Temple courts with the teachers of the Law (Luke 2:33, 49-50). Even though Jesus had already outgrown his parent's ability to understand him, he went back to Nazareth and *was submissive to them*. This was the point at which Jesus left his studies at the synagogue in *Beth Sefer* and was trained by his father and uncles into the family construction business (Mark 6:3). For the next eighteen years, *Jesus increased in wisdom and in stature and in favor with God and man.* (Luke 2:52)

The first three decades of Jesus' life are sometimes called the hidden years, and if we don't look closely it is easy to miss what Jesus was going through during this period. He lived in Joseph's extended family house and devoted himself to the family business, but ultimately he knew he had to be about his heavenly Father's business and had to be in his heavenly Father's house. Mary and Joseph didn't understand his wider calling, and yet Jesus chose to submit to them for eighteen years and wait for the right time to fulfill that wider calling. This took extraordinary patience and humility. As we noted earlier, the writer of Hebrews described Jesus when he wrote, *Although he was a son, he learned obedience through what he suffered.* (Hebrews 5:8) Surely that suffering was fulfilled on the cross, but it must have begun in Nazareth as Jesus bided his time year after year, waiting for the Father to release him into his calling.

OUR NEIGHBORHOOD

We often miss that Jesus was already setting an example for us to follow while he was a young man in Nazareth. These hidden years of Jesus show us that it takes time, a lot of time, to prepare for the things God has created us and called us to do. We must first allow God to do in us what we want him to do through us. It took thirty years for Jesus to be ready to answer his Father's call. It took thirty years of submitting to his parents, even when he was misunderstood. It took eighteen years of learning to be a builder in the family business. It took many years of exercising patience while learning to discern and follow his Father's leading. How long will it take for us to prepare to fulfill our Father's calling? How will we need to submit? What training do we need to receive? How much patience will we need to exercise?

When I look back on my walk with Jesus, I can see how God has used each chapter of my life to prepare me for the mission that lay ahead. My dad was an airline pilot, and so we lived overseas in different cultures when I was young. I can see now that God used those formative experiences to prepare me for the cross-cultural mission that Pam and I are living now. I spent ten years in college, graduate, and post-graduate studies, which prepared me for a lifetime of teaching. During those ten years, I spent my summers working in residential construction, which prepared me for twenty seasons of leading house-building missions in Mexico. I spent twenty-five years leading churches, which prepared me for my current calling to train pastors and church leaders. And so on. God doesn't waste anything if we will submit to him. He uses it all, if we will let him.

Once Jesus began his public mission, he said, *"Truly, truly, I say to you, the Son can do nothing of his own accord, but only what he sees the Father doing. For whatever the Father does, that the Son does likewise."* (John 5:19) How did Jesus learn to see what his Father was doing and hear what his Father was saying? It was through years of submitting, waiting, and trusting his Father. Jesus described the result of those years of waiting when he said, *"Everyone who comes to me and hears my words and does them, I will show you what he is like: he is like a man building a house, who dug deep and laid the foundation on the rock."* (Luke 6:47-48) As we have seen, that is exactly how the three houses in Nazareth were built, with foundations laid directly on the bedrock of that sloping hill! Perhaps Jesus was remembering these years spent living in just such a house when he gave us this picture of learning to hear and respond to the Word of God.

God has created you for a purpose bigger than yourself. Jesus is calling you to fulfill a purpose that will matter for eternity. The question is whether you are willing to go through the process necessary to prepare you to fulfill that calling. It may take a long time. Will you let God use it to prepare you? You may have to submit to others who don't understand you. You will have to trust God and wait on his timing. You will need to learn how to see what your Father is doing and hear what your Father is saying. Anything less than this means your house will be built on sand and the inevitable storms of life will bring it tumbling down. If you are willing to follow Jesus in his hidden years, you will learn how to build a house on bedrock. A house like the house of Jesus. A house that will stand through the toughest storms. A house that can nurture a family that will change the world!

CHAPTER SIX

JESUS' BAPTISM AND TEMPTATION: BIBLICAL BOOT CAMP

a voice from heaven said, "This is my beloved Son, with whom I am well pleased."
(Matthew 3:17)

 **THE WAY**

MESSIANIC PREPARATIONS

As far back as the Exodus, God promised to send a leader like Moses to come and lead his people out of bondage into freedom. Beginning with the Babylonian exile, under the preaching of the prophets, the anticipation of a liberating king from the line of David grew exponentially. By the time of Jesus, the expectation of a coming *Messiah* (Hebrew for "Anointed One") was deeply embedded in the Jewish consciousness. As we have discussed, many different Messianic theologies had bubbled up in first-century Palestine, variously promoting a royal Messiah, a priestly Messiah, a prophetic Messiah, and a military Messiah. The Sadducees played down these Messianic expectations in an attempt to keep the peace and hold on to power. The Pharisees prepared for Messiah by strict legal observance and teaching. The Essenes prepared for their dual Messiahs by living lives of extreme ritual purity. The Zealots forcefully set the stage for Messiah by acts of violence.

But one preparer stood out from the rest: John the Baptist. As we have seen, John probably spent some time in the Essene community at Qumran, but he appeared in the desert a unique figure. Dressed like the prophet Elijah, who was to be a forerunner of the Messiah, John also prepared for the coming Messiah, but with a markedly different message. John did not focus on the technicalities of legal observance, nor the minutiae of esoteric rituals. He did not promote armed resistance—in fact he even addressed Roman soldiers in his preaching. John prepared for the coming Messiah by addressing the hearts of people. He invited them to be immersed in the Jordan River as a sign they were turning of their lives back to God.

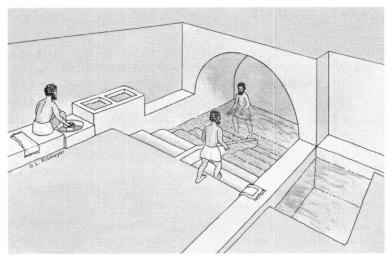

JEWISH RITUAL BATH

Beginning in the first century BC, ritual immersion in stepped pools (Hebrew plural: *mikvot*) had become a regular part of Jewish life. They used immersion in a *mikveh* to regain a ritual state of purity after touching a dead body, eating unclean food, experiencing skin disease, coming into contact with anyone in one of these states, or touching anything those people had touched. Women took ritual baths following menstruation and childbirth; and men immersed themselves after an emission of semen. Ritual impurity was not about moral acts or thoughts or attitudes; it was seen as an external kind of impurity that you could catch unaware, similar to the way modern people think of germs.

Mikvot are a common feature in archaeological excavations of first-century sites all around Israel, pointing to their importance in Jewish life at the time of Jesus. To be considered effective, a ritual bath was supposed to contain "living water," meaning naturally running water, as in a stream or lake or ocean. To achieve this in an arid environment where running water was extraordinarily scarce, they built small cisterns or placed a clay pot next to the *mikveh* with a narrow channel connecting the two. Opening a valve allowed a trickle of water to flow into the ritual bath, transforming the stagnant water into "living water." For the bath to be effective, every part of the body had to be immersed in the water. If even a wayward hair remained above the surface, the ritual bath was considered null and void. Because it was required that nothing come between your body and the water, *mikvot* were enclosed for privacy, men and women bathed separately, and an observer verified the complete immersion of each person.

A River Runs Through It

Although a number of smaller tributaries flow into it, such as the Yarmouk and the Jabbok, the Jordan is the principal river that flows 156 miles through the ancient land of Israel. Beginning with powerful springs at the base of Mount Hermon near the modern border of Israel and Lebanon, it runs south into the lake we call the Sea of Galilee, and then flows from that lake through a deep rift valley and empties into the terminal salt lake called the Dead Sea, the lowest place on the face of the earth. Although it is not very impressive compared to the mighty Tigris and Euphrates Rivers further east, the Jordan River is the largest river in the area. It formed the eastern boundary of ancient Canaan.

THE JORDAN RIVER AT QASR AL YAHUD

When Moses led the people of Israel through the wilderness toward the Promised Land, he stood on Mount Nebo looking west over the Jordan Valley into the land of Canaan. After Moses' death Joshua led God's people to the eastern bank of the Jordan River, the flow of which was miraculously interrupted so they were able to cross and begin their conquest of the land. Bethabara (Hebrew for "House of the Ford") is this spot on the eastern bank, and John refers to it as "Bethany beyond the Jordan" (John 1:28). The western bank of this same spot on the river is known as *Qasr al Yahud* (Arabic for "Castle of the Jews"), and it marks the traditional site of Jesus' baptism. Several churches and monasteries were built here on both sides of the river during the Byzantine era, and their ruins are still visible today. Since 1967, this had been a closed military zone, but the governments of Jordan and Israel have recently developed facilities on both sides of the river and opened them to the public.

To the west of the baptism site at *Qasr al Yahud* lies the ancient city of Jericho. Powerful springs water this area through extensive aqueducts, turning it into a fertile oasis. First settled as early as the ninth century BC, Jericho is the oldest continuously inhabited city in the world. It was famous in antiquity for its extensive date plantations. To the west of Jericho, at the mouth of the dry river bed known as *Wadi Qelt,* Hasmonean rulers of Israel built a palace complex a hundred years before the time of Jesus, complete with colonnaded halls and a swimming pool. Water for the palace and the pool were supplied by two long aqueducts built into the steep sides of the Wadi Qelt, as they brought water from a spring six miles up the valley. Further west beyond the palace stretches the vast Judean desert wilderness riven with deep ravines, a harsh and inhospitable territory with very little water supply. This made the Wadi Qelt an especially significant area because of its precious springs and the open aqueducts that flowed through it for miles.

When Herod the Great took control of the area in 37 BC, he greatly expanded the Hasmonean palace at Jericho and strengthened the aqueducts which supplied it. Herod built a bridge across the Wadi Qelt that connected his renovated palace to a sunken garden and pool on the other side of the dry riverbed. The primary road that led from Jericho in the deep Jordan Valley up to Jerusalem is known in the Bible as the "Ascent of Adummim." It ran south and west from Jericho, directly past Herod's palace, and then up onto the southern ridge above the Wadi Qelt toward Jerusalem. (cf. Joshua 15:6-8). This is the road Jesus and his family used every year on their pilgrimage from Nazareth to Jerusalem. It is the road in which Jesus' parable of the Good Samaritan is set. It is also the road Jesus and the disciples followed as they made their way from Jericho to Jerusalem for Jesus' final Passover.

 # THE TRUTH

WHAT HAPPENED AT THE RIVER?

When John the Baptist appeared in the desert just east of Jericho, where Joshua had led the people of Israel over the Jordan River, it was as if he were calling Israel back to where they had begun. As he challenged people to confess, repent, and be baptized, it caused quite a stir. Mark tells us that *all the country of Judea and all Jerusalem were going out to him* (Mark 1:5). When self-righteous Pharisees and sanctimonious Sadducees came to listen, he called them out as a "brood of vipers." When oppressive tax collectors and abusive soldiers came, he challenged them not to misuse their positions. John was not calling them to be immersed in the waters of Jordan River for ritual purification, as in a *mikveh*. His baptism was pointing to something much bigger. John's baptism symbolized a response of the heart to what God was saying.

Josephus describes John's influence this way, "[John the Baptist] was a good man, and commanded the Jews to exercise virtue, both as to righteousness towards one another, and piety towards God, and so to come to baptism; for that the washing with water would be acceptable to him, if they made use of it, not in order to the putting away of some sins only, but for the purification of the body; supposing still that the soul was thoroughly purified beforehand by righteousness. Now when others came in crowds about him, for they were very greatly moved by hearing his words, Herod, who feared lest the great influence John had over the people might put it into his power and inclination to raise a rebellion..."[26]

But John was clear about the limits of his mission. His baptism was just the precursor to something far greater. He was preparing people to receive and respond to the Messiah who would soon appear. He said, *"I baptize you with water for repentance, but he who is coming after me is mightier than I, whose sandals I am not worthy to carry. He will baptize you with the Holy Spirit and fire."* (Matthew 3:11) John was very clear that he was not the Messiah but was pointing to the Messiah. Later he told his disciples in reference to Jesus, *"He must increase, but I must decrease."* (John 3:30)

---

26 Flavius Josephus, *Antiquities of the Jews,* trans. William Whiston, (Delmarva, 2016), Book 18, Chapter 5, Section 2, Digital.

At this time Jesus' hidden years in Nazareth were coming to an end, and he was about to complete his long season of preparation with two defining experiences. Luke tells us Jesus was about thirty years old when he left his home and family in Nazareth to begin his public ministry. We might have expected him to head to Jerusalem to launch his mission with a big splash among the crowds at the Temple Mount, but instead he traveled south from Nazareth into the barren Judean desert and found that spot at the Jordan where his cousin John was baptizing. When John saw his cousin coming, he suddenly had a prophetic insight and declared, *"Behold, the Lamb of God, who takes away the sin of the world!"* (John 1:29) There was no human way John could have known that in a few years' time Jesus would suffer and die as the perfect atoning sacrifice for the sins of all humanity. Neither he nor those who heard him could comprehend the meaning of this profound statement until years later.

John was understandably reticent to baptize Jesus because he realized in that moment Jesus was a far greater prophet than he was. And yet Jesus pressed him for baptism, saying, *"Let it be so now, for thus it is fitting for us to fulfill all righteousness."* (Matthew 3:15) The word translated "righteousness" (Greek: *dikaiosune*) here is a covenantal word, pointing to the right relationship that a covenant creates between two parties. A covenant is a biblical way of establishing a personal connection that shapes our identity. Jesus was explaining to John that his baptism would serve as an example for others to follow into a new kind of covenant relationship with God.

Jesus chose to launch his mission by being baptized to show us he was inaugurating a new covenant. He was fulfilling God's promise of a renewed relationship that came hundreds of years earlier through the Prophet Jeremiah: *"Behold, the days are coming, declares the Lord, when I will make a new covenant with the house of Israel and the house of Judah… I will put my law within them, and I will write it on their hearts. And I will be their God, and they shall be my people. And no longer shall each one teach his neighbor and each his brother, saying, 'Know the Lord,' for they shall all know me, from the least of them to the greatest, declares the Lord. For I will forgive their iniquity, and I will remember their sin no more."* (Jeremiah 31:31, 33-34) Jesus asked John to baptize him to invite others into this new kind of covenant relationship. And so, John relented and immersed Jesus in the waters of the Jordan.

As Jesus emerged from the water, the synoptic Gospels (Matthew, Mark, and Luke) record two phenomena which reflected the cosmic shift taking place between heaven and earth. First the sky was torn open, and the Holy Spirit was poured out on Jesus in a visible form that looked like a descending dove. John tells us this was not just a temporary filling of the Spirit that we see from time to time in the Hebrew Scriptures. He said, *"I saw the Spirit descend from heaven like a dove, and it remained on him."* (John 1:32) Jesus was establishing a permanent connection between heaven and earth. Jesus, although fully human, was permanently filled with the Holy Spirit, and God was continually present to those who were with him. The supernatural power that flowed through Jesus into the lives of others was not exclusively due to his divine nature and thus unavailable to us. This infilling by the Holy Spirit empowered Jesus to do all that he did. Soon the Holy Spirit would be poured out on all those who put their trust in Jesus, empowering them follow his way of life. That same power to do God's will is still available to those of us who follow Jesus post-Pentecost!

The second thing that happened was a declaration of the Father from heaven about Jesus: *"You are my beloved Son; with you I am well pleased."* (Mark 1:11) A biblical covenant creates a connection that establishes our identity. Having poured out his Spirit on Jesus, the Father now declared Jesus' true identity in relationship to himself. Jesus is God's own Son. It is important to note that this was not a prearranged meeting or a rehearsed plan between Jesus and John. John twice says he did not know until the moment of his baptism that Jesus was the Messiah. He said, *"I myself did not know him, but he who sent me to baptize with water said to me, 'He on whom you see the Spirit descend and remain, this is he who baptizes with the Holy Spirit.' And I have seen and have borne witness that this is the Son of God."* (John 1:33-34)

In his baptism we discover Jesus' true identity. In our baptism we discover our true identity. Jesus is unique in all of creation and history because he is the eternally preexistent second person of the Trinity, the Word made flesh, Emmanuel, the incarnate Son of God. And yet God chose to empty himself in Jesus and take on our humanity in order to show us the Way. Jesus lived every aspect of his life as an example for us to follow, and his baptism is no exception. Jesus invites us to follow him into the waters of baptism so that we might be filled with his Spirit, be established in a covenantal connection with our heavenly Father, and discover who we really are as the sons and daughters of God!

PASSING THE TEST

Jesus' baptism as the beloved Son was only half of his final preparation experience. The Spirit who remained on him drove Jesus from the banks of the Jordan westward, past the ancient city of Jericho and into the barren wadis stretching into the Judean desert. Now, aside from wild animals eyeing him and angels ministering to him, Jesus could be completely alone with his heavenly Father who had just declared unconditional love and approval, and with the Spirit who remained on him. In this harsh and foreboding wilderness, Jesus began to fast.

The Gospel writers do not specify exactly where Jesus was led by the Spirit, but the natural way into the Judean desert from this part of the Jordan River was the Ascent of Adummim, which ran west from Jericho along the southern ridge of t*he Wadi Qelt*. After passing Herod's palace outside of Jericho, a traveler can veer off the road and into the deep wadi itself. We can have some confidence that this is the area where Jesus spent his forty days in the wilderness because the springs of Wadi Qelt and the two aqueducts that run through it are the most accessible water source for many miles in every direction. While Jesus was abstaining from food, he would still need regular access to drinking water. It makes the most sense that Jesus would have slept in one of the many caves along the Wadi Qelt and drawn water from the aqueducts during his time of fasting in the desert.

MONASTERY OF ST. GEORGE IN WADI QELT

It is no accident that, in the early centuries of Christianity, many ascetics came to this very wadi and lived in its caves, as they sought to imitate Jesus' time of testing in the wilderness. Saint George's Monastery, built in the fifth century directly onto the sheer cliffs of Wadi Qelt, is a vivid testimony to this tradition of fasting and prayer which continues in the desert today. Fasting is an ancient spiritual discipline that leads us to a deeper experience of our dependence on God for all things. The fact that Jesus spent forty days fasting tells us he was profoundly aware that depending on his Father was the only way he would be able to fulfill his calling. Later he expressed this when he said, *"Truly, truly, I say to you, the Son can do nothing of his own accord, but only what he sees the Father doing… I can do nothing on my own. As I hear, I judge, and my judgment is just, because I seek not my own will but the will of him who sent me."* (John 5:19, 30)

The synoptic Gospels tell us that, after forty days in the desert with no food, when Jesus was physically in his weakest and most vulnerable state, the devil began to tempt him. The Greek word *peirazo*, translated "tempt" in these passages, carries both a positive and a negative sense. The positive sense of *peirazo* is when someone offers a challenge meant to demonstrate what you have learned and to establish you in that skill or knowledge. The best translation for this positive sense is "test," because the one offering the challenge wants you to succeed.

The negative sense of *peirazo* is when someone is trying to entice you away from what is good and into what is destructive. This usually happens through a series of seemingly small compromises. The best translation for this negative kind of challenge is "tempt." The Spirit led Jesus into the desert for a challenging time of testing in order to establish him more fully in the Father's authority and power. The devil, however, was using this as an opportunity to co-opt Jesus for his own purpose by tempting him to serve himself and seek his own glory.

The tempter came to Jesus and said, *"If you are the Son of God, command these stones to become loaves of bread."* (Matthew 4:3) When you are standing on the ridge overlooking Wadi Qelt, the devil's initial tactic becomes immediately obvious, for stones are scattered on the hillsides as far as the eye can see. We can well imagine these stones appearing as countless loaves of bread to someone who has gone without food for forty days. The devil begins by appealing to Jesus' appetites. We can all be driven by hungers and desires, longing to be fulfilled in the things of this world. Forty days of relying on his Father alone had made it crystal clear to Jesus that the love and approval of our heavenly Father poured into our hearts through the indwelling Holy Spirit is the only thing that will truly satisfy the hunger inside us. Every other appetite is a counterfeit for the one thing that we truly need.

It is instructive to note the devil began his attack by calling into question what the Father said so clearly about Jesus' identity, *"If you are the Son of God…"* It is reminiscent of the serpent's words to Eve in the Garden of Eden, *"Did God actually say, 'You shall not eat of any tree in the garden'?"* (Genesis 3:1) Satan will twist the Word of God at every opportunity, because deception is the devil's primary weapon. In this case the deceiver was trying to get Jesus to misuse the covenant identity he had received from his Father. But Jesus responds by quoting Deuteronomy 8:3, *"It is written, 'Man shall not live by bread alone, but by every word that comes from the mouth of God.'"* (Matthew 4:4) Jesus refuses to operate on his own authority, but instead chooses to act as a representative of his Father the King by speaking God's words rather than his own.

The devil was not easily discouraged. He took Jesus to the *"pinnacle of the Temple"* and dared him to jump off, claiming that God's angels would catch him. We can't be sure exactly which part of the Temple complex this was, but the nature of the temptation gives us a strong clue. If Jesus were to jump from the southwest corner of the Royal Stoa, the highest point on Herod's massive Temple Mount, and be caught by angels, it would happen right in the very center of Jerusalem's busiest and most visible intersection. Such a miracle would have made Jesus an instant celebrity and the most talked about person in Jerusalem.

The offer of fame and the approval of others at the expense of our integrity is a powerful temptation, because it seems to validate us and increase our value as a person. Jesus had already received the full approval of his heavenly Father, and it set him free from the allure of this seductive trap. When the King of the universe is your Father who is already proud of you, any kind of human approval pales in comparison! In our brokenness we all long to receive

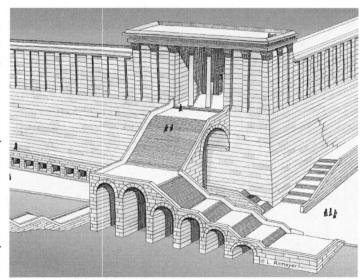

SOUTHWEST CORNER OF TEMPLE MOUNT

approval from those we admire. The more deeply rooted we become in our Father's unconditional approval and his lavish love for us, the more we will become free to submit our will to God alone. This time the devil tried to beat Jesus at his own game by quoting Scripture, but Jesus was not fooled and again spoke his Father's words in reply, rejecting the temptation outright.

The tempter took one more shot at Jesus and this time he laid his cards on the table. On an unnamed mountain peak, the devil showed Jesus all the kingdoms of the world and their glory. He said, *"All these I will give you, if you will fall down and worship me."* (Matthew 4:9) Although later tradition placed this temptation at the top of Mount Quarantal overlooking Jericho, the location of this temptation is not known. We don't even know the nature of these visits. Is Satan able to physically translocate Jesus, or are these some kind of a vision that Jesus experienced? Either way, this third temptation was a raw offer of earthly authority and power in exchange for complete submission. The devil was appealing to Jesus' ambition in order to undermine his submission to the Father. He knew this was the only way he could thwart Jesus' mission.

Just think of what Jesus could have done with all that temporal authority and power. He could throw down tyrants from their thrones. He could bring justice to countless oppressed people. He could provide food, shelter, and security to those who had none. The justifications go on and on, but in the end the enemy would have won. Whoever or whatever we give first place in our heart is the thing that rules us. The simple fact remains that there is only one true King. Every other power that does not submit to him is a counterfeit and a fraud. Jesus was fully submitted to his Father, the King of the universe, and filled with the Holy Spirit. That was the source of his extraordinary authority and power.

This temptation had no power over Jesus because his greatest ambition was simply to do the will of his King, even if that meant dying on a cross. When you are submitted to the King who happens to be your Dad, you have the authority to speak and act on his behalf. That is why Jesus could say *"Be gone, Satan!"* and Satan had to go. Jesus quoted Scripture a third time to show us that he did not speak by his own authority or by any other earthly authority. He chose again to represent his Father the King of the universe. Near the end of his earthly life, Jesus explained it this way, *"For I have not spoken on my own authority, but the Father who sent me has himself given me a commandment—what to say and what to speak. And I know that his commandment is eternal life. What I say, therefore, I say as the Father has told me."* (John 12:49-50)

Jesus knew who he was, the Son of the Father—and he knew who his Father was, the

King of the universe. The Holy Spirit remained on Jesus and filled him. Because Jesus was so deeply rooted in his true identity and so completely submitted to his role as a representative of the King, the greatest force of evil in the world could not overcome him. The devil slinked away as angels ministered to Jesus. Satan knew that he was beaten for the time being, and he waited for an opportune time to strike again.

 ## The Life

Preparation for Battle

Boot camp has two purposes: to demonstrate who is really suited for military service and to prepare them with the fundamental tools and skills they will need to navigate the rigors that are to come. Jesus' baptism at the Jordan and temptation in the wilderness served as a kind of biblical boot camp to identify him and prepare him for the battle ahead. His baptism was an opportunity to demonstrate and receive confirmation of his true identity as the Son of God. His time of temptation was an opportunity for Jesus to demonstrate his submission to the King of the universe and confirm that God's authority and power are infinitely stronger than the fearsome enemy he faced. Untold challenges still lay ahead of him, but Jesus emerged from his boot camp ready to overcome them all. No wonder the Gospel writers describe Jesus coming out of the wilderness *"in the power of the Spirit"* as he was led back to his hometown in Galilee.

Every one of us needs to go through our own biblical boot camp if we are going to be ready for what lies ahead. To go on this journey, we need to consider two crucial questions: Am I rooted in my true Covenant identity given to me in relationship with my heavenly Father? Do I know how to operate in the Kingdom authority and power given to me by my Father the King? If we intend to follow Jesus in the power of the Spirit to Galilee, first we will have to follow him into the waters of the Jordan to find our true Covenant identity. Then we will have to follow him into the formidable desert wilderness to learn how to exercise Kingdom authority. This is the preparation we need for the journey of discipleship that lies ahead.

The starting point on this journey is our identity. Everything else that matters flows from this. No human being can tell you who you really are. Nothing on this earth can truly define you—neither your past nor your present; neither your possessions nor your pedigree; neither your friends nor your family; neither your failures nor your finest moments. The Creator is the one who defines his creation. The one who made you is the one who knows you fully. Your heavenly Father is the only one who can tell you who you really are. It is important to note that Jesus had not yet accomplished anything of significance when his Father made this declaration about him. He had not preached any profound sermons, fed any multitudes, healed any lepers, or released anyone from demonic oppression. And yet the Father loved him, was proud of him, and claimed him as his own Son! The same is true of you.

You can't earn your identity as God's daughter or son. It is not something we can manufacture or create. Our identity is a gift of grace given to us by a generous Father who loves us and is proud of us regardless of anything we have done or not done. Those who have children know that a child cannot earn their parents' love and acceptance, nor can they lose it. That unconditional love is simply an inevitable byproduct of the relationship. We love our kids because they are our kids! The same is even more true of us in relation to our heavenly Father. As Jesus said, *"If you then, who are evil, know how to give good gifts to your children, how much more will your Father who is in heaven give good things to those who ask him!"* (Matthew 7:11) Ultimately Jesus died and rose again, and the Spirit was poured out to permanently establish our new identity in Christ as sons and daughters of the Father by his grace.

Where do you find your identity? It is in your job? Too often we let our titles tell us who we are only to discover we were fooled. Do you find your value in the accomplishments you have achieved, especially the ones you have done for God? Perhaps you have identified yourself with what you have amassed: your house, your car, your clothes, or your bank account. Maybe it is the school you graduated from or the neighborhood you live in. Is it your appearance, how much weight you have been able to keep off, or how much hair you have held onto? Or maybe it is your relationships, having the right friends, being married to the right person, coming from the right family, or producing the right kind of children.

When we say it out loud, we know these things don't define us, but how subtly we submit to those lies without noticing! The deceiver will use anything to convince us that this is what defines us. The only antidote to the bondage of this subtle deception is wading into a muddy river with Jesus and looking up into a torn open sky. Those false identities will have to be drowned one by one. If we are going to learn to live in our true identity, we will need ears to hear what the Father is saying. We will need a heart that is open to receiving the Spirit who remains. We will need to begin exercising the faith that the Word and the Spirit of God create within us. Can you hear what the Father is saying to you right now? "This is my beloved son. In him I am well pleased. This is my beloved daughter. In her I am well pleased." Are you listening? Can you feel the wings of the dove fluttering in your heart of hearts? The Holy Spirit is present and working. Are you receiving him and responding?

The Power to Overcome

One of the things that sets Jesus apart from every other figure in human history is that he was not only a brilliant teacher who taught profound truths, but he was also a practitioner who had the power to do the very things he talked about. It is one thing to philosophize hypothetically about concepts and ideas. It is another thing to walk your talk and implement the vision you proclaim. Jesus did not just proclaim the Kingdom of God; he demonstrated it. He did not just philosophize about a new kind of Covenant relationship with God; he embodied it. Jesus spoke of Living Bread and then fed hungry people. He spoke of the Light of the World and then opened the eyes of the blind. He called his disciples to take up their cross and then died on a cross and rose from the dead. Jesus is not just the Truth; he is also the Way and the Life!

As the incarnate Son of God, Jesus is unquestionably unique in all creation and all human history. One of the biggest mistakes we can make is assuming that Jesus' divinity separates us from the life he lived. We have discussed earlier our propensity to mitigate Jesus' call to do what he does by ignoring his full humanity and imagining an impossible chasm between us and his Way of Life. If it is true that God emptied himself in becoming fully human (Philippians 2:7) and promised we would do even greater things than him (John 14:12), then Jesus' followers have to take seriously the call to imitate him in every aspect of his life. The question is, then, how did Jesus do the amazing things he did if he had become fully human like us? The answer can be found in his baptism in the Jordan and testing in the wilderness.

Jesus lived the amazing life he lived not because he had access to some kind of power that is not available to us, but because he knew who he was and he knew who his

Father was, and because he was filled with the Holy Spirit who spoke faith into his heart. When the devil came to him, questioning his identity and twisting the Word of God, Jesus simply responded in faith as a Spirit-filled Son of his heavenly Father who had decided to submit himself to represent his Father the King. Over and over again, Jesus made it clear that he did not speak or operate on his own behalf, but as the Son who was speaking for and representing his Father. So *Jesus said to them, "When you have lifted up the Son of Man, then you will know that I am he, and that I do nothing on my own authority, but speak just as the Father taught me. And he who sent me is with me. He has not left me alone, for I always do the things that are pleasing to him."* (John 8:28-29)

This was the secret of Jesus' great power! The reason Jesus could cast out demons, heal the sick, feed the multitudes, walk on water, give sight to the blind, and raise the dead was that he refused to represent himself, operate on his own authority, or carry out his own will. Instead he trusted his identity as the Son and by faith exercised the authority given to him by his Father the King. The result was divine power flowing through Jesus to do the will of God no matter what the obstacles. This way of life is available to all those who trust Jesus and submit to his indwelling Spirit.

After the day of Pentecost, Jesus' disciples learned to live out of their true identity so they could do the things Jesus did. This newfound identity and authority completely changed them and changed their way of life. John describes the transformation this way: *See what kind of love the Father has given to us, that we should be called children of God; and so we are. The reason why the world does not know us is that it did not know him. Beloved, we are God's children now, and what we will be has not yet appeared; but we know that when he appears we shall be like him, because we shall see him as he is. And everyone who thus hopes in him purifies himself as he is pure.* (1 John 3:1-3) The assurance of their true identity in Christ produced in them in the present what they would become fully in the future. This is how the ordinary men and women who followed Jesus were able to live the Life they saw in him. They knew who they were and they knew who their Father is.

If you trust and believe that you have been made a daughter or son of God by grace in Jesus and that his Spirit lives in you, then it is time to step into the authority Jesus has given you to follow him and to learn to do the things he does. This journey begins by recognizing who your Father is. He is the King of kings and Lord of lords, Creator of heaven and earth, in whom all authority in heaven and earth resides. This is your Dad! Everywhere the son or daughter of an earthly king goes, people recognize them as a representative of their father the king because of their relationship to him. The same is true of you. He has given you, as God's son or daughter, full authority to represent your Father and do his will on earth as it is in heaven. The question is whether you will trust him and submit to his will by exercising that authority.

For the first thirty years of my walk with Jesus, I grew in my knowledge that the grace of God had made me his son. But it has only been in the past decade or so that I have come to understand that this identity brings with it the inherent authority of Jesus to do all the things he did. Through discipling relationships, I have been learning to operate in that authority, and see now God's power flowing through me and those who are close to me in ways I had never seen before. Prophetic images and words have become a daily blessing and resource in the work we do. We regularly see physical healings, in addition to spiritual, emotional, mental, and relational healings, on our trips and in the trainings we lead. We have found the power to do God's will in ways we never did before simply because we are learning to live out of our identity in the authority Jesus has given us.

Jesus was very clear that the authority given to him as the Son of God and the resulting power that flowed through him to do God's will is also available to us. When he sent his disciples out on mission, Luke tells us, *he called the twelve together and gave them power and authority over all demons and to cure diseases, and he sent them out to proclaim the kingdom of God and to heal.* (Luke 9:1-2) This power and authority was not limited to just the twelve disciples. In the next chapter, Luke tells us Jesus gave the same power and authority to the seventy-two whom he sent out as a second generation of disciples (Luke 10:19). When the risen Jesus breathed the Holy Spirit on the disciples, he made it clear that our mission is to do exactly what he did when he said, *"As the Father has sent me, even so I am sending you."* (John 20:21) When he was giving us the great commission to make disciples Jesus used the simple phrase *"Go therefore…"* to pass on to us all the authority of heaven and earth which his Father had given to him (Matthew 28:19).

Living in a Covenantal relationship with God as our Father means exercising faith in his promise through Jesus and leads us to submit to his will. The result is a new identity as a member of the eternal family of God. The same is true of living as a Kingdom representative of your Father the King. It means trusting that you have been given his authority as a son or daughter and submitting to his will by stepping into that authority as his Spirit leads and empowers you. The result is that God's power will flow through you, empowering you to do his will in ways you never could before.

Do you trust the identity Jesus has given you as a daughter or son of God? Do you know your Father as the King of the universe? Do you believe the Holy Spirit lives in you? Do you trust Jesus has given you the authority to represent your Father the King? Are you willing to submit to the Father and learn to speak and act on his behalf? Are you willing to take the risk of exercising the divine authority given to you so God's power can flow through you by the Spirit who lives within you?

As you reflect on these questions, I invite you to ask the Holy Spirit to speak faith into your heart as you listen for what Jesus is saying, so you can learn to exercise the authority of your Father the King more fully. This is the only way we can follow Jesus as he returns from the Jordan and the wilderness to launch his mission in Galilee.

PART III

JESUS' MISSION:
RELATIONSHIP AND REVOLUTION

Soon afterward he went on through cities and villages, proclaiming and bringing the good news of the kingdom of God. (Luke 8:1)

A Rabbi and His Disciples

CHAPTER SEVEN

JESUS' FAMILY: THERE'S NO PLACE LIKE HOME

"My mother and my brothers are those who hear the word of God and do it." (Luke 8:21)

BACK TO GALILEE

Emerging from the cool waters of his baptism and the heat of his testing in the wilderness, Jesus returned to Galilee with great authority and a crystal-clear sense of purpose. Luke tells us he preached along the way in many of the synagogues of Galilee, and his reputation began to spread. John tells us he attended a wedding celebration of a family friend in Nathanael's hometown of Cana, just a few miles north of Nazareth. There, at his mother's urging, Jesus performed his first recorded miracle, saving the wedding party by turning water stored in stone purification jars into the most delicious of wines. In addition to delivering a family from crippling shame in front of their entire village, Jesus set the tone for a way of life that celebrates the multiplication of God's abundance, even while recognizing the inevitable costs of seeking God's Kingdom in a world fundamentally opposed to God's rule.

From Cana Jesus visited Capernaum and then made his way back to his hometown of Nazareth. There, among the members of his extended family and the people who knew him his whole life, we first hear Jesus' vision articulated and begin to sense the obstacles that lie ahead. Let's go now with Jesus and explore the region of Galilee that was so critical to his life and mission.

THE WAY

GALILEE OF THE GENTILES

Galilee is the northern region of Israel, encompassing the area between the Mediterranean Sea and the Jordan River, running north from the Jezreel Valley up to the base of Mount Hermon. With Hermon and other volcanoes to the north, it is not surprising that the area is liberally scattered with black basalt stone, an important building material in this area. This extremely hard volcanic stone is prevalent, in addition to the ubiquitous cream-colored limestone which is found nearly everywhere in Israel just beneath the thin layer of soil. The mountainous terrain of Galilee creates a typical elevation between 1500-2300 feet above sea level, which contributes to lower temperatures and higher rainfall than much of the country.

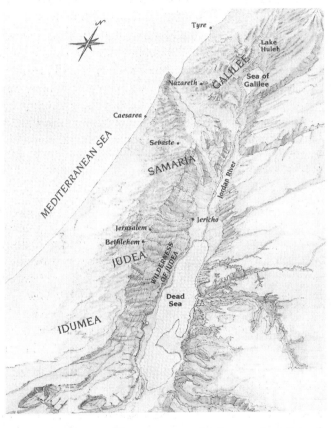

Three powerful springs, one at the base of Mount Hermon, one in the ancient Israelite city of Dan, and another in the Lebanese village of Wazzani, feed streams that form the upper Jordan River and flow into the Sea of Galilee, the largest freshwater lake in the region. This abundance of fresh water, combined with the lower temperatures and higher rainfall, contribute to making Galilee the most lush and fertile region of the Holy Land.

In ancient Israel, Galilee was surrounded on three sides by Gentile nations, and it was the first region to fall to the invading Assyrian armies in the eighth century BC. In the Hellenistic period, the area was dominated by the ten large Greek cities of the Decapolis. By the first century, these regional pagan influences contributed to the common stereotype of Jewish Galileans as country hicks who were religiously suspect to the Jerusalem elite. Perhaps these suspicions were exacerbated by the fact that Galilee is the region of Israel most distant from Jerusalem and its Temple sacrifices, which made it more challenging for the Jewish inhabitants of Galilee to follow the complex cultic rituals of the Sadducees and the legal minutiae of the Pharisees. Archaeology demonstrates these denigrating stereotypes were markedly unjustified. Many of the Jews of Galilee demonstrated at least as strong, if not stronger, commitment to their faith than their southern counterparts. In spite of this, the religious opponents of Jesus in Jerusalem used his Galilean heritage against him, claiming that no genuine prophets ever came from Galilee. His followers were even unfavorably identified by their Galilean accent (John 7:52; Matthew 26:73).

Nazareth was located in the ancient territory settled by the Israelite tribe of Zebulun, while Capernaum, on the north shore of the Sea of Galilee, was in the territory of Naphtali. The ancient trade route called the *Via Maris* (Latin: "Way of the Sea") ran near Nazareth and directly past Capernaum on its way north to Damascus. Matthew ties all these regional factors together when he introduces Jesus' Galilean mission by quoting Isaiah 9:1, *And leaving Nazareth he went and lived in Capernaum by the sea, in the territory of Zebulun and Naphtali, so that what was spoken by the prophet Isaiah might be fulfilled: "The land of Zebulun and the land of Naphtali, the way of the sea, beyond the Jordan, Galilee of the Gentiles—the people dwelling in darkness have seen a great light, and for those dwelling in the region and shadow of death, on them a light has dawned."* (Matthew 4:13-16)

THE HEART OF GALILEE

The Sea of Galilee was, and is still today, the heart of Galilee. For obvious reasons the region surrounding this large freshwater lake has been inhabited for countless millennia. One of the oldest human settlements ever discovered is situated near its southeastern shore. Boasting plentiful water teeming with fish and surrounded by lush valleys and fertile plains, the Sea of Galilee was home to numerous towns and villages that enjoyed the abundance of this inviting area. Remains of at least fifteen first-century harbors dot its shores, testimony to the level of development around the lake in the time of Jesus and the importance of the lake to the economy of that period. Three

THE SEA OF GALILEE

of these harbors on the eastern shore served three of the ten Hellenistic cities of the Decapolis, indicative of the Gentile culture that characterized that side of the lake. The Gospel writers often refer to this eastern shore as "the other side." Magdala, on the northwest shore, was the largest Jewish city on the lake at the time of Jesus, although it was eventually sur-passed by Tiberius, the new capitol Herod Antipas built just south of Magdala and named after his Roman benefactor. The area where the Jordan River flowed into the north end of the lake provided the most nutrients and therefore the best fishing, and so the towns on the northern shore were home to most of the fishing families.

The Sea of Galilee is also referred to in the New Testament as "the Sea of Tiberias" (John 6:1) and "lake of Gennesaret" (Luke 5:1). The Hebrew name of the lake is the Kinneret, based on the word for "harp" which some have claimed reflects the shape of the lake. More likely it is simply based on the name of the Bronze and Iron Age city of Kinneret or Ginosar, which lay in the plain of the same name on the northwest shore of the lake. The Sea of Galilee is thirteen miles long, eight miles wide, and 140 feet deep. Surrounded by steep ridges that drop down to its shoreline, the surface of the lake currently lies about 700 feet below sea level, making it the lowest freshwater lake in the world.

In the first century, the Sea of Galilee may have been home to as many as 25 species of fish, and today 18 different kinds of fish swim its clear waters. Three species were most important to the economy of Jesus' day and are still the primary fish caught today. The bliny (Barbels) is a large member of the carp family and is served by Jews for Sabbath meals and feasts. These predators could be caught on a hook, so this was probably the fish with the coin in its mouth that Jesus told Peter to catch by casting a line into the lake (Matthew 17:24-27). The Kinneret sardine is a small fish which was abundant in New Testament times and is still caught with nets by Galilean fishermen in large quantities today (Matthew 15:34; Mark 8:7). These fish were preserved by drying or pickling, making them perfect for long-range shipping, and so they became a favorite all over the Roman Empire. The most served Galilean fish today is called musht (Arabic: "comb"), referring to its spiny dorsal fin. It is popularly known as St. Peter's Fish. This Galilean tilapia is coveted for its small bones and excellent taste and is probably the fish used by Jesus in the feeding of the 5,000 (Matthew 14:17).

ANCIENT GALILEAN SYNAGOGUES

When the Babylonians destroyed the Temple in Jerusalem and carried the leaders of Israel off to captivity, the Jewish people began to gather in houses for times of prayer and teaching. Eventually, they began to build special buildings for these Sabbath gatherings called *"Beth Knesset,"* which is Hebrew for "house of gathering" (Greek: *sunagoge*). By the time of Jesus, the synagogue had taken on a significant role in the life of Jewish towns and villages in Galilee. Many ancient synagogues have been discovered in Galilee dating from two to five hundred years after the time of Jesus. However, because these later synagogues were built over the earlier ones, often destroying them, only a handful of first-century synagogues have been discovered.

Construction of a new guesthouse on the shore of the Sea of Galilee about six miles southwest of Capernaum in 2009 brought ancient ruins to light. When archaeologists investigated, just a few feet below the surface they found the heart of the first-century city of Magdala, hometown to Jesus' disciple

MAGDALA SYNAGOGUE

Mary Magdalene. As excavations continued, they uncovered a wealthy residential area, a thriving commercial district, an industrial section, and warehouses at the waterfront. Most spectacular of all, they discovered a beautiful first-century synagogue, complete with mosaic floors, colorful frescos on the walls, and a beautifully carved limestone scroll table sitting in the middle of the hall. One of only five synagogues from the time of Jesus discovered in the Holy Land and the only one found in Galilee so far, it features columns that supported a raised central roof, benches around the perimeter, and a stepped floor surrounding the central area. As Magdala is the nearest city to Capernaum, we can be confident that Jesus taught in this synagogue. It may be where he first encountered his disciple Mary and liberated her from seven demons (Luke 8:1, 2).

Based on the excavation of these five first-century synagogues, we know that synagogues from the time of Jesus were rectangular in layout with a U-shaped row of columns that held up a higher central roof, with windows letting light into the interior of the building. The entrance was normally at the open end of the U-shaped row of columns. Around the outer walls was built-in, stepped seating. At the front of the building these seats formed platforms that flanked either side of the entrance. People sat on the stepped seats or the floor during the weekly prayer service. Sometime after the second century, women were segregated from men during the synagogue services, but

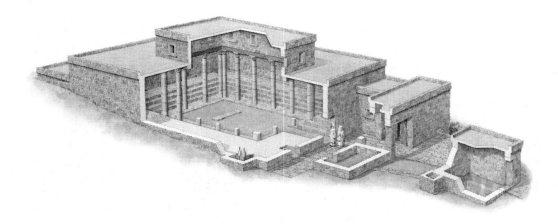

FIRST-CENTURY SYNAGOGUE IN GAMLA

in the time of Jesus men and women gathered together in the synagogue, seated in their extended families. Often families from the same trade guilds sat together as well.

Other features we find in these first-century synagogues include a small room built into one wall to secure a cabinet containing the biblical scrolls. For the Sabbath prayer service, this "Torah Ark" would be rolled out or carried onto one of the platforms flanking the entrance. This is where the biblical scrolls would be accessed by the synagogue attendant for reading during the weekly prayer service. A scroll table near the center of the room is where the rabbi would unroll the scroll and read from it before it was returned to the scroll cabinet (cf. Luke 4:16-20). The recently discovered synagogue in Magdala features a highly decorated scroll table carved from a single block of limestone. The platform on the opposite side of the main entrance held a special chair designated as the "Moses Seat," from which the rabbis would sit and teach (cf. Matthew 23:2). A Moses Seat carved from a block of black basalt stone was discovered in the ancient Galilean synagogue of Chorazin, one of the three Galilean towns where Jesus spent the most time.

During this period synagogues were not built exclusively for religious activities. They served as community centers for general usage as well. As we have seen in Chapter 5, the synagogue is where the children and teens were educated in *Beth Sefer*, *Beth Midrash*, and *Beth Talmud*. The carvings on five sides of the first-century scroll table in the Magdala synagogue depict images from the Temple in Jerusalem, indicating that the synagogue still functioned as a surrogate place of worship for those with limited access to the Temple. The synagogue was seen as the heart of any Jewish community at the time of Jesus, particularly those at a distance from Jerusalem.

THE TOWN OF CAPERNAUM

A mid-sized town with more than 1500 inhabitants located on the northern shore of the Sea of Galilee, first-century Capernaum (Hebrew for "Village of Nahum") enjoyed relative prosperity due to an active and diverse economy. Its position on the north shore of the Sea of Galilee made it particularly attractive to fishing families due to the abundance of fish there. The importance of this industry is demonstrated by the large first-century wharf discovered on the waterfront of the town. But fishing was not its

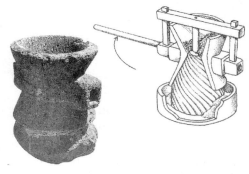

ANCIENT FLOUR MILL

only industry in the first century. In addition to anchors, fish hooks, and net weights, archaeologists have also unearthed many flour mills, olive crushing stones, oil presses, and evidence of glass manufacturing.

THE SYNAGOGUE AND HOUSES OF ANCIENT CAPERNAUM

Fishermen sold their catch, grain was ground into flour, olives were pressed for their oil, glassware was blown, and international goods passed along continually on the nearby *Via Maris,* the famous trade route connecting Egypt with Damascus. Just to the east of Capernaum, the Jordan river entered the lake and served as the boundary between the territory of Herod Antipas in the west and Herod Philip's territory in the east. The fishing town of Bethsaida that stood just east of this boundary was the original hometown of Simon and Andrew before they moved to Capernaum. This is where the disciple Philip lived, and Jesus ministered and performed miracles there. Recent excavations along the lakeshore just east of the Jordan have uncovered Roman baths and a Byzantine church dedicated to these followers of Jesus, confirming this as the site of ancient Bethsaida. Josephus describes Herod Philip's Romanization of the Jewish villages in his territory when he writes, "When Philip also had built Panias, a city at the fountains of Jordan, he named it Caesarea. He also advanced the village Bethsaida, situated at the lake of Gennesaret, unto the dignity of a city, both by the number of inhabitants it contained, and its other grandeur, and called it by the name of Julias, the same name with Caesar's daughter."[27]

Capernaum's location on the famous Via Maris trade route and sitting just west of the boundary between Herod Philip and Herod Antipas' territories made it an important site for the collection of Herodian and Roman taxes. This is the setting for Jesus' scandalous decision to call the local tax collector Matthew (Levi) as one of his closest disciples and then spend time with other tax collectors in Matthew's extended family home (Matthew 9:9-10). Capernaum's strategic location also explains the presence of

27 Flavius Josephus, *Antiquities of the Jews,* trans. William Whiston, (Delmarva, 2016), Book 18, Chapter 2, Section 1, Digital.

a Roman centurion here. In the first century he commanded a small garrison whose camp has been discovered just to the east of Capernaum. Surprisingly, this Roman centurion financed the building of a large synagogue right in the middle of the town. A number of Roman soldiers were drawn to the monotheistic God of Israel, and this centurion was likely one of those believing Gentiles known as "God-fearers" (Mark 15:39, Acts 10:1-2). This influential Roman military commander asked Jesus for help when his servant was dying, and Jesus healed him from a distance (Luke 7:1-10).

Entering the excavated site of Capernaum today, the visitor's eye turns immediately to the impressive ruins of a white limestone synagogue dating from the fourth century AD. It is one of the larger (70 x 100 feet) and more elaborately decorated synagogues from this period during which rabbinical Judaism flourished in Galilee and many synagogues were built there. This white limestone building is not the synagogue where Jesus preached, healed, and cast

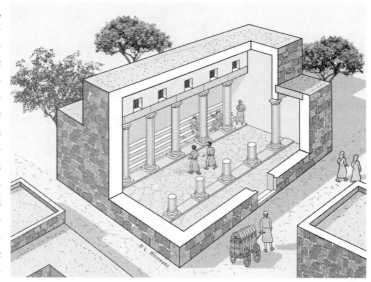

FIRST-CENTURY SYNAGOGUE IN CAPERNAUM

out demons. However, lying beneath this beautiful structure are the foundations of the black basalt synagogue from the time of Jesus, built by the God-fearing Roman Centurion. The fourth-century synagogue was built directly on the footprint of this first-century synagogue and so, although its decorations are more elaborate, the ruins of the later building still form the outline of the earlier one. This first-century black basalt synagogue is the largest so far discovered anywhere in Israel from the time of Jesus, reflecting the patronage of the wealthy Roman who built it. This is where Jesus taught, healed, and cast out demons (Mark 1:21, Luke 4:31-35).

The House of Simon and Andrew

As we discussed in Chapter 5, people in biblical culture lived together in multigenerational extended families which the New Testament refers to in Greek as an *oikos*. The two primary reasons for this

WHITE LIMESTONE SYNOGOGUE IN CAPERNAUM

were protection and provision. Most of us in the modern world assume the protection of a legal system and law enforcement, but in the first century no police patrolled neighborhoods. If bandits attacked your house and you were living as just a nuclear family, you were vulnerable. You needed the strength of an extended family to protect yourself. Likewise, modern westerners tend to assume the provision of a social safety net, but this was completely lacking in the ancient world. If the parents of a nuclear family fell ill during harvest season, who would bring in the grain? There were no health insurance or disability policies to protect them from unseen circumstances. In the first century you needed the strength of an extended family to provide for yourself. For this reason, the extended family,

FIRST-CENTURY HOUSES IN CAPERNAUM

not the nuclear family, was the primary place where people found their identity and placed their priority.

This social reality shaped the residential architecture of the ancient world. First-century houses were designed for protection with an outer wall built of solid stone and no windows, featuring only a single door that gave access to a central courtyard. This wall enclosed a series of smaller rooms which all faced inward, opening into the courtyard. The courtyard is where the extended family cooked and ate their meals together. The smaller rooms accommodated the various nuclear families, slaves, and workers in the

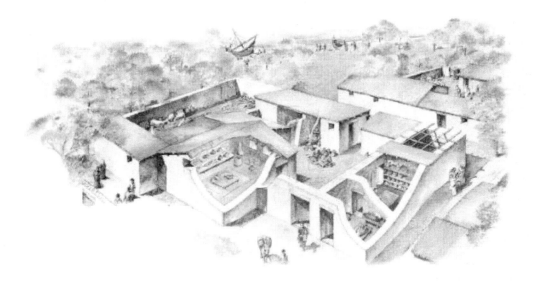

HOUSE OF SIMON AND ANDREW IN CAPERNAUM

family business who made up that *oikos*. The heavy outer door to the courtyard could be securely barred and bolted, creating something like a small family fortress. If bandits attacked the extended family would be able to defend itself and protect its members. The houses were also designed for a shared vocational life that could provide for an extended family. In the modern western world most people leave their home and their family to go to work. In the ancient world people lived a much more integrated life and worked side by side as part of an extended family business. There was a role for all the generations. In Capernaum many of the families were built around a fishing business. The courtyard house of the *oikos* was the headquarters of such a business. This is where members of the family and those who worked for them tied and repaired the nets, carved stone weights and wooden floats, and cleaned and dried fish. From here they went out to catch and sell the fish. The extended family home and business provided for and protected the members of the *oikos*. Simply put, the *oikos* existed for the sake of the *oikos*.

Through extensive excavation archeologists have uncovered numerous blocks of *oikos* houses in the heart of Capernaum from the time of Jesus. These blocks of extended family homes are called *insula* and were arranged within a grid-pattern of perpendicular streets, much like a modern town might be laid out. One block south of the synagogue, directly opposite the waterfront and wharf, archaeologists excavated one of the largest extended family homes discovered so far. It consists of eight rooms opening into a central courtyard with a pen for animals on the south side. Like other *oikos* homes in Capernaum, this house contained fish hooks, anchors, net weights, and various types of domestic pottery typical of a first-century fishing family. Excavation of this extended family home in Capernaum has not only demonstrated it was the home of a Jewish fishing family from the first half of the first century, but specifically identified this as the very house of the extended family of Simon and Andrew which Jesus made his own home. Within a decade of his death and resurrection, this home was being used as a place of worship for the earliest followers of Jesus!

By the fourth century, the house had been modified to accommodate more worshipers. The ceiling of the main room was raised and supported with a stone arch. An atrium and entrance were added through the room to the east of this main room. A strong perimeter wall was added to enclose the entire compound as sacred space. By the fifth century, the walls of the original house church were completely dismantled, and a larger, octagonal church was built over its foundations. Octagon-shaped buildings from this early Byzantine period indicate the commemoration of significant events, as with the Constantinian church built over the cave in Bethlehem to commemorate Jesus' birth. The central space of this new church in Capernaum was built directly over the main room of the original house and was surrounded by two concentric octagonal rows of arches. The floors were paved with mosaics depicting the flora and fauna of Galilee.

It is no wonder that this house was converted to a sacred place of worship, because it was here that Jesus was invited into the extended family home of Simon and Andrew, shared meals with them, healed the sick, delivered people from demonic oppression, proclaimed the Good News, and started a movement that would change the world forever!

 # THE TRUTH

JESUS' MISSIONAL STRATEGY

One of the most compelling characteristics of Jesus was his integrity to live out so completely the amazing truths he powerfully proclaimed. When Jesus launched his public mission, he demonstrated an intentional strategy he would later teach his followers. Jesus first explained this strategy to his twelve full-time disciples when he trained them and sent them out on mission, and again when he trained and sent out a wider group of 72 disciples on mission as well (see Luke 9:1-6; 10:1-12).

Jesus began by pointing out the importance of recognizing seasons of harvest and acknowledging the intimidating forces arrayed against their mission. He also gave the disciples the counter-intuitive challenge to intentionally put themselves in a position of dependence upon God and others by leaving their money, knapsack, and extra sandals at home. Then he told them, *"Whatever house you enter, first say, 'Peace be to this house!' And if a son of peace is there, your peace will rest upon him. But if not, it will return to you."* (Luke 10:5) The greeting *Shalom!* (Hebrew for "Peace!") was and still is an invitation to friendship. When you offer your *shalom* to someone, you are wishing them wholeness. It is a way of saying, "I would like to be your friend."

When Jesus told his disciples to greet people by saying *"Peace be to this house"* he was training them to start their missional efforts by simply offering their friendship to people in an *oikos*. When he said that their peace would *"rest"* on a *"son of peace,"* he was using a Middle Eastern idiom which means some people will receive and reciprocate that offer of friendship. Jesus was saying not to worry about those who don't respond positively because your peace *"will return to you"* and you are to *"shake the dust from your feet."* Instead, he told his disciples to focus on the ones who did respond positively.

Notice Jesus is telling us to offer our peace to *"this house."* The Greek word for *"house"* here is *oikos*. As we have seen, this denotes an extended family and the multi-room courtyard house where they share life and work together. By challenging these disciples not to take money and extra provisions with them on their mission, he was putting them in a position where they would have to rely on the hospitality of those whom they were trying to reach. When they entered an extended family home, they had the opportunity to offer their friendship to all who lived there and see who would respond positively. This was not an individualistic mission of one person trying to reach one other person in isolation. Both by his words and his example Jesus trained his disciples to do mission in the context of an extended family.

Jesus went on to tell his disciples what to do when they found a *"son of peace"* who responded positively to their offer of friendship, *"And remain in the same house, eating and drinking what they provide, for the laborer deserves his wages. Do not go from house to house. Whenever you enter a town and they receive you, eat what is set before you."* (Luke 10:7-8) Itinerant rabbis in the first century often visited as many families in a town as possible to increase their income base. Jesus trained his disciples to do the opposite. He told them to focus on the "people of peace" who were responsive and invest in a deeper relationship with them.

Sharing a meal with someone in that culture was a covenantal act. This is how people affirmed their connection and friendship. Jesus is telling us to stay with those who respond positively to our peace and eat with them. In eating the meal they set before us, we find out that they not only welcome us, but will even serve us. What a revolutionary approach to evangelism! Simply offer your friendship to those you meet and look for those who reciprocate by showing you they welcome you, they will listen to you, and they will serve you. These are your people of peace. Don't worry about those who don't respond. Invest in the people who do. There are no leaflets or bullhorns here, simply an offer of friendship. Suddenly a missional life starts to seem more attainable.

Up to this point, Jesus' approach to mission was very low challenge. Who can complain about finding families who will welcome you, feed you, and respond to your invitation to friendship? But then Jesus' teaching got more challenging, *"Heal the sick in it and say to them, 'The kingdom of God has come near to you.'"* (Luke 10:9). After establishing a covenantal friendship, Jesus told his disciples to both show and tell them about the coming of God's Kingdom. This is exactly the pattern of Jesus' own life. He continually showed people what the Good News of the Kingdom looked like by his actions and then explained the principles of the Kingdom to them with his words. Jesus said his followers are to do the same. By the authority given to us as God's daughters and sons, we are to love people enough to allow God's power to flow through us to touch, heal, and restore those who are hurting. Then we are to explain where this power comes from and what it means for them.

Too often our approach to mission is to try and attract people by offering things that we think will meet their perceived needs and then explain the nature of the Gospel to them as effectively as possible. The problem is that this approach reduces the Good News of God's Kingdom to a hypothetical set of ideas that produces consumers rather than disciples. When the crowds started becoming attracted to Jesus because of the things he could provide them, he said, *"Truly, truly, I say to you, you are seeking me, not because you saw signs, but because you ate your fill of the loaves."* (John 6:26) Jesus went on to increase the challenge of his teaching until most of this consumeristic crowd and even some of his disciples had gone away. Then he asked his closest disciples if they were going to leave as well. Peter responded, *"Lord, to whom shall we go? You have the words of eternal life, and we have believed, and have come to know, that you are the Holy One of God."* (John 6:68-69) These were the people of peace in whom Jesus invested everything! [28]

Jesus' First People of Peace

Once we understand the principles behind Jesus' strategy for mission, we suddenly notice Jesus using this very same approach over and over throughout the Gospels to find and invest in people of peace. Because the Synoptic Gospels first describe Jesus' interaction with the disciples after his return to Galilee, we sometimes forget he had already met five of his future disciples down south in Judea at the Jordan when he was baptized. The fourth Gospel tells us that, after John the Baptist declared Jesus to be the Lamb of God, Andrew and an unnamed disciple (probably John, the author of the Gospel) sought Jesus out, asking where he was staying. Jesus responded with the simple invitation, *"Come and you will see."* (John 1:39) Bringing along Andrew's brother Simon, they spent the afternoon with Jesus. We don't know what they talked about or how long they stayed, but cultural expectations would have demanded that Jesus offer them a meal.

[28] See Mike Breen, *Building a Discipling Culture,* 3rd edition (Pawleys Island, 3DM Publishing), 113-121.

PEOPLE OF PEACE: JESUS' MISSIONAL STRATEGY FROM LUKE 9-10

SIGNS OF PEOPLE OF PEACE	INVEST IN PEOPLE OF PEACE
THEY WELCOME YOU THEY LISTEN TO YOU THEY SERVE YOU	GO WITH THEM STAY WITH THEM EAT WITH THEM HEAL THEM TELL THEM GOOD NEWS

Now we start to see what Jesus was doing. To find people of peace, first you have to be a person of peace. Jesus was offering these three men his peace. By inviting them in, spending time with them, and presumably serving them a meal, he was offering them friendship. He was serving them. He was being a person of peace to them. By responding to Jesus' invitation, spending time with him, and sharing this meal, they were indicating their openness to him. But they had not yet taken the step of inviting Jesus into their home and serving him. If that happened, then he would know that they were truly people of peace to him.

The next day Jesus met two more Galileans who were down in Judea, Philip from Bethsaida, the fishing town just east of Capernaum, and Nathanael from Cana, just west of Capernaum. Jesus gave them a similar invitation into his life as he did to the three from Capernaum. He overcame Nathanael's initial reticence by sharing a prophetic insight about his character and a vision of him under a fig tree. Faith surged in both of their hearts, and Jesus gave them a glimpse of a possible future when he told them, *"You will see greater things than these."* (John 1:50) It seemed as if Jesus had found two more possible people of peace, but only time would tell if they were going to reciprocate and serve him.

As Jesus headed north, we are not sure if all five of these Galileans returned with him, but it is interesting that Jesus' next stop was Nathanael's hometown of Cana, where he attended the wedding of a family friend. After that, John says Jesus went to Capernaum, the hometown of Simon, Andrew, and John. It sounds like he was visiting the hometowns of his new friends as they returned to their families. Luke tells us Jesus taught in the synagogues of various towns along the way, but that he was ultimately heading to Nazareth. By the time Jesus arrived in his hometown, he was alone, and on the Sabbath day he attended the prayer service at his home synagogue.

An Unexpected Homecoming

We all tend to read the Gospels with our own cultural assumptions in place until we intentionally begin to remove them. Modern western readers like myself will tend to picture Jesus going to the synagogue by himself, because we come from an individualistic culture. However, the original readers of the Gospel would assume, unless they are told otherwise, that Jesus stayed in the home of his extended family and that they attended the synagogue together as an *oikos*. The only people in that culture who did not live as part of an extended family were outcasts, the destitute, or victims of a terrible tragedy, because you needed the strength of an *oikos* to survive and thrive. And so our assumption would be, unless told otherwise, that Jesus went to the Nazareth synagogue with his extended family.

Synagogues in the time of Jesus were overseen by a council of elders called the "synagogue rulers." These people were responsible for organizing the prayer services and arranging the teachers and the readers. There were also "synagogue attendants" who were responsible for maintaining the building and protecting the valuable scrolls. Each Sabbath a reader read aloud a passage of the Torah as well as a passage from the Prophets (Acts 13:15). We don't know if, at the time of Jesus, the readings from the Prophets were designated for a certain day, as they were later using a three-year cycle of readings that was established after the destruction of the Temple. Jesus was not a trained rabbi in the traditional system; on the contrary, he was described by the Gospel writers as a *tekton*, a "builder" (Mark 6:3). As we saw in Chapter 4, that means he would have left *Beth Sefer* (primary school) around the age of twelve and gone to work as an apprentice in the family construction business. Later, when Jesus was teaching in the Temple courts, the people said of him, *"How is it that this man has learning, when he has never studied?" So Jesus answered them, "My teaching is not mine, but his who sent me."* (John 7:14-16)

Although Jesus was not formally trained as a rabbi, his reputation as a teacher and healer was already growing quickly. By the time he arrived in Nazareth, the ruler of the synagogue invited him to teach on the Sabbath. Based on Luke's description, we can assume the reading from the Torah had already been read by the reader for that day, and then Jesus stood up to read from the Prophets. The synagogue attendant handed Jesus the substantial scroll of Isaiah, Jesus laid it down on the scroll table in the middle of the room, and *He unrolled the scroll and found the place where it was written, "The Spirit of the Lord is upon me, because he has anointed me to proclaim good news to the poor. He has sent me to proclaim liberty to the captives and recovering of sight to the blind, to set at liberty those who are oppressed, to proclaim the year of the Lord's favor." And he rolled up the scroll and gave it back to the attendant and sat down. And the eyes of all in the synagogue were fixed on him. And he began to say to them, "Today this Scripture has been fulfilled in your hearing."* (Luke 4:17-21)

What an electrifying statement for Jesus to make about this powerful vision of Messianic jubilee! After centuries of oppression by a succession of pagan invaders, most recently the Romans, first-century Jews were longing for the divine liberation promised by the prophets. As they labored under the crushing taxation of the decadent Herodians, they had a growing sense of desperation for something to change. Jesus was personalizing this Messianic statement, *"The Spirit of the Lord is upon me,"* and announcing the beginning of a new era by proclaiming, *"Today this Scripture has been fulfilled in your hearing."*

We can just imagine the feelings welling up inside the people of Nazareth as they heard these words. Hope! Excitement! Joy! Luke tells us at this point Jesus had suddenly become the most popular guy in Nazareth, *And all spoke well of him and marveled at the gracious words that were coming from his mouth. And they said, "Is not this Joseph's son?"* (Luke 4:22) If Jesus had simply stopped there, he could have dined in a different *oikos* as the guest of honor every night that week. But he didn't stop there.

Jesus responded to their praise by prophesying that they would soon change their tune and reject him. He began to explain what he meant when he said that this great promise was now starting to be fulfilled. He lifted up two examples from the Hebrew Scriptures, the widow of Zarephath and Naaman the Syrian. He pointed out that in the time of Elijah, there were many Jewish widows to whom God could have sent the Prophet Elijah, but instead God sent him to minister to a Gentile widow who lived on the Phoenician coast north of Israel, between the great pagan cities of Tyre and Sidon. There Elijah miraculously fed this woman and then raised her son from the dead. He went on to point out that there were many Jewish lepers that God could have healed through the Prophet Elisha, but it was a Gentile nobleman from Syria who was healed.

Jesus' point was obvious to everyone in the synagogue that day. Although God chose the descendants of Abraham as his own people, we can see from these biblical examples that he also shows love and mercy to Gentiles. Jesus was clarifying that the Messianic jubilee he embodied and proclaimed was not just to benefit the children of Israel, but pagan Gentiles as well! Suddenly the joy and excitement everyone felt was overcome by the deep-seated resentments and long-nurtured bitterness they felt toward the Gentiles, whom they blamed for all the injustices they had suffered. That resentment and bitterness overflowed in violent rage toward Jesus. How could our own villager betray us like this? How dare he suggest Gentiles will benefit from the coming of Messiah!

It is easy to assume what happened next was mindless mob violence, but in fact the people of Nazareth were following the rabbinical interpretation of how to carry out the execution of a heretic or blasphemer, as it was commanded in the Torah (Exodus 19:13; Leviticus 20:27). The rabbis taught that the person being executed should have his hands tied behind his back and be pushed from a height at least twice the height of a man. If the fall did not kill them, then they were to drop stones on him from that height until he was dead.[29] This is a biblical stoning in the first century. When the people of Nazareth took Jesus to one of the nearby ridges that drop down into the Jezreel Valley, their intent was to stone him as a heretic. This is certainly the most complete and intentional rejection of Jesus' Messianic vision that they could have given!

One question the modern western reader usually forgets to ask is where Jesus' *oikos* was. Remember, one of the reasons for living in an extended family was protection. The members of Jesus' extended family were sitting there, watching all this take place. Jesus' family business was construction and he had five brothers, not to mention uncles and cousins, who would have worked in the business as stone masons. By definition these were physically powerful men. Why weren't they surrounding Jesus and protecting him? Why wasn't Mary clinging to Jesus' leg and screaming "Don't you dare hurt my son!"?

As we understand the cultural context of Luke's narrative more clearly, we begin to see that not only did the people of Nazareth reject Jesus' Messianic vision, but the members of his own family rejected it as well. Jesus described his rejection in Naza-

---

[29] Jacob Neusner, ed., *The Mishnah: A New Translation* (New Haven: Yale University, 1988), Sanhedrin 6.4, 7.4-8.7, Digital.

reth by saying, *"A prophet is not without honor, except in his hometown and among his relatives and in his own household."* (Mark 6:4). The Greek word translated "household" in this verse is *oikos*. The reaction of his mother and brothers later in the Gospel accounts confirms this. John tells us, *For not even his brothers believed in him.* (John 7:5) Mark tells us that when his family heard of Jesus' ministry, Mary and Jesus' brothers *went out to seize him, for they were saying, "He is out of his mind."* (Mark 3:21) Jesus shared the vision of his mission in his hometown to the people who knew him best, even to his own extended family, and he was profoundly rejected. John describes it this way: *He came to his own, and his own people did not receive him.* (John 1:11) This must have been one of the most painful experiences in Jesus' earthly life.

A New Kind of Family

Without explanation Luke describes Jesus' mysterious escape from the crowd in Nazareth and then simply tells us *he went down to Capernaum, a city of Galilee.* (Luke 4:31) It was painfully obvious that the people of Nazareth and his own family were not people of peace, so Jesus simply shook the dust off his feet and moved on. But, why did Jesus head straight to this fishing town on the northern shore of the Sea of Galilee? Now that we understand the missional strategy of Jesus, the most obvious answer is that Jesus thought he may have some people of peace there. If you remember, that is where Simon, Andrew, and John all lived! And so Jesus returned to Capernaum, where he was invited to speak in their synagogue on the Sabbath. Jesus startled the people, not only by teaching with authority, but also by demonstrating that authority in the deliverance of a demonized man. The people in Capernaum reacted to Jesus quite differently than those in Nazareth: *And they were all amazed and said to one another, "What is this word? For with authority and power he commands the unclean spirits, and they come out!"* (Luke 4:36)

After a visiting rabbi taught on the Sabbath, it was expected that he would dine in the home of one of the rulers of the synagogue or another leading family. But as the synagogue service was ending, the fisherman Simon invited Jesus into his family's home to dine with them. Inviting someone into your *oikos* to share a meal was a significant statement. It was a cultural way of inviting someone to be closely connected with you and your family. Jesus had invited Simon and Andrew in for a meal down at the Jordan River, and now they were reciprocating that invitation. For Jesus this confirmed that Simon and Andrew were people of peace to him, so he did exactly what he would later tell them to do when they found a person of peace: *"remain in the same house, eating and drinking what they provide... Heal the sick in it and say to them, 'The kingdom of God has come near to you.'"* (Luke 10:7-9)

We have seen that Simon and Andrew's *oikos* lived in a very nice extended family home, one block south of the synagogue, near the waterfront. As Jesus entered the courtyard of their home, he heard the news that Simon's mother-in-law was sick, and so he healed her. This powerful act demonstrated the authority they had seen in the synagogue, but also his love for their family. Something profound was beginning to happen in this home! Simon's newly energized mother-in-law promptly took the lead in serving the Sabbath meal. As they ate together, the covenantal bond between them grew stronger. Like the people in the Nazareth synagogue during the first half of Jesus' message, the *oikos* of Simon and Andrew must have had nothing but glowing things to say about Jesus. But then he did something that tested their new friendship to the core. After dinner Jesus invited the entire town to join them in the courtyard of their home!

Normally, you would be very careful about who you invited into your *oikos*. In the first century and still today, Middle Eastern people live in an honor/shame culture. It was considered an honor to be invited into someone's family home, and a person of good standing in the community could bring honor to the family by accepting such an invitation. But if someone whom you invited into your home acted shamefully, it would bring shame on the entire family. This was considered one of the worst things you could do. However; it is clear that Jesus invited *everyone* into their home, because some of the guests were demon-possessed. Later Jesus would go so far as to invite even Matthew, the hated local tax collector, into their home and spiritual family!

In doing so, Jesus challenged a status-based system in which people were welcomed according to their religious and social standing, and he laid the foundation for a whole new understanding of what family is meant to be. As Jesus began to reshape the culture of Simon and Andrew's *oikos,* he turned their attention outward. He gave them a vision of God's Kingdom as an invitation for everyone to become a part of God's big family. Jesus described his mission in the *oikos* of another hated tax collector named Zacchaeus when he said, *"for the Son of Man came to seek and save the lost."* (Luke 19:10) And as people gathered in the courtyard of Simon and Andrew's house, their lives were fundamentally transformed. Just as Jesus had declared in the synagogue of Nazareth, the blind received their sight, the oppressed were liberated, and the poor heard Good News!

This radically inclusive invitation filled the courtyard of Simon and Andrew's house with people, so that they were overflowing out the door that led into the street. Mark's gospel uses a bit of hyperbole when he reports, *And the whole city was gathered together at the door.* (Mark 1:33) But this was not a one-time occurrence. Once we understand the layout of *oikos* houses, we start to recognize a consistent pattern of Jesus' life in the Gospels. Again, and again, Jesus gathered his disciples together in a house so full of people that no one could enter the courtyard through the outer door. Sometimes there were so many they couldn't even cook meals! (cf. Mark 2:1-2; 3:20; etc.) The house of Simon and Andrew served as the headquarters and base of operations for Jesus' mission. Here he welcomed in the outcasts. Here he gave people access to his life and trained them. From here he took his disciples out to seek and save the lost. This house was much more than a base of operations for Jesus; it was where he was forming a new kind of family.

When news of Jesus' teaching and healing ministry reached the ears of his extended family back in Nazareth, they became concerned. These reports were so unlike the Jesus they thought they knew that they began to wonder if he had lost his mind (Mark 3:21). Finally, his mother Mary took her four other sons and traveled to Capernaum with a plan to return Jesus to Nazareth and nurse him back to health. When they arrived at the house of Simon and Andrew, once again the courtyard was so full of people that they could not make their way in to where Jesus was sitting and teaching. When the crowd passed word to Jesus that his family was outside asking for him, Jesus replied, *"Who are my mother and my brothers?" And looking about at those who sat around him, he said, "Here are my mother and my brothers! For whoever does the will of God, he is my brother and sister and mother."* (Mark 3:33-35) In a culture where loyalty to your biological *oikos* was universally considered your highest obligation, this was nothing less than a scandalous response!

Jesus demonstrated by his own actions that our commitment to our spiritual family on mission needs to take priority over even our biological family commitments if the two are in conflict. He explained the inherent conflict of these two understandings of family when he said, *"For I have come to set a man against his father, and a daughter against her mother, and a daughter-in-law against her mother-in-law. And a person's enemies will be those of his own household. Whoever loves father or mother more than me is not worthy of me, and whoever loves son or daughter more than me is not worthy of me."* (Matthew 10:35-37) Once a would-be disciple responded to Jesus, *"Lord, let me first go and bury my father."* Shockingly Jesus said to him, *"Follow me, and leave the dead to bury their own dead."* (Matthew 8:21-22) The great New Testament scholar, N. T. Wright, commented on this statement: "The only explanation for Jesus' astonishing command is that he envisaged loyalty to himself and his kingdom-movement as creating an alternative family." [30]

By these declarations Jesus made it clear that he was establishing a whole new way of being a family. Not a family defined by blood, but by the doing of God's will. Not a nuclear family, but an extended family. Not a biological family, but a spiritual family. Not an exclusive, inward-facing family, but an inclusive, outward-facing family. Not a family focused on providing for and protecting its own, but a family focused on seeking and saving the lost. Jesus was showing us that we are meant to live as part of an extended spiritual family that is living on mission together! [31]

TO THE ENDS OF THE EARTH

The central importance of living as an extended spiritual family was not lost on the men and women who followed Jesus. After his resurrection and the outpouring of the Holy Spirit, the disciples of Jesus took the Good News of his Kingdom to the ends of the earth, just as he foretold. As they went, they imitated the pattern Jesus had set for them. They gathered people into extended family homes where outsiders were welcomed and from which they would go out on mission. As Luke describes the spread of the Gospel after Pentecost, he first reports the multiplication of disciples gathering in extended family homes across Jerusalem (Acts 2:46), and then tells us how the apostles gathered new disciples in places like Lydia's *oikos* in Philippi and Titius Justus' *oikos* in Corinth (Acts 16:15; 18:7). This is what Luke refers to repeatedly as "churches" (Greek: *ekklesia*). These were not steepled buildings where professional staff organized and led programs. The first churches were extended spiritual families living on mission together. As we read on in the New Testament, we discover that the disciples of Jesus continued using the familial language their Rabbi had employed to describe his core community of followers. In his letters the Apostle Paul repeatedly refers to his "churches" as the gathering of spiritual families in the *oikos* of people such as Phoebe, Aquila and Priscilla, Nympha, and Philemon, to name a few (Romans 16:1; 1 Corinthians 16:19;

---

30 N. T. Wright, *Jesus and the Victory of God* (Minneapolis: Fortress, 1996), 401, Digital.

31 For this language, see Mike and Sally Breen, *Family on Mission*, 2nd ed. (Pawleys Island, 3DM Publishing, 2018).

Colossians 4:15; Philemon 1:1-2). Paul uses parental and/or sibling language to describe the members of the communities to whom he is writing in all thirteen of his letters. In these letters he employs familial language over 280 times! In just three verses of his letter to the followers of Jesus in Corinth, Paul calls Timothy "my beloved and faithful child in the Lord," refers to the Corinthians as his children, and himself as their "father" (1 Corinthians 4:14-17). The Apostle John refers to the people in his community as his "little children" eighteen times in his three short letters. Peter, James, and the writer of Hebrews also use familial language to describe their communities. Ironically, the only New Testament letter that doesn't use familial language of father, child, son/daughter, brother/sister is Jude, the only one written by a member of Jesus' actual biological family!

This understanding of the church as extended family did not die with the original Apostles. For the next three centuries, this is how the church was defined and functioned—multiple generations of people from every imaginable background coming together in homes to learn the way of Jesus and to carry out his mission as extended spiritual families. Even the opponents of Christianity recognized this as the primary expression of Jesus' movement. Lucian of Samosata wrote of the early Christians that Jesus "persuaded them that they are all brothers of one another... Therefore they despise all things indiscriminately and consider them common property."[32] In his thoroughly researched book *When the Church Was a Family* New Testament professor Joseph Hellerman concludes, "Jesus and His followers took their culture's strong group approach to family life, appropriated it as the preeminent social model for their local Christian communities, and lived with one another like Mediterranean brothers and sisters. And the early Christians turned the world upside down. When the church was a family, the church was on fire."[33] In light of this picture of the church Jesus started and which the Apostles multiplied, we have to ask ourselves if we have forgotten what it means to be a Jesus-shaped church today.

[32] Lucian, *The Passing of Peregrinus*, vol. 13, Loeb Classical Library (Cambridge, Harvard Press, 1926), 13, Digital.

[33] Hellerman, Joseph H., *When the Church Was a Family* (Nashville, B&H Publishing, 2009), 205, Digital.

 # THE LIFE

EXAGGERATED INDIVIDUALISM

I am the third generation of my family born in the same town in northwestern Montana. Although I lived in Hong Kong and West Berlin when I was young, I spent most of my formative years growing up in a rural area east of Seattle. Looking back I can see that, for all the diversity of my experiences, I was still fundamentally shaped by western culture. As such, I have come to realize that I am profoundly individualistic in my basic assumptions and psychology, particularly compared to people from biblical cultures as well as those from non-western cultures today.

My great-grandfather Phil Cole came to Montana from Iowa in the late nineteenth century to stake his claim, and he established a successful sheep ranch where he raised my grandmother. Montana was the frontier of the Wild West. In frontier culture the ideal is the rugged individualist who is independent and strong enough to make it on his own. We picture the Marlboro Man sitting alone on his horse, watching cattle in the wide-open expanses of the West. This is how the West was won, by strong pioneering individuals like my great-grandfather who were brave or foolish enough to strike out on their own into unknown territory. I grew up shaped by the assumption that independence is always a virtue and that self-sufficiency is the true sign of maturity. Growing up meant proving I could stand on my own two feet, separate from my family of origin.

Of course, the roots of western individualism go back much further than Montana, to the enlightenment and the industrial revolution in Europe. The rise of industrialized cities with cash-based economies drew people off their farms and into urban neighborhoods where they lived in apartments and worked in factories. This meant that more and more people moved away from their extended families and learned to live on their own. When they married and had children, they no longer saw themselves as part of a multi-generational, interdependent wider family, but came to define "family" as parents and children, or the independent nuclear family. Social systems evolved to support the disconnected nuclear family in ways that the extended family had once. Police forces, fire departments, insurance companies, large corporations, and agribusiness gradually replaced the extended family home and the family business as the primary source of protection and provision.

My parents both grew up in independent nuclear Montana families. Although they loved their extended families, they were only intermittently connected to their grandparents, aunts, uncles, and cousins. When my parents came of age and married, they moved far away from home and proved they could make it on their own. My sister and I grew up assuming we would follow the same pattern, and we did. After college graduation we each moved away, established careers, married, had kids, and bought single-family homes. We proved we could make it on our own and celebrated this as success! For all my life, I lived in a different state than my grandparents, aunts, uncles, and cousins. Although we are a very close, loving family, for most of my life all four members of my immediate family of origin have lived in different states.

Most of us who are shaped by modern, western culture don't realize that we are the products of an exaggerated individualism. There is, of course, much to be said positively about healthy individualism. Western culture has taught us the importance of each person taking responsibility for themselves. Western democracy has demonstrated the power of individual rights to combat tyranny and create a more free and fair society. Of course, we need to teach our children to take responsibility for themselves so they mature into the fulness of their constructive potential. Of course, we affirm the freedom for each person to follow their conscience. However, those of us in the modern West have to ask ourselves if this cultural trend has gone too far. Have we missed a crucial ingredient of a healthy, fruitful life?

While the modern redefinition of the family as parents and children has put a greater emphasis on personal responsibility and freedom, it has also put greater pressure on those same parents and children. Never before in history has the nuclear family suffered the level of disintegration that we have seen in the past fifty years in the West. The statistics tell us that the pressure of mom and dad raising kids on their own is a weight we were never intended to bear. That pressure has fractured many families with devastating effects personally and socially. The research demonstrates that more people experience isolation and loneliness in our society today than ever before.

From the beginning we were meant to grow up with grandparents, aunts, uncles, and friends helping our parents nurture and challenge us, so that we might mature into the people we are intended to become. As teens mature into adults, they need to be able to differentiate from their parents without becoming disconnected from them. This is the classic role of a trusted uncle or aunt who can provide the connection and guidance that helps adolescents figure out who they are and what they are meant to do with their lives. When all we have is a nuclear family, it is difficult to differentiate without disconnecting, because the other adults to whom we naturally turn are often distant or absent.

As the extended family has faded into the background in western culture, we have compensated in various ways. In the church we have created programs to help parents raise their children in the faith. Often the result has been the outsourcing of parental discipleship to children's workers and youth ministers and college ministries. I have spent many years leading such ministries and can testify that they can provide wonderful resources to teens and their families. But we can also see that our need for such programs is a symptom of a deeper problem. We need to reclaim intergenerational extended spiritual family as the cornerstone of healthy community and relationships. Recent research has demonstrated that the chemicals in our brain that represent the experience of joy dramatically increase when three generations are interacting together.[34] Having recently become a grandfather, I can certainly attest it is true for me! Perhaps we have lost sight of how family is meant to function. If so, Jesus shows us a better way.

A BETTER WAY

It is no accident that Jesus centered his life and mission around a new kind of extended spiritual family in Capernaum. He had experienced firsthand the kind of dysfunction that can infect and divide a biological extended family. His own relatives in Nazareth did not embrace his vision or stand with him when he faced the threat of death. But that didn't mean that Jesus gave up on extended family and decided to go it alone. Instead, he decided to demonstrate a whole new way to be a family. Jesus found people of peace who embraced his vision and were willing to follow him. With them he formed a new kind of *oikos* that was focused on doing the will of God and that became the basic unit of his world-changing movement! Extended spiritual family is the way Jesus carried out his mission.

Since the adoption of Christianity by Constantine in AD 313, followers of Jesus have tended to center their spiritual life around public church buildings and have focused

---

[34] James Wilder, *Joy Starts Here* (Pasadena, Life Model Works, 2013), 8, 91.

their mission on convincing lost people to join them there for services and programs. Of course, gathering together with crowds of people in public spaces for worship, teaching, and prayer is a wonderful thing to do. It is clear from the Gospels that Jesus participated regularly in the public Sabbath services in the synagogue and attracted crowds of people. However, as the way of Jesus becomes clearer to us, we start to realize that Jesus did not center his spiritual life or mission around the synagogue in Capernaum, although it was just one block from his adopted home. The Gospels never describe Jesus urging the crowds to attend the synagogue, nor did he instruct his disciples to recruit people in the Sabbath prayer services. Instead, Jesus centered his life and mission around the extended family home of Simon and Andrew. When he called the notorious tax collectors Matthew and Zacchaeus, he didn't convince them to come to the synagogue. Instead, he accepted an invitation into their *oikos*, which was completely forbidden according to the rabbinical rules of ritual purity.

It took over three hundred years before the followers of Jesus began constructing public buildings for worship. Without the "benefit" of facilities, programs, and clergy, the church continued to reach the lost, multiply disciples, and change its world at an astonishing rate despite massive religious and cultural pressure, not to mention periods of brutal persecution. Rodney Stark estimates that by the early fourth century, the movement of Jesus had reached over 50% of the Roman empire![35] Apparently public buildings and religious programs are not necessary for the movement of Jesus to reach the lost and change the world.

I vividly remember the day when I was reading the Gospels and this realization hit me like a ton of bricks. I had spent my entire adult life seeking and saving the lost by trying to get them to come to the programs and services held in our church buildings, but that is not the way Jesus did it! Jesus invited people into his home and extended spiritual family, in order to show them and share with them the Good News. My home was a fortress where I hid out with my nuclear family to recover from my stressful programmatic, church-centered life. Jesus said the greatest commandment is to love God and love our neighbor. The only neighbors on my entire block that I even knew, much less, loved, were the ones who went to my church. I was too busy participating in the many programs of our church to build relationships with my unbelieving neighbors.

35 Rodney Stark, *The Rise of Christianity* (San Francisco, Harper, 1997), 6-20.

As Pam and I learned how to follow the way of Jesus more intentionally, we began to open up our home and invite people in. We started to gather there with brothers and sisters in Christ in order to learn how to function more like an extended spiritual family. We didn't limit it to a small group of believers where outsiders would feel uncomfortable, as we had done for so many years. We opened it up so that it was more like a multi-generational extended family. We found a new sense of joy in being together, not just for our sake, but for the sake of those who are lost. We asked God to show us how to connect with our neighbors. As we invited them into our extended spiritual family, they began to invite us into their families. We started to identify which ones were people of peace to us. We grilled hot dogs together and watched their children for them. We heard their stories, celebrated their victories, and shared their struggles. We prayed for them and showed them the Good News of Jesus. When they were ready, we told them about Jesus. Some began to trust him and follow him.

We decided we were not going to live as rugged individuals trying to make our own way in the world. No longer were we going to function as isolated nuclear families, hiding out in our homes trying to recover from our over-programmed lives. We still gathered with our wider spiritual family at the church facility, but we cut back on what we did there so we could invest more time in building a spiritual family and connecting with those outside the church. We still worshiped, prayed, and shared Scripture together, but we learned how to do it in a way that newcomers would be able to understand and participate. We found we were able to connect with people who were far from God in a way we never had before. We had a place to welcome those who were people of peace to us and build deeper friendships. Through these friendships we found opportunities to both show and tell them the Good News of Jesus. Because this happened in the context of an extended spiritual family, those who came to believe in Jesus also began learning how to follow him as a daily way of life.

Recently Pam and I have embarked on a new season of life and mission. Feeling called to invest full-time in our wider ministry of training of leaders, we stepped down from local church leadership, sold our home, and moved into a new neighborhood. Before we had finished unpacking, we were already meeting our new neighbors and inviting them into our home. What a joy to get to hear their stories and begin to get to know them. We found a little church at the end of our block and have decided to make that our place of weekly worship. Now we have the challenge of a busy travel schedule and are trying to establish regular rhythms to build genuine friendships with the people who live where God has planted us. We have started gathering regularly with our neighbors who are not yet part of God's family. We have also invited a small group of Jesus-followers to join us in our mission as disciples. Our goal is to form an extended spiritual family where those who don't yet know Jesus are welcomed and can learn to follow him.

Our way of life is changing because we are allowing the Spirit of Jesus to shape and guide our way of living by his Way. This means breaking out of the cultural expectations of our western individualism and learning to live as an extended spiritual family on mission. Wherever we live, whatever jobs we have, whatever stage of life we are in, this is the way we have decided to live. It has not been an easy journey, because it means breaking old habits, learning new ways of functioning, taking risks, feeling awkward, and making sacrifices. But we have also found that there is no better, more fulfilling, or more exciting way to live. Pam and I are still learning this Jesus-shaped way of life, but it is already bearing more and better fruit than our own way ever did. What about you? Does your own family look more like the ideals of western individualism or the new kind of extended spiritual family Jesus built? Is your way of life producing the same kind of fruit that Jesus' Way produced in the lives of those who first followed him? Do you feel the Spirit of God stirring in you a desire to live a more fruitful, meaningful, impactful life? [36]

As we continue to explore Jesus' Way in Galilee, we will take a closer look at how he formed a core for this new kind of family and trained them to build missional families of their own.

[36] If you are interested in more practical strategies for living this way of life, see Bob Rognlien, *A Jesus-Shaped Life* (Pawleys Island: 3DM Publishing, 2016). If you want a more in-depth resource for leaders, try Bob Rognlien, *Empowering Missional Disciples* (Pawleys Island: 3DM Publishing, 2016).

CHAPTER EIGHT

JESUS' CALL: FOLLOW ME

Jesus said to them, "Follow me, and I will make you become fishers of men." (Mark 1:17)

 THE WAY

THE RABBI-DISCIPLE RELATIONSHIP

In the first century the term *Rabbi* (Hebrew for "teacher") was an honorific title of respect given to teachers, scholars, and scribes, but it had not yet become an official office as it would in later Judaism. Before the destruction of the Temple in AD 70, Jewish teachers were also called *hakamim* or sages (Hebrew for "the wise"), and this was interchangeable with the term rabbi. As we saw in Chapter 5, rabbis educated the Jewish children at the synagogue by teaching them the *Torah* in *Beth Sefer* (Hebrew for "house of the book"), starting at about age 5. Instruction consisted primarily of reading aloud and memorizing the first five books of the Hebrew Bible.

At about age 12, the boys completed their studies and transitioned into the family business, being recognized as fully participating members of society who were responsible to follow the Torah they had studied. However, the best students could apply to learn the Oral Law in *Beth Midrash* (Hebrew for "house of interpretation") for a few years. They would debate the meaning and application of the various rabbinical interpretations of the Torah that were passed down by memory. By AD 200 these oral traditions had been written down in the Mishnah, which became the basis for the Talmud, the defining document of Orthodox Judaism today. At age 15 the best of these midrashic students could apply to become the disciple of a rabbi and enter into *Beth Talmud* (Hebrew for "house of instruction").

A RABBI AND HIS DISCIPLES

If these students were accepted as a *talmid* (Hebrew for "disciple"), they moved away from their family to live with the rabbi and his extended family for a period of time. Their sole focus was to be as close as possible to the rabbi. Functioning as part of his *oikos*, they listened to their rabbi's teaching and studied what the rabbi said, so they could learn to know what the rabbi knew. They watched how the rabbi lived, studying his way of life, so they could learn to do what the rabbi did. At first their role was passive, listening and watching, but over time the rabbi invited them to participate more and more in the things he was doing. He engaged them in conversation and debated with them on the meaning and application of Jewish law. As the disciples processed this information, they then imitated the way their rabbi was living out these teachings in his daily life.

All Jewish teachers in this period had disciples, not just Jesus. The Gospels repeatedly refer to the disciples of John the Baptist, one of whom was Andrew son of Jonah, and the disciples of the Pharisees (John 1:35, 40; Matthew 9:14, Mark 2:18, Luke 5:33). Discipleship was the primary way rabbis trained leaders and promoted their way of life. In the modern world we think of teaching taking place as a lecture in a school building or a classroom. While elementary instruction in the first century did typically take place in the synagogue, discipleship was much more of a conversation that took place along the way while walking on roads, shopping in marketplaces, and sitting in extended family homes. Many of the rabbinical teachings recorded in the Mishnah are described as dialogues happening in the *oikos*. The famous blessing of Yose ben Yoezer, a rabbi who lived in the second century BC, describes this setting: "Let your house be a gathering place for sages. And wallow in the dust of their feet. And drink in their words with gusto."[37]

This saying envisions the rabbi seated on a stool in the courtyard or main room of the *oikos* house, having a conversation with his disciples while they are seated on the dusty floor around his feet. This is how Paul of Tarsus describes his rabbinical training: *"I am a Jew, born in Tarsus in Cilicia, but brought up in this city, educated at the feet of Gamaliel according to the strict manner of the law of our fathers…"* (Acts 22:3). The Gospels repeatedly describe Jesus seated in the main room of Simon and Andrew's house in Capernaum, surrounded by disciples sitting in the rooms and courtyard, listening to his teaching and dialoguing with him. This is exactly the position Mary took when Jesus visited her *oikos* in Bethany: *Now as they went on their way, Jesus entered a village. And a woman named Martha welcomed him into her house. And she had a sister called Mary, who sat at the Lord's feet and listened to his teaching.* (Luke 10:38-39)

Another primary context for discipleship was while walking from place to place. The Hebrew word translated "wallow in the dust" in the blessing of Yose ben Yoezer refers to the fine powder-like dust that accumulated along ancient roads and was kicked up when people walked along (See Ezekiel 26:10, Nahum 1:3). For that reason, some scholars believe "walk in your teacher's dust" was the original intent of this phrase.[38] Thus this saying can be paraphrased, "May you follow your rabbi, drink in his words, and be covered by his dust." This sounds like the account of three rabbis discussing Exodus 31:13: "Once Rabbi Ishmael, Rabbi Eleazar, and Rabbi Akiva were walking along the road followed by Levi the net-maker and Ishmael the son of Rabbi Eleazar. The following question was discussed by them: 'Whence do we know that

[37] Jacob Neusner, ed., *The Mishnah: A New Translation* (New Haven: Yale University, 1988), Pirke Avot 1:4, Digital

[38] See Shmuel Safrai, *The Jewish People in the First Century* (Philadelphia: Fortress Press, 1976) 958-69, Digital.

the duty of saving a life supersedes the Sabbath laws?"[39] We can see that the disciples Levi and Ishmael were simply following closely enough behind their rabbis on the road to listen and learn from the conversation about this theological issue. Along the way they were caked with the fine powder kicked up by their rabbi's feet, a vivid picture of how their lives were being shaped by their rabbi's way of life.

This is exactly the way Jesus taught his disciples as they walked from place to place. Luke tells us about a dialogue Jesus had with the Pharisees as they were walking through a grain field one Sabbath day (Luke 6:1-2). John describes Jesus walking in the Portico of Solomon on the Temple Mount as he taught and answered the questions of those who walked with him (John 10:23-25). We can easily miss that Jesus' amazing teaching about the vine and the branches took place on Passover Eve while Jesus was walking from the upper room in Jerusalem, through the Kidron Valley, to the Garden of Gethsemane. It is likely he was pointing to a vineyard they passed by when he said, *"I am the vine; you are the branches."* (John 15:5)

Following a rabbi and becoming his disciple meant submitting yourself to the yoke of Torah. Rabbi Nechunia son of Hakanah said, "Anyone who accepts upon himself the yoke of Torah removes from himself the yoke of government duties and the yoke of the way of the world; but one who casts off the yoke of Torah accepts upon himself the yoke of government and the yoke of the way of the world."[40] This saying evokes the famous image the prophet Isaiah used for the pagan nations that oppressed the people of Israel: *For the yoke of his burden, and the staff for his shoulder, the rod of his oppressor, you have broken as on the day of Midian.* (Isaiah 9:4) Disciples were those who chose to take up the yoke of the Torah by following their rabbi, rather than submitting to a yoke of slavery imposed by the world around them. Jesus characterized his interpretation of the Torah and his subsequent way of life: *"Take my yoke upon you, and learn from me, for I am gentle and lowly in heart, and you will find rest for your souls. For my yoke is easy, and my burden is light."* (Matthew 11:29-30) Jesus made it clear that following him was costly—in fact it would cost you your very life—but it was not the burdensome legalistic yoke of the Pharisees. To be yoked to Rabbi Jesus was to be lifted up and carried along into a whole new way of life.

---

39 Neusner, *The Mishnah*, Mekhilta, *Shabbeta* 1, Digital.

40 Neusner, *The Mishnah*, *Pirkei Avot* 3:5

This is the picture of biblical discipleship: an invitation to the closest kind of relationship in which the disciple shares daily life with the rabbi as part of his extended family, eating what he eats, going where he goes, and sleeping where he sleeps. With this intimate invitation into the very life of the rabbi and the challenge to imitate his example, his disciples not only learned their rabbi's teaching but also his very way of life. The goal of this process was for the disciples to become rabbis themselves, so they could continue to clarify and sharpen this teaching of the law and its application to daily life. At that point they would, of course, consider the applications of potential disciples and begin to invite younger apprentices into their *oikos* to learn this teaching and this way of life. A rabbi was successful when his disciples were recognized as rabbis and began to accept disciples who would follow them.

FISHING ON THE SEA OF GALILEE

The people of Israel generally saw the sea as a place of danger and evil and as such did not develop a strong maritime culture or a fishing industry along their Mediterranean shore, leaving that to the Phoenicians and others who had come from across the sea.

FIRST-CENTURY GALILEAN FISHING BOAT

However, the settlements around the Sea of Galilee gradually embraced this abundant food source, and by the time of Jesus a large and vibrant fishing industry had developed. The ancient Jewish historian Josephus Flavius tells us that about 230 fishing boats sailed the waters of the Sea of Galilee in the first century, seeking its abundant catch. Two of these boats were owned by the fishing families who became central to Jesus' mission.

The fishing industry of first-century Galilee was primarily carried out as an extended family business, as it often still is today. While the men did the actual fishing, every member of the extended family contributed to the effort by repairing the boats, chiseling stone weights, carving wooden floats, tying flaxen nets, drying fish, and selling the catch. Often extended families formed partnerships or even larger cooperatives (Greek: *koinonoi*) to increase their efficiency and gain negotiating power with commercial fish processors and distributors. Luke tells us that the extended families of Simon and Zebedee from Capernaum had formed such a fishing partnership (Luke 5:10). When business was good, families hired workers who lacked an effective family business of their own, as was the case with the family of Zebedee (Mark 1:20).

In January 1986 two members of a local kibbutz were walking along the northwest shore of the Sea of Galilee and noticed some soggy wood planking protruding from the mud. It looked significant to them,

GALILEAN FISHING BOAT

and archaeologists confirmed it was, in fact, an ancient fishing boat from the first century. Winter rains prompted an emergency reclamation to preserve this unprecedented find from the rapidly rising waters of the lake. After nearly a decade of careful preservation efforts, the hull of this unique boat is now on display in a specially constructed museum near the place it was discovered. The remains of the boat measure 27 feet long, 7.5 feet wide, and 4.3 feet high. The hull is constructed out of cedar planks that were edge-joined together using pegged mortise and tenon joints. Curved ribs were added inside to strengthen the hull, and a lengthwise keel was added to the bottom for stability. Originally it was fitted with fore and aft decks, four oars for rowing, and a steering oar in the rear. It had a removable mast that carried a square-rigged sail. Although there is no evidence linking this boat directly to Jesus and his disciples, it was in use on the lake during their ministry and is precisely the kind of boat referred to in the Gospels some 50 times.

There were three primary types of nets used by Galilean fishermen in the first century: the casting net, the dragnet, and the trammel net. The casting net was a circular net about 20 feet in diameter. It was used by a single fisherman from the shallows or from a boat. The middle of the net was drawn up over the shoulder or arm of the fisherman, who would then throw the weighted perimeter of the net out in a circular fashion. The spinning weights extended the net to its fullest size and then dropped to the bottom, trapping fish underneath the net. The fisherman then stripped naked and dove down to the bottom, either placing the fish into a pouch or gathering the net together like a bag to retrieve the fish. This was probably the technique used by Simon and Andrew when Jesus called them while they were casting nets from the shore (Mark 1:16).

The dragnet (or seine net) was a long net with floats along the top edge and weights along the bottom edge. Fishermen in a boat pulled the net out into the water from the beach and then looped back to shore, forming a semicircular wall in the water. A crew of men then dragged the net up onto the beach, trapping a large number of fish. This is the type of net envisioned in Jesus' parable about sorting different kinds of fish after they are caught (Matthew 13:47-50).

The trammel net (or gill net) was the most common type used on the Sea of Galilee in Jesus' time. It is a three-layer net consisting of two larger looped nets with a finer looped net in the middle. With floats on the top and weights on the bottom, it formed a wall in the water like the dragnet, but in this case the fish swam through the loops in the larger net and got caught in the smaller looped net as they tried to escape. This net was let out behind the boat as it was rowed parallel to the shore, forming a wall stretching from the surface to the bottom. Then the fishermen disturbed the water on the shore, driving fish into deeper water where they were caught in the net. This was the type of net the disciples of Jesus used most often and is the net Jesus told Simon to *"Put out into the deep and let down your nets for a catch."* (Luke 5:4)

Net fishing was normally done at night when the fish are more active and when the nets are less visible. Smaller scale fishing was done with barbed hooks on lines, fish traps, and spear fishing with three-pronged tridents. Stone fishing weights and iron hooks were discovered by excavators in the home of Simon and Andrew in Capernaum.

ROMAN TAX COLLECTORS

As we saw in Chapter 1, the Roman Empire conquered territory in order to maximize the taxes it could produce to swell the coffers of the wealthy landowners of Rome. To ensure the most effective collection of these taxes, they employed local citizens as their representatives and made them responsible for meeting the quota of expected tax revenues. Each tax collector was assigned an area and an amount of taxes to collect from the people in that area. Anything these people collected above that amount constituted their own profit, creating a system that encouraged abuse. The local tax collectors were accountable to a chief tax collector who oversaw the collection of an entire region and was responsible for delivering the quota to the Herodians, who took their cut and then passed it on to the Romans. Luke tells us that Zacchaeus, to whose house Jesus invited himself, was just such a chief tax collector (Luke 19:2).

The Roman system of taxation was complex. The primary taxes, charged for land owned and goods produced, could be shockingly high. The tax on grain could be one third of the produce, while the tax on fruits and nuts could be one half of the produce! In addition, there were taxes on basic necessities such as water, salt, meat, and fish. Taxes were levied on goods transported between geographical districts and for the use of roads and bridges. Matthew's presence outside of Capernaum in a tax booth indicates he was collecting taxes that were charged on goods being transported along the Via Maris, from Herod Antipas' territory into Herod Philip's. Gamaliel, the famous first-century rabbi who taught Saul of Tarsus, reportedly commented on the extent of Roman taxation when he said, "By four things does the empire exist: by its tolls, bathhouses, theatres, and crop taxes." [41]

Historical references to the abuse and violence of Roman tax collectors are abundant. Philo of Alexandria, the first-century Jewish philosopher, reported the tension between Roman tax collectors and their subjects when he wrote, "for cities usually

---

41 *The Fathers according to Rabbi Nathan* 28; Yale Judaica Series, trans. Goldin (New Haven, Yale University Press, 1955), 116, Digital.

furnish them [taxes] under compulsion, and with great reluctance and lamentation, looking upon the collectors of the taxes as common enemies and destroyers, and making various excuses at different times, and neglecting all laws and regulations, and with all this obfuscation and evasion do they contribute the taxes and payments which are levied upon them."[42] An official complaint was lodged with the local Roman centurion in Arsinoe, Egypt, in AD 193 by a farmer and his brother against two collectors of the grain-tax and their scribe who physically assaulted the complainants' mother because she had only paid 90% of the taxes demanded of them. [43]

Tax collectors are rarely popular in any culture, but in first-century Judaism they were hated with a special vengeance because they were seen not only as corrupt, but also as traitors. The degree to which a tax collector prospered was the degree to which he added to the already crushing tax burden imposed by the Romans and the Herodians on the Jews. Even more, a tax collector was branded a traitor by his fellow Jews for colluding with the pagan invaders who oppressed God's people. The animosity toward tax collectors took on a religious expression as well. The rabbis taught that synagogues could not accept contributions for the poor from tax collectors, since their money was assumed to be illegally earned.[44] They also taught that, if a tax collector entered your home, everyone and everything in it automatically became unclean.[45] The presence of a tax collector in the Temple courts, was considered an act of defilement.

All of this demonstrates just how shocking it was when Jesus invited Matthew, the local tax collector of Capernaum, into his inner circle of full-time disciples and then went and spent time in Matthew's *oikos* with the wider community of tax collectors (Matthew 9:9-10). It also points out what an affront it was to the religious leaders of Jericho when Jesus chose to dine and spend the night in the home of Zacchaeus, the chief tax collector, rather than in the home of the leading rabbi (Luke 19:5-7). As we will see, Jesus was a Rabbi unlike any who had come before him, and he called disci-

---

42 Philo, *The Works of Philo*, Special Laws, translated by C. D. Yonge. (Peabody, MA: Hendrickson, 1993), 1.143, Digital.

43 *Select Papyri, Berlin Griechische Urkunden* no. 515, Volume II. Loeb Classical Library, translated by A. S. Hunt and C. C. Edgar (Cambridge, Harvard Univ. Press, 1934), 277, Digital.

44 Neusner, *The Mishnah*, m. B. Qam. 10:1.

45 Neusner, *The Mishnah*, m. Tehar. 7:6.

ples that no one would have dreamed of calling. The result was that their lives were radically transformed, and they were able to live the life Jesus modeled for them and pass it on to others who could do the same.

 # THE TRUTH

THE GOOD NEWS OF THE KINGDOM

When Jesus returned to Galilee, he began to proclaim the Good News that God's Kingdom was finally beginning to come. This was the long-awaited fulfillment of the biblical promise that God would one day reassert himself as the true Ruler of the universe and that the righteous principles of heaven would invade and transform this dark and broken world. As we have seen in the synagogue in Nazareth, this was understandably a very popular message among Jews who had been oppressed for centuries, at least until Jesus took the radical stance of saying this new Kingdom was for everyone, not just the Jewish people. This was not always popular among those who had become deeply embittered yet entitled.

As Jesus announced this Good News of the Kingdom, he called it a *kairos*, which is a moment of opportunity in which God is breaking in and doing something new. He invited people to take advantage of this in-breaking *kairos* by responding to the Good News in two specific ways: *"The time is fulfilled, and the kingdom of God is at hand; repent and believe in the gospel."* (Mark 1:15)

The Greek word we translate "repent" (*metanoia*) means literally to have your thinking changed. Jesus is telling us that the Good News of God's in-breaking Kingdom has the power to completely change our mindset and give us a whole new perspective. The first question is whether we are listening to what God is saying and allowing him to give us a new perspective. The Greek word we translate "believe" (*pisteuo*) is the verb form of the word for faith. In English the word faith has no verb form, so we resort to the word believe, but that sounds like simply agreeing with an idea. *Pisteuo* is more than agreeing with an idea; it means putting faith into action, taking a step of faith. Jesus is saying that the Good News of God's in-breaking Kingdom has the power to give us a whole new perspective if we are listening and receptive. This new perspective creates faith inside of us (cf. Romans 10:17). The second question is whether we will exercise that faith and respond to what Jesus is saying.

Earlier we noted Jesus' parable based on the setting of the house in Nazareth where he grew up. This story gives us a vivid picture of repenting and believing: *"Everyone then who hears these words of mine and does them will be like a wise man who built his house on the rock. And the rain fell, and the floods came, and the winds blew and beat on that house, but it did not fall, because it had been founded on the rock. And everyone who hears these words of mine and does not do them will be like a foolish man who built his house on the sand. And the rain fell, and the floods came, and the winds blew and beat against that house, and it fell, and great was the fall of it."* (Matthew 7:24-27) Jesus is telling us that hearing his word produces the faith we need to do what he says. If we are listening to Jesus' word (repenting) and responding in faith (believing), we will build a whole new way of life on the secure foundation of an immovable rock.

This is the very heart of how Jesus lived and taught his disciples to live. Jesus said, *"Truly, truly, I say to you, the Son can do nothing of his own accord, but only what he sees the Father doing. For whatever the Father does, that the Son does likewise."* (John 5:19). He also said, *"The words that I say to you I do not speak on my own authority, but the Father who dwells in me does his works."* (John 14:10) It is clear that Jesus listened to what his Father was saying, watched what his Father was doing, and simply responded to that in faith. Repenting and believing was at the very center of the incredible life Jesus lived.

Jesus called his followers to do the same when he said both, *"Listen!"* and *"Follow me"* (Mark 4:3, 8:34). He told his disciples to listen and receive his word: *"He who has ears to hear, let him hear."* (Mark 4:9) But he also challenged them to respond in faith by following his example: *"For I have given you an example, that you also should do just as I have done to you."* (John 13:15) Jesus' call was for people to listen to what God was saying through him and to respond by exercising the faith that word produced. This is the heart of Jesus-shaped discipleship. It is a relationship of faith that shapes our character and guides our life. As we hear his word and then do it by faith, we build our house on solid rock. Jesus didn't only tell us the way; he showed us the way. It is not only Jesus' spoken words that create faith, but the visible example of his life that we are called to imitate. This process of repenting and believing is how Jesus trained the disciples to live the life he was living and pass that life on to others.

A NEW KIND OF RABBI

Of all the incredible things Jesus did, none was more strategically important than making disciples. From the very beginning this was his key priority in establishing his mission. When Jesus made his first public appearance at the River Jordan, he met and invited into his life five men who would later become some of his closest disciples: Andrew, Simon, Philip, Nathanael, and probably John (John 1:35-51). When Jesus returned to Galilee from the Jordan, they traveled with him, and he visited some of their hometowns as he made his way back to Nazareth. When he was rejected by the people of his own village and abandoned by his extended family, Jesus came to Capernaum and began to build a new kind of extended family in the house of Simon and Andrew. It is significant that the Gospel writers refer to the men and women who filled the courtyard and rooms of that house as "disciples." (Matthew 12:49). Luke describes this same group as "a great crowd of disciples." This certainly constitutes the seventy-two that Jesus eventually sent out on mission (Luke 6:17; 10:1).

We have seen how radical it was for Jesus to welcome everyone into the house of Simon and Andrew, regardless of their religious or social standing. Now we see it is even more radical that this group of people were recognized as his "disciples." In first-century Jewish culture, being a disciple of the rabbi meant being recognized as the cream of the crop, the best of the best, those who met the highest religious and academic standards. Every Jewish boy dreamed of the status and recognition that came with being a disciple of the rabbi. It would never even occur to Jewish girls to wish for such a position. But when his mother and brothers came to Capernaum to take him back to Nazareth, Jesus looked around at the courtyard full of men and women and recognized them, not only as his true family, but also as his disciples!

There were no female disciples in ancient Judaism. The prevailing prejudice against women precluded this from even being considered. The status of women in first century Judaism had declined from the Old Testament era due to the influence of Greek culture. For instance, mimicking an earlier Greek prayer, the Jewish morning prayers in the first century included the statement, "Blessed are you O God, King of the Universe, who has not made me a woman." Women were largely confined to the private sphere of their home and family. As one rabbi put it, "It is the way of a woman to stay at home and it is the way of a man to go out into the marketplace."[46]

46 Neusner, *The Mishnah*, Bereshit Rabbah 18:1; cf. Taanit 23b.

194

If women did go out in public, they were expected to cover themselves and avoid interaction with men.

Jesus did not conform to these prejudicial views. We see him interacting freely with women in many different contexts and consistently demonstrating their dignity and equal value with men. Jesus affirmed the hemorrhaging woman who secretly touched his robe, he commended the Syrophoenician woman for her faith, he engaged in dialogue with the Samaritan woman at Jacob's Well, he praised the sinful woman who showed more gratitude than Simon the Pharisee, he protected the woman caught in adultery from stoning, and he recognized Mary of Bethany's anointing as a prophetic act. Luke names Mary Magdalene, Joanna the wife of Chuza, and Susanna as three of the upper-class women from Galilee who supported Jesus' mission financially and traveled on mission with him and the twelve full-time male disciples (Luke 8:1-3).

The Gospels use discipleship language when they report that Mary Magdalene and a large number of women from Galilee "followed" Jesus to Jerusalem (Matthew 27:55; Mark 15:41; Luke 23:49). Jesus explicitly affirmed Mary of Bethany when, despite her sister Martha's protestations, she scandalously took the posture of a disciple and sat at his feet. Perhaps it was Jesus' affirmation of and investment in these women that emboldened Mary Magdalene and the other women followers to venture out to the tomb that first Easter morning when the male disciples were still hiding in fear. The Gospel writers show us that Jesus clearly welcomed women as disciples and affirmed them as a critical part of his family and mission. This recognition of women followers was unprecedented for a first-century Jewish rabbi.

In this way and so many others, Jesus was a rabbi unlike any that had come before. All other Jewish rabbis waited for students to come to them and apply to become disciples. Jesus went to those who would never think of applying for discipleship and invited them to follow him. All other Jewish rabbis applied the strictest religious and social criteria to selecting a few favored applicants. Jesus welcomed everyone from Pharisees to tax collectors and demonized people into his family of disciples and challenged them to respond to his call. Jesus invited all who would believe in him and were willing to function as part of his family to become his disciples.

Often, when we read the phrase "his disciples," we assume the writer is referring only to Jesus' twelve closest disciples. In fact, the same phrase refers to the larger houseful in Capernaum as well as his inner circle; they are all considered Jesus' disciples. This does not mean that Jesus lowered the standards for discipleship; it just means that he transformed the criteria from social status and academic ability to total commitment and surrender. To those who would answer his invitation, Jesus gave the highest challenge: *"whoever does not take his cross and follow me is not worthy of me. Whoever finds his life will lose it, and whoever loses his life for my sake will find it."* (Matthew 10:38-39) This was a gracious invitation and an exhilarating challenge to which everyday people could respond. When people approached Jesus to apply for discipleship, he tested their motives by giving them extremely high challenge. He challenged the rich young ruler to sell everything. He told another would-be disciple there was nowhere to lay his head. To another he dismissed a father's funeral as a reason to delay responding and didn't even allow for a quick farewell to the extended family. As Jesus put it, *"No one who puts his hand to the plow and looks back is fit for the kingdom of God."* (Luke 9:57-62)

Although Jesus invited anyone who was willing to become a disciple, there is a clear distinction between the houseful of disciples, who constitute an extended spiritual family, and the twelve disciples, who function more like a nuclear family. Luke tells us, *In these days he went out to the mountain to pray, and all night he continued in prayer to God. And when day came, he called his disciples and chose from them twelve, whom he named apostles* (Luke 6:12-13). These twelve disciples are a subset of Jesus' larger family of disciples and are given a special role as "apostles." Clearly, Jesus is intentionally calling an inner circle of twelve full-time disciples to a higher level of commitment. The larger group of followers are those who had come to trust Jesus, listen to him, pattern their lives after him, and join in his mission locally while still functioning in their extended family and family business as they had before. The twelve apostles recognized that, for them, answering Jesus' call meant leaving their family business so they could travel out of the area on mission with Jesus. This was certainly the case for the fishing disciples who *left their nets and followed him,* and Matthew/Levi the tax collector who, *leaving everything, rose and followed him.* (Mark 1:18; Luke 5:28).

One of the common misconceptions in an excessively individualistic culture is that Jesus' call to discipleship took people out of their families. In fact, the opposite is true. Jesus entered into their families and taught them a whole new way to be a family on mission together. For Simon and Andrew, this was especially true, because their extended family home became the central gathering point for the new family of disciples Jesus was building. But, it was also true for someone like Matthew/Levi, who welcomed Jesus into his *oikos* so that his extended family and tax collector friends could also be exposed to Jesus' call to discipleship (Mark 2:15).

The reason the twelve disciples had to step down from their full-time involvement in their family's business was because they were signing up to travel with Jesus. This doesn't mean that they abandoned their families; it simply means that they went away periodically on mission trips but would regularly return to their home *oikos* in Capernaum. Most likely this would not have been popular with some of their extended family members who had to pick up the slack in the family business. Presumably Zebedee had to hire more men to keep their fishing business productive once James and John went full time with Jesus. Someone like Matthew/Levi would have had an even bigger challenge, because following Jesus certainly meant shutting down his questionable family business altogether.

A NEW WAY TO LIVE

Jesus' call to discipleship was not a call out of their family, but a call to transform their family. One morning Jesus left the house of Simon and Andrew in Capernaum and went to the shore of the lake to teach a crowd gathered there. Nearby were the fishing

SOWER'S COVE ON THE SEA OF GALILEE

disciples, Simon, Andrew, James, and John, who were cleaning up after a bad night of catching no fish. The crowd was overwhelming Jesus, and so he asked Simon to take him out from the shore in his boat. From there he could project his voice to the many people who had gathered. The crowd sat down on the steeply sloping hillside surrounding the cove, and Jesus began to tell them a story about a sower who went out to sow his seed.

Just half a mile east of Capernaum on the northern shore of the Sea of Galilee is a small cove with a steep bowl-shaped hillside rising away from the lake. In 1972

Cobbey Chrisler and Mark Myles conducted acoustical tests in this cove. They confirmed that 5,000-7,000 people could sit in this natural amphitheater and clearly hear an unamplified voice of someone speaking from a boat in the cove. It is highly likely that this was the location where Jesus taught from Simon and Andrew's boat. Since Matthew and Mark tell us this is when Jesus told his famous parable of the sower, it has come to be called the Sower's Cove.

When Jesus finished teaching from the boat and the sun had climbed high in the sky, he gave some unconventional fishing advice to his host on the boat: *"Put out into the deep and let down your nets for a catch."* (Luke 5:4) Simon was understandably reluctant. Who was this Nazarene stone mason to tell him, a professional, when and where to fish? Everyone knows you don't fish in the middle of the day when the fish are sleeping, and you certainly don't let your trammel nets down into deep water! But despite his well-honed fishing instincts, Simon decided to follow Jesus' direction anyway, *"Master, we toiled all night and took nothing! But at your word I will let down the nets."* (Luke 5:5)

Up to this point Simon had demonstrated he was a person of peace to Jesus. Simon welcomed Jesus into his home, listened eagerly to his teaching, and served Jesus in any way he could, even letting him use his fishing boat as a pulpit. But now Jesus was inviting Simon to become more than his friend; he was challenging him to become a follower. A friend will serve, but a follower submits.[47] Simon the fisherman submitted to the fishing advice of Jesus the stone mason. And to his shock, and the amazement of all who looked on, this submission paid off outrageously! They snagged a school of fish so large it literally broke their nets. Simon and Andrew called upon their business partners James and John for help, and they brought out a second boat to land this record-breaking catch. There could be no clearer lesson than this—submitting to Jesus and following him leads to the most fruitful kind of life we can live! Simon was learning what it means to be a disciple.

When Simon fell down before him in the midst of all those flopping fish, Jesus said something truly remarkable: *"Do not be afraid; from now on you will be catching men."* (Luke 5:10) Jesus had entered Simon's *oikos* and turned their lives inside out. No longer was their family home a fortress to keep out strangers, but a refuge to welcome the hurting

---

47 Mike and Sally Breen, *Family on Mission,* 2nd ed. (3DM Publishing: Pawleys Island, 2018), p. 27.

and lost into a new kind of family. They had built a comfortable, secure way of life by catching lots of fish, cleaning them, drying them, and selling them in the market. But now Jesus was inviting them to do something far more significant. He was transforming their family business into a Kingdom business. He was calling them to join him on his mission to seek and save the lost. He was inviting them into a life of discipleship in which they would learn how to live a life as fruitful as this boat full of flopping fish.

Jesus-Shaped Discipleship

Everyone who claims a biblically based faith in Jesus recognizes the importance of discipleship. Jesus made it crystal clear that this is to be our top priority when he commissioned his followers, *"Go therefore and make disciples of all nations, baptizing them in the name of the Father and of the Son and of the Holy Spirit, teaching them to observe all that I have commanded you. And behold, I am with you always, to the end of the age."* (Matthew 28:19-20) The question is not whether we should make disciples; the question is what does that mean? How should we do it?

In the modern West, we tend to reduce discipleship to an intellectual exercise. Our discipleship strategies center around books, videos, curricula, classes, and church programs. This reflects our concept of information-only discipleship. We assume if we can get the right information into people's brains, they will become disciples. As a result, our primary strategy tends to be organizing our churches in a way that we can deliver more effective disciple-making systems which we assume will produce more mature disciples of Jesus. But this is the opposite of Jesus' strategy for disciple-making!

Jesus never once told his disciples how to organize the church, nor did he ever tell his disciples to try and get as many people as possible to attend the programs at the synagogue—even when he was teaching there! Instead, Jesus looked for friends—people of peace—who responded positively to his offer of friendship. Then he invited them into a home where he was building a new kind of family. In the context of that extended family where everyone was welcome, he called people into the deeper, committed relationship of disciples following their rabbi. He challenged them, just as he did Simon in the boat, to move from being a friend who would serve him to being a follower who would submit to him. Luke describes the response of Simon, Andrew, James, and John to this incredible invitation: *when they had brought their boats to land, they left everything and followed him.* (Luke 5:11)

Biblical discipleship certainly involves good information, for Jesus is the greatest teacher who ever lived. However, it must involve much more than simply words, no matter how good they are. Jesus-shaped discipleship combines revelatory *information* from God with the opportunity for real-life *imitation*.[48] It was not enough for the followers of Jesus to simply sit and listen to him talk; they also needed to watch how he lived. As they listen and watched, then Jesus invited them to participate.

Once, while Jesus was teaching a crowd of 5,000 men plus women and children and healing the sick in an undeveloped area, the day was dragging on and the people were getting hungry, so he challenged his disciples to feed them. When they protested that they only had five loaves of bread and two fish (which they pinched from a little boy who was nearby), Jesus proceeded to show them how to do it. He looked to heaven, prayed a prayer of blessing to God, and broke the bread and fish into pieces. Then Jesus put this paltry offering into their hands and sent them into the hungry crowd. To their amazement, when the dust settled, the entire crowd was well-fed, and they still had twelve baskets of bread left over (Matthew 14:13-21). As the disciples followed Jesus' example and instructions, they got to participate in the miracle. They were learning Jesus' remarkable way of life, not just by listening to his words, but by following his example. Jesus made disciples who could do what he did by giving them powerful *information*, but also a concrete opportunity for *imitation*.

Here we see that Jesus' goal was not just to help his disciples understand the content of his teaching, but for them to learn how to do the things that he did. Information-only discipleship often leads us to the conclusion that the goal of discipleship is simply to take on the character of Jesus. If we can understand his teaching better, perhaps that will help us take on some of Jesus' characteristics, like becoming more loving, more generous, more faithful, etc. While character formation is certainly an important aspect of biblical discipleship, Jesus was not only forming the *character* of his disciples, but he was developing their *competency* as well. Jesus' goal was that his disciples would know what he knew and become like him, so they could do the same things that he did. Not just some of what he did, but everything he did.

It is reductionistic to conclude that disciples of Jesus are to learn how to do some of

---

48 For more on this approach to discipleship see Bob Rognlien, *Empowering Missional Disciples* (Pawleys Island, 3DM Publishing, 2016), 145.

what he did, but not all of it. Through his words and deeds Jesus regularly operated in supernatural authority and power for the sake of others. After teaching in the synagogue in Capernaum Luke reports, *they were all amazed and said to one another, "What is this word? For with authority and power he commands the unclean spirits, and they come out!" And reports about him went out into every place in the surrounding region.* (Luke 4:36-37) Many assume we should learn to teach the Bible, feed the hungry, welcome outcasts, and forgive sinners. But when it comes to healing the sick, delivering the spiritually oppressed, and raising the dead, we often assume that is the kind of work that only Jesus can do. An imbalanced Christology contributes to this false conclusion.

As we have seen in Chapter 4, if we over-emphasize the full divinity of Jesus to the detriment of his full humanity, we will end up concluding Jesus did things we can never do because he had access, in his divine nature, to authority and power that is not available to us. However, this is to misunderstand the nature of incarnation. Jesus said exactly the opposite, *"Truly, truly, I say to you, whoever believes in me will also do the works that I do; and greater works than these will he do, because I am going to the Father."* (John 14:12) Jesus trained his disciples to heal the sick, cleanse lepers, cast out demons, and raise the dead (Matthew 10:8). When they came back from their mission, they joyfully reported, *"Lord, even the demons are subject to us in your name!"* (Luke 10:17) The followers of Jesus continued to operate in his supernatural power as the movement spread across the Mediterranean world. As we learn to be disciples and make disciples the way that Jesus did, more and more we will learn to live the life that Jesus modeled for us.

 # THE LIFE

ACCIDENTAL VS. INTENTIONAL DISCIPLESHIP

My dad learned to ski on the powdery slopes of northwest Montana before skiing was a mainstream sport. He went on to become a competitive racer and won a skiing scholarship to Montana State College in Bozeman. I received my first pair of skis for Christmas when I was five years old. We lived in Europe at the time, so I learned to ski in Austria. I can still remember my dad hunched over in an exaggerated snow plow, looking over his shoulder, urging me to follow him down the slope. I took a deep breath, pushed off with my poles, and simply tried to do what I saw him doing. It wasn't long before I was flying down the mountains of Kitzbuhel in the most daring snow plow ever! Over time I became a confident skier, went on to teach ski lessons, and have enjoyed the sport ever since. We all need good examples to follow. This is the first and most important job of parents: showing and telling our children the way to live a fruitful life. Whether we realize it, we all end up imitating our parents. Then, for better or worse, we set an example that our children will follow. I remember the pang of responsibility I felt when I realized my toddler son was simply imitating everything I said and did. It certainly made me think more carefully about my words and actions! Jesus offered the best example ever given. The first step of discipleship is to imitate Jesus. It is telling that the best-selling Christian book of all time (after the Bible) is *The Imitation of Christ* by Thomas à Kempis, written in 1418. Soren Kierkegaard wrote, "To be truly redeemed by Christ is, therefore, to impose on oneself the task of imitating him; As a man Jesus is my model because as God he is my Redeemer; Christianity can be defined as a faith together with a corresponding way of life, imitation of Christ." [49]

It is no accident that Jesus called the disciples his "*little children*" (John 13:33). Just like a good father, he explained things to them and then he showed them what it looked like in action. He was setting an example for them to follow. And they did! They learned to live the way Jesus lived and passed this way of life on to their spiritual children, who eventually did the same. As we learn to imitate Jesus, the next step is for us to offer an example of Jesus that others can follow. This is what Jesus-shaped discipleship looks like. We learn the way of Jesus from our spiritual parents, and then we pass that way on to our spiritual children. To be a disciple is to learn how to become a rabbi. To become a rabbi is to call disciples to follow you. This is how the movement of Jesus continued to multiply in the face of massive resistance. Jesus' disciples kept multiplying Jesus-shaped disciples!

When I came to faith in Jesus, I had no understanding of biblical discipleship. I was taught the Good News that Jesus was God in human flesh who died on the cross to pay the price for my sin, so I could be forgiven and live in a personal relationship with God, filled with the Spirit. It was wonderful to say yes to Jesus, receive his grace, feel the presence of his Spirit, experience the joy of Christian community, and begin to worship, read the Bible, and pray. However, no one offered to disciple me. No one

---

[49] Dupré, *Kierkegaard as Theologian*, (New York, Sheed & Ward, 1963), 172, Digital.

explicitly challenged me to follow their example as they followed Jesus. But I did have some great role models. My pastor and my youth director both set an example that I could follow. I had some friends who were a little older than I was who sought to live out their faith as a daily way of life. Without realizing it, I was patterning my Christian walk after the example of these people in my life. Looking back, I would call it accidental discipleship!

Once I had finished college, seminary, and graduate school, I can say that I no longer had any spiritual role models in my life, intentional or accidental. For most of my adult life, I tried to grow in my faith and learn to follow Jesus on my own. I had lots of friends in the faith and fellow travelers for the journey, but no one who invited me to follow their example. It wasn't until I was in my early 40s that I began to understand the true nature of discipleship as Jesus lived it out. For the first time in my life I had people who invited me into their lives, who were willing to set an example and challenge me to follow it. Through this process I found my walk with Jesus growing by leaps and bounds. Although I had already completed a decade of theological training and spent another fifteen years in full-time church leadership, I found the fruitfulness of my life increasing exponentially. I felt like Simon in a boat full of fish, wondering why I hadn't let my nets down into the deep earlier in life!

Once I was receiving more intentional, relational discipleship, I found I was able to offer that to others. At first it felt very awkward. I was reluctant to intentionally disciple others because I had always thought of that as something Jesus did, not me! But the more I came to understand biblical discipleship, the more I realized that being a genuine disciple means seeking to become a rabbi; and all rabbis have disciples who follow them. For the first time the Great Commission made sense to me. Jesus wasn't telling us to recruit people into church services and programs, as helpful as those can be. He wasn't telling us to simply convince people the truth of various doctrines, as important as that can be. Jesus was commissioning us to do with others what he did with his disciples: to invite people of peace into our lives as part of an extended spiritual family, invest in them, and challenge them to follow us as we are learning to follow Jesus. This is discipleship. This is the Way of Jesus.

A PERFECT EXAMPLE VS IMPERFECT EXAMPLES

One of the biggest roadblocks for me in learning to make disciples was my sense of unworthiness. I didn't feel qualified to challenge people to follow my example, because I was vividly aware of my faults and shortcomings. But then I came to understand we don't need to be a perfect example to make disciples. Jesus is our perfect example to whom we always point people. What we need to offer others is not a perfect example, but a living example of the perfect life Jesus lived. Jesus is directly accessible to us in the pages of the Gospels and in the power of his Spirit, but we all need a Jesus with "skin," a Jesus-shaped example that we can see with our eyes, hear with our ears, and follow with our life.

Jesus said he would come back in the power of the Spirit to make his home inside of us: *"In that day you will know that I am in my Father, and you in me, and I in you… If anyone loves me, he will keep my word, and my Father will love him, and we will come to him and make our home with him."* (John 14:20, 23) If Jesus is alive in you, then your life can be a living example of Jesus to others, even if that example is imperfect. When you call someone into a discipling relationship, you are inviting them to follow the Jesus who they can see showing through your life, despite your shortcomings. Paul, who was profoundly aware of his faults and failures, said it this way to his spiritual children in Corinth: *Be imitators of me, as I am of Christ.* (1 Corinthians 11:1). Being a discipling spiritual parent is offering your life as an imperfect example of Jesus for others to follow.

As I have followed the example of those who have invited me into discipling relationships, I have learned to simply include others in what I am doing so they get more access to imitate those parts of my life that look like Jesus. This means breaking old habits and establishing new and better ones. It takes intentional choices to do this. As a pastor I realized I was training others to do most of the things I was doing except for preaching. So, I started to be more intentional about inviting younger leaders to join in the preaching ministry and grow in their communication skills. When the time came for me to step down from leading that church, we had a team of excellent preachers who could carry the ball forward without me there! When I realized I was maxing out my capacity to lead our unique pilgrimages in the Footsteps of Jesus, I decided to start inviting other leaders to come back and learn how to do what I do. Now I have two fully-trained Footsteps of Jesus leaders and six more in the process of being trained. In our new neighborhood we are reaching out to our neighbors who don't know Jesus and inviting them into our extended spiritual family, but we have also invited other believers to join us in this mission so they can learn to do the same.

This is how the first disciples of Jesus fulfilled the Great commission. They followed the example of Jesus as the Spirit empowered them to do. As they learned to do what Jesus did, they welcomed people of every walk of life into their spiritual family. They looked for people of peace and began to invest in those relationships. Those who were responsive were offered full access to their lives and challenged to follow their imperfect example of the perfect life of Jesus. They taught them the profound information they had learned from Jesus, but also challenged them to intentional imitation. This means they had to open up their lives, homes, and families, so their disciples could not only come to understand what Jesus taught, but also learn to do what Jesus did. These disciples grew up to become spiritual parents who did the same with others. That is how extended spiritual families reached the lost, multiplied, and became established churches in countless towns and cities across the Roman Empire.

Jesus-shaped discipleship is the key to fulfilling the mission Jesus has entrusted to us. It doesn't matter how many people we recruit into our churches and programs. If we are not intentionally inviting people into such close relationships that they can see Jesus in us and learn to follow that example, we are not fulfilling the Great Commission. Dietrich Bonhoeffer underscored the indispensable nature of biblical discipleship when he wrote, "Christianity without the living Christ is inevitably Christianity without discipleship, and Christianity without discipleship is always Christianity without Christ."[50] If we are going to be true to Jesus' call and actually follow him, we will have to learn a way of life in which intentional, relational discipleship is at the very core.

[50] Dietrich Bonhoeffer, *The Cost of Discipleship*, (New York, Macmillan, 1937), 64.

CHAPTER NINE

JESUS' RHYTHMS: THE SECRET TO A FRUITFUL LIFE

"Come away by yourselves to a desolate place and rest a while." (Mark 6:31)

 ## THE WAY

THE GIFT OF SABBATH

It is hard for modern people to imagine a world without weekends, but the ancient world had no concept of days off. Most people worked from sun up to sun down every day, except for an occasional religious feast or festival. The wealthy and powerful could afford to take vacations and live a life of leisure, but the vast majority of the population lived in a daily grind, with one day of labor blurring into the next. It is significant that in chapters one and two of Genesis, the Creator is depicted taking a day of rest

SABBATH FAMILY MEAL

after creating human beings as the pinnacle of his creation. It is fascinating that immediately after giving men and women the job of stewarding his creation, God gave them a day of rest—before they had even begun working. He was showing us how to work from rest, rather than simply resting from our work. This rhythm of a day of rest, followed by six days of fruitful activity, followed by a day of rest, became the rhythm of life for the people of Israel.

This principle became so important to the people of Israel that it was applied to everyone in their community and included as number four in the top ten list of God's laws: *"Remember the Sabbath day, to keep it holy. Six days you shall labor, and do all your work, but the seventh day is a Sabbath to the Lord your God. On it you shall not do any work, you, or your son, or your daughter, your male servant, or your female servant, or your livestock, or the sojourner who is within your gates."* (Exodus 20:8-10). This weekly 24-hour period of rest from sundown to sundown was one of the key distinctives by which other cultures identified the Jewish people as unique, and it continues to be a cornerstone of Orthodox Jewish observance today.

Other rhythms of rest were built into the Jewish calendar as well, including a Sabbath Year every seventh year in which the land was allowed to lie fallow and no new crops were to be planted (Leviticus 25:1-7). In addition, every seventh Sabbath Year was celebrated as a Year of Jubilee in which no crops were to be planted, all debts were released, and any sold land was returned to its original owner (Leviticus 25:8-17). The Sabbath Year continues to be practiced by many Orthodox Jews today, and its principles are reflected in the modern practice of crop rotation. However, the Year of Jubilee was much more difficult to implement, and most scholars believe it was never actually observed, even in ancient Israel.

By the time of Jesus, weekly Sabbath observance had become highly regulated by the many rabbinical rules dictating what kinds of activity were prohibited or allowed on the seventh day of the week. This included how many steps you could take, how many letters you could write, how meals were prepared, and what you could touch and carry. Jesus was not bound by these specific interpretations of Sabbath in the Oral Law, but he did practice the biblical rhythms of Sabbath rest and applied these principles to the way of life he modeled for his disciples.

A NATURAL RETREAT

In a small valley on the northwest shore of the Sea of Galilee, just one and a half miles west of Capernaum, is a cool, well-watered area known as Tabgha, named after the seven strong springs that flow from the base of the hills into the nearby lake. In later centuries these springs were harnessed to irrigate the surrounding fields, but in the time of Jesus they watered the abundant grass and trees that created a natural park-like setting. The water channels carrying the cold spring water into the lake acted as a natural air conditioner, lowering the temperature under the shade of trees, even in the hot summer months.

The high water table softened the soil in this area, discouraging construction of buildings, so it retained its isolated nature despite its appealing atmosphere. It appears this was a favorite place where Jesus brought his disciples for special times of retreat and rest after busy seasons of ministry. The earliest traditions locate here the miraculous feeding of the 5,000, which took place during an interrupted time of rest Jesus had planned for his disciples.

The Gospels specify this took place in an area that was both isolated and lush, where *"there was much grass in the place."* (John 6:10; cf. Matthew 14:13, 19; Mark 6:32, 39) In the fourth century, a Christian pilgrim named Egeria visited this place and wrote in her journal, "Not far away from there (Capernaum) are some stone steps where the Lord stood. And in the same place by the sea is a grassy field with plenty of hay and many palm trees. By them are seven springs, each flowing strongly. And this is the field where the Lord fed the people with the five loaves and two fishes. In fact the stone on which the Lord placed the bread has now been made into an altar. Past the walls of this church goes the public highway on which the Apostle Matthew had his place of custom. Near there on a mountain is a cave to which the Savior climbed and spoke the Beatitudes."[51]

Shortly before Egeria's visit, a small church was built in Tabgha, centered around the large rock which she identified as the place where Jesus blessed and broke the bread before distributing it to the crowds. In the fifth century, a larger church was built around that same rock, preserving a now famous mosaic floor depicting the two fish and a basket of loaves Jesus used to feed the multitudes. It is likely that this was the place where Jesus took his disciples for short local retreats to rest and be restored after a busy season of mission.

Gentile Urban Centers

As we noted earlier, the area east of the Sea of Galilee was dominated by ten Hellenistic city-states which had formed a military and economic alliance described by Pliny in his *Natural History* as the Decapolis (Greek for "ten cities"): Philadelphia, Gerasa, Pella, Scythopolis, Gadara, Hippos, Dion, Canatha, Raphana, and Damascus. These were established after Alexander the Great conquered the Middle East in the fourth century BC and exported Greek culture and population around the region. They were generally large, wealthy cities which featured strong military defenses, monumental Greek architecture, and thriving trade-based economies.

The city of the Decapolis closest to Jesus' Galilean mission field was called Hippos (Greek for "horse"). It is clearly visible from Capernaum. Built on a steep ridge on the eastern shore of the Sea of Galilee, Hippos was one of the most defensible of the Greek cities of the Decapolis. The city enjoyed commanding views over the lake, and stone hydraulic pipes brought pressurized water from springs to the east into its elaborate water system. One of the wealthiest cities in the region, Hippos was adorned with beautiful pagan temples, a vast marketplace, and a recently discovered theater and bath house. Near the main city gate a large bronze mask of the god Pan was also found,

---

[51] *Egeria's Travels,* trans. John Wilkinson, as quoted in Jerome Murphy-O'Connor, *The Holy Land* (Oxford, Oxford University Press, 2008) Digital.

indicating the theater may have been part of a pagan worship complex just outside the city walls.

All three synoptic Gospels describe Jesus calming a storm and then landing on the shore with his disciples in the region of the Decapolis. There

MAIN STREET OF HIPPOS

Jesus encountered a terribly demonized man whom he dramatically delivered, sending a legion of demons into a herd of pigs who promptly drowned themselves in the lake. Matthew 8:28 tells us it was "the country of the Gadarenes" where this took place, but the textual variants of "Gerasenes" and "Gergesenes" indicate that this geographical identification was questioned by early scribes due to the fact that Gadara was located some 30 miles from the lake (cf. Mark 5:1; Luke 8:26). The region of Gadara that borders the southern shore of the Sea of Galilee is the most likely location for this event, since it is the next closest city of the Decapolis to the lake after Hippos.

The ancient Phoenician cities of Tyre and Sidon on the coast north of Israel comprised another area which was populated primarily by Gentiles. These ancient Canaanite cities were colonized by early Greek settlers and became wealthy and powerful centers of maritime trade. The region came to be called Phoenicia (Greek for "purple") by the Greeks, because of its trade in the prized murex sea snails that provided the precious purple dye worn by the nobility. Under Roman rule Tyre and Sidon reached the peak of their wealth, prospering from east-west trade as major Roman port cities. Today few ancient remains are visible in Sidon because the modern city covers the ancient site, but Tyre boasts numerous impressive Roman ruins, including one of the bestpreserved Roman hippodromes (athletic stadium) in the world. Jesus periodically brought his disciples into this area on longer retreats. It was here that Jesus healed the Syrophoenician woman's daughter (Matthew 15:21-28; Mark 7:24-30).

CAESAREA PHILIPPI AND CAVE OF PAN

On the very northern border of Israel, not far from the Israelite city of Dan, in the foothills of Mount Hermon, stood the Greek city of Panias. Following the death of Alexander in 323 BC, when the Selucids took control of this area, the Greeks were drawn to the massive springs that flowed from a large cave at the base of Mount Hermon. At 9,332 feet this is the highest peak in all of Syria, and the spring that flows from its base is the primary source of the Jordan River. The Greeks built a sanctuary here to worship the nature god Pan, and they believed the cave was a gateway to the underworld.

After Herod the Great subdued the local population in 23 BC, Caesar Augustus gave the northern Golan Heights, including Panias, to Herod. Josephus tells us that Herod built a white marble temple near the cave of Pan and dedicated it to Augustus. The remains discovered directly in front of the cave match this description. When Herod the Great died, his territory was divided between three of his sons, with Philip receiving the Golan Heights, including Panias. He renamed the city Panias-Caesarea in honor of his Roman patron Tiberias Caesar, as Josephus explains, "When Philip also had built Panias, a city at the fountains of Jordan, he named it Caesarea."[52] Since his father had also named the port city he built on the coast Caesarea, this city came to be called Caesarea Philippi.

The Banias Stream flows from the springs about a half mile south where it falls 33 feet over a basalt shelf forming the Banias Falls, the largest in the entire region. This lush gorge, shaded from direct sun and cooled by the falling water, is an ideal place for retreat and refreshment. Both Matthew and Mark specify that Jesus did not take

---

52 *Antiquities of the Jews, 18.2.1*

them into the city of Caesarea Philippi itself, but rather to a district of that city. This beautiful waterfall is a logical candidate for the place where Jesus took his followers to rest and reflect.

BANIAS FALLS NEAR CAESAREA PHILIPPI

THE FAMILY BUSINESS

Like the Greeks and Romans, and nearly all the cultures of their time, most Jews in the first century lived as part of an extended family that was supported by a commonly held business. In the modern world, we generally think of our job as something separate from our family, but in the biblical world your family was primarily shaped by its vocation, and everyone in the family was expected to be part of it. As we've seen, Jesus' extended family was centered around a lucrative construction business. Simon, Andrew, James, and John all grew up in families with a successful fishing business. Saul of Tarsus' extended family became wealthy enough through their tent-making business to send their son to train with the most famous rabbi of their time, Gamaliel. In the first century your family was primarily defined by its vocational mission.

Some families were centered on less honorable professions. Matthew and Zacchaeus were tax collectors. They made a lot of money, but their families were branded shameful traitors because of it. Others were not part of a family with a stable business and suffered as a result. The so-called "sinful woman" who wept over Jesus' feet at the house of Simon the Pharisee was likely driven by necessity to prostitution because she lacked the protection and provision of an effective *oikos* (Luke 7:37-38). The Samaritan woman who met Jesus at Jacob's well had been a part of five different families and now was living outside the security of a recognized marriage covenant (John 4:16-19). Being part of a family with an effective business was critical to support and well-being in the first century. For Jesus this became a central metaphor to explain the nature of his call to discipleship.

 # THE TRUTH

FRUITFUL RHYTHMS OF RETREAT

Jesus was a master at using ordinary experiences to help everyday people apprehend powerful Kingdom truths. On the last night he was with them before his arrest and crucifixion, Jesus walked with his disciples from the Jerusalem home of Mary, the mother of John Mark, through the Kidron Valley heading north towards the Mount of Olives. He was weighed down with the realization that the painful fulfillment of his destiny was upon him, but still he was sharing profound spiritual insights with his closest friends. They were likely passing by vineyards when he said, *"I am the vine; you are the branches. Whoever abides in me and I in him, he it is that bears much fruit, for apart from me you can do nothing."* (John 15:5). This would have been a vivid image for people who grew up surrounded by the grain fields, olive groves, and vineyards that supplied the staples of their middle eastern diet. But the message would have been even more vivid for them because Jesus was describing a way of life they had watched him live and had already been learning themselves.

Mark records what Jesus did the morning after his very first night in the extended family home of Simon and Andrew in Capernaum: *rising very early in the morning, while it was still dark, he departed and went out to a desolate place, and there he prayed.* (Mark 1:35) Jesus was showing his future disciples one of his primary rhythms of life—a daily time of solitude and prayer to "abide" with his heavenly Father. Jesus was practicing what he would later preach. If we hope to produce something good in our lives, we must be intentional about staying connected to the One who is the source of all good things. Jesus knew a daily rhythm of abiding with the Father was critical for him to be able to do the things he did and overcome the inevitable obstacles he faced. When the disciples came looking for Jesus that morning, he didn't resist the many people who were looking to him for help. He stepped from his place of private abiding with the Father into the fruitful public work that the Father was calling him to do. This was Jesus' *daily* rhythm.

Luke tells us that it was Jesus' "custom" to attend the synagogue on the Sabbath day (Luke 4:16). It goes without saying that this took place in the context of Jesus' faithful observance of a weekly day of rest. Starting with sundown on Friday night and following through to sundown on Saturday night, Jesus would have taken time to rest, reconnect with the people close to him, and abide at a deeper level with his heavenly Father. This doesn't mean that Jesus was worried about following all the extra religious rules that had been imposed on Sabbath observance. In fact, we see Jesus regularly come into conflict with the religious leaders because he refused to let these man-made traditions stand in the way of what he saw the Father doing.

When someone was sick or injured on the Sabbath, Jesus did not hesitate to heal them, regardless of the Pharisees' reaction. When he was walking through a grain field with his disciples on the Sabbath, Jesus defended their right to pluck heads of grain to eat, based on a biblical precedent set by David (Matthew 12:1-12). Jesus was clear that the Sabbath was meant as a gift to bless and nurture a fruitful life, not as a legalistic burden to weigh people down. He said it this way, *"The Sabbath was made for man, not man for the Sabbath."* (Mark 2:27) Jesus observed a weekly day of rest, not to fulfill legalistic religious rules, but in order to abide more deeply with his Father and his family, and so to live a more fruitful life. This was Jesus' *weekly* rhythm.

As Jesus' notoriety grew, the Gospel writers describe the pressure on him and his disciples to meet the demands of the rapidly expanding crowds. They couldn't meet in towns anymore because there was not enough room for those who gathered. Sometimes they missed meals because of the demands placed upon them. After particularly busy, demanding seasons of ministry, Jesus made it a point to take his disciples away to a nearby place for an extra day of retreat and abiding. After his twelve disciples returned from their first mission trip apart from him, Jesus said, *"Come away by yourselves to a desolate place and rest a while."* (Mark 6:31) These local retreat days gave them an opportunity to rest physically and to be spiritually renewed. This was Jesus' *occasional* rhythm.

On this particular occasion, Jesus' local retreat with the disciples was interrupted by crowds of people desperate to receive more teaching about the Kingdom of God. In this case, Jesus changed his plans, ministered to the crowds, and ended up miraculously feeding them with five loaves and two fishes.

TABGHA LOAVES AND FISH MOSAIC

In the 18th century, a German Catholic organization purchased a large property on the northwest shore of the Sea of Galilee known as Tabgha, where seven strong springs flow. When they began to build a guesthouse for pilgrims there, they discovered ancient remains, but the Ottoman government prevented further excavation.

In 1932, under British rule, German archaeologists discovered the fourth century church, built around a large rock, and the larger fifth century church built over the same rock which served as the altar for both churches, that we discussed earlier. This discovery fit perfectly with the accounts of early pilgrims who visited these churches to remember Jesus' miraculous feeding of the 5,000. The floor of this church was covered by an extensive "Nilotic" mosaic depicting a typical scene along the Nile River. However, in this scene, the flora and fauna are representative of the setting around the Sea of Galilee, and the mosaic in front of the ancient rock altar features the famous fish and loaves. That marks this as the site of Jesus' miraculous feeding of the 5,000. This ancient church has been beautifully restored, painstakingly preserving the original Byzantine design and the mosaics.

At other times Jesus was aware that he and the disciples needed a longer period of abiding, and he knew the only way they would be able to get it was to get completely out of the area and go somewhere they would not be readily recognized. They did take trips to Jerusalem seasonally for the great festivals, but these hardly allowed time for rest or retreat. Since Jesus' self-identified missional focus was *"the lost sheep of the house of Israel"* (Matthew 15:24), he knew he needed to get away into a primarily Gentile area for a more in-depth time of retreat. At various times the Gospels record Jesus taking the disciples east into the area of the Decapolis and north to the region of Tyre and Sidon. There Mark tells us *he entered a house and did not want anyone to know* (Mark 7:24). Jesus was taking them on longer retreats designed to provide them the time and anonymity to really unwind, rest, and abide deeply with the Father. This was Jesus' *seasonal* rhythm.

JESUS' ABIDING RHYTHMS

DAILY	Time alone with the Father	Mark 1:35: *And rising very early in the morning, while it was still dark, he departed and went out to a desolate place, and there he prayed.*
WEEKLY	24-hour Sabbath rest	Luke 4:26: *And as was his custom, he went to the synagogue on the Sabbath day...*
OCCASIONAL	Local retreats around the lake	Mark 6:31: *And he said to them, "Come away by yourselves to a desolate place and rest a while."*
SEASONAL	Longer retreats in Gentile areas	Mark 7:24: *And from there he arose and went away to the region of Tyre and Sidon. And he entered a house and did not want anyone to know...*

PRUNING FRUITFUL BRANCHES

As Jesus' mission in Galilee continued to unfold, his popularity with the crowds grew exponentially, as did his unpopularity with the religious and political leaders. The more miracles he performed, the more the crowds came looking for displays of spiritual fireworks, and the more the threatened leaders plotted against him. After the miraculous feeding of the multitude, people also began looking for the practical benefit of a free lunch! Jesus called out their consumerism in the synagogue at Capernaum when he said, *"Truly, truly, I say to you, you are seeking me, not because you saw signs, but because you ate your fill of the loaves."* (John 6:26) When the crowds responded by demanding more miraculous signs, Jesus did something completely unexpected.

Instead of performing tricks for the crowd, Jesus began to give them more challenging teaching. He started by telling them they didn't need him to give them bread, because he was the bread of heaven that came down for them. When the crowd objected that he couldn't come from heaven because they knew his parents in Nazareth, Jesus said something shocking to Jewish sensibilities: *"I am the living bread that came down from heaven. If anyone eats of this bread, he will live forever. And the bread that I will give for the life of the world is my flesh."* (John 6:51) When they balked at this provocative statement, Jesus went even further: *"Truly, truly, I say to you, unless you eat the flesh of the Son of Man and drink his blood, you have no life in you."* (John 6:53) At that many in the crowd walked away, and even some who were part of the houseful of disciples no longer followed Jesus. Only his core group of disciples stuck with him. As Simon said, *"Lord, to whom shall we go? You have the words of eternal life, and we have believed, and have come to know, that you are the Holy One of God."* (John 6:68-69)

When we look ahead to Jesus' teaching about the vine and the branches, it starts to become clear what he was doing in this challenging exchange. That final night in the Kidron Valley Jesus told his disciples, *"Every branch in me that does not bear fruit he takes away, and every branch that does bear fruit he prunes, that it may bear more fruit."* (John 15:2). We can see that Jesus was cutting off and pruning the consumerist crowds in order to make sure that his disciples were truly learning to live the kind of fruitful life that he modeled for them, a life that produces good fruit that bears the seeds of reproduction. Jesus was not interested in attracting the largest number of people possible to his gatherings—he was focused on making disciples who knew how to live a fruitful life that would reproduce good fruit again and again.

In the end Jesus had a relatively small circle of disciples with him in Jerusalem. By the Day of Pentecost, Luke tells us that only 120 people gathered in the upper room, but they were fruitful disciples who had been trained to reach the lost and make more disciples. These 120 people turned out to be enough to bring the Good News of the Kingdom to the ends of the earth. These men and women were branches that had been pruned back so they would produce good fruit that lasts. They had learned to follow the rhythms of Jesus' life, daily, weekly, occasionally, and seasonally. They knew how to abide in Jesus so that their lives would produce more and better fruit, fruit with seeds that would be planted all the way to the ends of the earth!

THE FINAL RETREAT

Once Jesus knew the time was coming for him to set his face toward the destiny that awaited him in Jerusalem, he took his disciples on one final retreat. They traveled northward on a two-day journey to the region of Panias, the pagan center for the worship of Pan. Festivals of debauchery, featuring drunkenness, orgies, and bestiality took place there in open courtyards to honor this god of nature. Ancient Greeks pictured Pan living in caves that communicated with the underworld. The priests of Pan offered sacrificial animals to the god by throwing their carcasses into the powerful spring that flowed from the Cave of Pan.

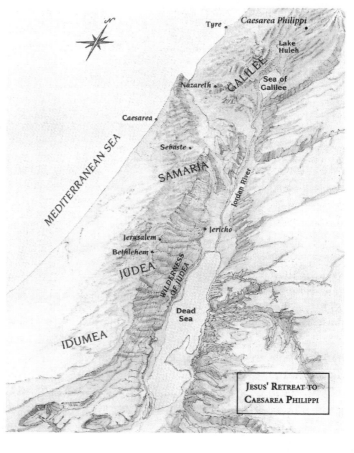

JESUS' RETREAT TO CAESAREA PHILIPPI

As we discussed above, it is highly unlikely that Jesus would have taken his disciples directly into this pagan worship center, but rather would have found a restful place somewhere nearby in *"the district of Caesarea Philippi"* (Matthew 16:13). The waters that flow from the Cave of Pan become the powerful Banias Falls which pour into a nearby gorge, creating a cool, lush environment, not unlike the area of Tabgha by the lake. It is easy to picture Jesus and the disciples taking time for retreat and rest in this beautiful place. Often, times of retreat and abiding lead to revelation, and that is exactly what happened for Simon. Jesus was dialoguing with his disciples in typical rabbinical fashion, and he asked them the pointed question, *"But who do you say that I am?" Simon Peter replied, "You are the Christ, the Son of the living God."* (Matthew 16:15-16) Jesus affirmed this profession of faith as a revelation from his heavenly Father and then gave Simon a new name, Peter (Greek: *petros*), which can be translated "little rock."

FALLS NEAR CAESAREA PHILIPPI

In the Hebrew Scriptures, God is repeatedly referred to as the big rock, as in Psalm 18: *The LORD is my rock and my fortress and my deliverer, my God, my rock, in whom I take refuge, my shield, and the horn of my salvation, my stronghold.* (Psalm 18:2) Taking a common family name is an ancient and modern symbol of Covenant relationship. When Jesus gave Simon the name Peter, it was as if he was giving Simon his heavenly Father's name as a sign of the profound family Covenant between them. Jesus went on to declare: *"you are Peter, and on this rock I will build my church, and the gates of hell shall not prevail against it."* (Matthew 16:18)

It is no coincidence that, speaking near the Cave of Pan, Jesus described their opposition as "the gates of hell." But Jesus tells us that he is the builder of a church so powerful it can storm even the demonic strongholds of paganism itself. Jesus went on to offer Peter the keys to the Kingdom of heaven, a symbol of the authority to represent their Father the King and exercise his authority. This is where we find the power to overcome even the gates of hell.

We should remember Jesus was trained as a builder and came from an extended family of builders in Nazareth. Clearly, he was evoking his earthly family's business, as well as his heavenly family's name, in this profound declaration. When he entered into Simon and Andrew's extended family and called them to follow him, he used the imagery of their family business, fishing. Jesus transformed their family business into a Kingdom business when he told them he would teach them to fish for people. Now Jesus is inviting them into his heavenly family and inviting them to be part of his Father's family business, building.

We have noted that when Jesus was twelve and his parents found him among the rabbis in the Temple courts, his response to them can be translated two ways: *"Did you not know that I must be in my Father's house?"* or *"Did you not know that I had to be about my Father's business?"* (Luke 2:49) Even at this young age, Jesus was clear that God was his Father and that his life was to be about fulfilling his Father's business. When Jesus began to proclaim, *"the Kingdom of God has come near,"* it was nothing less than the declaration that the Father's business is the rebuilding of the entire created order!

Jesus' definition of the "Kingdom of God" is where God's will is being done on earth as it is in heaven (Matthew 6:10). Ever since the fall of Adam and Eve, the universe has been thrown into chaos, and God's perfect intention for his creation has been thwarted. But now Jesus declared that things were going to change, that heaven was invading earth, and that God has begun restoring his creation to his original design. Years later, the risen and glorified Jesus gave a powerful vision to John in which the Father declares from his throne: *"Behold, I am making all things new."* (Revelation 21:5) What is Jesus' plan for making all things new and fully establishing the reign of God as King? Building the church. And what is the church that Jesus is building? It is a new kind of extended family that seeks and saves the lost, where everyone is graciously welcomed, and where disciples learn to make disciples who are trained to carry out Jesus' mission. Paul describes this epic rebuilding project when he tells the Ephesians that Jesus has made us *members of the household of God, built on the foundation of the apostles and prophets, Christ Jesus himself being the cornerstone* (Ephesians 2:19-20).

Whether Peter fully comprehended all this at the time is unclear, but it is clear he took his Covenantal oneness with Jesus to heart. Jesus went on to tell the disciples that he had to go to Jerusalem and there he would suffer, die, and rise again. When Peter heard this, he did what any good Covenantal partner would do—he stood up for his rabbi: *"Far be it from you, Lord! This shall never happen to you."* (Matthew 16:22) Remember, this is what family is, protection and provision. Peter was determined that no one was going to hurt Jesus on his watch. We can see that Peter, along with the rest of the disciples, still did not understand the true nature of Jesus' Kingdom. Contrary to their assumptions, he was not going to Jerusalem to move into the Palace of Herod, throw out the Romans, and set up a temporal kingdom. The Way of Jesus is the way of the cross. Jesus was going to lay down his life to establish a Kingdom that nothing and no one could thwart, a Kingdom that will result in the reconstruction of the entire created order.

When Peter rebuked Jesus, he was literally tempting Jesus to deny the difficult destiny he dreaded, the path so painful he would sweat blood seeking to avoid it. Jesus' response reflected the importance of understanding how the Father's cosmic rebuilding project would be undertaken: *"Get behind me, Satan! You are a hindrance to me. For you are not setting your mind on the things of God, but on the things of man."* (Matthew 16:23) The word translated "hindrance" here is *skandalon*, which literally means "stumbling stone." Jesus was making it clear to Peter and all the disciples that they had a choice. They could submit to sacrifice as the way of Jesus and be shaped into a building block in his new creation, or they could resist Jesus' call to lay down their lives and become a stumbling stone, hindering the coming of God's Kingdom. Jesus made the nature of his call crystal clear: *"If anyone would come after me, let him deny himself and take up his cross and follow me."* (Matthew 16:24)

We each need to consider Jesus' words carefully. It is not enough to simply welcome Jesus into what we are doing and ask him to bless it. Jesus is inviting us to join the Father's great family, and he's challenging us to join in his family business. Are we going to be building blocks or stumbling stones? Are we going to be about our business or the Father's business? Are we going to build our own kingdom or allow Jesus to use us in the building of his Kingdom? The question is ultimately whether we are willing to take up our cross and follow him.

 # THE LIFE

THE BEAT OF A DIFFERENT DRUM

Patience has never been a particularly abundant virtue in my life. I usually have a pretty good idea about how things should be, and I am generally motivated to move things in that direction. Normally, I want that to happen as soon as possible. The result is that I often move too fast, push too hard, and work too long. This has contributed to what I acknowledge as my workaholic tendencies.

Another factor is that I generally want people to like me. I like approval, especially from people I respect. This often drives me to be ambitious and seek success, whatever the price. Growing up mostly in American culture only reinforced these tendencies. In America we are lauded for ambition, drive, and success. Whether it was winning a horse show ribbon, getting good grades, making the first string on the football team, or simply beating my sister at Monopoly, I was willing to work hard and make sacrifices in order to succeed.

What drives you? I would like to think that my motivations in life have matured over time. I hope that I am more compelled by love for God, compassion for others, and faith in the possibilities of God's purposes than I used to be. But I recognize those less admirable motivations are still at work in my soul. We are complex people, and there is never just one thing that shapes our character and actions. One way to consider your motivations is to look at the rhythms of your life. How you spend your time will tell you what you actually value.

When we were first married, Pam and I were both aware of my tendency to overcommit and overwork. As a young pastor, I was passionate about the work I was called to, but I recognized that my marriage and family were more important than my ministry at church and had to come first. We talked about strategies for achieving healthy balance between work and family. These mainly involved setting up boundaries to protect our marriage and family from the imbalance that often seems to plague church leaders and threaten their families. This approach usually left Pam responsible for patrolling our boundaries and me focused on walking the tightrope of balance in the midst of a demanding ministry. With great effort we momentarily achieved the elusive "healthy balance," but then something happened to knock us off kilter. I would careen into being too busy, Pam would feel resentful and reassert our agreed-upon boundaries, and I would repent and get back on the tightrope. It felt exhausting and we never seemed to make much progress… until we decided to pattern our lives after Jesus' fruitful rhythms.

Jesus lived the most fruitful life in all of human history. No one has impacted the world and the people in it for good more significantly. The secret of Jesus' "success" was not trying harder and working longer hours. As we have seen, Jesus often started by resting, not working. He launched his public ministry with a quick dip in the Jordan River followed by more than a month of solitude in the desert. His follow-up to his debut in Capernaum was spending the next morning alone with God. Despite greater demands than most of us will ever experience, Jesus maintained a rhythm of abiding and bearing fruit that literally changed the world and continues to transform countless lives today. Jesus lived out the principle he taught his disciples, that choosing to abide regularly with the Father leads to a healthier, more fruitful life. Once Pam and I came to understand the secret of Jesus' fruitfulness, we have been pursuing that way of life one step of faith at a time. It has been an incredible blessing.

First, we started by establishing a daily rhythm of abiding in Scripture reflection and prayer together. We had always sought this pattern, but were never very consistent, primarily because we were doing it alone and had no supportive accountability. We decided to get on the same daily Bible reading plan and to support each other in making this a consistent rhythm. Next, we decided to observe a 24-hour day of rest each week, from sundown to sundown, and treat it as a gift from God that we needed to protect from the enemy who wanted to rob us of this weekly blessing. Now we look forward to this abiding time as the best day of the week. Our one "rule" is that we can only do things we genuinely want to do on the Sabbath. We continued by becoming more proactive about our schedule and recognizing coming seasons that would be especially busy, preempting them with additional days of rest and retreat to abide. We also started planning a year ahead to make sure that our more significant times of rest and abiding were strategically placed to bring the most fruitfulness.

One of the advantages of Jesus' rhythms was that unexpected events didn't seem to affect him the way they did me on my precarious tightrope. When the crowd rushed around the shore of the lake and met Jesus and the disciples at their Tabgha retreat center, Jesus was able to see what the Father was doing and respond with *compassion for them, because they were harassed and helpless, like sheep without a shepherd.* (Matthew 9:36) Likewise, when they went away to Tyre and Sidon because no one knew them there, Jesus was able to respond positively to the Syrophoenician woman's request for her daughter's healing once she expressed her faith (Mark 7:24-30). As Pam and I started to more intentionally follow the rhythms of Jesus daily, weekly, occasionally, and seasonally, our marriage and family life became healthier and more fruitful. This newfound health and fruitfulness were more durable to the rough and tumble realities of real life than boundaries and balance ever were.

The more I learn to live in Jesus-shaped rhythms, the more I find my soul freed from the unhealthy things that used to drive me. I am less frantic about trying to succeed because I am more connected to a Father who loves me just as I am. I am less driven to meet the expectations of others because I am more in touch with the Father's calling in my life. When I think of these rhythms like a pendulum swinging back and forth between abiding and bearing fruit, a certain kind of momentum builds, and it is not difficult to maintain the rhythms once they are going. If something happens to knock us out of rhythm for a moment, that momentum picks up and the pendulum comes back into a healthy rhythm. [53]

WHAT ARE YOU BUILDING?

One of the reasons I have come to believe that rhythms are so important in the life of a Jesus follower is that our rhythms reflect what we value. They can be a barometer to help you measure what you are investing your life in and why. If you are primarily focused on your own success and the approval of others, your rhythms are likely to reflect that in being driven, working too hard, and ultimately hurting the people close to you. But maybe you have the opposite challenge. Maybe you find yourself apathetic, unmotivated, and struggling with laziness. This can reflect a narcissistic tendency in which we are self-focused and driven more by hedonistic values than Kingdom values. Many of us have made it a goal to establish the most comfortable, secure, stress-free life possible. Our choices revolve around how things make us feel and what serves our own perceived best interests.

[53] See Mike Breen, *Building a Discipling Culture,* 3rd ed. (Pawleys Island, 3DM Publishing, 2016), 123-137.

To follow Jesus is to reject both of these motivations in life. Discipleship is the decision not to build your own kingdom, be it a kingdom of achievement or a kingdom of comfort. The Way of Jesus is to seek God's Kingdom above all else. This will profoundly shape our motivations and the rhythms they produce. Jesus said it this way: *"Therefore do not be anxious, saying, 'What shall we eat?' or 'What shall we drink?' or 'What shall we wear?' For the Gentiles seek after all these things, and your heavenly Father knows that you need them all. But seek first the kingdom of God and his righteousness, and all these things will be added to you."* (Matthew 6:31-33) You can worry, or you can live in peace. You can be a stumbling stone, or you can be a building block. You can seek your own kingdom, or you can seek God's Kingdom.

In the end it comes down to the question Peter had to answer. Am I willing to take up my cross and follow Jesus all the way to Jerusalem, no matter the cost? Peter made the right choice, and we would be wise to follow his example.

PART IV

JESUS' TRIUMPH:
THE END IS THE BEGINNING

"See, we are going up to Jerusalem, and the Son of Man will be delivered over to the chief priests and the scribes, and they will condemn him to death and deliver him over to the Gentiles. And they will mock him and spit on him, and flog him and kill him. And after three days he will rise."
(Mark 10:33-34)

PILGRIMS ENTERING JERUSALEM

CHAPTER TEN

JESUS' CAPITOL: CITY OF DESTINY

From that time Jesus began to show his disciples that he must go to Jerusalem... (Matthew 16:21)

THE END OF THE STORY?

Jesus spent the vast majority of his thirty-some years on earth living in Nazareth, studying at the synagogue and working in the family business. John reports three different Passovers during the public ministry of Jesus, so we can assume about three years passed between his baptism and his resurrection. The lion's share of these years was spent in the towns and villages of Galilee, seeking after what Jesus referred to as *"the lost sheep of the house of Israel"* (Matthew 15:24). It is instructive to note that all four Gospel writers devote a disproportionate amount of words to describe the last weeks of Jesus' earthly life as he traveled to Jerusalem to spend his final Passover in the Holy City. This reminds us that the final events of Jesus' life are what make the rest of his extraordinary life so revolutionary and world-changing.

Jesus lived to show us how we are meant to live, but he is much more than just a great teacher with unique spiritual and ethical insights. Jesus called us to follow him, but he is much more than another Jewish rabbi with a new interpretation of the Law. The eyewitness accounts are unanimous in reporting that Jesus was nailed to a cross and died; and that, three days later, he rose from the dead, gloriously alive and eternally transformed. The cross and the empty tomb definitively confirm that Jesus is who he claimed to be, the divine Son of Man, God incarnate, who fully submitted to his Father's will and defeated the power of evil that has held the whole creation in bondage since the fall of Adam and Eve. Jesus triumphed over sin, death, hell, and the devil.

Jesus has not only accomplished the salvation of the world by his gracious sacrifice and inaugurated God's victorious reign, but he also shows us that those who decide to follow him will inevitably have to take up a cross and die to themselves if they hope to live the life he lived. It also means that those who follow him can learn to walk in the same power that raised him from the dead, live a life that reflects his will on earth as it is in heaven, and know that their eternal destiny lies in the fulness of the Kingdom of God!

For some, Jesus' extraordinary life is little more than a historical curiosity to admire and discuss. But those who understand how his story ends realize that Jesus is the key to discovering how our story is just beginning. And so, with Jesus, we set our faces toward Jerusalem to discover all that he has for us there.

 THE WAY

THE PILGRIM ROUTE

We noted that Jesus grew up making the journey from Nazareth to Jerusalem with his family every year for the great Passover festival. Jesus' family traveled south and east from Nazareth through the Jezreel Valley, connecting with the pilgrimage route that ran down through the Jordan Valley on the west bank of the river. This route was longer than the road which went directly south through Samaria, but it avoided the rigors of the mountainous terrain in the central part of the country and allowed them to minimize confrontations with less-than-friendly Samaritans. Once arriving in Jericho, they turned westward and took the Jericho-Jerusalem road that ran along the southern ridge of the Wadi Kelt, leading to Bethany, Bethphage, and then over the Mount of Olives into the city of Jerusalem. This final stretch of the journey was the Ascent of Adummim (Hebrew for "red"), a name that evoked the color of the limestone mountains through which it passes (Joshua 15:7). It may also have had a double meaning as the "ascent of blood," because it was a notoriously dangerous stretch of road.

The journey from Nazareth to Jerusalem is about 100 miles, which means it would have been a five-day journey on foot, longer if you stopped to visit family and friends along the way. The route from Nazareth to Jericho follows a drop of 1,700 feet in elevation, but the final day's journey, 15 miles from Jericho over the Mount of Olives, entails a climb of 3550 feet. This was not an easy journey, but Jesus made dozens of these trips in his lifetime. John tells us that during Jesus' public ministry, he made at least four trips to Jerusalem, participating in two Passovers, the Feast of Dedication (Hannakah), and an unnamed feast (John 2:13, 10:22, 12:12. Cf. a third Passover in 5:1). Each time he visited the Holy City, Jesus went into the courts of the Temple to teach the crowds that had gathered there for the festival.

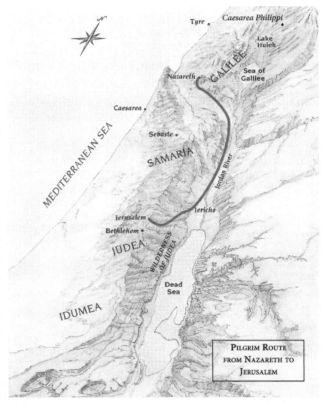

PILGRIM ROUTE FROM NAZARETH TO JERUSALEM

This pilgrim road running through the Jordan Valley was the normal route for Jesus and the disciples as they made their way back and forth between Galilee and Jerusalem, as it was for most Galilean Jews. However, John tells us that on at least one occasion Jesus *had to pass through Samaria* on his way back to Galilee (John 4:4). This is not describing a geographical necessity, but a divine imperative. The Spirit of God was leading Jesus to take the more challenging central route through Samaritan territory, apparently so he would encounter the Samaritan woman at the well who would in turn transform her entire town (John 4:1-42).

On his final journey to Jerusalem, Jesus and the disciples took the familiar pilgrim route through the Jordan Valley, but apparently that was not Jesus' initial plan. Luke tells us that when Jesus set out for Jerusalem, he sent messengers ahead into a Samaritan village to make arrangements for them there, but the people would not receive them because they were on a pilgrimage to Jerusalem (Luke 9:51-53). James and John wanted to retaliate with spiritual fireworks, but Jesus simply changed course and headed south through the

Jordan Valley. Luke devotes the next ten chapters of his Gospel to describing events as they made their way to Jerusalem, but it is clear that he is including thematic passages that probably took place at other times in Jesus' ministry as well (cf. Luke 10:38-42).

Regardless of different chronologies, Matthew, Mark, and Luke are unanimous in describing Jesus' visit to Jericho just before he and his disciples made their final ascent up the Jericho-Jerusalem pilgrim road. In Jericho Jesus healed blind Bartimaeus and shockingly spent the night in the home of the notorious chief tax collector Zacchaeus, before heading up the Ascent of Adummim to Bethany. As they left Jericho, Jesus and the disciples passed Herod's winter palace, turned west and began the steep climb up the desert road to Jerusalem, along with the throngs of Passover pilgrims who would have been traveling the same route. This road is the setting of Jesus' famous parable of the Good Samaritan, which was fitting because it was known as a dangerous area where bandits were waiting to attack wealthy pilgrims carrying offerings for the Temple (Luke 10:30-37).

ACCOMMODATIONS IN JERUSALEM

When Jesus' family visited Jerusalem on their annual Passover pilgrimage, they would have stayed with relatives in the area, if possible. Mary's relatives, Zechariah, Elizabeth, and their son John lived in the hill country just outside of Jerusalem. If it wasn't too

HEROD'S WINTER PALACE AND THE ASCENT OF ADUMMIM

far away, we can presume they would have stayed with them. When Jesus and his disciples visited Jerusalem, they seemed to stay with the extended family of Mary, Martha, and Lazarus in the village of Bethany, on the eastern slope of the Mount of Olives opposite Jerusalem. We don't know how they first connected, but John described the depth of their relationship when he wrote, *"Jesus loved Martha and her sister and Lazarus"* (John 11:5). In the first half of his Gospel, Luke tells us about an incident that took place in their home when Martha was critical of her sister, but Jesus affirmed Mary's choice to assume the position of a disciple at his feet (Luke 10:38-42). This must have taken place during one of Jesus' earlier visits to Jerusalem. Later in Jesus' ministry, John tells us of an emergency visit he and the disciples made to Bethany to visit Mary and Martha due to Lazarus' death, despite the growing danger from the religious leaders nearby in Jerusalem (John 11:1-16). All four Gospel writers confirm that Jesus and the disciples stayed with Mary's family in Bethany during their final Passover visit, and John specifies that they arrived there six days before the festival began (John 12:1).

JERUSALEM AND THE MOUNT OF OLIVES

Their daily rhythm during that final Passover was to walk the 1.75 miles over the Mount of Olives, through the Kidron Valley, and up into the Temple courts, where Jesus would teach each day. At the end of the day, they made their way back over the Mount of Olives to Bethany to stay with the extended family there (Mark 11:11-12). Luke indicates that sometimes they would stay the night on the Mount of Olives instead of going all the way back into Bethany, as they did on the night of Jesus' arrest (Luke 22:39). Just as Jesus entered into the extended family of Simon and Andrew and their *oikos* became his base of operations, so it seems that this family in Bethany functioned in the same way when Jesus and the disciples were visiting Jerusalem.

A CITY LIKE NO OTHER

From the time King David and his elite troops scaled up the water system, captured the city of Jebus, and made it the capital of Israel, the city of Jerusalem has played a central role in the story of God's people. The Jebusites had fortified a steep ridge bounded by the Kidron Valley and the Tyropoeon Valley, next to the Gihon Spring, just a few miles north of Bethlehem near the border between the territory of Benjamin and Judah. David built his palace at the north end of the newly captured city. Then he purchased the threshing floor of Aruna, a little further north on the top of Mount Zion, as a building site for the Temple. David's son Solomon built the first Temple there,

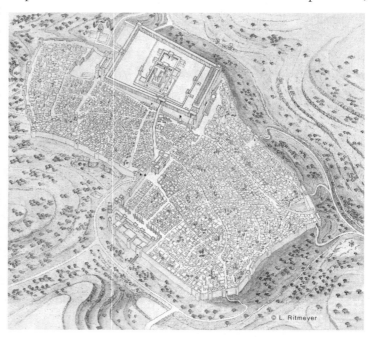

with the huge flat rock at the top of the mountain serving as the floor of the Holy of Holies. This cemented Jerusalem's place as the Holy City where people could come from all over the world to meet with God.

Solomon extended the walls of the city northward to include Mount Zion and the newly built Temple. As the Israelites centralized their sacrificial system at the Temple, Jerusalem became increasingly important. The priests traveled to Jerusalem twice a year to carry

JERUSALEM IN THE TIME OF JESUS

out their two weeks of annual service in the Temple courts. Great throngs of Jewish pilgrims came every year for the three great festivals, *Pesach* (Passover), *Shavuot* (Pentecost), and *Sukkot* (Tabernacles). Huge crowds gathered in the courtyards surrounding the Temple to hear rabbis teach and participate in the rituals. This is how Jesus came to know Jerusalem, as his family came from Nazareth for Passover every year.

Over the centuries Jerusalem expanded onto the ridge west of the City of David, between the Tyropoeon and Hinnom Valleys. After the devastating Babylonian destruction of the city and its Temple, the city shrank back to its original size, gradually expanding again after the Jews' return from exile and the rebuilding of the Temple. By the time of Jesus, the walls of Jerusalem enclosed a larger city than ever. Herod the Great had built his enormous palace on the height of the western hill and developed an advanced water system bringing in water to all parts of the city from the abundant springs south of Bethlehem. But the greatest of all Herod's impressive building projects was the rebuilt Temple and expansion of the Temple courts.

THE TEMPLE MOUNT

Mount Zion is a ridge that drops steeply into the Kidron Valley on the east and less steeply into the Tyropoeon Valley on the west. When Solomon built his Temple at the top of this ridge, he had to build large retaining walls to support a level courtyard surrounding the sacred precinct, since the hill sloped away in every direction. When the exiles returned from Babylon and rebuilt the Temple under Zerubbabel, they were poor and could only afford a pale reflection of Solomon's glory. Some five hundred years later, Herod was determined to outdo the glory of Solomon by rebuilding the Temple, training priests as stonemasons so the sacrifices would not cease during construction.

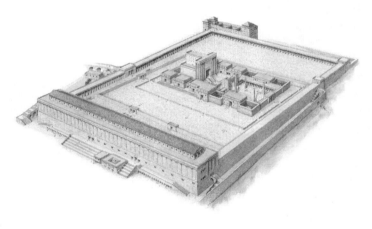

HEROD'S TEMPLE MOUNT

Josephus described Herod's daunting project this way, "And now Herod, in the eighteenth year of his reign, and after the acts already mentioned, undertook a very great work, that is, to build of himself the temple of God, and make it larger in compass, and to raise it to a most magnificent altitude, as esteeming it to be the most glorious of all his actions, as it really was, to bring it to perfection; and that this would be sufficient for an everlasting memorial of him... He also encompassed the entire temple with very large cloisters, contriving them to be in a due proportion thereto; and he laid out larger sums of money upon them than had been done before him, till it seemed that no one else had so greatly adorned the temple as he had done. There was a large wall to both the cloisters, which wall was itself the most prodigious work that was ever heard of by man." [54]

SOLOMON'S PORTICO ON THE TEMPLE MOUNT

Herod expanded the courts surrounding the Temple to the size of twenty-five American football fields, nearly engulfing the entire mountain. On the eastern, southern, and western sides, he built retaining walls reaching more than 100 feet high to support this huge courtyard. To stabilize these massive walls, he used enormous blocks of limestone cut from the nearby hills, the largest of which weighs over 500 tons!

Herod built 30-foot-tall double-wide porticoes surrounding the massive courtyard, the roof of which was supported by beautifully carved stone pillars, creating nearly a mile

[54] Flavius Josephus, *Antiquities of the Jews,* trans. William Whiston, (Delmarva, 2016), Book 15, Chapter 3, Section 1, Digital.

of covered space, protected from sun in the summer and rain in the winter. The acoustics of the solid back wall and open front wall of a portico was well-suited to public speaking. In these huge porticoes surrounding the Temple the crowds gathered to listen to Jesus teach and watch him debate the religious leaders. John specifies that Jesus taught in "*Solomon's Portico*" during the Feast of Dedication, which fell in December at that time (John 10:23). This was the eastern portico which would have shielded the crowds from the cold easterly winds so common in the winter. Luke tells us that Solomon's Portico is where the early church continued to gather in large groups to hear the teaching of the Apostles (Acts 3:11; 5:12).

The south end of the Temple platform was spanned by the towering Royal Stoa, some 800 feet long and rising another 100 feet above the Temple courts. According to Josephus 162 columns supported the roof, each one so large it took three men to reach their arms around the circumference. On the northwest corner of the Temple Mount, Herod built a large stronghold with four towers and named it the Antonia Fortress, after his friend and patron Mark Antony. This served as the garrison for the Roman legions who watched over Jerusalem, and it gave them immediate access to the Temple courts.

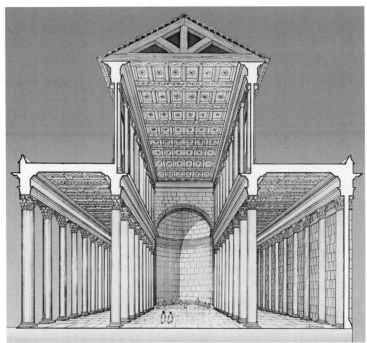

ROYAL STOA ON THE TEMPLE MOUNT

Entrance to the Temple platform came through eight monumental gates: four in the western wall, two in the southern wall, and two in the eastern wall. Three of these gates, Warren's Gate, Barclay's Gate, and the Golden Gate, stood over 25 feet high and opened into subterranean staircases which led to the top of the platform. On the western side, the Zion Bridge spanned the Tyropoeon Valley, giving access directly at the level of the plat-form. This bridge carried an aqueduct and was designed for the High Priest and Chief Priests to enter the Temple from the upper city without becoming ritually unclean from having to walk through the streets. In the south-west corner was a huge staircase carried by a massive barrel vault, known as Robinson's

THE WESTERN WALL OF THE TEMPLE MOUNT

Arch. It gave access directly into the Royal Stoa. This would have been the preferred entrance for those going to the Temple to conduct business or meet with someone.

The focus of religious Jews in Jerusalem today is a 187-foot long stretch of a monumental wall located on the western side of the Temple Mount between Warren's Gate and the Zion Bridge. Its base consists of 24 courses of enormous limestone blocks cut by Herod's stonemasons in the first century. On top of this sit courses of smaller stones from the Early Muslim through the Ottoman periods. The Western Wall is a small section of the 1600-foot long western retaining wall that Herod built to support his expanded plaza surrounding the Temple above. Jews come here to pray because it is as close as they can get to the ancient Holy of Holies, and they believe the presence of God is available to them here in a way he is not present anywhere else in the world. The practice of placing prayers written on small pieces of paper into the crevices of the wall originated with Jews who could not visit Jerusalem and thus asked pilgrims to take their prayer to the wall in the hope that God would hear and answer.

Along the southern wall stood two enormous staircases which led to two tunnels that followed the slope of the mountain and opened up in the midst of the outer Temple courts. Known as the Hulda Gates in the Mishnah, Josephus refers to the westernmost tunnel as the Double Gate and the easternmost tunnel as the Triple Gate, reflecting their design. These served as the primary entrance and exit for pilgrims going to the Temple for religious reasons. It is up these staircases and through these tunnels that Jesus and the disciples would have entered and exited the Temple courts when he taught in Jerusalem. Given the size, scope, and intricate design of this gigantic complex, it is little wonder the Galilean disciples of Jesus looked around at all of this and said, *"Look, Teacher, what wonderful stones and what wonderful buildings!"* (Mark 13:1) Still today the ruins of this great structure evoke similar wonder and amazement. This is where Jesus centered his teaching ministry while in Jerusalem.

THE WATER SYSTEM

The original Jebusite city was located on the ridge that rises up next to the sole spring in this area, named the *Gihon Spring* (Hebrew for "gushing") due to its intermittent flow. The ancient Jebusites and Israelites went to great lengths to fortify this spring, since it was their only source of water. In the face of an impending siege by the Assyrians, King Hezekiah dug an elaborate tunnel, bringing the water inside the walls

THE POOL OF SILOAM

of the city to the Pool of Siloam (2 Kings 20:20). This rock-cut passage runs for a third of a mile, and it is still possible to walk through it today. For many years the small pool at the end of Hezekiah's Tunnel was assumed to be the ancient Pool of Siloam, but recently the first-century pool has been discovered just to the south of the tunnel's terminus. It is a stepped pool abutting the southern city wall with a colonnaded building at the northern end. For centuries this was the only source of fresh water in Jerusalem, and it was still a major source of water in the time of Jesus. This is the pool where Jesus sent the blind man to wash, and he came back seeing (John 9:1-7).

A long stepped first-century street was also recently discovered, leading north from the Pool of Siloam up the City of David to the Temple Mount. This was the street used by the Chief Priests during the festival of *Succoth*. They processed to Siloam each morning, and the High Priest scooped up water in a golden pitcher and returned to the Temple to pour the water into the silver basins at the altar. In the drainage channel underneath this street, archaeologists discovered a tiny golden bell, just like those sown into the hem of the High Priest's robe. We can imagine it coming loose during one of those processions, dropping through the street drain, and lodging between the stones in the channel below, only to be discovered 2000 years later. John tells us that it was during the festival of *Sukkoth*, precisely when these rituals were being carried out, that Jesus stood up in the Temple courts and cried out, *"If anyone thirsts, let him come to me and drink. Whoever believes in me, as the Scripture has said, 'Out of his heart will flow rivers of living water.'"* (John 7:37-38)

By the first century BC, Jerusalem had outgrown its water supply, so Herod the Great, building on the earlier work of the Hasmoneans, devised an elaborate system to bring water from several large springs south of Bethlehem into the city. They constructed three huge rock-cut storage pools ten miles south of Jerusalem, erroneously called Solomon's Pools. These pools were fed by four springs and could hold 75 million gallons of water. Utilizing advanced Roman engineering, five aqueducts carried this water through some fifty miles of rock-cut tunnels, over arched bridges, and through sealed stone hydraulic pipes into Jerusalem. This water flowed first into the Sultan's Pool, just outside of the western wall of the city, then into Hezekiah's Pool, the Struthion Pool, the Sheep's Pool, and the Pools of Bethesda, before filling the huge cisterns cut in the rock underneath the Temple Mount.

John tells us that five porticoes surrounded the Pools of Bethesda. Many scholars questioned the historicity of this description, since no pentagon-shaped pools or porticoes are known from the ancient world. However, once the archaeologists began to excavate, they found two pools end to end, with porticoes around all four sides, and one across the dam separating the two pools, thus confirming two pools with five porticoes! Even more interestingly, they discovered a large pagan healing shrine dedicated to the god

Asclepius beside the pools.

This shrine consisted of a small temple, a series of smaller pools, and small caves. Sick and injured people would come here desperate for healing. They made an offering to the god, took a bath in one of the small pools, partook of a halluci-nogenic drink, and fell

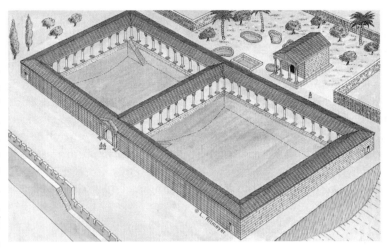

POOLS OF BETHSEDA

asleep in a small cave where they hoped Asclepius would come in their dreams and heal them. Next to this healing center in one of the porticoes surrounding the Pools of Bethesda is the place where Jesus came to heal the paralyzed man in spite of his utter lack of faith (John 5:1-9).

As we can see, even at first glance, Jerusalem is a singularly unique and sacred city with a history like none other. This is where Jesus came with his disciples to celebrate his final Passover festival and fulfill his ultimate destiny.

 # THE TRUTH

JESUS' JERUSALEM OIKOS

When Jesus entered Jericho, his final journey to Jerusalem was almost complete. In an honor/shame culture where hospitality is the highest value, the privilege of hosting a visiting dignitary is a jealously guarded feather in your cap. We can be sure the leading Pharisee of Jericho had already prepared a banquet in the dining room of his *oikos* home and invited the leading citizens in anticipation of hosting Jesus and his disciples for the night. He would have sought the honor bestowed by Jesus' presence in his home. By contrast the leading tax collector of the region, Zacchaeus, was humiliating himself by climbing a tree just so he could see Jesus pass by. Even today in the Middle East, climbing a tree is considered child's play. A grown man climbing a tree is seen as foolish and weak. Apparently, Zacchaeus didn't care! When Jesus entered Jericho, he saw who his real person of peace was. Jesus shocked the entire city and offended the religious elites by calling Zacchaeus down from his tree and inviting himself over for dinner (Luke 19:1-10). Everyone tried to figure out what this unconventional Rabbi from Nazareth was doing. However, Jesus was continuing the same pattern he had followed since the beginning of his public ministry: offering his peace, looking for those who respond positively, then going, eating, and staying with his people of peace, regardless of their moral reputation or social standing (Luke 10:5-9).

The fact that Zacchaeus hurried down from his tree, threw an impromptu banquet for Jesus, and made such a dramatic pledge to right his countless wrongs to the people of Jericho is simply a measure of what a radical act of grace it was for Jesus to invite himself into that extended family home. It was the last thing anyone expected, and the people of Jericho would certainly never forget what he did! This is the Way of Jesus. Again and again we see him welcoming the outcasts, touching those the religious leaders labeled unclean, entering the homes of those considered immoral, and demonstrating the lavish acceptance of the New Covenant and the radical inclusion of the Kingdom of God. Those who follow Jesus will learn to do the same.

However, Jesus did not stick around to watch Zacchaeus' new way of life take shape, because his face was set toward Jerusalem, and he knew his destiny awaited him there. So Jesus led his disciples out of the city, followed the Roman road as it turned west past Herod's winter palace at the mouth of Wadi Qelt, and began the arduous climb through the murderous red rock hills of the Ascent of Adummim, as he had done so many times before. As they walked the Jerusalem-Jericho road, it seems likely the disciples would have recalled Jesus' vivid story of the unlikely Samaritan who stopped along this way to bandage the wounds of the beaten traveler that the Priest and Levite had left for dead.

As they climbed the eastern slope of the Mount of Olives and finally saw the town of Bethany up ahead, even these hardened travelers would have been glad for the thought of a warm meal and a comfortable bed. If all we had was the Synoptic Gospels, we would assume they proceeded directly to Jesus' dramatic entrance into Jerusalem on a donkey, but John tells us they stopped in Bethany for a banquet six days before the Passover (John 12:1-2). Given all the other references we have to Jesus' relationship with Mary, Martha, and Lazarus, we can safely assume that Jesus and the disciples stayed with them in Bethany.

The *oikos* of these three in Bethany had become Jesus' home base during his various visits to Jerusalem. However, Matthew and Mark tell us this welcome banquet in Bethany was hosted not by Jesus' Jerusalem *oikos*, but by someone named Simon the Leper (Matthew 26:6-13; Mark 14:3-9). Since this man was able to host a banquet in his home without transmitting uncleanness to all his guest, he must be one of the lepers Jesus healed, showing gratitude to his healer! John tells us that Lazarus was also an invited guest at this banquet, while his sister Martha was helping to serve the meal. This sets the stage for Mary's dramatic act of devotion at the dinner.

During an earlier visit when Jesus was teaching in their home, Mary broke the expected cultural norms by sitting at Jesus' feet, which was explicitly the posture of a disciple (Luke 10:38-42; Acts 22:3). Since women were never recognized as disciples, this was a radical demonstration of Mary's determination

THE CHURCH OF LAZARUS IN BETHANY

to follow Jesus regardless of the cultural obstacles. While most people interpret Martha's objection to her sister's posture as purely a practical matter of needing more help with the meal, it is clear from a cultural perspective that Martha was also prompting Jesus to scold Mary for her impertinence in assuming the position of a disciple. Instead Jesus reproved Martha and affirmed Mary as a female disciple when he said, *"Martha, Martha, you are anxious and troubled about many things, but one thing is necessary. Mary has chosen the good portion, which will not be taken away from her."* (Luke 10:41-42)

This final banquet at Simon the Leper's home took place six days before the Passover (John 12:1-8). Although the Passover dinner began after sundown and the Sabbath meal could take place at midday, in first-century Palestine a banquet normally began in the late afternoon. This allowed guests to travel to the host's home during the daylight, even though the meal often stretched on past midnight. As we discussed in Chapter 3, Jesus and the disciples celebrated the Passover on a Thursday night/Friday, which puts this banquet on a Saturday if it took place at midday or in the afternoon. This means that Jesus and the disciples would have arrived in Bethany at the end of a long travel day on Friday, spent the night in the *oikos* of Mary, Martha, and Lazarus, and then attended this banquet at the home Simon the Leper the following afternoon.

Once again Mary broke the cultural norms when she appeared at the banquet, not serving like her sister, but preparing to make a dramatic demonstration of her devotion to Jesus. Perhaps she had heard reports of the "sinful woman" in Galilee who had broken down in tears of gratitude during a banquet for Jesus in the home of Simon the Pharisee, wiping his feet with her hair and anointing him with perfumed ointment (Luke 7:36-38). The only women who were normally present at a first-century banquet, besides those who served, were prostitutes who wore their long hair down and uncovered. Apparently, Mary was less concerned about her reputation than showing her devotion to Jesus!

It was customary at a special banquet for each guest to receive a drop of scented oil on his head as a sign of blessing and to add a sweet aroma to the proceedings. Mary went much further when she broke open this stone vial of precious ointment, costing nearly a year's wages! Breaking the vial tells us that she didn't hold back any but poured all of it out on Jesus' head and feet. Then, adding to the shock of this act, she uncovered and let her hair down to wipe Jesus' feet, demonstrating the unbridled nature of her love and devotion for Jesus. It seems to evoke King David's lack of concern that he might be considered *"contemptible"* when he expressed his devotion to the Lord by dancing before the Ark of the Covenant as it was also about to enter Jerusalem (2 Samuel 6:12-22).

Like David's critical wife Michal, Judas voiced the criticism others were thinking, that this was a wasteful act of decadence. But, once again, Jesus defended Mary's provocative actions, interpreting it as a prophetic demonstration when he said, *"Why do you trouble the woman? For she has done a beautiful thing to me. For you always have the poor with you, but you will not always have me. In pouring this ointment on my body, she has done it to prepare me for burial. Truly, I say to you, wherever this gospel is proclaimed in the whole world, what she has done will also be told in memory of her."* (Matthew 26:10-13) Jesus was right; he was soon to die, and we are still talking about this remarkable woman two thousand years later! Mary is truly an example of a disciple who was completely devoted to following Jesus and was willing to offer everything she had to demonstrate her love for him, regardless of the consequences. What are we willing to offer, and what consequences are we willing to face?

A DRAMATIC ENTRANCE

It was probably the next day, a Sunday, when Jesus chose to make a deliberately symbolic entrance into Jerusalem. Appropriately, this entrance is traditionally recounted every year on Palm Sunday. The prophet Zechariah foretold that the Messiah would

JERUSALEM FROM THE MOUNT OF OLIVES

enter Jerusalem over the Mount of Olives, *"On that day his feet shall stand on the Mount of Olives that lies before Jerusalem on the east..."* (Zechariah 14:4). He also proclaimed the Messiah would enter Jerusalem on a young donkey: *"Rejoice greatly, O daughter of Zion! Shout aloud, O daughter of Jerusalem! Behold, your king is coming to you; righteous and having salvation is he, humble and mounted on a donkey, on a colt, the foal of a donkey."* (Zechariah 9:9) It is no accident that Jesus chose to enter Jerusalem in exactly the place and the way that Zechariah foretold!

The fact that there was a young donkey tied up in the nearby village of Bethphage and that there was a set password (*"the Lord has need of it"*) that compelled its owners to release it tells us that Jesus carefully planned his entrance as a public announcement that he was, indeed, the long-awaited Messiah foretold by the prophets and anticipated by the Jewish people. (Luke 19:31) By contrast, Jesus repeatedly told those he healed not to tell anyone what he had done for them in an attempt to keep his popularity from overwhelming his mission. John tells us that after the miraculous feeding of the 5,000, the crowd was going to compel Jesus to claim his Messianic role, but Jesus slipped away from them (John 6:15). The question of Jesus' identity had swirled around him ever since his baptism, and theories of his significance had only multiplied since then (John 1:36-41; Matthew 16:14). Now Jesus wanted to make it crystal clear to all in Jerusalem what Simon Peter had come to recognize in Caesarea Philippi—that he was coming as their true King to save them. And so Jesus rode over the Mount of Olives into Jerusalem on the colt of a donkey.

This message was not lost on the crowds, who immediately responded by crying *"Hosanna"* (Hebrew for "save us!") and joyfully chanting the Messianic Psalm 118, *"Blessed is he who comes in the name of the Lord!"* (Mark 11:9) They spontaneously gave Jesus a royal welcome by laying their cloaks down on the road, the equivalent of a red-carpet reception in the modern world. It was traditional for religious pilgrims to carry palm branches and wave them in celebration as they entered Jerusalem. These too became part of Jesus' royal reception. About 190 years earlier during the Maccabean Revolt, when Judas Maccabeus triumphantly entered Jerusalem as a conqueror after driving out the pagan Seleucids, the book of Maccabees records, "Therefore, carrying ivy-wreathed wands and beautiful branches and also fronds of palm, they offered hymns of thanksgiving to him who had given success to the purifying of his own holy place" (2 Maccabees 10:7).

A conquering king entered the city on a war horse, but a king who came in peace entered on a donkey. By custom, no one else was to sit on the king's mount. Jesus' decision to enter Jerusalem over the Mount of Olives on a young, unridden donkey was a deliberate symbolic declaration that he was coming as a King—not as a conquering warrior like Judas Maccabeus, but as the Prince of Peace who would lay down his life to save his people. He was prophetically hinting to the crowds what he had explicitly told his disciples three times, *"See, we are going up to Jerusalem. And the Son of Man will be delivered over to the chief priests and scribes, and they will condemn him to death and deliver him over to the Gentiles to be mocked and flogged and crucified, and he will be raised on the third day."* (Matthew 20:18-19) In five short days that wrenching prediction was to be fulfilled.

WHAT JESUS DID IN THE TEMPLE COURTS

The Gospels tell us that Jesus descended the Mount of Olives, crossed the Kidron Valley, and entered the huge courtyard that surrounded the Temple in the heart of Jerusalem. There were two entrances on the eastern side of the Temple Mount, a

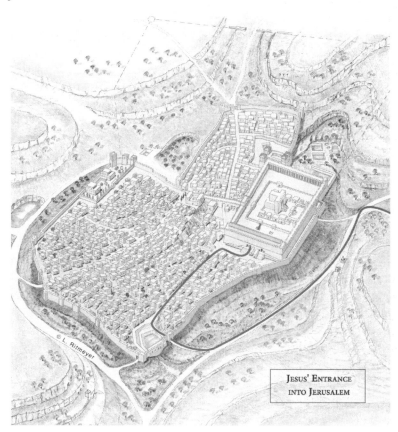

JESUS' ENTRANCE INTO JERUSALEM

monumental staircase in the southeast corner and a massive entrance north of that, which today is called the Golden Gate. After the complete destruction of the Temple by the Babylonians, the Prophet Ezekiel had a vision in which God gave him a walking tour of the rebuilt Temple. When Ezekiel came to the eastern gate in that vision, God said to him, *"This gate shall remain shut; it shall not be opened, and no one shall enter by it, for the Lord, the God of Israel, has entered by it. Therefore it shall remain shut. Only the prince may sit in it to eat bread before the Lord. He shall enter by way of the vestibule of the gate, and shall go out by the same way."* (Ezekiel 44:2-3) This gave rise to the later Jewish tradition that the Messiah would enter the Temple through the Golden Gate. For that reason, some have claimed that Jesus entered through this gate when he made his symbolic entrance, but there are two reasons to doubt this assumption.

First of all, it is clear that this is a later Jewish tradition that arose after the time of Jesus. If it was current in Jesus' time and he went to such great lengths to fulfill Zechariah's Messianic prophecies, surely he would have also made it a point to enter the Temple through this gate. However, none of the Gospels specify which gate Jesus used when entering Jerusalem, which tells us that there was no symbolic significance to the gate Jesus did use. Second, by the time of Jesus, the Golden Gate was only used for ceremonial purposes on the Day of Atonement and for the Sacrifice of the Red Heifer. If Jesus had somehow forced his way through this ceremonial gate, likewise the Gospel writers would have recorded such a radical act. The pilgrim entrance to the Temple

SOUTHERN STEPS TO THE TEMPLE MOUNT

Mount was up the huge staircases at the southern wall and through the Double and Triple Gates, which opened to tunnels that led up onto the Temple platform. Jesus would have descended into the Kidron Valley, turned left, followed the road to one of the southeastern gates in the city wall, and then followed the city streets leading back up the hill to the Double and Triple Gates. From here Jesus and the disciples climbed thirty steps up the 200-foot wide staircase and entered the Temple courts through one of the pilgrims' tunnels.

Although the timing varies, all four Gospels describe the provocative act Jesus carried out in the Temple courts when he turned over the tables of those changing money and selling sacrificial animals, driving them out of the plaza. Why did Jesus do this? Worshipers needed to be able to buy sacrificial animals at the Temple, since many came from too far away to transport their own animals. The annual half-shekel tax that was due at the time of the Passover could only be paid in Tyrian shekels, so money-changers were needed to convert local currencies into the required one. Recent archaeological discoveries have confirmed that this kind of trade was happening in the Royal Stoa, the enormous building that stretched across the southern end of the Temple Mount. A huge staircase at each end of the Royal Stoa allowed people to access this area directly for business without disrupting the religious rituals of the temple. This is most likely where Jesus turned over the tables. All of this raises the question why Jesus would act in such a confrontive and disruptive way if these were necessary and appropriate functions for the Temple.

Jesus quoted Isaiah and Jeremiah while he was doing this, *"Is it not written, 'My house shall be called a house of prayer for all the nations'? But you have made it a den of robbers."* (Isaiah 56:7; Jeremiah 7:11) Many have interpreted *"den of robbers"* as Jesus' protest against unfair business practices in which these sellers were taking advantage of the pilgrim's needs and overcharging them. While this is probably part of the picture, it is clearly not the whole story. Mark tells us Jesus was driving both the sellers and the buyers from the Temple, so it was not just an indictment of those profiting from these sales (Mark 11:15-17). Furthermore, we can see that Jesus' action is more symbolic than practical. If Jesus had tried to drive all the sellers and buyers out of the Temple courts, it would have caused such a commotion that the Roman soldiers stationed at the Antonia Fortress would have come pouring out onto the plaza to violently put down the disruptors (for an example of this, see Acts 21:30-36).

Following Mary of Bethany's prophetic act at Simon the Leper's house and Jesus' own dramatic entrance into the city, Jesus' clearing of the Temple seems to be another prophetic action in the tradition of the great biblical prophets. Whether it was Isaiah walking around Jerusalem naked (Isaiah 20), Jeremiah smashing a clay pot (Jeremiah 19), or Ezekiel eating a scroll (Ezekiel 3), a prophetic act is when a prophet does something out of the ordinary or even shocking to vividly demonstrate what God is saying to his people. But what was Jesus' message in this prophetic act?
It is significant that the Temple was surrounded by increasing levels of restriction. While anyone could enter the colonnaded outer courts, only Jews could enter the central area. A fence surrounding the inner courts had warnings written in Greek and Latin threatening death to Gentiles if they came any closer to the Temple. Josephus described it this way, "there was a partition made of stone all round, whose height was three cubits: its construction was very elegant; upon it stood pillars, at equal distances from one another,

declaring the law of purity, some in Greek, and some in Roman letters, that 'no foreigner should go within that sanctuary'" (*War of the Jews*, 5.2).

In 1871 the French archaeologist Charles Simon Clermont-Ganneau discovered a large inscribed limestone tablet built into the wall of a Muslim school just north of the Temple Mount. The Greek inscription still bears traces of red paint highlighting the

WARNING INSCRIPTION FROM THE TEMPLE

letters and reads, "No stranger is to enter within the balustrade round the temple and enclosure. Whoever is caught will be responsible to himself for his death, which will ensue." A partial fragment of the same inscription was found in 1936 by John H. Iliffe, an Australian archaeologist, while excavating nearby at the Lions' Gate in Jerusalem. These inscriptions are currently displayed in the Istanbul Archaeological Museum and the Israel Museum respectively.

Even Jews who passed beyond these warning signs were restricted access. Female Jews could only go as far as the Court of Women. Male Jews could only go as far as the Court of Israel. Only Priests could enter the area around the Temple itself. Only the priest chosen for that day by drawing lots could enter the Sanctuary of the Temple. Only the High Priest could enter the Holy of Holies, and even he only once a year on the Day of Atonement. These restrictions reflected an emphasis on ritual purity and a sense that God's holiness needed to be protected. Jesus was protesting this religious restriction when he turned over the tables in the outer courts.

Jesus did not follow the Pharisaical rules of ritual purity. He regularly touched those who were considered unclean, even lepers. He rejected extra-biblical washing rituals and ultimately declared all foods clean (Mark 7:1-30). Although his missional focus was on *"the lost sheep of the house of Israel,"* he healed and delivered Gentiles and said of the Roman Centurion who asked healing for his servant, *"Truly, I tell you, with no one in Israel have I found such faith."* (Matthew 8:1-13) When Jesus entered the Temple courtyard and

INNER COURTS OF THE TEMPLE

saw all the levels of religious restriction, and the inscriptions threatening death to Gentiles, it would have struck him how different this was from Solomon's vision that the Temple would be a place where Jews and Gentiles alike could come to know God. In his dedication prayer for the first Temple, Solomon prayed, *"Likewise, when a foreigner, who is not of your people Israel, comes from a far country for your name's sake (for they shall hear of your great name and your mighty hand, and of your outstretched arm), when he comes and prays toward this house, hear in heaven your dwelling place and do according to all for which the foreigner calls to you, in order that all the peoples of the earth may know your name and fear you, as do your people Israel..."* (1 Kings 8:41-43).

Surely Jesus was calling for a return to this vision when he quoted Isaiah 56 in which the Prophet is describing how God will welcome *"foreigners"* and bring them *"to my holy mountain, and make them joyful in my house of prayer; their burnt offerings and their sacrifices will be accepted on my altar; for my house shall be called a house of prayer for all peoples."* (Isaiah 56:7-8) Near the end of his earthly ministry, Jesus recalled the vision he cast in Nazareth at the very beginning, that the New Covenant of God's Kingdom that he was inaugurating is not just for Jews, but for all people! This should cause us to consider the barriers we have unwittingly constructed that keep those who don't know Jesus from entering into his family.

HEALING IN JERUSALEM

During his final days in Jerusalem, Jesus and his disciples made the journey from Bethany or the Mount of Olives into the city each morning and then back again each evening. They spent their days primarily in the Temple Courts teaching the crowds, but as he did throughout his ministry, Jesus also continued to heal those who were sick and suffering. Matthew tells us that immediately following Jesus' action in the Temple courts, *the blind and the lame came to him in the temple, and he healed them.* (Matthew 21:14) John describes in great detail two particular healings Jesus carried out during earlier visits to Jerusalem, both associated with the city's water storage pools. The first of these was at the Pools of Bethesda just north of the Temple, when Jesus was visiting Jerusalem for one of the Jewish feasts (John 5:1-17). As we discussed, a pagan healing shrine stood beside these large storage pools. Because John does not give any particular reason for Jesus to be present in this area, we can conclude that he came intentionally seeking out the *multitude of invalids—blind, lame, and paralyzed* who were lying in the colonnades around the pools (John 5:3). Jesus didn't seem to be bothered that these people had turned to a false, pagan god for healing rather than the God of Israel. He was more interested in showing them God's mercy and power.

Jesus asked a lame man who was lying there a probing question: *"Do you want to be healed?"* (John 5:6) He was pointing to the deeper issues that were keeping this man from physical healing. It is reminiscent of the paralyzed man whose friends lowered him through the roof of Simon and Andrew's house in Capernaum. Jesus began by forgiving his sins and then followed by physically healing his legs (Mark 2:1-12). In this case, however, the lame man completely missed Jesus' point. Rather than expressing a desire to be healed, he began to complain about all the reasons why he had not been healed in 38 years: *"Sir, I have no one to put me into the pool when the water is stirred up, and while I am going another steps down before me."* (John 5:7)

This man was putting his trust in local superstition and false gods, yet Jesus neither condemned him or corrected him. He simply healed him. Astounding! Often when Jesus healed someone, he gave them credit for exercising their faith. Sometimes Jesus looked at a person intently before healing them, as if to discern their faith. Mark tells us that Jesus could not do many miracles in Nazareth because of their lack of faith (Mark 6:5-6). But in this instance, Jesus healed this man despite his misplaced trust and complete lack of faith! Later we discover this man didn't even know who Jesus was. Sadly, the newly healed man didn't

PREPARING FOR THE FESTIVAL OF BOOTHS

respond to this incredibly gracious and powerful act of healing by trusting and following Jesus. Instead, he reported Jesus to the religious authorities for not following their Sabbath rules (John 5:15-17).

On another visit to Jerusalem, this time for the Festival of Booths (Hebrew: *Sukkoth*), Jesus drew on the imagery of the Temple rituals when he said, *"If anyone thirsts, let him come to me and drink. Whoever believes in me, as the Scripture has said, 'Out of his heart will flow rivers of living water.'"* (John 7:37-38) Each morning of the festival, the people had watched the High Priest scoop water from the Pool of Siloam and pour it out at the Temple into the silver basins at the altar. This image was vivid as they listened to Jesus teach. Similarly, Jesus went on to say, *"I am the light of the world. Whoever follows me will not walk in darkness, but will have the light of life."* (John 8:12) In the inner Court of the Women stood four monumental oil-fed lampstands over 75 feet tall. Each evening during the Festival of Booths during the ceremony called the "Illumination of the Temple," these huge oil lamps were lit to remind the people of the pillar of fire that guided Israel in the Sinai wilderness. Josephus says they burned all night long, illuminating the entire city. If Jesus was teaching after dark, this would have been a particularly powerful image.

Not long after that, Jesus encountered a man who was born blind. In response to a theological question from his disciples Jesus repeated his declaration, *"...I am the light of the world."* Then he spit on the ground, made mud, and spread it on the man's eyes saying, *"Go, wash in the pool of Siloam"* (John 9:5-7). Thanks to recent archaeological discoveries in the far southern tip of the City of David, we can walk on part of the very stepped street this blind man took to the Pool of Siloam and can sit on the very stone steps of that first-century pool where he washed! Walking that "Pilgrimage Road" today offers a profound reminder of just how difficult it would have been for this blind man to obey Jesus' directive to wash in the pool. Even with perfect sight, this is a difficult route to travel because it follows the contours of the Tyropoeon Valley, climbing the steep ridge on which the City of David was built, leading up toward the Temple Mount. As this blind man made his way down that steep, stepped street, he had to navigate the steps, the crowds, and the inevitable obstacles along the way.

FIRST-CENTURY SILOAM PILGRIM ROAD

John described this man's response with sparse prose when he wrote, *So he went and washed and came back seeing.* (John 9:7) It's quite a contrast to imagine him stumbling his way down this street in perpetual darkness, kneeling down on the steps of the pool to splash water in his eyes, blinking, walking, then running back up that stepped street, seeing everything around him for the first time in his life! In contrast to the lame man at the Pools of Bethseda, this man is a powerful example of responding to Jesus in faith. It would have been far easier for him to dismiss this strange act of anointing with spit-mud and simply go back to his routine of begging and foraging. Instead he responded to Jesus' word by exercising faith, no matter how hard it was to make his way down that stepped street.

Jesus said that even a mustard seed of faith is enough to move a mountain (Luke 17:6). Paul wrote, *So faith comes from hearing, and hearing through the word of Christ.* (Romans 10:17) When we hear what Jesus is saying to us, it creates faith in our hearts. When we respond by exercising even a mustard seed of that faith, incredible things can happen! As Jesus said to the man who came to him for his son's deliverance, *"All things are possible for one who believes."* (Mark 9:23) We are all a mixture of faith and doubt. Doubt does not negate faith; it is the context in which faith is meant to be exercised. When we take Jesus at his word and exercise the faith his word creates, even in the face of our doubts, miracles happen. The man born blind must have had lots of doubts coursing through his mind as he stumbled his way down that street, but he chose to act in faith anyway. We can choose to do the same. What is Jesus calling you do in faith today?

SHOWDOWN AT THE TEMPLE

Although we are told that Jesus healed people during these final days in Jerusalem, we aren't told any of those details. What the Gospel writers did record was the profound teaching and the intense debates that went on in the Temple courts as Jesus spent his days there interacting with the crowds, the religious leaders, and the political operators. Jesus told parables, addressed theological questions, thwarted attempts to trap him, spoke of the end of history, and promised his eventual return. In the midst of all this, the leaders of Jerusalem continually plotted how to arrest and kill Jesus.

Even before Jesus came to Jerusalem, the religious and political elite were threatened by his authority and popularity, so they tried to figure out how to eliminate that threat. Jesus was aware of these plots and was very careful about timing his appearances in Jerusalem, not wanting to be arrested before he could accomplish his mission. As he told his unsympathetic brothers who were baiting him to go to Jerusalem, *"my time has not yet come…"* (John 7:1-9) The raising of Lazarus finally moved the Jerusalem elite to official action. The Sanhedrin convened under the leadership of Caiaphas the High Priest and made a specific plan to arrest and execute Jesus (John 11:45-57). By the time Jesus made his dramatic entrance into Jerusalem for this final visit, the Herodians,

Sadducees, and Pharisees were all working together to eliminate him. Only Jesus' popularity with the huge Passover crowds kept them at bay. Luke summarized the situation this way: *and he was teaching daily in the temple. The chief priests and the scribes and the principal men of the people were seeking to destroy him, but they did not find anything they could do, for all the people were hanging on his words.* (Luke 19:47-48)

As Jesus and the disciples made their daily trek from Bethany over the Mount of Olives, they came to the Temple Courts each day. We have seen that this enormous plaza was surrounded by nearly a mile of 30-foot-tall porticoes supported by huge columns, providing shade, shelter, and acoustic amplification. The crowds gathered to hear Jesus' parables, ask him questions, and watch him debate representatives of the hostile authorities. When a Pharisee tried to trap him with a question about which commandment is most important, Jesus gave his famous teaching on loving God completely and loving our neighbor as ourselves (Matthew 22:34-40). Jesus told the parable of the tenants who ultimately killed the vineyard owner's son, clearly foretelling his impending death. As an interpretation of this story, *Jesus said to them, "Have you never read in the Scriptures: "'The stone that the builders rejected has become the cornerstone; this was the Lord's doing, and it is marvelous in our eyes'? Therefore I tell you, the kingdom of God will be taken away from you and given to a people producing its fruits. And the one who falls on this stone will be broken to pieces; and when it falls on anyone, it will crush him."* (Matthew 21:42-44) The Pharisees were vividly aware of what Jesus was saying, that they were the ones who would reject the cornerstone, which in turn would ultimately crush them!

Rather than try to placate the religious leaders, Jesus only intensified his criticism of their hypocrisy as this impending conflict grew. Finally, throwing all subtlety aside, Jesus lashed out directly at the Pharisees calling them *"hypocrites," "child of hell," "blind guides," "blind fools," "blind men," "white-washed tombs," "serpents," "brood of vipers,"* and *"sons of those who murdered the prophets"* (Matthew 23:1-36). It is hard to imagine a more provocative declaration! Clearly Jesus was not going to relent in his authoritative proclamation of the truth and his fearless confrontation of the temporal and spiritual powers that held the people captive and hindered God's Kingdom. One day, as they left the Temple courts heading for the Kidron Valley, the disciples admired the awe-inspiring architecture and engineering of Herod's massive Temple Mount. Jesus used this as an opportunity to foretell the impending disaster that was soon to engulf Jerusalem and to teach them about the ultimate end of all things. They sat down on the western slope of the Mount of Olives, looking out over the massive Temple complex and the entire walled city of Jerusalem, and Jesus began to describe the disasters that were to come. Jesus expressed both his heartfelt sorrow over the suffering that the people of Jerusalem would endure at the hands of the Romans some forty years later, as well as promising his eventual return to, once and for all, right every wrong and fully establish God's rule on earth as it is in heaven.

It is hard to imagine the pressure Jesus must have felt to soften his message and compromise just enough to preserve his life and freedom. And yet Jesus did exactly the opposite. The more the opposition intensified, the more determined and focused Jesus became. There was no question of compromise. Jesus knew his entire earthly life had led him to this point and that his destiny was to complete his mission here in Jerusalem. Ever since Simon Peter's declaration at Caesarea Philippi, Jesus had repeatedly prophesied to his disciples how difficult that destiny would be for all of them. Now Jesus understood his public teaching ministry was completed and his time had finally come. Matthew reports, *When Jesus had finished all these sayings, he said to his disciples, "You know that after two days the Passover is coming, and the Son of Man will be delivered up to be crucified."* (Matthew 26:1-2) Jesus knew his next chapter was going to be the darkest of all.

 # THE LIFE

THE ROAD LESS TRAVELED

Most of us tend to take the path of least resistance. We generally want to feel good, maintain control, receive affirmation, and get our own way. These desires cause us to avoid conflict and find non-confrontive ways to accomplish our will. Often this requires us to compromise our integrity. Who we are on the outside does not match who we are on the inside. Sometimes we will violate our values to keep the peace or get our way. This can easily lead us into manipulation and outright dishonesty. The end of this path never turns out well.

As a kid I was deeply affected by a sense of rejection from my peers. I always felt like the odd man out, like I didn't fit in, like I didn't have any friends. I desperately wanted people to like me and include me; so I did what I thought would cause them to accept me. I dressed a certain way and acted in ways that matched prevailing trends. I acquired certain possessions and engaged in certain activities that I thought would earn the approval of others. There were also things I desperately wanted to have and to do. It was like a gnawing hunger inside of me. Sometimes I stole to acquire what I wanted. Sometimes I lied to accomplish my goals. I was unconsciously driven by forces I did not understand.

One day a boy in my class named Carlos brought an old coin from his dad's collection to our classroom for Show and Tell. It was large and silver and covered with intricate designs. He stood at the front of the room, held up the coin, and told us about its history and value. Suddenly, I felt I had to have it. It was an irrational compulsion. After his presentation the coin was passed around the room, from desk to desk. I was sitting in the back of the room and the coin came to me last. Rather than pass it on or return it, I slipped it in my pocket. When the class period was ending, Carlos suddenly realized the coin had not been returned to him. No one seemed to know where it was. I acted as surprised as everyone else. Walking home with the coin in my pocket, I was so pleased at how clever I was to get what I wanted. However, I didn't realize I wasn't clever enough to hide what I had done from my own parents! That evening my dad drove me to Carlos' house and I found myself knocking at the front door, literally shaking with fear as I held the coin in my hand, terrified at the realization that my true character was about to be exposed.

I learned a difficult lesson that day about the powerful forces that can control me and shape my decisions. What drives you? What motivates you? What leads you to make the decisions you make every day? If we are honest, we will have to admit many complex forces lead us to choose the things we do. Jesus was clear about the driving force of his life: *"I can do nothing on my own. As I hear, I judge, and my judgment is just, because I seek not my own will but the will of him who sent me... For I have come down from heaven, not to do my own will but the will of him who sent me."* (John 5:30, 6:38) This was ultimately what set Jesus apart from other people—he knew the Father's will and yielded himself completely to that will.

Jesus left the familiar comfort of Galilee and set his face toward Jerusalem, although he knew what awaited him there. When Jesus entered Jericho to great fanfare, there was a blind beggar who refused to be quiet, no matter how many people tried to silence him. Any ordinary dignitary would have ignored him and turned his attention to the influential leaders of the city who were waiting to wine and dine him. But Jesus stopped and did his Father's will by healing the man (Luke 18:35-42). As he went on, he saw the most hated man in Jericho, the diminutive chief tax collector Zacchaeus, humiliating himself by climbing a tree. Instead of ignoring him or ridiculing him, Jesus honored him by dining at his house (Luke 19:1-9). Jesus was always surprising people because he was not driven by the same things that drive everyone one else.

This pattern continued as Jesus entered Jerusalem. Most people, knowing power brokers were plotting to kill them, would keep a low profile and try to avoid detection. Jesus did the opposite. He attended a banquet in Bethany. He provocatively rode a donkey over the Mount Olives to the adoring cheers of the crowd. He knocked over tables in the center of the power brokers' base. He fearlessly confronted their oppression and hypocrisy, publicly taking them to task in full sight of all the people. The more they threatened him, the stronger his resolve became. Who does that? Only someone who is marching to the beat of a different drummer, in this case, the will of the Father who sent him! Jesus said, *"Enter by the narrow gate. For the gate is wide and the way is easy that leads to destruction, and those who enter by it are many. For the gate is narrow and the way is hard that leads to life, and those who find it are few."* (Matthew 7:13-14)

I wonder if Robert Frost had this saying in the back of his mind when he penned the iconic line, "Two roads diverged in a wood, and I—I took the one less traveled by, and that has made all the difference."[55] Jesus consistently took the road less traveled because he was not following his own will, but the will of the one who sent him. Powerful freedom comes when we let go of our own way and yield to Jesus' way.

I was recently traveling with a pastor from India, and he told me of a colleague who was ministering in a very difficult part of India where he faced constant persecution and death threats from fundamentalist Hindus. My friend described the fearless peace and unwavering determination of this man to continue carrying out the calling he had received. When asked how he could continue in such difficult and dangerous circumstances with such unwavering and joyful resolve, he replied, "I have already died with Christ and it is no longer I who live. What can they do to me? They can take nothing from me, I have already given up my life!" This is the freedom of complete surrender to the will of the Father, and it stands in stark contrast to a life bound

55 Robert Frost, *Mountain Interval* (New York, Henry Holt, 1916), 1, Digital.

by the competing desires and motivations of our broken, sinful condition. Jesus lived in this kind of freedom and it made him fearless in the face of opposition!

One night in Jerusalem, Jesus invited the Pharisee Nicodemus to enter into a whole new way of life by being born again from above. When Nicodemus struggled to understand how this is possible, Jesus explained, *"Truly, truly, I say to you, unless one is born of water and the Spirit, he cannot enter the kingdom of God. That which is born of the flesh is flesh, and that which is born of the Spirit is spirit."* (John 3:5-6) A whole new life emerges when we move from the way of the flesh to the way of the Spirit. The Apostle Paul learned this Way of Jesus, this way of the cross. Through many difficulties he came to understand that to be born of the Spirit is to die to the flesh. He wrote to his disciples in Galatia, *"But I say, walk by the Spirit, and you will not gratify the desires of the flesh... And those who belong to Christ Jesus have crucified the flesh with its passions and desires."* (Galatians 5:16, 24) Paul was teaching them to follow the Way of Jesus. Jesus had surrendered his own will completely to the Father and so was able to walk fully in the Spirit. This is why no one could intimidate him, manipulate him, or distract him from fulfilling his destiny.

Jesus explained how to yield to the Father and walk in the Spirit when he said, *"Truly, truly, I say to you, the Son can do nothing of his own accord, but only what he sees the Father doing. For whatever the Father does, that the Son does likewise."* (John 5:19) Later he told his disciples, *"The words that I say to you I do not speak on my own authority, but the Father who dwells in me does his works."* (John 14:10) This is the secret to the extraordinary life Jesus lived. He continually listened to what his Father was saying, watched for what the Father was doing, and responded by doing and saying those things, no matter what the opposition or consequences.

What is driving you? Are you listening for the Father's voice, or are you following another voice? Are you born of the flesh or born of the Spirit? Are you walking in the flesh or walking in the Spirit? What needs to be put to death in you, for you to come more fully alive? You have a destiny. God has a good purpose and calling for you. Will you set your face toward Jerusalem and follow Jesus all the way to the fulfillment of that destiny, or will you play it safe in your comfortable Galilee and continue seeking your own ends? We all wish that following Jesus would be easy and comfortable, but as Jesus explained, that way leads to destruction. The way that leads to life is narrow and hard. Following Jesus will cost us everything, we will have to take up a cross and die with Jesus. Our flesh will need to be nailed to that cross so we can learn to walk in the Spirit. But the more that old self dies with Jesus and the more our true self comes alive in the Spirit, the more fully we will be living the abundant life of Jesus!

FACING OPPOSITION

I was ordained into pastoral ministry at the age of 27 and was hopelessly naïve about the nature of people in our church and the obstacles we faced in our mission. I figured all the members of my church loved God and were seeking his purposes, so I assumed everyone would get along and we would be able to happily carry out our mission together. I remember a volunteer in our youth program chuckling at my naivete and asking if I had ever heard of church politics before. I was saddened by how cynical she sounded, but it wasn't long before I began to understand what she was talking about. It was shocking how many different agendas were at work in our church and the ugly things people did and said when those agendas clashed. As a student of the New Testament, I shouldn't have been so shocked. From the beginning of his ministry Jesus faced opposition from within the religious and political establishment. After his first recorded sermon, in his hometown synagogue, they tried to kill him! Paul's letters give testimony to the ongoing division and conflicts that threatened the very first communities of Jesus' followers. It didn't take long before I realized the obstacles we faced in our church were not just due to broken and sinful people, but that something even deeper was happening behind many of the divisive behaviors.

The year I was ordained was the same year an African-American man named Rodney King was brutally beaten by four white Los Angeles police officers. Because the beating was captured on video, it became a media sensation. The officers' acquittal at trial sparked six days of rioting in which 63 people were killed, 2,373 injured, over 1,000 buildings were burned, and over one billion dollars of property damage occurred. When King was interviewed during the riots, he voiced his dismay over the violence saying, "Can't we all just get along? …We can get along here, we all can get along… let's try to work it out." I am writing this some 27 years later, and it is painfully clear that police brutality and racial injustice are still tearing at the fabric of our society. Unfortunately, Rodney King's naïve hope has proven to be false. Despite all efforts to the contrary, we just can't seem to get along. We are up against deeper, more sinister forces than many people recognize.

Because Jesus willingly laid down his life, some people assume he was a compliant doormat who allowed anyone to do anything to him and those around him. We have seen how this assumption is far from the truth. From the beginning of his public ministry, Jesus actively confronted the hypocrisy and deception of the religious establishment, even to the point of his radical action in the Temple courts. Although he rejected a political role and refused to be identified with any political party, he courageously stood up to the political forces that sought to silence him. When religious and political agents in the crowds sought to trap Jesus with trick questions, he brilliantly deflected their manipulation by pronouncing profound truths. But all this was more than religious deception and political power plays; the spiritual powers of darkness were at work behind these other players.

Jesus was vividly aware he faced both human and spiritual opposition. His human opponents were pretty obvious. They came from the powerful groups of his time: the Herodians, the Sanhedrin, the Sadducees, the Pharisees. They often confronted him publicly in front of the crowds, even as they secretly plotted against him. His spiritual enemies were also overt, which is why Jesus so often cast out demons and delivered people from bondage to unclean spirits. Sometimes demons even addressed Jesus directly, confirming his identity as *"the Son of God"* (Mark 3:11). When interpreting his parables, he identified our enemy as the devil (Matthew 13:39; Luke 8:12). When confronted by antagonistic crowds on the Temple Mount, he said, *"You are of your father the devil, and your will is to do your father's desires."* (John 8:44) He even recognized demonic influences within his inner circle of disciples, identifying Peter with "Satan" and calling Judas "a devil." (Matthew 16:23; Luke 22:31; John 6:70).

It is no surprise that Jesus was equipped to recognize and deal with demonic forces. As we saw in Chapter 5, Jesus faced intense spiritual opposition at the beginning of his mission during his time of testing in the wilderness. In the desert he learned to operate out of his identity as the Son of the Father and exercised the authority that came from the fact that his Father is the King of the universe. This source of Jesus' divine power is how he overcame his enemies, both natural and spiritual. By watching what the Father was doing and listening to what the Father was saying, he put himself in the position of a representative of his Father the King. He did not speak for himself, he spoke for his Father. He did not act on his own, he acted in concert with his Father.

Following Jesus means learning to do the same. Those who trust Jesus and follow his way receive the indwelling presence of the Father and the Son through the power of the Holy Spirit. As Jesus promised his disciples the night he was arrested, *"And I will ask the Father, and he will give you another Helper, to be with you forever, even the Spirit of truth, whom the world cannot receive, because it neither sees him nor knows him. You know him, for he dwells with you and will be in you… In that day you will know that I am in my Father, and you in me, and I in you… If anyone loves me, he will keep my word, and my Father will love him, and we will come to him and make our home with him."* (John 14:16-17, 20, 23) Discipleship is learning to follow Jesus in the power of the Holy Spirit by listening for what the Father is saying and doing what we see the Father doing. We learn this way of life by reading God's written Word, listening for God's spoken Word, and imitating God's living Word, as we see him embodied in both the imperfect examples around us and the perfect example of Jesus.

The simple truth is that those who decide to follow Jesus will face both natural and spiritual opposition. That same night in the upper room, Jesus went on to tell his followers, *"If the world hates you, know that it has hated me before it hated you. If you were of the world, the world would love you as its own; but because you are not of the world, but I chose you out of the world, therefore the world hates you. Remember the word that I said to you: 'A servant is not greater than his master.' If they persecuted me, they will also persecute you."* (John 15:18-20) Like Rodney King, we would love it if everyone could just get along. As I thought as a naïve young pastor, it would be great if we could all just love God and do his will. But we don't live in a neutral world. Forces are arrayed against those who seek to do the will of God on earth as it is in heaven.

When we seek God's Kingdom by following Jesus, we come up against three primary obstacles: the world, the flesh, and the devil. Ever since Adam and Eve decided to choose their own will over God's will, the perfect world God created has become deeply broken. Every minute of every day things are happening in this broken creation that are not God's will, and we often suffer the consequences of this chaotic broken world. This is the battlefield where we live. Likewise, as the children of Adam and Eve, we have inherited that same brokenness of sin within ourselves. We are not yet as we are meant to be. A battle rages within us between the flesh and the Spirit. Death and resurrection is the only way that the Spirit wins out over the flesh. This is why we must take up our cross to follow Jesus. Finally, we have an adversary, the devil, the enemy of our soul, that fallen angel who rebelled against God, was cast out of heaven, and has been seeking to usurp the children of Adam and Eve as the rightful rulers of this world. As Jesus said, his purpose is *"to steal and kill and destroy"* the abundant life for which we were created (John 10:10). We must come to recognize his presence and learn to fight the demonic work.

The Good News is that Jesus died and rose from the dead to defeat our enemies and overcome these obstacles to God's Kingdom coming more fully. That is why we don't have to be afraid in the face of these adversaries. The hard truth is that those who seek to be part of God's coming Kingdom will have to take up their cross and follow Jesus to Jerusalem. We will have to let go of our will and yield to the will of our Father. We must learn how to function as a representative of our Father the King and exercise the spiritual authority he has given us. Ultimately, we have to learn how to face both natural and spiritual opposition and overcome the same way Jesus did; by confronting the lies, standing up for the truth, and being willing to lay down our lives. During Jesus' final days in Jerusalem he showed us how to complete our mission as he completed his. We turn now to those fateful last days.

CHAPTER ELEVEN

JESUS' SACRIFICE: COUNTING THE COST

Now before the Feast of the Passover, when Jesus knew that his hour had come to depart out of this world to the Father, having loved his own who were in the world, he loved them to the end.
(John 13:1)

 **THE WAY**

THE COVENANTAL MEAL

The miraculous liberation of the twelve tribes of Israel from slavery in Egypt was a shared experience that forged the national identity of the people of Israel and defined their relationship with God. At the heart of this experience was the covenantal meal that saved them from the final and most terrible of the ten plagues that God sent in judgment upon Egypt, death of the firstborn males. Through Moses God gave his people specific directions for how this meal was to be prepared and eaten. At twilight on the 14th of the month of Nisan, they were to take an unblemished yearling lamb (or kid) and slaughter it. God said, *"Then they shall take some of the blood and put it on the two doorposts and the lintel of the houses in which they eat it. They shall eat the flesh that night, roasted on the fire; with unleavened bread and bitter herbs they shall eat it."* (Exodus 12:1-8)

They were to eat the meal with their extended family, dressed and ready to travel in anticipation of their impending liberation. God promised that death would "pass over" each home marked by the blood of a lamb and that through this experience they would be set free. Through Moses God went on to explain that this meal would be repeated each year on the same day and would initiate a week-long festival; *"This day shall be for you a memorial day, and you shall keep it as a feast to the Lord; throughout your generations, as a statute forever, you shall keep it as a feast. Seven days you shall eat unleavened bread.*" (Exodus 12:14-15) They were to remove all yeast from their homes in preparation for this special meal and celebrate it with at least ten people. Over the centuries that followed, the annual Passover meal became the most important religious observance for the people of Israel as they reaffirmed their Covenant relationship with God and each other every year.

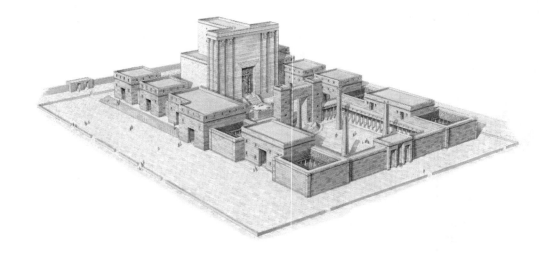

INNER COURTS OF THE TEMPLE

By the time of Jesus, the Passover traditions had evolved significantly. Because the annual slaughter of lambs had become a religious sacrifice, Jerusalem was the only place they could rightly celebrate the Passover, because that is where the Temple stood. At noon on the 14th of Nisan each year, all work ceased, and by 3:00 PM each family sent a male representative to the Temple courts with a sacrificial animal to be slaughtered. These men took a ritual bath for purification (Hebrew: *mikveh*) at the south end of the Temple Mount, entered the Double Gate, and ascended through the tunnel up to the courtyards above. They passed the barrier warning Gentiles to go no further and entered the inner courts on the eastern side through the monumental Beautiful Gate. At the western end of the Court of Women, they waited their turn to ascend the semi-circular staircase to the Nicanor Gate, where they handed the lamb to a priest who took it into the Court of Priests where the open-air altar of sacrifice stood. A priest slit the throat of the animal, sprinkling its blood on the altar. Then the entire carcass of the lamb, with head still attached and legs unbroken, was returned to the man, who then retraced his steps back to the family home to butcher and roast the lamb for their Passover meal.

Meanwhile, the room where the meal was to be held was swept clean of all leaven, and a low-to-the ground, three-sided, u-shaped table was arranged, surrounded by pillows on which the diners would recline with their legs extending away from the table. This three-sided table is called a triclinium and is the way people all around the ancient Mediterranean world ate on special occasions. The diners leaned on their left

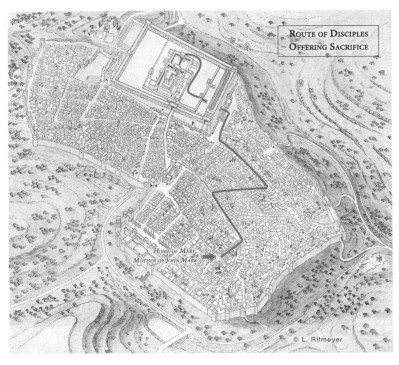

arm and ate with their right hand, facing to the right. The table was set with baskets of unleavened bread, bowls of bitter herbs, platters for the roast lamb, and cups for wine. It is possible there were also bowls with greens, a sweet mixture of apple and nuts, and salty water, although we can't be sure if these elements were included in the first century.

After sunset, on the beginning of the 15th of Nisan, extended family and friends gathered and reclined on the pillows around the triclinium. In Roman culture, the patriarch of the family took the second to last place on the left side of the table as viewed from the open end. The guest of honor was seated on his left side, and the next highest place of honor was on his right, sometimes reserved for his wife. Roman historians disagree about the exact order of the remaining seats, but they had a definite ranking from highest to lowest honor. There was also an honor ranking of seats in Jewish culture, as we see when Jesus criticized the Pharisees because, "*they love the place of honor at feasts*" (Matthew 23:6). Once, when they were at a wedding feast, Jesus noticed people vying for the seats of highest honor. He told his disciples, "*when you are invited, go and sit in the lowest place, so that when your host comes he may say to you, 'Friend, move up higher.' Then you will be honored in the presence of all who sit at table with you.*" (Luke 14:10) In this Jesus was applying the proverbial wisdom of Solomon who said, *Do not put yourself forward in the king's presence or stand in the place of the great, for it is better to be told, "Come up here," than to be put lower in the presence of a noble.* (Proverbs 25:6-7).

Once everyone was reclining around the table, the Passover meal began with a hand-washing ceremony. The "seder," or order, of the Passover meal was not yet firmly established in the first century, so the details could vary. We do know that the meal consisted of unleavened bread, bitter herbs, and roast lamb, framed by four special cups of wine. During the course of the meal, the story of the Exodus was recounted and celebrated with great joy. As the meal unfolded, the host interpreted the various elements of the meal. The unleavened bread was symbolic of the haste with which the people of Israel had to be ready to depart Egypt. The bitter herbs symbolized their suffering under slavery. The roast lamb reminded them how the blood of the lamb saved each family from the tenth and most terrible plague. It is possible that the first-century meal also included some of the elements that later became part of the fixed Passover Seder, such as greens dipped in salty water symbolizing the tears of Jewish slaves, and a sweet apple-nut mix symbolizing joy found in the midst of sorrow. It is likely that some of the Hallel Psalms (113-118) were sung during the course of the meal.

In the Middle East, sharing a meal together is a significant act that reinforces friendship. In biblical culture meals were often used to ratify a covenant relationship between two people or extended families. The Passover meal was an annual celebration of God's saving act and a renewal of the Covenant relationship God established with his people when he redeemed them from slavery in Egypt, gave them the terms of the Covenant on Mount Sinai, and ultimately led them through the wilderness and into the Promised Land. Annual participation in this covenantal meal in Jerusalem was the highlight of the year for Jews in the first century. Jesus grew up coming to

Jerusalem each year and sharing in this meal there with his extended family, but his final Passover meal was the most significant of all. Jesus went to great lengths to make sure nothing would interfere with this last supper.

THE GARDEN OF GETHSEMANE

Just across the Kidron Valley, to the east of the Temple near the base of the western slope of the Mount of Olives, a large grove of olive trees stood in the first century. This area was known for the growing of olives and also for the production of olive oil. Olive oil was produced by crushing the olives with a large rolling stone into a pulp. This was transferred into doughnut-shaped woven baskets which were stacked up on a flat stone with a channel carved into its perimeter. The weight of the baskets themselves caused the first oil to seep out and collect in an underground vat. This was considered "extra virgin" oil and was reserved for special uses, such as anointing people of honor and burning in the Temple lamps. Then a long beam was placed across the baskets as a lever and weights were hung from the beam to increase the pressure. This "second press" oil was the standard grade used for cooking, medicine, perfume, and cos-

GETHSEMANE OLIVE OIL PRESS

metics. More weight was added to the lever for a third and final pressing. This lower quality "third press" oil was burned in oil lamps and used to make soap.

Today, at the base of the Mount of Olives stands a small grove of extremely old olive trees, some more than 1,000 years old, tended by Franciscan monks. This is identified as the Garden of Gethsemane. While the original Gethsemane encompassed a larger area, this is the correct location. Josephus tells us the Romans cut down every tree on the Mount of Olives to build their siege works when attacking Jerusalem in AD 70, so

THE GARDEN OF GETHSEMANE

it is clear these trees do not date all the way back to the time of Jesus. But they are certainly the oldest olive trees in the world. Next to this ancient olive grove stands a large outcropping of rock traditionally associated with the prayer that Jesus prayed in the Garden the night he was arrested. A succession of churches have been built over this "rock of agony," and today the Church of All Nations enshrines the rock, beautifully recreating the feeling of an olive grove at night.

THE CHURCH OF ALL NATIONS

The name "Gethsemane" is based on the Hebrew words for "oil" and "press," so it is no surprise that archaeologists have discovered the ancient remains of several commercial oil presses in that area. Just to the north of the Franciscan Garden of Gethsemane lies a large natural cave which archaeologists have determined was enlarged and used for the production of olive oil in the first century. Archaeologists have found an olive oil press dating to the time of Jesus there. In the Byzantine period, this was turned into a chapel marking the place where the disciples stayed when Jesus went *about a stone's throw* away to pray (Luke 22:41). Although we can't be sure about the specific locations of each part of this event, the cave, the olive grove, and the rocky outcropping fit the narrative descriptions of Jesus' final night on the Mount of Olives when he was arrested by soldiers from the Sanhedrin.

THE JEWISH COUNCIL

Beginning in 63 BC, the Romans claimed sovereignty over the biblical land of Israel. Ruling through their client King Herod, they brutally repressed Jewish aspirations to independence and extracted maximum taxes from the people. As we saw in Chapter 1, following his death in 4 BC, Herod's territory was divided between his three sons. Archelaus did such a poor job ruling Judea, the southern region that included Jerusalem, that the Romans replaced him in AD 6 with Roman governors who ruled directly for Rome. During the entire time of Jesus' public ministry, Jerusalem was under the direct jurisdiction of Rome. While the Romans ruled directly, they ceded authority for what they considered internal matters, such as religion, to the Sanhedrin, the traditional council of seventy Jewish leaders in Jerusalem. Each city in Israel had its own "lesser" Sanhedrin, so the Sanhedrin in Jerusalem functioned like a supreme court for the people of Israel. This council was comprised of aristocratic, priestly, and scholarly leaders representing both the Sadducees and the Pharisees. The High Priest was the head of the Sanhedrin but was appointed by Rome and so subject to its political influence. Joseph Caiaphas was High Priest for 18 years, from AD 18-36, whereas the three High Priests before him lasted no more than one year each, which tells us volumes about Caiaphas' skill at giving the Roman Governor what he wanted.

The Sanhedrin had authority over the Temple and ruled in matters of Jewish law as it related to rituals, festivals, calendar, divorce, land disputes, and religious taxation. Although the Romans gave them freedom to pass judgment in these areas, they did not permit the Sanhedrin to implement the death sentence (see John 18:31). The Council normally met in the Chamber of Hewn Stone, which was one of the six rooms built into the wall of the inner court surrounding the Temple itself. There is some indication that about AD 26 the primary meeting place moved into a room in the huge Royal Stoa, which stretched across the entire southern end of the Temple Mount. The Sanhedrin had under their command a Levitical police force that was responsible for protecting the sanctity of the Temple, as well as a detachment of Roman soldiers, on loan from the Roman Governor, who were more heavily armed. These armed guards and soldiers were called upon to arrest those suspected by the Sanhedrin and enforce their judgments.

The Mishnah, a written compilation of oral rabbinical sayings from the first century BC and the first century AD, devotes one of its 63 Tractates to the functioning of the Sanhedrin. It lists six rules for trials conducted by the council:

1. All capital cases were to be tried during daylight hours and the verdict was to be reached during daylight.
2. Trials could be carried out on any day except a Sabbath or during a festival.
3. Capital cases were to begin with the accused presenting testimony for acquittal before testimony for conviction was presented.
4. Verdicts of acquittal could be offered on the same day as the trial, but guilty verdicts were to be finalized the day after the trial, after a night's sleep.
5. A guilty verdict required the agreement of at least two witnesses. If testimony was to be found false, the false witnesses were to suffer "same death penalty to which the accused had been made liable."
6. Trials were to be held in the public meeting place of the Sanhedrin, not in a private home.

Because the Mishnah was written down about AD 200 and none of its sayings are explicitly dated, it is difficult to know if this tractate accurately describes the rules of the Sanhedrin from the time of Jesus. However, it is likely that many, if not all, of these common-sense rules were in place during the first century. As we will see, even a cursory comparison to the Sanhedrin's trial of Jesus makes it obvious it was an invalid proceeding.

THE ROMAN GOVERNOR

Roman governors were responsible for ensuring the orderly collection and transfer of taxes to Rome. They acted as the commander of the Roman troops in their region, and they adjudicated local matters as judge, particularly in capital cases. Roman governors were expected to travel to the major cities of their region to oversee the functions of government and try legal cases. The Roman Emperor Tiberius Caesar appointed Pontius Pilate governor of Judea in AD 26, a position Pilate held until AD 36. Pilate owed his appoint-ment to Sejanus, the commander of the Praetorian Guard in Rome and a close confidant to the Emperor. The seat of Pilate's government of Judea was on the coast in Caesarea

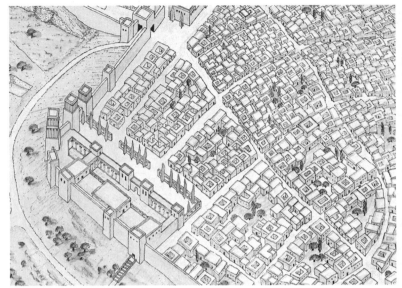

HEROD'S PALACE IN JERUSALEM

Maritima, where he lived in Herod the Great's seaside palace. During the Passover, Pilate traveled to Jerusalem, with a large military force and took up residence in Herod the Great's huge palace to oversee the festival.

On the western hill, the highest point in Jerusalem, Herod the Great built his palace overlooking the city and the Temple Mount. The north end of the palace was guarded by three gigantic towers. The largest of these towers reached 145 feet tall, and its base still stands at Jaffa Gate in the walled Old City, the so-called "Tower of David." The palace complex stretched 1,000 feet south along the western city wall and was 180 feet wide. Within this compound stood two large matching buildings, each of which con-tained banquet halls, Roman-style baths, and rooms that could accommodate hundreds of guests. Between these two buildings was a huge plaza with gardens surrounded by porticoes which contained groves of trees, canals, and ponds decorated with bronze fountains. At each end of this plaza, connected to the two buildings, stood large plat-forms facing paved areas where a crowd could gather and be addressed. Almost certainly this was where Pilate addressed the crowds as he considered the accusations brought against Jesus by the religious leaders.

BASE OF TOWER FROM HEROD'S PALACE

When he first came to Judea in AD 26, Pilate acted aggressively to impose his rule, even erecting pagan images in the Temple courts. This triggered such a violent reaction that the Governor had to eventually back down and remove the standards. There are other indications that Pilate ruled with a heavy hand and was not afraid to massacre crowds of people to demonstrate his resolve (see Luke 13:1). However, in AD 31 his patron in Rome, Sejanus, was accused of treason and executed, putting Pilate in a precarious political situation that caused him to tread very lightly. In an attempt to curry favor with the local population in Jerusalem Pilate began the practice of pardoning a popular prisoner at the time of the Passover festival. Based on Luke's historical statement that Jesus began his public ministry in "the fifteenth year of the reign of Tiberius Caesar," John's account of three subsequent Passovers, and the fact that his final Passover began on a Friday, we can determine Pilate condemned and crucified Jesus on April 3, AD 33. This tells us that Pilate's dealings with Jesus came after his patron Sejanus had been executed, at a time of great political uncertainty for him. This explains why the Governor offered to release Jesus at the request of the people, but the religious leaders prompted them to ask for the release of the murderer Barabbas instead. By AD 36 Pilate was called back to Rome and was never heard from again.

FLOGGING AND CRUCIFIXION

Roman rule of conquered territory depended on the intimidation of entire populations. This was achieved primarily through overwhelming military superiority, brutal repression of any hint of rebellion, and terrifying punishment for those who broke Roman law. Flogging was one of the most feared forms of Roman punishment. The flogging strap (Latin: *flagellum*) consisted of a wooden handle with strips of leather attached, each of which was embedded with sharp pieces of bone and metal. The convict was tied to a post with his back exposed to the flagellum. The spiked leather strips sliced through the skin leaving shreds of flesh exposed. Unlike the Jewish limitation of forty lashes, there was no limit to a Roman flogging. The repeated flaying often exposed bones and organs, leaving a person near death. It was not unusual for a flogging to be fatal. Roman law stipulated that anyone condemned to crucifixion must first be flogged.

The Romans employed various methods of capital punishment such as decapitation, being burned alive, condemnation to the arena or wild beasts, being cast from the Tarpeian Rock, "the sack," enforced suicide, and crucifixion. Crucifixion was considered the most brutal of these methods and was originally reserved for rebellious slaves. However, by the time of Jesus, the use of crucifixion had expanded to include freedmen, non-citizens and even citizens on rare occasions. Crucifixion was first developed by the Persians and Carthaginians and then adopted by the Romans as their favored method of deterrence. The most famous example of this took place about one hundred years before Jesus' crucifixion, following the defeat of Spartacus, the Thracian gladiator who led a massive slave revolt. To ensure such a revolt never happened again, the Romans crucified six thousand slaves defeated by the legions of Crassus, lining the Appian Way from Rome to Capua with their crosses.

In Roman practice the one being crucified was required to carry the crossbeam (Latin: *patibulum*) of his cross to the place of execution. They were stripped naked and either nailed through the wrists or tied to the crossbeam, which was then attached to a fixed upright post (Latin: *palus*). The crossbeam was fixed either on top of the post (T-shape) or on the side of the post (t-shape). Jesus' cross was apparently a small case t-shaped cross, because Pilate had a placard (Latin: *titulus*) affixed above his head reading *Jesus of Nazareth, the King of the Jews* in Latin, Greek, and Hebrew (John 19:19-20). The ankles or heels were then nailed to the post. As the weight of the crucified person's body pulled down on their arms, it constricted the muscles around the lungs, making it difficult to breathe. Fluid began to collect in the lungs, reducing the capacity of each breath. The crucified person lifted themselves up with their arms and legs to catch a breath, which pulled on the painful wounds of the nails. Sometimes a small seat or spike was affixed to the post to prolong death by providing a place to rest, even while causing more pain. Slowly the crucified person suffocated. The design of crucifixion was to publicly inflict brutal torture by prolonging a slow, excruciating death while exposing someone to maximum humiliation and terrifying all those who witnessed it.

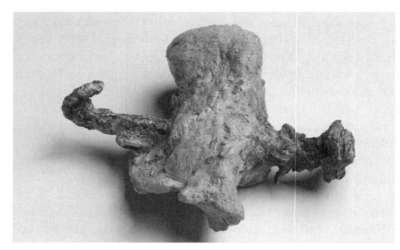

HEEL BONE OF CRUCIFIED MAN

When the Romans captured the land of Israel, they brought this brutal form of execution with them to help subdue the Jewish population. Josephus tells us that during the siege of Jerusalem in AD 70, the Romans crucified so many Jews in front of the city walls that they ran out of wood for crosses. In 1968 archaeologists discovered a rock cut tomb on Mount Scopus, just north of the Mount of Olives, containing the remains of a Jewish male, between the ages of 24 and 28, who was crucified about AD 70, grim testimony to this brutal practice in the time of Jesus. It was a typical first-century extended family tomb, with various chambers containing niches cut into the walls for the placement of bodies. It also contained ossuaries, the small stone boxes used to contain the bones after the bodies had decayed. The ossuary containing the bones of the crucified man had his name inscribed into the side: Yehohanan ben Hagkol (Hebrew for "Jonathan, son of Hagkol"). Yehohanan's right heel bone was pierced by a 6-inch iron spike, bent at the tip from hitting a knot in the wooden cross. Experts disagree whether the arm bones also show evidence of being nailed to the cross, but this discovery is the first concrete physical evidence we have for first-century crucifixions in Judea.

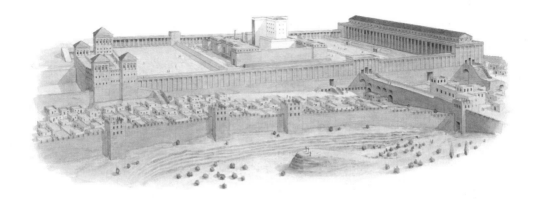

Rock Quarry with Golgotha

For the place of crucifixion in Jerusalem, the Romans chose a large, rock outcropping just west of the city wall, near one of the western gates. It was part of an abandoned rock quarry which had originally been used 500 years earlier to cut limestone blocks for the rebuilding of the Temple when the exiles returned from Babylon under the Edict of Cyrus. Limestone is a sedimentary rock that forms by pressure and results in rock of differing hardness. When the builders were cutting large building blocks from the quarry, they encountered a section of limestone that was soft, fissured, and crumbling; not suitable for building. As a result, they simply quarried around that section of stone, leaving a 20-foot-high rock outcropping.

Over the centuries that followed, wind blew soil and seeds into the quarry, causing plants and trees to take root within its sheer stone walls. By the first-century BC, the old quarry was transformed into an exclusive garden cemetery with large tombs cut into its rock faces. Its location just outside the city walls made it a prime location for family tombs, so it is no surprise that a wealthy and influential Jewish leader named Joseph of Arimathea chose this location to cut a new tomb for his extended family. It is also no surprise that the Romans chose this rock outcropping to carry out their brutal executions by crucifixion, as it was such a visible spot so close to the city and beside a well-traveled road. Little did they know that one of these crucifixions would literally change the course of human history.

THE TRUTH

PASSOVER PREPARATIONS

Much like his triumphal entry into Jerusalem, it is clear that Jesus made specific preparations to ensure he could celebrate his final Passover meal with the disciples in Jerusalem. Rabbis taught that the Passover could only be celebrated in the city of Jerusalem with at least ten people. However, by the time of Jesus, so many people came to celebrate the festival that the city couldn't contain the crowds. As a result, during the Passover they extended the city limits to encompass the villages around Jerusalem, including Bethany.

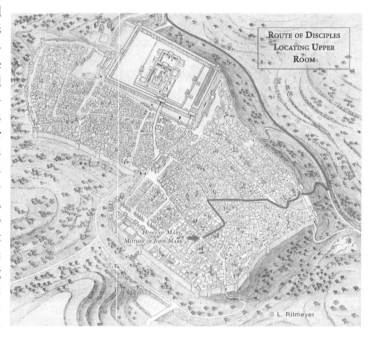

Although Jesus could have celebrated the Passover in Bethany, he made specific arrangements to eat in an upper room inside the city walls. He already knew one of his disciples was going to betray him, so he chose to keep the location of this meal secret even from them. As he sent two of them to make preparations, he said, "*Go into the city, and a man carrying a jar of water will meet you. Follow him, and wherever he enters, say to the master of the house, The Teacher says, 'Where is my guest room, where I may eat the Passover with my disciples?' And he will show you a large upper room furnished and ready; there prepare for us.*" (Mark 14:13-15) Coming from Bethany, these two disciples entered the city through one of three gates in the southeastern wall: the Fountain Gate by the Gihon Spring, the Water Gate by the King's Garden, or the Potsherd Gate near the Pool of Siloam.

All three of these gates opened into streets which were packed with people carrying jars of water from the Pool of Siloam back to their homes. The daily task of filling water jars was considered "women's work," so it would be an unusual sight to see a man carrying a water jar. Following the male water carrier and giving this password to the master of the house he entered was Jesus' way of directing these two disciples to their host home while preventing his betrayer from tipping off the authorities about their location. All of this was aimed at making sure Jesus would not be prevented from sharing this Passover meal with his disciples so he would be able to deliver the powerful teachings recorded in John 13-17. Jesus was determined not to let his betrayer interfere with these plans by disrupting this important meal. As Jesus said, "*I have earnestly desired to eat this Passover with you before I suffer. For I tell you I will not eat it until it is fulfilled in the kingdom of God.*" (Luke 22:15-16)

THE UPPER ROOM IN JERUSALEM

In the southwest part of Jerusalem, on what is today called Mount Zion, beneath the so-called "Tomb of David," lie the remains of a large first-century home that belonged to a wealthy Jewish family. Archaeologists discovered this home underneath the ruins of a series of churches built over it. The earliest of these churches shows signs of Jewish influence and dates as early as the second century. The church father Epiphanius notes that there was "a little church of God" built on this site from the time of the Emperor Hadrian's rebuilding of Jerusalem (AD 135). That makes this the first public space ever built as a place of worship for the followers of Jesus—the oldest church building in the world! These discoveries confirm the earliest traditions that indicate this was the extended family home of Mary, the mother of John Mark, who offered a large upper room of their fancy home to Jesus and the disciples to celebrate their final Passover meal together.

The upper room of this home continued to serve as the primary gathering place for the followers of Jesus in Jerusalem during the weeks and months after his death and resurrection (see Acts 1:13). This makes it highly likely it is the same place where Jesus appeared to the disciples on Easter evening, where the Holy Spirit was poured out on his followers on the Day of Pentecost, and where a group of believers gathered to pray for Peter's release when he was imprisoned by Herod Agrippa I. Luke identified this as the *house of Mary, the mother of John whose other name was Mark, where many were gathered together and were praying.* (Acts 12:12) The building that stands on this site today was built by the Crusaders in the 13th century AD and features a large upper room, mimicking the place where Jesus instituted the Last Supper.

A NEW PASSOVER MEAL

On Thursday of that final week in Jerusalem, Jesus brought the disciples to the upper room where two of them had prepared for the Passover meal. Luke tells us that even in these final hours, the disciples still did not understand the sacrificial nature of Jesus' call and were arguing about their relative positions of status in Jesus' coming Kingdom. Jesus told them they were not to operate like Roman benefactors who wielded power by keeping their clients dependent upon them. Instead, Jesus said, "*...let the greatest among you become as the youngest, and the leader as one who serves.*" (Luke 22:26) To make this point unmistakably clear, John tells us Jesus got up from the table and proceeded to shock the disciples by washing their feet, which would have been extended away from the triclinium as they were reclining on pillows. In Middle Eastern culture, feet are considered the most unclean and unmentionable parts of the body. The task of washing dirty feet was considered the least desirable household task, reserved for the lowliest of slaves. In a classic example of discipleship, Jesus challenged them to imitate his way of life when he said, "*If I then, your Lord and Teacher, have washed your feet, you also ought to wash one another's feet. For I have given you an example, that you also should do just as I have done to you.*" (John 13:14-15)

We have seen that the Passover meal consisted of at least unleavened bread, bitter herbs, roast lamb, and four cups of wine. The four cups of wine framed the retelling of the Exodus story by recounting four of God's key promises to the people of Israel; 1. The Cup of Sanctification: "*I will bring you out from under the burdens of the Egyptians*" 2. The Cup of Deliverance: "*I will deliver you from slavery to them*" 3. The Cup of Redemption: "*I will redeem you with an outstretched arm*" 4. The Cup of Praise: "*I will take you as my people*" (Exodus 6:6-8) As the meal progressed through the first two cups of wine, the Cups of Sanctification and Deliverance, Jesus took the bread in his hands, prayed the traditional prayer of thanks, "Blessed are you, O Lord our God, King of the Universe, who causes bread to come forth from the earth," and broke the loaf. Instead of the normal interpretation of unleavened bread as a reminder of the haste with which the children of Israel left Egypt, Jesus said, *"Take, eat; this is my body."* (Matthew 26:26) They were eating the roast lamb which was sacrificed earlier that day, but now Jesus was pointing to himself as the true sacrifice, as John the Baptist prophesied at his baptism, *"Behold, the Lamb of God, who takes away the sin of the world!"* (John 1:29) Jesus had also pointed ahead to this moment earlier when he told the crowds at the Temple, *"I am the living bread that came down from heaven. If anyone eats of this bread, he will live forever. And the bread that I will give for the life of the world is my flesh."* (John 6:51)

Luke tells us it was after the main part of the meal, when they had finished eating the lamb, that Jesus gave the third cup of wine a whole new meaning. He lifted the Cup of Redemption and prayed the traditional prayer of thanks, "Blessed are you, O Lord our God, King of the Universe, who creates the fruit of the vine." Then he passed the cup to them saying, *"This is my blood of the covenant, which is poured out for many. Truly, I say to you, I will not drink again of the fruit of the vine until that day when I drink it new in the kingdom of God."* (Mark 14:24-25) Just as the lamb's blood had been shed at the altar, Jesus was telling them his blood was about to be shed on the cross. His impending death would inaugurate the New Covenant foretold by the prophet Jeremiah, *"Behold, the days are coming, declares the Lord, when I will make a new covenant with the house of Israel and the house of Judah, not like the covenant that I made with their fathers on the day when I took them by the hand to bring them out of the land of Egypt, my covenant that they broke, though I was their husband, declares the Lord. For this is the covenant that I will make with the house of Israel after those days, declares the Lord: I will put my law within them, and I will write it on their hearts. And I will be their God, and they shall be my people. And no longer shall each one teach his neighbor and each his brother, saying, 'Know the Lord,' for they shall all know me, from the least of them to the greatest, declares the Lord. For I will forgive their iniquity, and I will remember their sin no more."* (Jeremiah 31:31-34)

Jesus told the disciples, *"Do this in remembrance of me."* (Luke 22:19; cf. 1 Corinthians 11:24-25) Just as the Passover meal gave the people of Israel an opportunity to remember what God had done for them, participate in that redemption, and renew their Covenant relationship with God, now Jesus was offering the same kind of experience for his followers in the New Covenant every time they shared this special meal

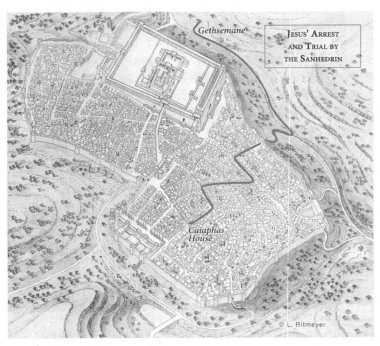

Gethsemane

JESUS' ARREST
AND TRIAL BY
THE SANHEDRIN

Caiaphas'
House

© L. Ritmeyer

of bread and wine. Paul explained the meaning of this covenantal meal when he wrote to the Corinthians, *The cup of blessing that we bless, is it not a participation in the blood of Christ? The bread that we break, is it not a participation in the body of Christ? Because there is one bread, we who are many are one body, for we all partake of the one bread.* (1 Corinthians 10:16-17) Jesus was giving his followers a powerful way to remember his sacrifice on the cross, receive the redemption that was purchased by his blood, and experience the oneness that this New Covenant makes possible with God and with one another.

At the end of the meal, Jesus shocked his disciples when he prophesied that one of them reclining at the table would betray him. John gives us an idea of the seating arrangement around the triclinium as he records their reactions, *One of his disciples, whom Jesus loved, was reclining at table at Jesus' side, so Simon Peter motioned to him to ask Jesus of whom he was speaking. So that disciple, leaning back against Jesus, said to him, "Lord, who is it?" Jesus answered, "It is he to whom I will give this morsel of bread when I have dipped it." So when he had dipped the morsel, he gave it to Judas, the son of Simon Iscariot.* (John 13:23-26) This description makes it clear that John (*the disciple whom Jesus loved*) was reclining on Jesus' right side in the seat of the co-host because, as he was resting on his left elbow, he leaned back against Jesus to ask him who would betray him. Peter must have been sitting in one of the "lower seats" on the opposite side of the U-shaped table because he had to motion with his hand to get John's attention. Judas had to be reclining on the left side of Jesus, because he was able to use his right hand to dip his bread into the same bowl that Jesus was using.

In light of what we have learned about the significance of seating positions, this tells us that Jesus seated Judas to his left, which was the seat of highest honor. It is incred-

THE LAST SUPPER

ible that Jesus not only washed his betrayer's feet and included him in this covenantal meal, but went so far as to put him at his side in the seat of honor! Jesus could have simply excluded Judas from the meal altogether to ensure he could not bring soldiers to interrupt them, but it is clear that Jesus was giving Judas every opportunity to repent and change course before it was too late. Despite Jesus' amazing acts of grace, Judas did not allow that extraordinary love to change his heart. Instead, Judas got up from the table and went to tell the authorities where they could come and arrest Jesus. It is interesting that John says it was that very moment that Satan entered into him (John 13:27). Perhaps this was the point of no return. After Judas left, Jesus told Peter, despite his protests, that he would deny him three times before the sun rose again. In contrast to Judas, Jesus knew that this would be a temporary failure on Peter's part. He predicted Peter's remorseful repentance and his restoration as leader of the disciples when he said, *"Simon, Simon, behold, Satan demanded to have you, that he might sift you like wheat, but I have prayed for you that your faith may not fail. And when you have turned again, strengthen your brothers."* (Luke 22:31-32)

After Judas left, Jesus shared with the disciples some of his most profound teachings about loving each other and the promise of a place in the Father's great extended family home. As the meal concluded, they sang the final Hallel from Psalm 118 and left the upper room, followed the stepped streets east down through the City of David, exited the city walls through one of the southeastern gates, turned north and headed up the Kidron Valley with the Temple Mount on their left and the Mount of Olives on their right. As they walked along under the light of the full moon, Jesus continued to teach them, sharing some of his most powerful insights about fruitfulness and promising the indwelling of the coming Holy Spirit. He concluded with a powerful prayer of oneness for the disciples and those who would follow them (John 14-17). This brought them to the Garden of Gethsemane at the base of the Mount of Olives and the beginning of Jesus' final test.

THE PRESSURE OF GETHSEMANE

On the lower western slope of the Mount of Olives in a grove of olives trees, they arrived at the Garden of Gethsemane next to the rock where Jesus prayed his agonizing prayer of submission to his heavenly Father. While the tour busses line up to deliver hordes of tourists to visit this profoundly significant site, a stone's throw away there is a first-century cave that was converted into a small chapel in the Byzantine period which goes largely unnoticed. Archaeologists have confirmed that this cave was used in the time of Jesus to press olives in the production of olive oil. Although Jesus and the disciples were staying in the extended family home of Mary, Martha, and Lazarus, Luke tells us that Jesus and his disciples sometimes spent the night on the Mount of Olives rather than returning over the mountain all the way to Bethany after dark. He goes on to say Jesus withdrew *"about a stone's throw"* from the rest of the disciples to pray. Since Jerusalem was inundated with so many pilgrims during Passover, many people rented out rooms in their homes, or other shelters they owned, to accommodate visiting pilgrims. The fact that Jesus and the disciples were heading to the Garden of Gethsemane that night indicates this is where they stayed when they spent the night on the Mount of Olives. It is possible they rented this olive oil production cave just north of the Garden of Gethsemane as a place to stay.

In any case, when they reached that area, the main group of disciples settled down for the night, but Jesus took his three closest disciples, Peter, James, and John, with him as he withdrew to pray. Asking them to stand with him in prayer, he confessed to the deep inner struggle he was facing, *"My soul is very sorrowful, even to death; remain here, and watch with me."* (Matthew 26:38) Jesus then withdrew further into the grove of olive trees and threw himself on the ground, agonizing in prayer to the Father.

What was Jesus struggling with that night? When you have traveled from Jericho to Jerusalem and you stand in the Garden of Gethsemane, it becomes evident how easy it would have been for Jesus to avoid the suffering he knew awaited him. If you continue walking up the Mount of Olives for ten minutes, you reach the crest, and then stretching out to the east as far as you can see is a desert wilderness riven by countless wadis and filled with hidden caves. Jesus spent forty days in that very wilderness and knew exactly where he could hide and still survive. How tempting it must have been for Jesus to simply slip away into the night, never to be seen again! When he first predicted his death to the disciples in Caesarea Philippi, Jesus recognized Peter's objection as a temptation straight from Satan himself. Now Jesus was in the midst of that same spiritual battle, pitting his human survival instinct and the pull of his enemy against submission to the will of his Father. Luke tells us the pressure was so great that drops of blood began to form on Jesus' skin like sweat, a documented condition known as hematidrosis, where extreme anguish or physical strain causes one's capillary blood vessels to dilate and burst, mixing sweat and blood. Just as huge stones in that "Garden of Olive Pressing" crushed olives and squeezed oil from them, so Jesus was being pressed under an unimaginable weight.

How did Jesus fight that battle and overcome the pull of his natural human desires and the temptation of the devil? He did it the same way he had lived his entire life on earth—through honesty and submission. Jesus did not hide his feelings from the Father or hold them back. Just like the Psalmists of old, Jesus poured out his authentic fears and desires in prayer, but then trusted his Father by choosing to submit. He prayed, *"Abba, Father, all things are possible for you. Remove this cup from me. Yet not what I will, but what you will."* (Mark 14:36) Submission is an act of faith in which we decide to trust God regardless of our feelings or the circumstances we face. Jesus lived his entire life this way, trusting his Father and submitting to his will. But now he was facing the ultimate test. Would he fully submit all the way to the end? This was as difficult for Jesus as it would be for you or me. No wonder he asked his closest friends to help him fight the battle, even knowing they might not pass the test themselves. As he told them,

"The spirit indeed is willing, but the flesh is weak." (Mark 14:38) Jesus persisted in prayer just as he taught us to do, praying the same prayer of submission three times. Finally, the power of the tempter and his own desires broke, and Jesus was ready to face his final fate. From this point on, Jesus never wavered or looked back, but resolutely yielded to the Father and fulfilled his mission regardless of the cost.

About this time the darkness of the olive grove was shattered by the fire of torches and the sound of an armed crowd. Jesus saw Judas coming to greet him with a kiss and knew exactly what was happening. Peter, roused from his sleepy prayers also understood, and reacted by drawing his sword, ready to fight for Jesus. He still needed to learn what his Rabbi had been trying to teach him ever since Caesarea Philippi—that the way of Jesus is the way of self-sacrifice, not the way of the sword. In the ensuing scuffle, Peter cut off the ear of Malchus, a slave of the High Priest, and Jesus responded by ordering Peter to sheath his weapon and promptly healing the man's ear. The fact that John names such a minor figure in the story tells us he must have become part of the community of Jesus' followers in Jerusalem who gave first-person testimony to these events. As Jesus yielded to his captors without a fight, the Gospel writers record their own cowardice when they report, *Then all the disciples left him and fled.* (Matthew 26:56) This was exactly what Jesus had predicted: *"You will all fall away because of me this night. For it is written, 'I will strike the shepherd, and the sheep of the flock will be scattered.'"* (Matthew 26:31) Mark alone adds a puzzling detail, *And a young man followed him, with nothing but a linen cloth about his body. And they seized him, but he left the linen cloth and ran away naked.* (Mark 14:51-52)

Many have wondered about this strange anecdote, but its meaning becomes clear if we are correct in concluding that the Last Supper was held at the extended family home of Mary, the mother of John Mark. Mary and John Mark were part of a wealthy Jewish merchant family from Cyprus who built a large home in Jerusalem. They are relatives of Barnabas, who later invited the young John Mark to join him and Paul on their first missional journey to Cyprus. Even later, John Mark became a disciple of Peter and, according to the church historian Eusebius, based his composition of the Gospel of Mark on Peter's preaching in Rome. This means that John Mark was a young man living in Jerusalem during these final events of Jesus' life who included this anecdote in his Gospel. If the Last Supper was happening in the upper room of his large home and stretched late into the night, it is reasonable to assume the young man had fallen asleep on his bed. In the warmer months of the year, it was typical for people to sleep naked with just a linen sheet at night. Because Judas left the dinner to notify the authorities of Jesus' whereabouts, it follows that he would have led them back to the upper room. The noise caused by soldiers pounding on the door and demanding custody of Jesus would have certainly awoken John Mark. Once he realized they were heading to the Garden of Gethsemane, he could have wrapped himself in his linen sleeping sheet and tried to get to the Garden ahead of the soldiers to warn Jesus and the disciples. Apparently, he arrived too late, hid in the bushes, and then fled naked when discovered. Perhaps this is Mark's way of telling us he was an eyewitness to these very events.

RELIGIOUS LEADERS AND ROOSTERS

The soldiers and officials from the Sanhedrin seized Jesus and led him back the way he had come through the Kidron Valley, into the city, and along stepped streets up a southwest hill to the extended family home of Annas and Caiaphas the High Priest. Annas was the first High Priest appointed by the Roman Governor Quirinius in AD 6 after the Romans deposed Herod's son Archelaus and imposed direct rule over Jerusalem. Although he was deposed by Gratus in AD 16, Annas continued to exert significant political influence through his five sons who were appointed High Priest at various

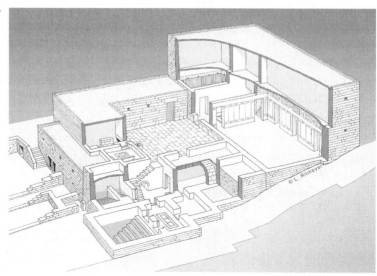

THE PALATIAL MANSION

times over the next 50 years. But his son-in-law Joseph Caiaphas held the office of High Priest longer than any of these and proved to have the greatest impact on history. Like former US Presidents, former High Priests generally retained their title for life, even if not their office. Thus, John tells us that they brought Jesus to Annas first, before bringing him to Caiaphas, the current High Priest (John 18:13; cf. Luke 3:2).

It is clear from the Gospel accounts that, like the nearby house of Mary and John Mark, the house of Caiaphas was a large, two-story home built around a central courtyard with an outer gate. It appears that Annas may have also lived in this same extended family compound. Late that night Caiaphas gathered select members of the Sanhedrin in an upper room of that house which looked down into the courtyard. In 1974 archaeologists excavating in the Jewish Quarter of the Old City uncovered the largest private residence ever discovered in first-century Jerusalem, aside from Herod's palace. It was a two-story compound with over 12,000 square feet of living space, centered on a large courtyard with basements, an enormous cistern for water storage, and no less than four private ritual baths (Hebrew: *mikvot*). The rooms were lavishly decorated with colorful frescos, the ceilings with elaborate stucco designs, and the floors with beautiful mosaics. None of the designs included any depictions of people or animals, and the furnishings included many stone vessels, including large stone jars designed to hold water for purification rites, exactly like the stone jars containing water at the wedding in Cana (John 2:6). From these artifacts we can conclude this was the extended family home of a wealthy and powerful priestly family, perhaps even the family of Annas and Caiaphas.

Although all the disciples abandoned Jesus and fled when he was arrested, John and Peter somehow regained their courage and followed Jesus as he was led away to Caiaphas' house. Apparently, John had a personal connection to someone in the High Priest's household, as he was able to gain access to the interior courtyard. When he realized that Peter was still waiting outside the gate to the house, he put in a word with the doorkeeper so that Peter was also able to enter the courtyard. Peter ended up standing with the guards and servants of the High Priest, warming himself around a charcoal fire that burned in the courtyard. We should not overlook the nerves of steel it took for him to stand there, right next to the very ones who had just arrested his rabbi.

Meanwhile, in a large room above the courtyard, Caiaphas and his hand-picked allies from the Sanhedrin were interrogating Jesus. They had recruited various "witnesses" with charges against Jesus, but none of their false testimonies agreed. The closest they could get was the charge that Jesus threatened to destroy the Temple and rebuild it in three days, but even in this there were discrepancies. If the Mishnaic rules for proceedings of the Sanhedrin were in force in the first century, it is clear that this was a completely invalid "trial" which violated all six of the stated requirements. Even if those rules date from a later period, common decency dictates that a fair trial take place during daylight hours in a public place where the defendant has access to counsel and is invited to make a reasoned defense. Jesus was given none of these basic rights, nor was there time or opportunity to appeal the capital verdict they delivered. It is no wonder Jesus refused to dignify these proceedings by answering his accusers. In the end Caiaphas asked him directly, "*Are you the Christ, the Son of the Blessed?*" And Jesus said, "*I am, and you will see the Son of Man seated at the right hand of Power, and coming with the clouds of heaven.*" (Mark 14:61-62)

Caiaphas finally had a basis to condemn Jesus on theological grounds. The Mosaic Law stipulated the death penalty for blasphemers and heretics. Jesus' Messianic claim and his use of the divine name "I AM" was enough to cause them to cry "blasphemy," tear their robes, and condemn him to death. They spat on him, mocked him, and beat him. Meanwhile, Peter was still out in the courtyard. In the light of the fire, one of the servant girls began to recognize his face and then his Galilean accent. When Peter was given the opportunity to testify to his relationship with Jesus, he denied it; not just once, but three times, swearing "*I do not know the man.*" (Matthew 26:74) At that moment the rooster crowed, *And the Lord turned and looked at Peter. And Peter remembered the saying of the Lord, how he had said to him, "Before the rooster crows today, you will deny me three times." And he went out and wept bitterly.* (Luke 22:61-62)

This was a transformative moment for Peter. He was forced to confront his own faithlessness, while coming face to face with Jesus' unwavering faithfulness. It is significant that Jesus refused to reply to the false accusations of the Sanhedrin, but he did not deny his true identity as the divine Son of God who came as Messiah to reestablish God's rule on earth as it is in heaven. In a letter to his disciple, Timothy, Paul quoted an early Christian saying which might have been based on this very event: *If we have died with him, we will also live with him; if we endure, we will also reign with him; if we deny him, he also will deny us; if we are faithless, he remains faithful—for he cannot deny himself.* (2 Timothy 2:11-13) Peter was crushed by his own faithlessness. Not only had he denied Jesus, but he denied himself as well. As he wept bitterly, he must have felt it was over for him. Little did he know that around another charcoal fire he would learn what Jesus meant earlier that night when he said, "*when you have turned again, strengthen your brothers.*" (Luke 22:32)

ON TRIAL WITH ROME

When the sun rose the next morning, Caiaphas and his accomplices gathered a larger group of the Sanhedrin to confirm their decision to put Jesus to death. However, since the end of Herod the Great's reign, the Sanhedrin was denied the authority to execute criminals. This was one of the ways the Romans demonstrated their absolute power. So, while it was still early morning, Caiaphas and his accomplices took Jesus to make a case before Pontius Pilate, the Roman governor, in order that he would execute Jesus. They also recruited a crowd of people subject to their influence to join them there. John said they went from Caiaphas' house to the governor's headquarters (Latin: *praetorium*) and

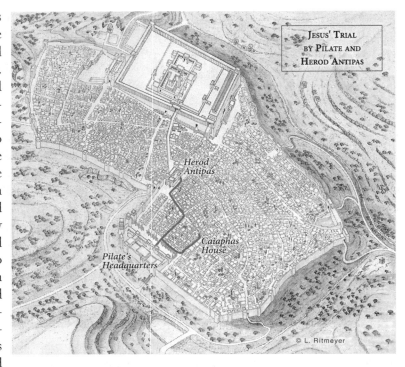

described the place where they gathered as the Stone Pavement (Aramaic: *gabbatha*). The religious leaders would not enter into the palace buildings for fear they would become ritually unclean during the Passover, so Pilate came out and addressed them in the plaza from a platform which John described as the judgement seat (Greek: *bema*). (John 18:28-29, 19:13). This description fits perfectly with what archaeologists have discovered about Herod's huge palace on the western hill of Jerusalem. The Stone Pavement is an apt description of the vast paved area that stretched between the two main palace buildings. Each of those buildings had a large platform facing the central plaza, which looked very much like the judgment platforms featured in every Greek and Roman town square.

Knowing Pilate would not care about Jewish charges of blasphemy or heresy, Caiaphas and the chief priests had to construct a different charge that would warrant a Roman execution. Pilate's primary concern was to keep the local population subjugated to Roman rule and productive enough to generate taxes, leaving zero tolerance for any hint of insubordination to Caesar. The religious leaders brought various accusations against Jesus, which he ignored, but the one that caught Pilate's attention was the charge that Jesus was *"saying that he himself is Christ, a king." And Pilate asked him, "Are you the King of the Jews?" And he answered him, "You have said so."* (Luke 23:2-3) Once again, although he could ignore false accusations all day long, Jesus could not deny who he is.

We might imagine that this oblique admission on Jesus' part as enough to convince Pilate he needed to execute him, but something deeper was happening. Pilate was a savvy politician, and he could recognize a setup when he saw it. Moreover, something about Jesus intrigued the cynical Roman governor. John tells us Pilate withdrew inside his headquarters to have a private conversation with Jesus away from the crowds and religious accusers. *Then Pilate said to him, "So you are a king?" Jesus answered, "You say that I am a king. For this purpose I was born and for this purpose I have come into the world—to bear witness to the truth. Everyone who is of the truth listens to my voice." Pilate said to him, "What is truth?"* (John 18:37-38) The governor could sense a deeper reality at work in all these events but could not quite grasp it. His curiosity turned to fear when his wife sent a warning to him, *"Have nothing to do with that righteous man, for I have suffered much because of him today in a dream."* (Matthew 27:19)

As the proceedings went on, Pilate kept protesting, *"I find no guilt in this man,"* but the religious leaders and crowd kept pressing for Jesus' condemnation. When he realized that Jesus was a Galilean, Pilate sent him over to Herod Antipas, ruler of Galilee, who was in Jerusalem for the Passover, hoping to pass off this political hot potato. But when Jesus refused to do magic tricks for him, Herod simply returned him to the governor. Next Pilate decided to draw on Jesus' huge popularity with the crowds and offer Passover amnesty to Jesus. Instead, the hand-picked crowd, stirred up by the religious leaders, called for the release of Barabbas, a notorious rebel and murderer. It is clear Pilate was torn between his sense of justice and his fear of the political fallout of making an unpopular choice, particularly when the city of Jerusalem was filled with nationalistic Jews celebrating their most patriotic holiday. On top of this, the governor was painfully aware of his own precarious political position, his patron Sejanus having recently been executed himself back in Rome. Perhaps what pushed him over the edge was the overt questioning of his loyalty to Rome. Someone in the crowd cried out, *"If you release this man, you are not Caesar's friend. Everyone who makes himself a king opposes Caesar."* (John 19:12) "Friend of Caesar" became a technical term for those recognized as allies of the Emperor and beneficiaries of his favor. Tiberius was known for applying swift and brutal consequences for any sign of disloyalty. In the end, although convinced of his innocence, Pilate vainly tried to wash his hands of Jesus, had him flogged according to Roman law, and condemned him to death by crucifixion.

A Brutal End

The soldiers took Jesus back inside the Palace building and began abusing him. Pilate's cohort, comprised of hundreds of Roman soldiers, gathered around to join in

the game of mocking the condemned man, as they were known to do. They stripped him naked, draped a soldier's dark red cloak on his bloody shoulders as a royal robe, wedged a cruel crown of thorns on his scalp, and shoved a reed into his hand as a mock scepter. They laughed at him, they spit on him, and they beat him. Then they put his own clothes back on him, laid the crossbeam on his shoulders, and led him into the streets of Jerusa-

THE VIA DOLOROSA IN JERUSALEM

lem, heading toward Golgotha. A large crowd of Jesus' admirers followed after him, crying out in grief at the scene unfolding before them.

Since the Middle Ages, Christian pilgrims have retraced the route Jesus followed, carrying his cross from the place of his condemnation to the place of his crucifixion. They assumed Pilate would have been staying at the Antonia Fortress, so the traditional Via Dolarosa (Latin for "Way of Suffering") starts in the northwest part of Jerusalem just north of the Temple Mount and makes its way to the Church of the Holy Sepulcher in the western part of the city. However, Jesus was actually condemned in the Palace of Herod, so he carried his cross from there north through the streets of the city, exiting out the gate in the western wall of that time, ending at the large rock outcropping in the old quarry converted into a cemetery.

Of the fourteen "Stations of the Cross" along the traditional Via Dolorosa, nine are based on the Gospel accounts. The rest are plausible but not specified in the biblical accounts. Clearly, Jesus was massively weakened by his night of beatings at the hands of the religious leaders and the brutal flogging by the Romans, which certainly tore flesh from his back and caused significant blood loss. When the Roman soldiers realized Jesus was incapable of carrying the crossbeam all the way, they conscripted a man from the crowd to carry it in Jesus' place. The Synoptic Gospels record his name: Simon of Cyrene, the father of Alexander and Rufus. This indicates that he, and perhaps his sons, had a continuing presence in the early community of Jesus' followers. Simon had a literal experience of Jesus' call to discipleship, *"If anyone would come after me,*

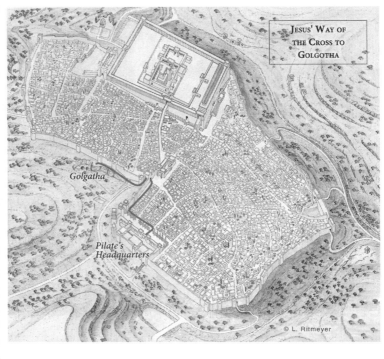

let him deny himself and take up his cross and follow me." (Mark 8:34) Apparently, this up-close encounter with Jesus in his weakened state of suffering was so powerful it brought Simon, and perhaps his extended family, to faith in Jesus.

As he continued his agonizing journey, Jesus addressed the disproportionate number of women who were in the grieving crowd pressing in all around him, *"Daughters of Jerusalem, do not weep for me, but weep for yourselves and for your children. For behold, the days are coming when they will say, 'Blessed are the barren and the wombs that never bore and the breasts that never nursed!' Then they will begin to say to the mountains, 'Fall on us,' and to the hills, 'Cover us.' For if they do these things when the wood is green, what will happen when it is dry?"* (Luke 23:28-31) In the midst of the nightmarish fog of suffering swirling all around him, Jesus continued to be a man for others. Rather than focus on his own pain, he turned his heart toward the cries of his female followers and prophetically anticipated the suffering that awaited them in the coming destruction of Jerusalem by the Romans. Once again, even to the very end, we see Jesus counter-culturally affirming women as disciples and people of significance in the community.

Passing outside the city walls, they came into the area of the old Temple quarry. Though this crumbling, off-white stone was not suitable for building, as we men-

TOP OF THE ROCK OF GOLGOTHA

tioned before, it served the Romans well as an executioner's platform. Since it was located just outside the city walls on the road that ran west to Jaffa from the Gennath Gate, it was also a perfect location to give Roman crucifixions maximum exposure. The vertical posts fitted into the top of the stone projected upward, visible to all those who passed by. Perhaps the bone color of this rock or its grisly function earned it the nickname Golgotha (Aramaic for "place of the skull"). The crossbeam was laid out on the rock, and Jesus was stripped of his clothing. Out of deference, artists typically depict Jesus on the cross wearing a loincloth, but in reality he would have been exposed for all to see, adding shame to his suffering. First-century Jews typically wore a loin-cloth, an inner tunic, an outer robe, a belt, a head covering, and sandals. The four Roman soldiers tasked with executing Jesus divided his clothes among them but decided to gamble for his seamless inner tunic. A Roman centurion oversaw the execution of Jesus and two other men convicted as revolutionary bandits.

The Roman soldiers stretched Jesus' arms out on the crossbeam, driving large iron spikes through his wrists, carefully placed to carry the weight of his body while missing the vital arteries. When Jesus showed Thomas the nail marks in his "hands," the word John used (Greek: *cheiras*) can mean hand or arm (John 20:20). Lifting him up, they hung the crossbeam on the upright post and nailed Jesus' ankles in place. The searing agony of iron splitting flesh and bone gradually gave way to burning pain in his shoulders and the pressure of muscles constricting his lungs. Pushing with his legs and pulling with his arms to relax the pressure and fill his lungs with air, and then sagging back down in exhaustion on the nails after each breath would have repeatedly exacerbated the pain in his ankles and wrists. This up-and-down movement dragged the wounds on his back against the rough post and drove the thorns of his "crown" deeper into his scalp. It is impossible to imagine the all-encompassing pain of this torturous dance, which only worsened as each breath became shallower and more difficult. Instead of cursing his tormentors, Jesus prayed, "*Father, forgive them, for they know not what they do.*" (Luke 23:34)

It appears that none of Jesus' male disciples except for John followed Jesus all the way to Golgotha, but a large number of Jesus' courageous female followers were there, including Mary Magdalene, Salome the mother of the sons of Zebedee, Mary the wife of Clopas, Mary the mother of James and Joseph, Joanna, and many other women who came up with him to Jerusalem (Mark 15:41). Although Jesus' mother Mary, along with his brothers, thought he was out of his mind and sought to bring him home to Nazareth earlier, now she had joined her son and his followers (Mark 3:21, 31). As Jesus hung on the cross, through the blinding pain he publicly recognized his mother's faith and inclusion in the extended spiritual family of his followers. Looking at Mary and John, he said, "*Woman, behold, your son!*" Then he said to the disciple, "*Behold, your mother!*" And from that hour the disciple took her to his own home. (John 19:26-27)

Earlier in Galilee, Jesus did not allow his biological family to derail his mission or compromise the spiritual family he was building, but he never closed the door for them to become part of a spiritual family defined by "*whoever does the will of God*" (Mark 3:35). As he was dying, Jesus wanted everyone in the community to be clear that his mother would now function as a part of their extended spiritual family. It is significant to note that, following his resurrection, Jesus appeared to his brother James, who went on to become the primary leader of the church in Jerusalem and wrote the New Testament letter of James. Another brother, Jude (or Judas), wrote a biblical letter as well. What a wonderful thing it is when our biological family also becomes part of our spiritual family!

As Jesus hung dying on the cross between two convicted criminals, passersby hurled insults at him and religious leaders mocked him. The soldiers added to the insults by offering Jesus wine spiked with gall, a bitter herb that can be poisonous. Luke tells us one of the crucified criminals joined the mockery of Jesus, while the other rebuked this man and defended Jesus' innocence. The repentant man turned toward him and said, "*Jesus, remember me when you come into your kingdom.*" Jesus replied with the powerful promise, "*Truly, I say to you, today you will be with me in paradise.*" (Luke 23:42-43) In the midst of unspeakable horror, Jesus offered this repentant man the simple but powerful promise of an indestructible life that transcends the worst kind of death imaginable.

It would be tempting to slip into an unbalanced Christology and take comfort in the thought that Jesus was somehow escaping the full impact of this suffering due to his divine nature. Nothing could be further from the truth. The fact that God emptied himself and became fully human in Jesus means he was experiencing the full force of physical agony that comes with such diabolical torture. Despite his faith and his promise to the repentant man, Jesus still faced a tidal wave of despair as his life slowly slipped away. Just like the lamenting Psalmists and his own prayer in Gethsemane, Jesus was not afraid to give voice to this experience of dereliction: *And about the ninth hour Jesus cried out with a loud voice, saying, "Eli, Eli, lema sabachthani?" that is, "My God, my God, why have you forsaken me?*" (Matthew 27:46)

Some have theologized these words of Jesus by claiming the Father turned away from the Son and forsook him when he was hanging on the cross. Clearly Jesus was dying a sacrificial death to atone for the sins of the world, but that does not mean his heavenly Father forsook him. That would be to break the often-repeated covenantal promise: "*He will be with you; he will not leave you or forsake you.*" (Deuteronomy 31:8) Jesus used the opening words of Psalm 22 to express his natural human feelings of forsakenness, even as he trusted his heavenly Father's faithfulness. In an oral culture, quoting the opening verse of a poem or song is a shorthand way of referring to the whole song. When you read Psalm 22, it describes almost exactly what Jesus was going through on the cross, but ends with a triumphant doxology praising God and proclaiming a victory that resounds through the ages: *it shall be told of the Lord to the coming generation; they shall come and proclaim his righteousness to a people yet unborn, that he has done it.* (Psalm 22:30-31) In the depths of his despair, Jesus continued to proclaim the victory that God was accomplishing through his suffering, a victory that would eventually be proclaimed to us, a people yet unborn as the psalmist says.

Some people who were crucified lingered for many hours and even days on the cross. Jesus, weakened by his beatings and flogging, lasted six hours. As his strength ebbed, he expressed his profound dehydration by saying, *"I thirst"* and receiving sour wine (John 19:28). Seeing the completion of his work drawing near, he said, *"It is finished"* (John 19:30). With his final breath, Jesus gave a triumphant victory cry: *"Father, into your hands I commit my spirit!"* (Luke 23:46) When the hardened Roman centurion responsible for these executions saw all that Jesus said and did on the cross, he could only respond, *"Truly this was the Son of God!"* (Matthew 27:54) At the moment of Jesus' death the huge tapestry curtain that separated the Holy of Holies from the Sanctuary of the Temple split in two, from top to bottom, a powerful testimony to the cosmic shift accomplished by Jesus' perfect sacrifice. Natural phenomena such as earthquakes and a solar eclipse reflected this earth-shaking event. The death of Jesus was changing everything!

 # THE LIFE

THE COST OF COVENANTAL ONENESS

When my wife Pam and I stood up at our wedding and exchanged lifelong, unconditional vows, we were being united in a profound covenantal bond that has only deepened and strengthened over more than thirty years of marriage. In modern western culture, marriage is one of the few examples of covenant relationship we have left, and even this one is threatened by changing values. In the biblical world people were used to entering into all kinds of covenants that defined their relationships with various people for various purposes. You made a covenant with your neighbors, promising to help one another when under attack. You made a covenant with a landowner if you were going to work their land for them. You made a covenant with your king when you entered military service under his reign.

God made Covenants with his people to build a deeper and stronger relationship with them. Covenants unite two people or groups of people together by the promises they make to each other and by exercising faith in those promises. When God made a Covenant with Abraham and Sarah, he promised them land, children, blessing, and a relationship with him. Their faith in those promises bound them to God. When Moses led the people out of slavery in Egypt to the foot of Mount Sinai, God fleshed out the nature of that relationship by making another Covenant with his people, giving them the Law as a guideline for how to live out that relationship in daily life. Sadly, this was a Covenant they were never able to fully keep. Still today Orthodox Jews focus all of their energy on trying to keep this Mosaic Covenant through countless additional laws and religious traditions.

At the Last Supper, Jesus made clear what had been implicit throughout his public teaching and ministry—that he was fulfilling the promise of Jeremiah and establishing an entirely New Covenant with God's people: *"This cup that is poured out for you is the new covenant in my blood."* (Luke 22:20) Often covenants were ratified by sacrifices, deeds, seals, and a meal. As Jesus reinterpreted the Passover meal that night, he inaugurated a new way of relating to God and each other. As Jeremiah said, this New Covenant would be written on human hearts, rather than tablets of stone. It would bring people of every background and status into a personal relationship with God; not an externally imposed religion, but an internally experienced oneness with God. This Covenant is based on God's gracious decision to forgive his people, not their ability to perfectly obey its stipulations (Jeremiah 31:31-34). That night around the table, Jesus described the oneness created by this New Covenant: *"I will not leave you as orphans; I will come to you. Yet a little while and the world will see me no more, but you will see me. Because I live, you also will live. In that day you will know that I am in my Father, and you in me, and I in you."* (John 14:18-20)

As Jesus demonstrated from the beginning in Nazareth, this New Covenant is good news for all people, not just the Jews. It is an invitation for people of every tribe and nation to be gathered into one family of God where we can reclaim the role of Adam and Eve, representing our Father the King and extending his Kingdom by carrying out his will on earth as it is in heaven. Jesus' entire life demonstrates how those who are part of the New Covenant can learn to live this kind of life. His call to discipleship is an invitation to learn this new way of life. His extended spiritual family on mission is the community in which this calling will be fulfilled. If we are going to learn how to follow Jesus in this kind of life, it will begin by entering into the New Covenant.

In the Last Supper, Jesus was not only showing his disciples what was about to happen in his death and resurrection; he was inviting all of us to participate in the New Covenant made possible by that same death and resurrection. Entering into Covenant oneness with Jesus means our lives will increasingly be shaped by his life. Participating in this New Covenant leads us to live as disciples who are learning this Way of Jesus and passing it on to others. It teaches us to multiply extended spiritual families, so we can carry out Jesus' mission to seek and save the lost. It empowers us to extend God's coming Kingdom to the last and the least. It assures us that Jesus has prepared a place for us in our Father's eternal oikos. Paul says that, by eating the bread, we participate in Jesus' broken body. By drinking the wine, we participate in his shed blood. This participation in Jesus' death is a picture of how we take up our cross and follow Jesus. This meal reminds us of our call to die to ourselves by being crucified with him, so we can also be raised with him and come alive to our true selves.

This is the cost of entering the New Covenant with Jesus. It is freely given to us as a gift of grace. We can never do anything to earn it or deserve it. It is far too expensive. But paradoxically, it costs us everything to accept such a priceless gift, because we have to give up what keeps us from receiving the gift. It costs us our self-determination. When Jesus was praying in Gethsemane, he was not afraid to express his natural human desires that were opposed to the Father's will, even as he submitted to that will. We too must recognize the tug of war going on inside of us every day. The pull of the world, the flesh, and the devil is constant and in opposition to the call of Jesus. What will it take for the Spirit to win that battle in our heart and mind, so that we can submit to God's will and fulfill our destiny as Jesus did? Paul described his own experience this way: *I have been crucified with Christ. It is no longer I who live, but Christ who lives in me. And the life I now live in the flesh I live by faith in the Son of God, who loved me and gave himself for me.* (Galatians 2:20)

The hard truth is that we are all implicitly in covenant with things that keep us from the Way of Jesus and his Kingdom. We make promises all the time and trust promises made to us, many of which stand in opposition to the New Covenant. We promise our boss to do whatever it takes to improve the bottom line. We believe the promise that the right purchase will bring us fulfillment. We promise to make our spouse happy all the time. We believe the promise that if we look better we will be better. We promise our kids they can be whatever they want. We believe the promise that moral compromise is worth the power it can bring us. We promise ourselves that if we try a little harder, God will approve of us more. These kinds of promises leave us in bondage when we make them and believe them. In the end we have to break these kinds of empty covenants if we are going to live in the New and infinitely better Covenant of Jesus. This is the dying that has to happen. This is the sacrifice that has to be made. This is the cross on which we must be crucified if we hope to be set free to live more fully in Covenantal oneness with Jesus and extend his Kingdom to more people.

As we begin to see the many ways we are in bondage to the false covenants of this world, we begin to understand the importance of the Last Supper for our journey of discipleship. We taste and see the price Jesus paid to redeem us. We taste and see the cost of following Jesus. We renew that Covenant relationship every time we participate in it.

The journey of discipleship is made one step at a time. Luke records Jesus' call as a daily invitation, *"If anyone would come after me, let him deny himself and take up his cross daily and follow me."* (Luke 9:23) Every day we can take a step of faith by denying another false promise and choosing to trust Jesus' promise instead. In his Small Catechism, the great Reformer Martin Luther, reflecting on baptism, wrote that "the old creature in us with all sins and evil desires is to be drowned and die through daily contrition and repentance, and on the other hand that daily a new person is to come forth and arise up to live before God in righteousness and purity forever."[56] Dietrich Bonhoeffer described the paradoxical cost of this free gift when he wrote,

> "Cheap grace is grace without discipleship, grace without the cross, grace without Jesus Christ, living and incarnate. Costly grace is the treasure hidden in the field; for the sake of it a man will go and sell all that he has. It is the pearl of great price to buy which the merchant will sell all his goods. It is the kingly rule of Christ, for whose sake a man will pluck out the eye which causes him to stumble; it is the call of Jesus Christ at which the disciple leaves his nets and follows him. Costly grace is the gospel which must be sought again and again, the gift which must be asked for, the door at which a man must

---

[56] Martin Luther, *The Small Catechism*, The Sacrament of Holy Baptism (St. Louis, Concordia, 2017) 23-24, Digital.

knock. Such grace is costly because it calls us to follow, and it is grace because it calls us to follow Jesus Christ. It is costly because it costs a man his life, and it is grace because it gives a man the only true life. It is costly because it condemns sin, and grace because it justifies the sinner. Above all, it is costly because it cost God the life of his Son: "ye were bought at a price," and what has cost God much cannot be cheap for us. Above all, it is grace because God did not reckon his Son too dear a price to pay for our life, but delivered him up for us." [57]

THE POWER OF SACRIFICE

My wife and I are serial remodelers. We always have an idea of how to make our house better. Since I have a background in construction, we tend to tackle these projects ourselves. After dealing with the ridiculous red tape and delay of our city's permit process on an earlier project, I thought I would try my next project without applying for a permit. "I am going to build it to code anyway," I reasoned to myself. Someone told me that if an inspector happened to come by and find out, there would be no fine. They would just make me stop the work and apply for a permit. Once I had my entire roof off, I discovered my neighbor was friends with a city building inspector. When the stop-work notice appeared on my house, I simply went down to the building office and applied for a permit, thinking it would be no problem. I discovered the building department can punish you in many ways besides charging a fine! Many months dragged by while I waited for permit approval, made endless required changes to my plans, and waited in vain for inspectors to sign off. My foolish impatience ended up adding at least six months to the project.

The flesh is always looking for a short cut. It is tempting to believe we can get what we want, when we want without having to give up anything. We are all prone to the allure of get-rich-quick fantasies. That is what drew thousands west during the gold rush. That is what keeps people coming back to the casino, no matter how much they lost last time. It is what keeps litigation lawyers buying billboard space. We all want something for nothing! Following his baptism, the devil showed Jesus all the kingdoms of the world and their glory. And he said to him, "*All these I will give you, if you will fall down and worship me.*" (Matthew 4:8-9) The lie was that Jesus didn't need to experience the challenges of his public ministry, face the opposition of those in power, and

[57] Dietrich Bonhoeffer, *The Cost of Discipleship* (New York, Touchstone, 1959), 45.

ultimately lay down his life. He could just accept the devil's shortcut and take up his rightful rule without sacrificing anything except his conscience.

What the devil didn't understand was that Jesus had already gotten something for nothing. He received his Father's unconditional love and gracious approval in the waters of the Jordan, which meant he had already been given everything. That is why Jesus could turn down the devil's shortcut without a second thought. He was already in Covenant with his heavenly Father, the King of kings, and the tempter could add nothing to that gift. It is interesting that immediately following this gift of grace, the Spirit led Jesus into a time of fasting in the desert. Fasting is the decision to willingly give up something to deepen our awareness of and dependence on God. Jesus knew that with the gracious gift of love comes the challenging call to sacrifice. Fasting for forty days and nights was his way of embracing that call. Jesus' ultimate submission to the Father in Gethsemane was the final outcome of this decision he made at the beginning of his ministry. Because he had received this gift from the Father in the Jordan, he could lay down his life at Golgotha.

Sacrifice is not a popular concept in a society that is based on producing ever more goods and services designed to entertain us and make us more comfortable. Talk of willing self-sacrifice brings up images of creepy monks in dark cells whipping themselves in a frenzy of self-hatred. If the devil can't get us to avoid sacrifice, he will try to get us to sacrifice the wrong thing. We are right to reject sacrifice for the sake of sacrifice. There is nothing intrinsically holy or virtuous about deprivation or pain. Jesus was not an ascetic. On the contrary, he celebrated God's goodness in creation and enjoyed the blessings of this life so much that he was falsely criticized for being a *"glutton and a drunkard"* (Matthew 11:19). There is no place for self-denigrating asceticism in a Jesus-shaped life. Jesus' famous great commandment includes the stipulation to *"love your neighbor as yourself"* (Mark 12:31). And yet, Jesus willingly chose to suffer on the cross and die. He could have escaped in Gethsemane, either by natural stealth or supernatural force. As he told Peter, *"Do you think that I cannot appeal to my Father, and he will at once send me more than twelve legions of angels?"* (Matthew 26:53) Jesus knew that faithfulness to his Father's will would inevitably force him to choose sacrifice over self-preservation. He chose sacrifice because of his great love for us.

People make sacrifices for different reasons. Some give up short-term comforts for their own long-term gains. Others seek the honor that comes to those who make dramatic sacrifices. Some try to influence others by their sacrifice. Co-dependents sacrifice out of guilt and shame, hoping to gain acceptance and approval. Narcissists are so self-absorbed they are unable to sacrifice for others. Jesus' sacrifice is different than all of these, because his is a sacrifice purely for others. The essence of true love (Greek: *agape*) is to seek the good of others, even when it costs you something. Love inevitably involves sacrifice. The power of Jesus' sacrifice is rooted in the depth of his love for us. John not only tells us that God loves the whole world, but also that God is love (John 3:16; 1 John 4:8). God's very identity is that he sacrifices for those he loves. Jesus made the ultimate sacrifice for us because he loves us completely. As Jesus explained to the disciples as they walked to Gethsemane that night, *"Greater love has no one than this, that someone lay down his life for his friends… I have called you friends"* (John 15:13, 15).

At Jesus' baptism John prophesied that he is *"the lamb of God who takes away the sin of the world!"* (John 1:29). The death of Jesus accomplished what the endless sacrifice of lambs could never do. He paid the price for the sin of the world that we could never have paid. He took the guilt and shame on himself that rightly belongs to us. He died the death that we deserved and in so doing broke the power of sin, death, hell, and the devil. It was God in human form laying down his life for ours. Everything turns on this incomprehensible act of selfless love. Without this perfect and ultimate sacrifice, Jesus' life and teaching would have amounted to little more than another footnote in history. Jesus being willing to die on the cross for us has changed everything! His blood ratifies the New Covenant. His death means we can live a whole new kind of life today and for eternity.

And yet, we miss the full meaning of Jesus' sacrifice if we stop there. In every way Jesus set an example for us to follow, including his death on the cross. We might protest that Jesus' unjust death on the cross was unique to him, but the very night he was arrested he told his disciples the destiny of those who follow him: *"If they persecuted me, they will also persecute you."* (John 15:20) Taking up our cross and following him not only means dying to ourselves; it also means sacrificing for others. Being a disciple of Jesus is living not primarily for ourselves, but for God first and then for others. John reflected on the implication of Jesus' death for those who follow him when he wrote, *By this we know love, that he laid down his life for us, and we ought to lay down our lives for the brothers.* (1 John 3:16) If we seek to follow Jesus in his extraordinary life, we will also have to learn to follow him in his sacrificial death.

Most of Jesus' closest disciples ended up being killed for following in their master's footsteps. Still today many disciples of Jesus pay for their faith with their lives. Thankfully most of us will never have to face that level of persecution, yet still today the Way of Jesus inevitably includes the way of sacrifice. Sacrifice can be as simple as letting your spouse have his or her way, or letting someone cut in front of you in line. It can be as significant as giving up cherished comforts and freedoms to care for and raise your children or your aging parents. It can be as mundane as getting up every morning and going to work to provide for your family, or as dramatic as putting yourself in harm's way to protect the innocent. Jesus-shaped sacrifice comes in many forms, but it is always about love. It is always about being willing to seek the good of another, even at your own expense. This is the power of willing sacrifice. Discipleship does not mean we sacrifice everything for everyone all the time. It does mean we listen to what God is saying, watch for what God is doing, and then willingly make the sacrifices Jesus leads us to make.

Once a rich young ruler came to Jesus asking about eternal life. Seeing he was in bondage to his wealth and possessions, Jesus challenged him: *"go, sell what you possess and give to the poor, and you will have treasure in heaven; and come, follow me." When the young man heard this he went away sorrowful, for he had great possessions.* When Peter was over-whelmed with the sacrifice Jesus asked of the rich young ruler and the sacrifices they had made as disciples, he exclaimed, *"See, we have left everything and followed you. What then will we have?" Jesus said to them, "…everyone who has left houses or brothers or sisters or father or mother or children or lands, for my name's sake, will receive a hundredfold and will inherit eternal life."* (Matthew 19:21-22, 27, 29) The rich young ruler did not understand the nature of sacrifice as a disciple of Jesus. He thought he would lose what was most precious to him, when in reality he missed the opportunity of a lifetime that was far more valuable than all the possessions he would have had to give up. Peter and the other disciples chose the way of sacrifice, and they received a hundred times more in this life and infinitely more in the life to come!

Pam and I have been learning Jesus' way of sacrifice at a new level recently. As I mentioned earlier, we felt led to quit our jobs and shift our full-time focus from local ministry to wider ministries we were engaged in. We wrestled with the decision for years because it meant giving up financial security we had worked all our lives to attain, medical benefits in the season we will most need them, along with a community and home we had come to love dearly. We had to make other kinds of personal sacrifices as well, and it was difficult. We each had a cross to bear, and there were many areas of dying along the way. But in the end, we knew this was the path Jesus was calling us to take. It has meant we are on the road most of the time and away from our children and grandchildren far more than we want. It has meant we live in a neighborhood that is less peaceful and more dangerous than what we had been used to. It has meant having to simplify our lives because we are not able to fully fund our salaries. We realize these sacrifices are nothing compared to the price many must pay to follow Jesus, and yet they are still real sacrifices that we have willingly chosen. It has not been an easy road for us; however, we would both say we have received far more than we have had to give up. I can honestly tell you I have neve had more fun, been more fulfilled, or seen as much good fruit in my life as I am enjoying right now! I feel I have been given a hundred times over what I have given up.

In the end, Jesus-shaped sacrifice is always about freely-given, unconditional love. This kind of love has the power to heal, transform, and set people free. The question is whether we have a surplus of love, so we can freely give it away to others. John answered that question: *God is love, and whoever abides in love abides in God, and God abides in him. By this is love perfected with us, so that we may have confidence for the day of judgment, because as he is so also are we in this world. There is no fear in love, but perfect love casts out fear. For fear has to do with punishment, and whoever fears has not been perfected in love. We love because he first loved us.* (1 John 4:16-19) Jesus laid down his life for us out of his great love for us. In doing so, he broke the power of sin and set us free. His perfect sacrifice is the ultimate expression of perfect love. The more we allow the Holy Spirit to pour that freely given gift of love into our hearts, the more we will be set free from the fear of losing what we have, so we can follow the way of Jesus and live a more complete life of sacrificial love for others. Jesus told us this is the most important thing in life, to love God and our neighbor! When we willingly choose loving sacrifice as Jesus did, it has the power to change lives. Are you willing to take up your cross and follow the sacrificial way of Jesus' love?

CHAPTER TWELVE

JESUS' VICTORY: THE SAME POWER

And he said to them, "Why are you troubled, and why do doubts arise in your hearts? See my hands and my feet, that it is I myself. Touch me, and see. For a spirit does not have flesh and bones as you see that I have." (Luke 24:38-39)

 THE WAY

FIRST-CENTURY JEWISH BURIAL CUSTOMS

Jewish funeral practices from the time of Jesus are well attested in the archeological record because those who could afford it were buried in extremely durable rock-cut tombs. For ancient Jews, and still for many Jews today, Jerusalem is the most sought-after place to be buried. Thus archaeologists have been able to identify over a thousand first-century Jewish graves in and around Jerusalem. Tombs from this period typically consisted of an entrance leading to an antechamber, which in turn led to multiple burial chambers. The bodies were either laid on shelves cut into the sides of the tomb (Latin: "*arcosolia*") or slid into narrow slots cut into the rock (Hebrew: "*kokhim*"). The *arcosolia* burial shelves are typically found in larger, more elaborate tombs because they take up more room than the *kokhim* slots. Larger tombs incorporated both types.

When a first-century Jew died, he was normally buried before the next sundown. The body was taken to the tomb where relatives washed and anointed their loved one with oil. If they could afford it, fragrant spices or lotions were added to mask the smell of the decomposing body. A linen burial shroud was placed over the corpse, passed around the feet and underneath the body, leaving the face uncovered. A separate piece of cloth was placed over the face. Then the entire body was wrapped in strips of linen, securing the shroud in place. The wrapped body was then slid headfirst into a burial slot or placed on a burial shelf.

On June 14, 2000, two archaeologists walked with a small group of their students through the Hinnom Valley, which runs south along the western edge of ancient Jerusalem. They were going to examine some elaborate tombs belonging to the Hasmonean period. Unexpectedly, they stumbled across an ancient tomb that had just been illegally opened and plundered by looters, sadly an all-too-common occurrence. Examining the tomb, they were shocked to discover the body of a first-century Jewish man who had died of leprosy and whose skeleton was still wrapped in the original burial shroud, the only one of its kind ever discovered. The tomb had remained sealed until these modern grave robbers broke it open. Unlike the spurious Shroud of Turin, an elaborate 14th century forgery claiming to be the burial shroud of Jesus, this shroud has been conclusively dated to the first century by carbon dating. The linen and wool shroud was made using a simple two-dimensional weave, characteristic of the first century. Rather than one continuous fabric, the first-century shroud was formed by smaller pieces sewn together. The face of this man was covered by a separate cloth, just as John describes Jesus' burial cloths. (John 20:6-7)

In our individualistic western culture, we normally think of a grave as belonging to one person, but ancient middle eastern tombs were always built for the extended family and were designed to receive multiple bodies at the same time. The larger and wealthier the family, the larger and more elaborate the family tomb. In first-century Judaism and still today, the Mount of Olives is the most coveted burial ground on earth. At the foot of the Mount of Olives on the east side of the Kidron Valley, enormous rock-cut funeral monuments mark the extensive family tombs of the Hasmonean elite from about a hundred years or more before the time of Jesus. Jesus referred to these outwardly impressive tombs when he was on the nearby Temple Mount and said to the religious leaders, *"Woe to you, scribes and Pharisees, hypocrites! For you are like whitewashed tombs, which outwardly appear beautiful, but within are full of dead people's bones and all uncleanness. So you also outwardly appear righteous to others, but within you are full of hypocrisy and lawlessness."* (Matthew 23:27-28)

Whether small and simple or large and impressive, these rock-cut tombs were designed to be sealed shut to contain the odor while the body decomposed and to protect the deceased from being disturbed by animals or scavengers. The rabbis also ruled that a

HASMONEAN TOMBS IN THE KIDRON VALLEY

sealed tomb did not leak defilement and a person could walk by or over such a tomb and be assured that they did not become ritually unclean. Sealing happened by sliding a large stone to the entrance of the tomb, wedging it into the opening, and sealing the edges with clay, as in the case of Lazarus' family tomb in Bethany (John 11:38-41). More elaborate tombs were designed with a large disc-shaped stone set into

a sloping trough cut parallel to the entrance. This heavy stone wheel, taller than the opening, would roll down the trough and across the entrance, sealing the tomb shut. With considerable effort the stone could be rolled back up the trough and wedged in place to open the tomb. Only noble and wealthy families could afford a rolling stone tomb, as with the newly cut tomb of Nicode-

FIRST-CENTURY ROLLING STONE TOMB

mus, a wealthy member of the Sanhedrin (Matthew 27:57-60). So it is interesting that the apparent extended family home of Joseph the *tekton* in Nazareth, where Jesus grew up, had a beautiful rolling-stone tomb cut underneath it (see Chapter 5).

Once the body was washed, anointed, wrapped, put in place, and sealed in the tomb, it was left for one year. The seven days following the death of a loved one were to be observed as a period of mourning called "*shiva*" (Hebrew for "seven," cf. Job 2:13). It was common for relatives to visit the grave of their loved one regularly during the three days following their death, to make sure they were really dead. The Rabbis explained it this way, "R. Abba b. R. Pappai and R. Joshua of Siknin said in the name of R. Levi: 'For three days [after death] the soul hovers over the body, intending to re-enter it, but as soon as it sees its appearance change, it departs'... Bar Kdappara said: 'The full force of mourning lasts for three days. Why? Because [for that length of time] the shape of the face is recognizable'"[58] The exception to this practice was if those three days fell on a Sabbath or festival. Since Jesus was buried just before sundown on a Friday, Sunday morning was the first opportunity for his disciples to visit his tomb. However, John and the women disciples had no question about Jesus' death after they saw the Roman soldier pierce his side with a spear, releasing *blood and water,* an apparent reference to the pericardial and pleural fluids that build up in the lungs and heart during crucifixion (John 19:34-35).

On the one-year anniversary of a loved one's death, the extended family gathered at the tomb to remember them, and the tomb would be unsealed and opened. The body would have fully decomposed by then, so the remaining bones were gathered together and placed into a small stone box called an ossuary. These were typically carved out of a solid block of limestone and fitted with a stone lid. In more elaborate burials, the ossuaries were carved with beautiful geometric and floral designs; for a simpler burials they were usually left plain. Often the person's name was scratched into the ossuary to identify their remains among the others. Once the bones were placed in the ossuary, it was typically set in the antechamber or in an open *kokhim* slot, and then the tomb was closed. Over time, a number of ossuaries collected in the family tomb as the generations were buried together. We can see this practice reflected in Paul's description of King David's death, "*David, after he had served the purpose of God in his own generation, fell asleep and was laid with his fathers.*" (Acts 13:36)

---

[58] Jacob Neusner, ed., *The Mishnah: A New Translation* (New Haven: Yale University, 1988), Lev. Rab. 18:1 on Lev. 15:1; cf. Eccl. Rab. 12:6., Digital.

FIRST-CENTURY TOMB WITH OSSUARIES

The Gospels record that Joseph offered his family burial site which was *a new tomb in which no one had yet been laid* (John 19:41). Further we are told that the women disciples who were sitting opposite the tomb watching Joseph and Nicodemus prepare Jesus' body, *saw the tomb and how his body was laid* (Luke 23:55). John says that when he first arrived at the tomb on that Sunday morning, bending over *to look in, he saw the linen cloths lying there, but he did not go in.* (John 20:5). The fact that Jesus' body could be seen from outside the tomb tells us Joseph's new tomb was still unfinished, consisting of only a single room. John goes on to tell us that when Mary Magdalene bent over to look inside the tomb, she saw *two angels in white, sitting where the body of Jesus had lain, one at the head and one at the feet.* (John 20:12).

Since angels could sit at either end of the place where Jesus' body had been laid, we know that this single burial chamber featured an *arcosolia* (shelf) rather than a *kokhim* (slot). This description fits precisely with the remains of the ancient tomb enshrined within the Church of the Holy Sepulcher in Jerusalem, which consists of only one room with one burial shelf cut into the northern wall. Presumably, Joseph's stone masons intended to cut two more shelves in the remaining walls, add burial slots, and possibly a passageway into a deeper burial room. But these plans were forever interrupted when Joseph took the brave step of offering his unfinished family tomb as a resting place for his crucified Rabbi.

An Ancient Jerusalem Cemetery

In the sixth century BC, when the Persian conqueror Cyrus the Great issued his edict allowing the Jewish exiles to return home, the Judean Governor, Zerubbabel, and his High Priest, Jeshua, oversaw the rebuilding of the Temple on Mount Zion. Persian King Darius received a report some years later this work was carried out with "huge stones" (Ezra 5:8). Many of these large building blocks were cut from the limestone hill just west of the city walls, the outlines of which may still be seen today underneath the Church of the Holy Sepulcher. Hundreds of years later, when this rock quarry had fallen into disuse, it was overgrown and converted into a garden cemetery with fine tombs cut into its stone walls. Situated just outside the western city walls and near the Gennath (Hebrew for "Garden") Gate, which opened onto the road to Jaffa, this coveted burial site attracted wealthy families like the family of Joseph of Arimathea to build tombs. Since Joseph's family lived some 30 miles west of Jerusalem and could afford it, we can understand why they would want a family tomb nearer to the holy city. They chose this well-placed cemetery located just outside the city walls on the road by which they would have normally entered Jerusalem and had a new family tomb cut there.

The Romans had chosen this same quarry as their place of crucifixion, due to its prominent location. As we explained in Chapter 11, a section of limestone in the quarry that was soft and flaky, not suitable for building, so the ancient temple builders cut around that section, leaving a large rocky outcropping overlooking the ancient quarry and subsequent cemetery. This outcropping, came to be called "place of the skull" both because of its appearance and the grisly executions that took place there. This means that the place of Jesus' crucifixion was only about 50 feet west of his burial place on the opposite side of the quarry, a detail captured by John's description of the tomb: *Now in the place where he was crucified there was a garden, and in the garden a new tomb in which no one had yet been laid. So because of the Jewish day of Preparation, since the tomb was close at hand, they laid Jesus there.* (John 19:41-42)

The fourth century Church of the Holy Sepulcher in Jerusalem is built over the site the earliest Christians identified as the Rock of Golgotha and the Tomb of Joseph, where Jesus' body was laid. The enclosure of this area by the city walls and the accumulation of centuries of tradition in this place have caused many to question its authenticity as the actual site of Jesus' crucifixion and resurrection. The shrine built over the remains of the tomb is called "The Edicule" (Latin for "little house"). In 2016 an extensive restoration of the Edicule was carried out, using cutting edge scientific methodologies. For the first time in over 800 years, the stones covering the tomb were removed, revealing the ancient remains beneath. This work confirmed that the Edicule is a fourth-century shrine built over a first-century tomb in a Jewish cemetery immediately outside the ancient walls of Jerusalem. These conclusions offer powerful support to the claim that this is actually the tomb of Joseph where Jesus' body was laid after his crucifixion on the nearby rock outcropping.

THE EDICULE BUILT OVER THE TOMB OF JESUS

In most parts of the Roman Empire, to further terrify the local population, crucified bodies were left on the crosses as carrion to be picked at by scavengers. However, in deference to Jewish sensibilities about caring for the bodies of the deceased, the Romans allowed families to take the bodies of their loved ones off the cross for burial. Joseph of Arimathea took a significant political and personal risk when he went to the Roman Governor Pilate requesting the body of Jesus, because he was aligning himself so closely with a man executed for treason. Although Joseph and Nicodemus kept their relationship with the Galilean rabbi secret up to this point, they were now going public as followers of Jesus (John 19:38-40). Perhaps Joseph was prompted to this courageous act by the realization that the new tomb he was building was within sight of Jesus' crucifixion. This was the best way he could demonstrate his devotion to his rabbi and serve Mary, whose family tomb was back in Nazareth underneath the family home.

SECURING THE TOMB

The Romans allowed the Jewish Sanhedrin to maintain the Temple Guard, a police force comprised of priests who were tasked with keeping the peace, protecting the High Priest, and punishing those who violated the sanctity of the Temple. Led by the Captain of the Temple, this Guard was the primary means by which the Sanhedrin exercised its authority and enforced its rulings (cf. Acts 4:1; 5:24). From time to time, for special purposes, the Romans assigned Roman soldiers to the Sanhedrin to reinforce their authority. John tells us that when the Sanhedrin sent its officers to arrest Jesus in the Garden of Gethsemane, they were joined by a cohort of soldiers, presumably Romans assigned by Pilate to the Sanhedrin (John 18:3). The day after Jesus was buried, the Jewish religious leaders came to Pilate requesting a guard of soldiers to secure the tomb and prevent his disciples from stealing the body and claiming resurrection (Matthew 27:62-64).

The Governor's response can be translated two ways, leaving us unsure of his exact meaning: *Pilate said to them, "You have* [or: *"take"*] *a guard of soldiers. Go, make it as secure as you can."* (Matthew 27:65) We can't be sure whether Pilate was telling the religious leaders to use their own security force to secure the tomb or authorizing them to take a guard of Roman soldiers for this task. Even if the correct translation is *"you have a guard of soldiers,"* this could still refer to the Roman soldiers previously assigned to the Sanhedrin to help with the arrest of Jesus two days earlier. Matthew tells us that this guard of soldiers affixed a seal to the rolling stone of the tomb (Matthew 27:66). A ribbon or rope was affixed at one end to the rolling stone and at the other end to the tomb itself by large wax seals. These seals bore the impression of either the Sanhedrin or the Roman Governor, threatening their punishment if the seals were broken.

When a Roman solider enrolled in military service, he swore an oath called the *sacramentum* to the Emperor and his General: "But the soldiers swear that they shall faithfully execute all that the Emperor commands, that they shall never desert the service, and that they shall not seek to avoid death for the Roman republic!"[59] This meant that a commanding officer had the right to summarily execute any solider under his command at his own discretion. The proscribed punishment for falling asleep during watch or allowing a prisoner to escape was death by beating. When the angel rolled

---

59 Publius Flavius Vegetius Renatus, *Epitoma Rei Militaris*, trans. N.P. Milner (Liverpool, Liverpool Univ. Press, 1996) 2.5, Digital.

back the stone and the guards saw the tomb was empty, they were so terrified that they passed out (Matthew 28:4). Because the guards were under the command of the San-hedrin, they reported this to the Chief Priests, who bribed them to tell the story that Jesus' disciples came and stole his body. Then they offered the soldiers an interesting reassurance, *"And if this comes to the gover-nor's ears, we will satisfy him and keep you out of trouble."* (Matthew 28:14) If these were soldiers from the Temple Guard, they would be liable to punishment from the Captain of the Temple. If they were Roman soldiers, they would have to answer to the Roman Governor, Pilate. The Chief Priests' assurance that they would intervene with Pilate tells us that, in fact, Roman soldiers were guarding the tomb of Joseph.

Matthew tells us that the Jewish religious leaders paid the Roman guards to spread the story, *"His disci-ples came by night and stole him away while we were asleep."* (Matthew 28:12-13) Apparently, they did a good job, since nearly a century later the rumor was still circulating among the Jewish community, as we can see Justin Martyr's comment to his imaginary Jewish opponent: "you have sent chosen and ordained men throughout all the world to proclaim that a godless

THE NAZARETH DECREE

and lawless heresy had sprung from one Jesus, a Galilaean deceiver, whom we crucified, but his disciples stole him by night from the tomb, where he was laid when unfastened from the cross, and now deceive men by asserting that he has risen from the dead and ascended to heaven."[60]

In the 19th century, a stone slab bearing a first-century Greek inscription was discovered in Nazareth. It records a decree from the Roman Emperor threatening death for those who would move a sealing stone to steal a body from a tomb. Normally graverobbing was considered a civic offense, but this edict makes it a capital offense. The decree concludes, "You are absolutely not to allow anyone to move those who have been entombed. But if someone does, I wish that violator to suffer capital punishment under the title of tomb-breaker."[61] Most scholars date this so-called "Nazareth Decree" to the reign of Claudius (AD 41-54). It is interesting that just when the news of Jesus' resurrection from the dead was spreading across the Roman Empire and both Jews and Gentiles were coming to faith by the thousands, the Roman Emperor found it necessary to make such a dire threat against tomb robbers and post it in Jesus' hometown. Perhaps this was an attempt by Claudius to prevent any other movements of resurrected Messiahs starting in Palestine!

 THE TRUTH

THE MEANING OF THE EMPTY TOMB

It was the third day of their week of mourning, but the Sabbath had prevented them from visiting Jesus' tomb even once. And so early that Sunday morning, while it was still dark, Mary Magdalene led a group of the women disciples from their hiding place in the southwest part of the city, through the streets of Jerusalem, out the Gennath Gate in the western city wall, to the ancient quarry-turned-cemetery. Included with

---

60 Justin Martyr, *Dialogue with Trypho,* from *Ante-Nicene Fathers*, Vol. 1, ed. Alexander Roberts, James Donaldson, and A. Cleveland Coxe. (Buffalo, NY: Christian Literature Publishing Co., 1885.) 108.2, Digital.

61 Clyde E. Billington, "The Nazareth Inscription: Proof of the Resurrection of Christ?," *Artifax* (Spring 2005), Digital.

ROCK QUARRY TURNED CEMETERY

Mary Magdalene in this group of female disciples were Joanna, the wife of Chuza (Herod Antipas' steward), Salome the wife of Zebedee and mother of James and John, Mary the mother of James and Joses, and Mary the wife of Clopas and mother of Simeon. Along with Jesus' mother Mary, they had watched Joseph and Nicodemus prepare Jesus' body and seal the tomb, but something felt unfinished. Taking spices, they were going to express their love for their rabbi by anointing his body; a final act of devotion. This demonstrated extraordinary determination and bravery on several levels.

THE TOMB OF JESUS

In that culture women normally did not go outside their homes when it was dark, certainly never alone, as it was seen to be inviting trouble. In addition, they were known associates of an accused revolutionary who had just been executed by the Romans. While women were less likely than men to be officially arrested and prosecuted, no Roman would blame a soldier who abused a woman associated with a crucified criminal. On top of all this,

Mary Magdalene led the women disciples straight to the place of Jesus' crucifixion to open his tomb—a tomb sealed and guarded by a squad of Roman soldiers. These courageous disciples had decided to take up their cross and follow their Rabbi no matter what the cost!

Arriving at the tomb, the women were confronted with the last thing they had expected. The huge stone sealing the entrance to the tomb was rolled back and propped open! The Roman guards were nowhere to be found. The synoptic Gospels jump directly to the account of the angelic messenger announcing Jesus' resurrection, but John tells us of an intervening episode. Mary Magdalene returned to the upper room where the male disciples were still in hiding and delivered the most obvious interpretation of the empty grave: *"They have taken the Lord out of the tomb, and we do not know where they have laid him."* (John 20:7-9)

This prompted a footrace between Peter and John, with the younger disciple John arriving at the tomb first. After examining the empty tomb, Peter returned home puzzled, while John came to a different conclusion. Recording his own first-hand experience, John recounts that something unusual about the way the burial shroud was lying on the *arcosolia* shelf caught their attention. John's description implies the shroud and wrappings were lying just as they had been placed on Jesus' dead body. And then Peter noticed *the face cloth, which had been on Jesus' head, not lying with the linen cloths but folded up in a place by itself. Then the other disciple, who had reached the tomb first, also went in, and he saw and believed; for as yet they did not understand the Scripture, that he must rise from the dead.* (John 20:7-8) John realized that no grave robber would take the time to unwrap the body and carefully rearrange the valuable linen wrappings on the burial shelf to be left behind. And why would the face cloth be carefully folded up (or "rolled up") and laid in a separate place?

Whatever John saw in that tomb precipitated his faith that Jesus' body had not been stolen, but that he had been miraculously raised from the dead. Perhaps the sight of the empty burial shelf and carefully arranged linens jogged his memory of all the times Jesus told the disciples plainly, *the Son of Man must suffer many things and be rejected by the elders and the chief priests and the scribes and be killed, and after three days rise again.* (Mark 8:31) During his ministry Jesus repeatedly used biblical images in his teaching that pointed to his resurrection. When the crowd asked him for a sign, Jesus told them, *"For just as Jonah was three days and three nights in the belly of the great fish, so will the Son of Man be three days and three nights in the heart of the earth."* (Matthew 12:40) Just the previous week, Jesus told a parable of tenants who took the vineyard owner's son outside vineyard walls and killed him. He concluded by quoting the famous Messianic Psalm 118: *"Have you never read in the Scriptures: "'The stone that the builders rejected has become the cornerstone; this was the Lord's doing, and it is marvelous in our eyes'?"* (Matthew 21:28-42)

After the fact, it might seem obvious to us what Jesus was talking about, but before it happened the disciples struggled to wrap their minds around his predictions of resurrection. When coming down the mountain following the transfiguration, Jesus told them not to speak of it until after he had risen from the dead. This only raised more questions in their minds: *so they kept the matter to themselves, questioning what this rising from the dead might mean,* and then they began to ask Jesus about Elijah, the prophet who didn't die, but was taken up into heaven (Mark 9:10-13). After his symbolic act in the Temple, Jesus said, *"Destroy this temple, and in three days I will raise it up."* But the disciples didn't understand what he meant until later. John notes, *When therefore he was raised from the dead, his disciples remembered that he had said this, and they believed the Scripture and the word that Jesus had spoken.* (John 2:19-22) Perhaps this moment in the tomb, seeing the undisturbed grave cloths, prompted John to remember and believe what Jesus had promised about his resurrection!

Resurrection of the dead was not a novel idea to first-century Jews. Although the Sadducees, who only accepted the first five books of the Torah, did not believe in life after death, the Pharisees accepted all the books of the Hebrew Bible and regularly taught the resurrection of the dead from Scriptures such as, *Your dead shall live; their bodies shall rise. You who dwell in the dust, awake and sing for joy! For your dew is a dew of light, and the earth will give birth to the dead.* (Isaiah 26:19) *And many of those who sleep in the dust of the earth shall awake, some to everlasting life, and some to shame and everlasting contempt.* (Daniel 12:2) On top of this, observant Jews were reminded of the resurrection three times a day in the second of their eighteen daily prayers, "Who is like You, Almighty, and who is compared to you, King, who kills and gives life and brings salvation to spring up? And You are reliable to give life to the dead. Praised are You, Lord, who gives life to the dead." [62] When Lazarus died and was in the tomb four days, Jesus came to Bethany and told his

---

[62] *Amidah,* "The Eighteen Benedictions," Second Benediction, from Emil Shuerer, *The History of the Jewish People in the Age of Jesus Christ,* ed. Geza Vermes (Edinburgh: T. & T. Clark, 1979) 455, n. 154.

sister Martha, *"Your brother will rise again."* Given the established Jewish teaching of resurrection, it is no surprise that Martha responded, *"I know that he will rise again in the resurrection on the last day."* But Jesus brought a radically new perspective when he declared in the present tense, *"I am the resurrection and the life"* and then went on to prove the irrefutable truth of those words by raising Lazarus from the dead! (John 11:17-44) The Old Testament always describes resurrection in an apocalyptic context at the end of human history, but by raising Lazarus Jesus demonstrated that this eschatological future is now breaking into the present. This is exactly what Jesus taught about the Kingdom

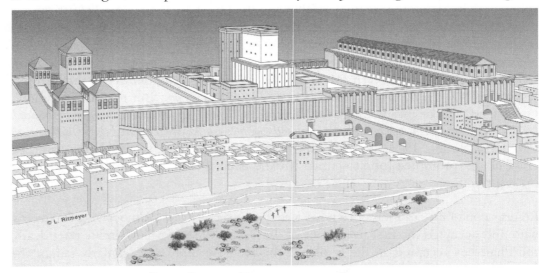

ROCK QUARRY TURNED INTO A CEMETERY

of God. God's full reign on earth as he reigns in heaven is a future reality that has now begun to unfold in the present, transforming those who will believe and follow Jesus. Jesus' resurrection from the dead is the definitive inauguration of this now-and-not-yet Kingdom in our present reality. When John stood in that empty tomb, looking at those undisturbed grave cloths, the transforming truth of this incredible new reality began to stir in his heart. But for most of Jesus' followers, the empty tomb and burial shroud were not enough. They needed something more.

ENCOUNTERS WITH THE RISEN JESUS

While Peter and John returned to the upper room of Mary's home in the southwest part of Jerusalem, pondering the meaning of the empty tomb, the female disciples lingered graveside, weeping over the presumed desecration of their Rabbi's body. But their grieving was suddenly disturbed by a dramatic and frightening angelic visitation. The angels that rolled the stone back now appeared to the women, first inside the tomb and then sitting on the rolling stone. One of the angels said to the women, *"Why do you seek the living among the dead? He is not here, but has risen. Remember how he told you, while he was still in Galilee, that the Son of Man must be delivered into the hands of sinful men and be crucified and on the third day rise."* (Luke 24:5-7) Both Matthew and Mark include the detail that the angels pointed to the empty burial shelf and said, *"Come, see the place where he lay"* offering visual confirmation of their message (Matthew 28:6; Mark 16:6).

For John, seeing the place where Jesus' body had been laid was enough, but the rest of the disciples needed more than an empty burial shelf to comprehend and believe that Jesus had risen from the dead. Certainly, this dramatic angelic visitation and proclamation was a turning point for the women disciples. In fact, Luke tells us this is the moment when the women *remembered his words*, meaning they recalled Jesus' predictions of his death and resurrection (Luke 24:8). The things Jesus had said were starting to make sense, and yet they were still filled with a dizzying array of conflicting thoughts and feelings. Mark tells us the angel's words filled the women with *trembling and astonishment* (Mark 16:8). Matthew describes their reaction as *fear and great joy* (Matthew 28:8). Luke says that when the male disciples heard the women's report of the angelic announcement, it *seemed to them an idle tale, and they did not believe them* (Luke 24:11). The angel's announcement contradicted the disciples' assumption that Jesus' body had been stolen and jogged their memory of Jesus' promise, but it did not fill them with faith that he was actually alive again.

Mary Magdalene still believed Jesus' body had been stolen, even after her encounter with the angels. As she was leaving the tomb with tears in her eyes, she saw a man whom she assumed to be the gardener of the cemetery and begged him to show her where the body was. But when she heard him speak her name, she suddenly realized it was Jesus speaking; *She turned and said to him in Aramaic, "Rabboni!" (which means Teacher).* (John 20:14-16) Matthew tells us that the risen Jesus appeared not only to Mary, but to all the women disciples who had come to the tomb that morning as well (Luke 24:10). It was one thing to find the tomb empty, notice the unusual arrangement of the burial shroud, and even hear the report of angels, but it was entirely another thing to actually encounter the risen Jesus! Jesus told the women not to cling to him, but *"go and tell my brothers"* what they had witnessed. So they ran back to the upper room and *Mary Magdalene went and announced to the disciples, "I have seen the Lord"* (John 20:17-18).

In addition to this appearance to the women at the tomb, the Gospels report six more appearances of the risen Jesus to the rest of his disciples. Paul confirms several of these and adds three more; Jesus' appearance to James the brother of Jesus, *to more than five hundred brothers at one time,* and to Paul himself on the road to Damascus (1 Corinthians 15:4-8). Luke recounts how that Sunday afternoon Cleopas and another unnamed disciple (his wife?) were walking from Jerusalem to Emmaus (their home?) and met the risen Jesus along the way. Once they recognized Jesus, he disappeared from their midst, and they returned with haste to report this to the other disciples in Jerusalem. When they arrived, the eleven and the other disciples shared their own Good News, *"The Lord has risen indeed, and has appeared to Simon!"* (Luke 24:13-35). This personal encounter between Simon Peter and Jesus is not recorded in the other Gospels, but Paul mentions this one first in his list of resurrection appearances (1 Corinthians 15:5).

MENSA CHRISTI AT THE SEA OF GALILEE

Luke tells us that while the disciples were having this conversation, presumably in the upper room of the house of Mary the mother of John Mark, suddenly *Jesus himself stood among them, and said to them, "Peace to you!"* (Luke 24:36). John records this same Sunday evening appearance to the fearful disciples hiding behind locked doors, followed by a second appearance the following Sunday in the same place, but this time with Thomas present (John 20:19-29). When Jesus appeared to the women at the tomb, he instructed them to tell the male disciples to meet him on a specific mountain in Galilee. The eleven disciples returned to Galilee, and when they met Jesus on the appointed mountain, he gave them the famous Great Commission, *"All authority in heaven and on earth has been given to me. Go therefore and make disciples of all nations, baptizing them in the name of the Father and of the Son and of the Holy Spirit, teaching them to observe all that I have commanded you. And behold, I am with you always, to the end of the age."* (Matthew 28:10, 16-20) We don't know which Galilean mountain this was, but it sounds very much like the slope rising above the northwest shore of the lake near Tabgha where Jesus reportedly took his disciples for the famous Sermon on the Mount (Matthew 5:1).

John describes another Galilean appearance that took place when Peter and six of the disciples decided to go fishing on the lake. They had a major déjà vu when, after fishing all night and catching nothing, the input of a mysterious figure on shore led them to another miraculous catch of fish. Realizing it was Jesus, they managed to drag their breaking nets to shore and ended up eating a fish breakfast with the risen Jesus.

They sat around a charcoal fire, reminiscent of the charcoal fire in the courtyard of the High Priest's house where Peter denied Jesus three times. But now, around this charcoal fire on the beach, Jesus brought Peter's deep shame into the healing light by asking him three times, *"Do you love me?"* Jesus went on to show amazing grace toward Peter by responding to each of his three affirmations of love with the mandate, *"Feed/tend my lambs/sheep."* (John 21:1-17) At their final Passover supper, Jesus spoke of this very moment when he prophesied, not only Peter's denials, but also his restoration: *"Simon, Simon, behold, Satan demanded to have you, that he might sift you like wheat, but I have prayed for you that your faith may not fail. And when you have turned again, strengthen your brothers."* (Luke 22:31-32) The risen Jesus was reinstating Peter as a leader and calling him to turn back from his spectacular failure so he could strengthen the other disciples.

About AD 384, a wealthy Christian woman named Egeria from western Europe took an arduous three-year pilgrimage through the Holy Lands. As she traveled, visited, and prayed at various sites, she wrote a detailed journal which has been preserved and serves as an invaluable source of information about biblical sites. Egeria reports visiting a site known as "Mensa Christi" (Latin for "Table of Christ") on the northwest shore of the Sea of Galilee, west of Capernaum near Tabgha. It consists of a large flat limestone rock on the beach with steps cut into the side of it. This was identified as the place where Jesus lit that charcoal fire on the beach, cooked the disciples a fish breakfast, and reinstated Peter. (John 21:9-19) About the time of Egeria's visit, a Byzantine church was built over that rock. It stood for over 900 years and by the ninth century was referred to as "the Place of the Coals." Today a small black basalt chapel called The Church of the Primacy of Peter stands on the rock to commemorate this event. We have little archaeological evidence to support this early tradition, but the location fits everything the biblical account describes.

The Nature of the Risen Jesus

It is apparent from the disciples' encounters with the resurrected Jesus that his physical appearance was somehow changed. When Mary Magdalene first met Jesus outside the tomb, she mistook him for the gardener (John 20:14-15). When Cleopas and the other disciple met Jesus on the road to Emmaus, they had a lengthy theological discussion about recent events, but did not realize they were talking to their Rabbi (Luke 24:13-16). When Jesus appeared to the disciples on the shore while they were fishing, they did not realize it was him telling them to let down their nets again (John 21:4). When Jesus met the disciples in Galilee on the mountain, some doubted it was really him (Matthew 28:17). And yet, in spite of this lack of recognition, it is also apparent that the risen Jesus still bore the wounds of his crucifixion. When he appeared to the disciples in the upper room, he showed them the wounds in his wrists and his side as verification that it was really him. John recorded their recognition and relief when he wrote, *Then the disciples were glad when they saw the Lord* (John 20:20). Although the appearance of Jesus' body had changed, it was undeniably the same body that had been nailed to a cross and pierced with a spear.

Not only was Jesus' outward appearance changed, but the nature of his body was also transformed. The angel who rolled back the stone revealed a tomb that was already empty, which means Jesus was able to leave the rock-cut tomb without opening it (Matthew 28:2-6). After Cleopas and the other disciple recognized Jesus in Emmaus, he suddenly disappeared from their midst (Luke 24:31). John tells us that on two occasions, both the outer door and the inner door of the house where the disciples were hiding out were locked, and yet Jesus suddenly appeared in their midst (John 20:19, 26) Some assume these phenomena indicate the risen Jesus was non-physical, what some would call a "spirit" or a "ghost." Others conclude the disciples were experiencing some kind of psychological projection or spiritual vision. And yet it is clear that, when the disciples met the risen Jesus, he was physically present to them in verifiable, tangible ways.

When Jesus met Mary Magdalene at the tomb, she must have embraced him, because he had to ask her not to cling to him (John 20:17). When the rest of the women met him, they fell down and took hold of his feet (Matthew 28:9). Jesus broke bread with the disciples in Emmaus, ate broiled fish in the upper room, and cooked fish for them on the shore of the Sea of Galilee. Luke explicitly addressed the nature of Jesus' body when he wrote, *But they were startled and frightened and thought they saw a spirit. And he said to them, "Why are you troubled, and why do doubts arise in your hearts? See my hands and my feet, that it is I myself. Touch me, and see. For a spirit does not have flesh and bones as you see that I have." And when he had said this, he showed them his hands and his feet. And while they still disbelieved for joy and were marveling, he said to them, "Have you anything here to eat?" They gave him a piece of broiled fish, and he took it and ate before them.* (Luke 24:37-43)

When God raised Jesus from the dead, he brought his whole person back to life: heart, mind, soul, and body. This is the promise of resurrection for us. The resurrected Jesus was a physical man, not a non-material spirit, but this is a new kind of physicality that defies the laws of our present reality. The fact that Jesus is now able to pass through solid rock could lead us to assume he has become somehow ethereal and less real, but *exactly the opposite* has taken place! Jesus has not become *less* physical; he has become *more* physical, a part of the new creation that has now begun with his resurrection.

In his Space Trilogy, C. S. Lewis points out that even in our world, a body passes through apparently "solid" materials if it is more substantive rather than less. When you drop a pebble in a glass of water, it sinks to the bottom because rock is more solid than the water. Therefore, the fact that the resurrected Jesus could pass through doors and walls implies that he was *more* physical, *not less*.[63] Nuclear physicists tell us that the vast majority of what appear to be solid objects are, in fact, comprised of nearly mass-less neutron clouds of atoms. What makes these atoms seem solid is the strong attraction between each atom's particles. Liquids and gases have weaker bonds, which is why solids can pass through them. It is not too big a leap to imagine the atoms making up Jesus' resurrection body having such strong bonds that his body could pass through the weaker bonded atoms of what seems solid to us. Lewis vividly illustrates this in his allegory, *The Great Divorce*, which depicts a bus tour from hell to the outskirts of heaven. The inhabitants of hell are semi-transparent, lacking substantive existence, while the inhabitants of heaven are described as "solid spirits." One of the travelers from hell

63 C. S. Lewis, *Out of the Silent Planet*, (New York, Macmillan, 1965) 95.

describes his first impression of heaven's outskirts; "It was the light, the grass, the trees that were different; made of some different substance, so much solider than things in our country that men were ghosts by comparison."[64]

The Apostle Paul grappled with this mystery when he was explaining the importance of Jesus' bodily resurrection to the Corinthians: *But someone will ask, "How are the dead raised? With what kind of body do they come?" You foolish person! What you sow does not come to life unless it dies. And what you sow is not the body that is to be, but a bare kernel, perhaps of wheat or of some other grain... So is it with the resurrection of the dead. What is sown is perishable; what is raised is imperishable. It is sown in dishonor; it is raised in glory. It is sown in weakness; it is raised in power. It is sown a natural body; it is raised a spiritual body. If there is a natural body, there is also a spiritual body.* (1 Corinthians 15:35-37, 42-44) The resurrection of Jesus marks the beginning of a new apocalyptic era in which the future is beginning to break into the present. The resurrected Jesus portends a future reality that is so much better than our present, as much better as a blossoming flower is more beautiful than the bare kernel from which it sprouts. Paul explains, *But in fact Christ has been raised from the dead, the firstfruits of those who have fallen asleep* (1 Corinthians 15:20). The *firstfruits* are the down payment assuring us of what is to come. The new creation that Jesus promised has now begun, and in his resurrection we see a brand-new present leading us into a glorious eternal future!

PHYSICAL EVIDENCE OF JESUS' RESURRECTION

The Gospel descriptions of Jesus' bodily resurrection confront us with a phenomenon so far outside our experience that we have to ask if there is any logical reason to trust the historical accuracy of these accounts. Some will simply dismiss the resurrection because it sounds too fantastic to be true, but we need to consider what the factual basis for this claim might be.

The first thing to ask is whether the Gospel accounts fit with what we know of the material remains related to the resurrection. We have already described the ancient stone quarry outside the western city wall of Jerusalem, subsequently turned into a garden cemetery by the first century BC. In AD 41-43, just a decade after Jesus' crucifixion, this northwest part of Jerusalem was enclosed inside the city walls by Herod Agrippa I. He built the

---

64 C. S. Lewis, *The Great Divorce*, (New York, Macmillan, 1946) 28-29.

foundations of what Josephus calls "the third wall," which ran north from the Hippicus Tower—what is today called the Tower of David at Jaffa Gate—to the enormous Psephinus Tower, which defended the northwestern corner of the city wall. This third wall meant that now the tomb underneath the current Church of the Holy Sepulcher was enclosed by the city walls within a decade of Jesus' burial. If the Christian community in Jerusalem did not know where the tomb in which Jesus was buried was located, they would never make up a site inside the walls of Jerusalem, because everyone knows that Jesus was buried outside the city!

In AD 70 the Romans attacked this third wall when they laid siege to the city during the first Jewish revolt, eventually destroying the Temple and burning the city to the ground. In AD 132, a Jewish revolutionary named Simon Bar Kokhba led a second revolt which was put down by the Roman Emperor Hadrian, who dispatched an overwhelming military force and destroyed the rebels by AD 135. In an effort to dispel Jewish nationalism once and for all, the Emperor expelled all Jews from Jerusalem, gave Jerusalem the new name Aeila Capitolina, and redesigned it as a Roman city, building new religious structures over existing religious sites. To commemorate his victory, Hadrian built a Roman-style triumphal arch called the "Ecce Homo Arch" which is still visible today north of the Temple Mount on the Via Dolarosa. Large statues of Jupiter and Hadrian were built on the still-ruined Temple Mount. In the northwest part of the city, a large commercial marketplace ("forum") was built adjacent to the stone-quarry-turned-cemetery. The ancient quarry was filled in, burying the cemetery and creating a platform on which a temple to Venus was constructed.

According to tradition, the earliest followers of Jesus returned to the site of Joseph's tomb on Sunday mornings to celebrate his resurrection, establishing the basis for the eventual designation of Sunday, rather than Saturday, as the primary day of Christian worship. For nearly two hundred years, the Christian community of Jerusalem continued to remember that the rock of Golgotha where Jesus was crucified and the tomb of Joseph were Jesus was buried were located underneath the massive platform of the temple of Venus. In the fourth century, when the Roman Emperor Constantine recognized Christianity as a legal religion of the Empire, he sent his devout mother Queen Helena to the Holy Land to build large churches on the three most important sites: the places of Jesus' birth, death and resurrection, and ascension. The result was the establishment of the Church of the Nativity in Bethlehem, the Church of the Holy Sepulcher in Jerusalem, and the Church of the Ascension on the Mount of Olives.

When Queen Helena came to Jerusalem in AD 326 and asked Macarius, the Bishop of Jerusalem, where the rock of Golgotha and the tomb of Jesus were located, he pointed to the pagan temple Hadrian built inside the city walls and told her that both were buried deep beneath its platform. If the early Christians of Jerusalem did not know the accurate location of the rock and the tomb, why would they fabricate a site inside the city walls

CHURCH OF THE HOLY SEPULCHER

and underneath a massive structure? Furthermore, how would they know there was a large rock and a first-century tomb buried deep underneath that pagan temple complex, unless the memory of the location had been preserved against all these seemingly contradictory indicators? This seems the most unlikely of locations to choose, unless it was based on an accurate historical identification.

The ancient church historian Eusebius, Bishop of Caesarea, accompanied Queen Helena and watched as the workmen cleared away the platform of the pagan temple, revealing what lay beneath. They were amazed to discover exactly what Bishop Macarius had described: a large rocky outcropping in an ancient cemetery containing a tomb marked with graffiti identifying it as the grave in which Jesus had been buried. Eusebius described their delight when he wrote, "as soon as the original surface of the ground, beneath the covering of earth, appeared, immediately and contrary to all expectation, the venerable and hallowed monument of our Savior's resurrection was discovered. Then indeed did this most holy cave present a faithful similitude of his return to life, in that, after lying buried in darkness, it again emerged to light, and afforded to all who came to witness the sight, a clear and visible proof of the wonders of which that spot had once been the scene, a testimony to the resurrection of the Savior clearer than any voice could give."[65]

Based on the testimony of the local Christian community and the corroborating evidence they discovered beneath the temple of Venus, Helena proceeded to build the massive Church of the Holy Sepulcher around this tomb and rock. Bishop Macarius of Jerusalem received the following letter from the Emperor Constantine, celebrating this confirming discovery and pledging his support in the building of the new church, "Such is our Saviour's grace, that no power of language seems adequate to describe the wondrous circumstance to which I am about to refer. For, that the monument of his most holy Passion, so long ago buried beneath the ground, should have remained unknown for so long a series of years, until its reappearance to his servants now set free through the removal of him who was the common enemy of all, is a fact which

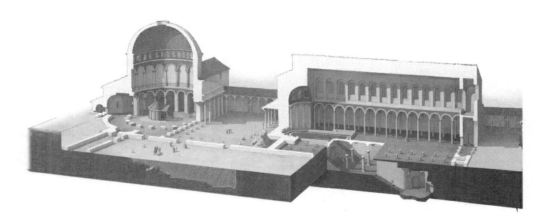

ORIGINAL CHURCH OF THE HOLY SEPULCHER

[65] Eusebius, *Life of Constantine*, trans. Bagster, rev. E.C. Richardson, Book 3, Chapter 28, Digital.

truly surpasses all admiration... And as to the columns and marble, whatever you shall judge, after actual inspection of the plan, to be especially precious and serviceable, be diligent to send information to us in writing, in order that whatever quantity or sort of materials we shall esteem from your letter to be needful, may be procured from every quarter, as required, for it is fitting that the most marvelous place in the world should be worthily decorated."[66]

This tells us there was a continuous testimony from the eyewitnesses of Jesus' death, burial and resurrection to the actual place where these things happened until the building of the Church of the Holy Sepulcher nearly 300 years later. The archaeological study of the physical remains underneath this ancient church fit perfectly with the testimony of the Gospels; just outside the city walls there was a rocky outcropping, reminiscent of a skull, which the Romans had chosen as their place of public execution. Nearby, in a garden cemetery, there was a newly cut tomb belonging to a wealthy Jewish family. Obviously, this physical evidence alone is not proof of Jesus' resurrection, but it is a powerful corroboration of the setting accurately described in the Gospel accounts of these events. Knowing that the physical evidence supports the accounts of Jesus' resurrection, we turn now to the historical evidence.

HISTORICAL EVIDENCE OF JESUS' RESURRECTION

It is striking that all four Gospels claim the female disciples first saw the empty tomb and heard the angelic announcement of Jesus' resurrection. Matthew, Luke, and John describe how these women encountered the physically resurrected and gloriously transformed Jesus. It is also surprising that all four Gospels depict the male disciples, by contrast, as hiding in fear and reliant on the report of the women to hear the news of an empty tomb. In first-century Judaism, women were not considered reliable witnesses, and their testimony was considered inadmissible in court. Josephus wrote, "Put not trust in a single witness, but let there be three or at the least two, whose evidence shall be accredited by their past lives. From women let no evidence be accepted, because of the levity and temerity of their sex."[67] Fabricating a story in which women were the primary witnesses was unthinkable in that culture.

---

66 Eusebius, *Life of Constantine*, Book 3, Chapters 30-32.

67 Flavius Josephus, *Antiquities of the Jews,* trans. William Whiston, (Delmarva, 2016), Book 4, Chapter 8, Section 15, Digital.

One of the most powerful indicators of historical accuracy is when writers record events that cast themselves in an unfavorable light. Both Matthew and John admit they were among the men hiding in fear in the upper room, while the women bravely went to the tomb. Luke reports that the male disciples did not believe the testimony of the women but dismissed it as *an idle tale* (Luke 24:11). He goes on to describe how Cleopas and his companion failed to recognize the risen Jesus on the road to Emmaus, even after extensive conversation with him (Luke 24:15-27). Matthew tells us that after the risen Jesus appeared to the male disciples in Galilee, *some doubted* (Matthew 28:17). The fact that these men recounted the circumstances of that morning in such unflattering terms is convincing evidence they are recording accurate historical facts, not constructing a fanciful tale.

Furthermore, the Gospels contain firsthand, eyewitness accounts of these events. This is not hearsay. Matthew and John reported what they themselves experienced. Mark recorded the firsthand testimony of Peter. Luke recounted the testimony of eyewitnesses he interviewed. The women watched Joseph and Nicodemus prepare Jesus' body, lay it in the tomb, and seal it with a stone. There was no question about which tomb they were to return to that Sunday morning. The women, Peter, Cleopas and the unnamed disciple, the twelve disciples, James, the wider family of disciples, and over

TOMB INSIDE THE CHURCH OF THE HOLY SEPULCHER

500 people at one time all encountered the risen Jesus over a period of forty days. They all saw him and spoke with him, some multiple times. Many of them touched Jesus' resurrected body. Jesus ate with them to make it clear he was not a ghost. He showed them his wounds to demonstrate he was the same person whom they had watched die on the cross. When they saw and heard Jesus, they were together with others who had the same experience, which is unmistakable evidence they were not seeing some kind of spiritual apparition or psychological projection, but encountering a mutually verifiable, resurrected Jesus.

John described this firsthand apostolic testimony as, *That which was from the beginning, which we have heard, which we have seen with our eyes, which we looked upon and have touched with our hands, concerning the word of life"*(1 John 1:1). Peter said it this way, *For we did not follow cleverly devised myths when we made known to you the power and coming of our Lord Jesus Christ, but we were eyewitnesses of his majesty.* (2 Peter 1:16) All trial lawyers know that eyewitness testimony is the most convincing, but they also understand human perception is limited and human memory faulty. Anytime multiple witnesses give the exact same account of an event, with little or no variation in detail, it immediately raises suspicion of witness coaching or collusion. When multiple witnesses describe the same basic events but differ on small details that can be explained by a difference in point of view or confusion of sequence, the testimony is considered solid and reliable. This is the kind of testimony we have in the New Testament about the resurrection of Jesus. The four Gospel accounts agree on the main points:

1. Jesus was really dead, and his body was sealed in a newly-cut rock tomb owned by Joseph of Arimathea.
2. A group of his female followers came to the same tomb on the third day and found the sealing stone rolled away and the tomb empty.
3. An angel told the women that Jesus was alive again and they were to go and tell the male disciples.
4. Jesus appeared to the women and then to the male disciples in various times and places.
5. The Jesus whom they saw alive was the same man they saw die on a cross two days earlier.
6. Jesus was physically present, but visibly different and able to come and go in a way he didn't before.

These four witnesses solidly agree on the key events that happened that first Easter day, and yet there are minor differences in the details. How many women went to the tomb that morning? Was there one angel or two at the tomb? Did the angel speak to the women before or after they went into the tomb? Did Peter run to examine the tomb before the women heard from the angel or after? These differing details don't compromise the core of their testimony - on the contrary, they add a credible texture to their testimony which affirms that these are real people recounting a genuine experience from their unique perspective and by their imperfect memory. If the disciples had conspired to steal Jesus' body and concoct a story of resurrection, surely their accounts would fit together more neatly than they do! In his book *The Jesus I Never Knew*, Philp Yancey explains why the conspiracy theory falls apart on closer examination of the Gospel accounts.

> ...if the disciples had set out to concoct a seamless cover-up story, they failed miserably. Chuck Colson, who participated in a feckless conspiracy after the Watergate break-in, says that cover-ups only work if all participants maintain a unified front of assurance and competence. That, the disciples surely did not do. The Gospels show the disciples cringing in locked rooms, terrified that the same thing that happened to Jesus might happen to them... The disciples seemed utterly incapable of faking a resurrection or risking their lives by stealing a body; nor did it occur to them in their state of despair... A deliberate cover-up would have put Peter or John or, better yet, Nicodemus in the spotlight, not built its case around reports from women. Since the Gospels were written several decades after the events, the authors had plenty of time to straighten out such an anomaly— unless, of course, they were not concocting a legend but recording the plain facts. A conspiracy also would have tidied up the first witnesses' stories. Were there two white-clad figures or just one? Why did Mary Magdalene mistake Jesus for a gardener? Was she alone or with Salome and another Mary? Accounts of the discovery of the empty tomb sound breathless and fragmentary. The women were "afraid yet filled with joy," says Matthew; "trembling and bewildered," says Mark. Jesus makes no dramatic, well-orchestrated entrance to quell all doubts; the early reports seem wispy, mysterious, confused. Surely conspirators could have done a neater job of depicting what they would later claim to be the hinge event of history.[68]

When examined on these points, the Gospel accounts of Jesus' resurrection appear to be an accurate record of credible first-hand testimony corroborating the fact that Jesus

---

[68] Yancey, Philip. *The Jesus I Never Knew* (Grand Rapids, Zondervan), 212-213, Digital.

really did rise from the dead. Luke sums it up this way: *He presented himself alive to them after his suffering by many proofs, appearing to them during forty days and speaking about the kingdom of God.* (Acts 1:3)

However, an even more convincing piece of historical evidence is the personal conduct of the first witnesses who reported experiencing all these things. Those who claimed to see Jesus alive again after he was killed spent the rest of their lives testifying to that fact and devoted themselves to sharing this Good News as far and wide as possible, no matter the cost. Luke tells us that Stephen was the first to pay for this testimony with his life (Acts 7:54-60). It is significant that, as Stephen was facing the enraged crowd, he was strengthened by a vision of the risen and ascended Jesus standing at the right hand of the Father. Luke goes on to tell us that James, the son of Zebedee, was beheaded by Herod Agrippa I (Acts 12:1-2). Josephus, the Jewish historian, records the execution of Jesus' brother James in Jerusalem; "Festus was now dead, and Albinus was but upon the road; so he assembled the sanhedrim of judges, and brought before them the brother of Jesus, who was called Christ, whose name was James, and some others; and when he had formed an accusation against them as breakers of the law, he delivered them to be stoned..."[69]

This deadly persecution did not come as a surprise to the followers of Jesus because he repeatedly told them they would face violence and hatred, and called them to take up their cross, a clear allusion to his own impending execution (Mark 8:34-35, 13:9-13, John 15:20). Jesus explicitly prophesied that Peter would be crucified in his old age in contrast to John (John 21:18-22). These periods of persecution pushed many of the followers of Jesus out of Jerusalem, across Judea and Samaria, and beyond. According to the earliest extra-biblical accounts, the original apostles intentionally struck out in different directions around the world, intentionally fulfilling Jesus' call to be his witnesses *"to the ends of the earth"* (Acts 1:8).

Various sources from the second and third centuries record the fate of these apostles as they carried out their mission in the face of continued opposition, persecution, and even martyrdom. Writers such as Polycrates of Ephesus (AD 130-196), Irenaeus of Lyon (AD 130-202), Dionysius of Corinth (AD 171), Clement of Alexandria (AD

[69] Flavius Josephus, *Antiquities of the Jews,* trans. William Whiston, (Delmarva, 2016), Book 20, Chapter 9, Section 1, Digital.

150-215), Tertullian of Carthage (AD 155-240), and Origen of Alexandria (AD 185-254) tell us of various apostles who died for their witness, but the church historian Eusebius of Caesarea (AD 260-341) gives the most extensive account of those who were martyred for their proclamation of the resurrection of Jesus. These ancient writers tell us Peter was crucified upside down in Rome, Andrew was crucified in Greece, Thomas was run through with a spear in India, Philip was crucified in Heliopolis, Matthew was run through with a spear in Ethiopia, Mark was dragged to death in Alexandria, and Paul was beheaded in Rome. In the end, of the original twelve disciples, only John is reported to have survived into old age to die of natural causes in Ephesus, after returning from his exile on the island of Patmos.

The determination and courage of these followers of Jesus is inspiring, to say the least, but it is also the most convincing evidence there is confirming the historicity of Jesus' resurrection. These men were among those who claimed to see Jesus dead and then alive again, who said they touched him, spoke with him, ate with him, and saw the wounds of his crucifixion. They alone knew whether or not their testimony was true and, in the end, not one of them recanted their story, even in the face of torture and death! Some people will lie for their own gain or to protect others. Conspirators will agree to join together in a lie to achieve a common goal. But who is willing to maintain a lie in the face of death when it is not in their own or a loved one's best interest? Some are duped into dying for something they believe to be true but are unknowingly being deceived by someone who knows it is a lie. The apostolic martyrs knew whether Jesus' resurrection was factually true, and they were willing to trade their own lives for the truth of that testimony. If these men had agreed to a grand conspiracy and were lying about their experience of the resurrected Jesus, what would motivate them to maintain that lie in the face of such pain and death? There was no worldly gain in store for them, they were not protecting others, nor were they achieving some kind of political end. The only hope they had was the certainty that a new and gloriously transforming life awaited them beyond the grave. It strains credulity to believe that not one of these who claimed to witness the resurrection would recant their testimony rather than die a slow, painful death… unless they knew it really is true.

No first century Jew would make up a story that was first witnessed by women who put their male counterparts to shame. No Roman guard would willingly allow a sealed tomb to be opened and robbed when he knew his life depended on preventing it. No grave robber would carefully unwrap and rearrange valuable grave cloths, leaving them behind in the tomb. No ghostly apparition would touch those to whom it appeared and eat food with them. No imposter would bear the wounds of the cross and be able to appear and disappear at will from a rock tomb and locked rooms. No conspiracy would ever promote and maintain a lie that consistently resulted in poverty, persecution, and painful death for themselves and their loved ones over many years. When we look at the Gospel accounts of Jesus' resurrection in the light of archaeology, history, and culture, we see that it constitutes clear and convincing eyewitness testimony that Jesus died, rose from the dead, was gloriously transformed, appeared to many of his disciples, and ascended into heaven.

 # THE LIFE

WHY THE RESURRECTION MATTERS

What are the moments that have shaped your identity and defined your life? I remember how the cold winter air felt in my throat the night I stood at the rail fence near our barn in rural Washington State, looked up into the brilliance of a billion stars, and knew for the first time that Jesus was the Creator of the universe who loved and accepted me without reservation. I remember the firm handshake Pam gave me and the look in her sparkling steel-blue eyes the Sunday morning we first met in a Dutch farmhouse near the Belgian border. I remember the blinding flash of light when my car hit a semi-truck head on at 60 miles per hour… and waking up in a hospital bed two days later, broken into thirty pieces. I remember the smell of spice in the air when I walked through Jaffa Gate into the Old City of Jerusalem for the first time and stopped to stare at the stones that had welcomed ancient priests, prophets, and kings. I remember the pushing and the yelling, followed by deafening silence… and the hot tears on my face when my blue-faced son finally took his first breath and let out the sweetest cry I had ever heard.

Some experiences in life are so significant they stick with you, because they have the power to shape you and define your path for years to come. When the disciples of Jesus saw the empty tomb, heard the proclamation of angels, and encountered the risen Jesus, it was the ultimate defining experience. Watching Jesus die a terrible death on the cross, and then seeing him unmistakably alive and radically transformed into a gloriously new kind of life literally changed everything. It was like pushing a massive reset button on a cosmic scale!

The disciples' entire framework for life had already been fundamentally altered by the singularly unique life Jesus shared with them. For three years they heard him teach with divine authority, watched him act in supernatural power, and learned an entirely new way to live. The resurrection put all these other experiences into perspective. The resurrection conclusively demonstrated that Jesus is in fact who he claimed to be: the Son of David, the Messiah of Israel, the Son of Man, yes, the incarnate Son of God. In the introduction of his letter to the Romans, Paul points to Jesus' resurrection as the defining proof of his true identity: *his Son, who was descended from David according to the flesh and was declared to be the Son of God in power according to the Spirit of holiness by his resurrection from the dead, Jesus Christ our Lord* (Romans 1:3-4). This is why establishing the truth of Jesus' resurrection is so important. It is not enough to say Jesus was a good man and a great teacher, or even a prophet of God. Jesus repeatedly claimed to be much more than that. From his messianic self-references, to his use of the title Son of Man from Daniel 7, to his seven "I AM" statements, to his claim to have existed before Abraham, Jesus clearly claimed to be more than just a man.

Once during the Feast of Dedication, Jesus taught in the eastern colonnade of the Temple courts, and when the people picked up rocks to stone him, he asked for which of his good works they were going to kill him. They replied, *"It is not for a good work that we are going to stone you but for blasphemy, because you, being a man, make yourself God"* (John 10:33). Jesus did not contradict their conclusion. The religious leaders understood the implications of Jesus' teaching, and the High Priest asked him directly before the Sanhedrin, *"I adjure you by the living God, tell us if you are the Christ, the Son of God." Jesus said to him, "You have said so. But I tell you, from now on you will see the Son of Man seated at the right hand of Power and coming on the clouds of heaven." Then the high priest tore his robes and said, "He has uttered blasphemy. What further witnesses do we need? You have now heard his blasphemy. What is your judgment?" They answered, "He deserves death."* (Matthew 26:63-66) Jesus was sentenced to die because of his claim of divinity. It is no wonder the natural response of those who encountered the risen Jesus was to fall at his feet and worship him! (Matthew 28:9, John 20:28)

Anyone can claim to be God, but only God can defeat death. In his full humanity, Jesus repeatedly pointed toward his full divinity. But his resurrection is the ultimate proof that Jesus is who he claimed to be—the preexistent Creator of the universe who entered into history by emptying himself and becoming fully human. He lived among us to show us how life is meant to be lived; he died as the perfect sacrifice to overcome the guilt and shame of our sin; and he rose from the dead in order to defeat the power of death itself. Jesus' resurrection is what makes his death effective as a perfect sacrifice, because it demonstrates that Jesus alone has the power to overcome the core effects of sin, death, and eternal separation from God. C. S. Lewis described it so well in his beautiful allegory where a white witch has kept the land of Narnia underneath her spell so that it is "always winter, but never Christmas." The dramatic end of the story comes when Aslan, the great Lion who is the Son of the Emperor from across the Sea, offers himself to the witch and allows her to kill him on the ancient stone table. Lewis introduces Aslan's dramatic return from the dead by explaining, "[The witch] would have known that when a willing victim who had committed no treachery was killed in a traitor's stead the Table would crack and death itself would start working backwards."[70] Jesus' death has begun to unravel the power of death and has inaugurated a whole new reality, which Jesus described as the coming Kingdom of God.

Jesus' resurrection literally changes everything. That is why it is so important to determine the historical reliability of the Gospel accounts. Paul described what is at stake in his letter to the Corinthians; *And if Christ has not been raised, then our preaching is in vain and your faith is in vain. We are even found to be misrepresenting God, because we testified about God that he raised Christ, whom he did not raise if it is true that the dead are not raised. For if the dead are not raised, not even Christ has been raised. And if Christ has not been raised, your faith is futile and you are still in your sins. Then those also who have fallen asleep in Christ have perished. If in Christ we have hope in this life only, we are of all people most to be pitied. But in fact Christ has been raised from the dead, the firstfruits of those who have fallen asleep.* (1 Corinthians 15:14-20) Paul had met the risen Jesus on the road to Damascus. He heard the personal testimony of Peter, James, John, and countless others who had encountered the risen Jesus in Jerusalem and Galilee. So he could say with certainty that *in fact* Christ has been raised from the dead.

Thomas was not present when Jesus first appeared to the disciples in the upper room. He told them, *"Unless I see in his hands the mark of the nails, and place my finger into the mark*

---

[70] C. S. Lewis, *The Lion, the Witch, and the Wardrobe*, (New York, Harper Collins, 1978), 164.

of the nails, and place my hand into his side, I will never believe." The following week Jesus appeared to Thomas and said, *"Put your finger here, and see my hands; and put out your hand, and place it in my side. Do not disbelieve, but believe." Thomas answered him, "My Lord and my God!"* Such undeniable proof that the same Jesus who was executed on the cross was now fully alive and radically transformed convinced Thomas that Jesus had risen from the dead and moved him to recognize Jesus as his Lord and God. It is easy for us who do not share in this rare privilege to have physically encountered both the historical and the risen Jesus to give excuses for our lack of faith. But Jesus made it clear that this privilege, beneficial as it might be, is not necessary to believe in him: *"Have you believed because you have seen me? Blessed are those who have not seen and yet have believed."* (John 20:25-29)

Jesus is warning us not to miss this blessing and make the mistake of Thomas by demanding physical proof of the resurrection in order to believe. Paul tells us, *faith comes from hearing, and hearing through the word of Christ* (Romans 10:17). John explains this is precisely why he wrote his Gospel; *Now Jesus did many other signs in the presence of the disciples, which are not written in this book; but these are written so that you may believe that Jesus is the Christ, the Son of God, and that by believing you may have life in his name* (John 20:30-31). When we read the eyewitness testimony of those who interacted with the risen Jesus, the Holy Spirit speaks to us through the words and actions of Jesus to produce faith in our hearts and minds. It is good to understand the factual and logical basis for the historical reliability of these accounts, as we have shown. It is good to visit Jerusalem to see with your own eyes and touch with your own hand the stone where Jesus was crucified and the tomb where he was buried. But, in the end, listening for the voice of Jesus as he speaks to us by his Spirit through the biblical witness of those who saw him resurrected produces the faith in us that we need.

We can all identify with Thomas in our struggle to trust and follow the risen Jesus, but rather than using him as an excuse for surrendering to doubt, we can see him as a role model for exercising faith. Thomas asked for what he needed to help him believe, and Jesus responded by giving him exactly what he needed. Earlier Jesus promised his disciples, *"And I tell you, ask, and it will be given to you; seek, and you will find; knock, and it will be opened to you"* (Luke 11:9). Thomas knocked and then walked through that opened door by exercising the faith Jesus gave him. The author of Hebrews put it this way: *without faith it is impossible to please him, for whoever would draw near to God must believe that he exists and that he rewards those who seek him* (Hebrews 11:6). If we ask Jesus to help us believe, he will plant in us the faith we need to trust and follow him; all it takes is a mustard seed!

Sometimes we mistakenly assume that faith is the absence of doubt and feel we can't believe until every hint of doubt is banished from our heart. When a man brought his son to Jesus for healing, he expressed both doubt and faith together: *"if you can do anything, have compassion on us and help us." And Jesus said to him, "If you can'! All things are possible for one who believes." Immediately the father of the child cried out and said, "I believe; help my unbelief!"* (Mark 9:22-24) Like this man we are all a mixture of faith and doubt; the question is to which we will respond. Doubt is not the absence of faith, it is the context in which faith must be exercised. Of course, we may still have doubts about the resurrection of Jesus, but we have abundant reason to trust and believe it is true. When we read these biblical accounts and listen to what Jesus is saying through the Spirit, faith is planted in our hearts. When we, like this desperate father, decide to exercise that faith even in the face of our doubts, our faith grows stronger. As we continue listening to Jesus through the words of the Scriptures, that faith is nourished. Every step of faith we take in following Jesus shapes us more and more into his image, and now our lives become a witness that plants faith in the hearts of others. This is how the Kingdom of God comes!

JESUS' RESURRECTION AND THE KINGDOM OF GOD

In Jesus the disciples met someone whose daily life was a perfect expression of the amazing words he spoke. He did not borrow derivative authority from the teachings of other rabbis but spoke directly out of his relationship with the Father. The disciples experienced unconditional love and gracious acceptance from Jesus that revealed their true identity as beloved children of God, and moved them to lay down their lives for others in love. Listening to Jesus, they received insights into the Scriptures that reflected the very heart of God and described life the way it is meant to be lived. The disciples were given a living example of that teaching and were empowered to imitate this Jesus-shaped way of life. Jesus broke down the barriers between them and welcomed his followers into a new kind of family, not defined by blood or religion or politics, but by a passionate pursuit of doing God's will on earth as it is done in heaven. They witnessed unexplainable acts of miraculous power that were motivated purely by compassion for the hurting and the outcast, and then learned how to do the same by walking and speaking in Jesus' authority. They were given a vision of a future in which God ultimately transforms and redeems all the pain and injustice of this broken creation, and ushers in the fullness of his righteous eternal reign.

All this was a powerful demonstration of Jesus' apocalyptic vision which he simply described as *"the kingdom of God."* In his words and actions, Jesus showed us what life looks like when God's will is done on earth as it is in heaven, even in a fallen world that is still subject to the power of the enemy. The life of Jesus is a picture of God's Kingdom breaking into the kingdoms of this world. This clash of kingdoms is why there is always so much opposition to Jesus and his followers. Jesus was restoring the reign of God on earth through his life and the lives of those who followed him, but the dominions and rulers of this world reacted by launching an all-out war in a desperate bid to hold on to power. Although it was intended to take him out, Jesus' death struck the decisive blow to the kingdom of darkness, which is the power behind these earthly kingdoms and rulers. As Paul wrote, *He disarmed the rulers and authorities and put them to open shame, by triumphing over them in him"* (Colossians 2:15). Jesus' resurrection demonstrated that the outcome of this cosmic war is already certain. Jesus will return in power and glory to finally vanquish sin, death, hell, and the devil once and for all! Paul describes the final victory: *Then comes the end, when he delivers the kingdom to God the Father after destroying every rule and every authority and power. For he must reign until he has put all his enemies under his feet. The last enemy to be destroyed is death.* (1 Corinthians 15:24-26) The resurrection of Jesus is our guarantee that Jesus has the authority and power to achieve this eternal victory and that we will be raised with him to participate in his triumph forever. The risen Jesus gave this powerful assurance to John when he was exiled to the island of Patmos: *"Fear not, I am the first and the last, and the living one. I died, and behold I am alive forevermore, and I have the keys of Death and Hades"* (Revelation 1:17-18)

The resurrection of Jesus not only assures us of how the story of fallen humanity will end; it also shows us our part in that redemptive story today. The men and women who followed the historical Jesus during his life on earth saw and learned how the Kingdom of God works in daily life, but it wasn't until Jesus was raised from the dead and the Holy Spirit came to permanently dwell in their hearts that these disciples were able to fully step into their apostolic calling. Before the resurrection and outpouring of the Spirit, the followers of Jesus were often afraid, confused, and unsure of what to do. After the combined impact of Easter and Pentecost, they were transformed into men and women who were filled with faith, following Jesus' way of life, and determined to bring the Good News of the Kingdom to the ends of the earth. What changed? The indwelling Spirit of God gave them the power of a whole new kind of life made possible by the death and resurrection of Jesus. Paul described it this way, *If the Spirit of him who raised Jesus from the dead dwells in you, he who raised Christ Jesus from the dead will also give life to your mortal bodies through his Spirit who dwells in you* (Romans 8:11).

In Jesus' life, death, and resurrection, and in the outpouring of the Holy Spirit, God's Kingdom has begun to break into this fallen world. When Jesus returns at the end of history, he will fully establish God's reign *in heaven and on earth and under the earth* (Philippians 2:10). But until that day comes, God's Kingdom will continue breaking into this broken world through those who are following Jesus in the power of the Spirit to do God's will on earth as it is in heaven. When Jesus said, *"Come, follow me"* he offered to show people what the inbreaking Kingdom of God looks like in daily life. When he said, *"Go and make disciples,"* he commissioned the disciples to be agents of that same Kingdom to the ends of the earth until he returns. Each of us who encounter Jesus by the power of the Spirit must decide how we will respond to those two callings.

- *"Come, follow me"* Will we enter into relationship with other followers of Jesus so we can see his Way in their lives and hear his Truth in their words, and so learn to live this truly abundant Jesus-shaped Life as part of a new kind of spiritual family?
- *"Go and make disciples"* Will we allow his Spirit to lead us as part of that family on mission to make disciples by inviting others to follow us as we follow Jesus and training them to do the things he did? If so, we will be part of God's coming Kingdom which even the gates of hell cannot overcome!

It is not enough to agree with the idea that Jesus is who he said he is and that he did what the Bible says he did. If we are going to live as part of his coming Kingdom, we will open ourselves to encounter the risen Jesus, learn to follow him in relationship with those ahead of us on the journey, and allow his Spirit to lead us in making disciples who are living out the will of God on earth as it is in heaven. This is what it means to live in the power of Jesus' resurrection.

EPILOGUE

JESUS' MOVEMENT: THIS IS JUST THE BEGINNING

"As the Father has sent me, even so I am sending you." (John 20:21)

STORY: A FAILURE ANSWERS THE CALL

Simon sat on the aft seat of the family fishing boat, hunched over the gunnel, trailing his hand in the water and watching the first streaks of light break over the eastern ridge. It had been years since he spent a night hauling nets on the Sea of Galilee, and he could feel it in his aching back and shoulders. It would be nice if he and his six friends had something to show for all their work, but they had caught nothing and now dawn had come. But his mind drifted away. It seemed like his head had been swimming ever since that Sunday morning Mary Magdalene woke them up with her mad pounding on the outer door. Simon could hardly remember all the unexpected things that had happened in the days that followed. *Who could have ever imagined it all!* Yet he was clear about the one undeniable truth he had experienced—the crucified Jesus was in fact alive again and was the same person they had known, physically present yet gloriously trans-formed.

Simon was shaken from his pondering by a voice calling to them from the shore, "Children, do you have any fish?" Thomas frowned and simply replied, "No," with a dis-dainful tone that warned the stranger not to rub salt in their wounds. The man on the shore said to them, "Cast the net on the right side of the boat, and you will find some." They all had the same thought. *Who has the audacity to tell us how to fish?!* But a memory stirred in Simon's mind. He caught John's eye. "Quick, help me lower these nets!" He and John dropped the long trammel net over the side while the others manned the oars. The net started to trail behind the boat, but it was barely in the water before the ropes began to pull tight. "Turn the boat! Turn the boat!" Simon gestured wildly. He could see the net was already full of fish. It was so full, the seven of them couldn't even lift it into the boat!

This had only ever happened one other time in his life, a few years earlier in a cove just a mile east of here. John must have remembered the same thing, because at that moment he grabbed Simon by the shoulders, pulled his face up close, and blurted out, "It is the Lord!" Before he could think twice, Simon pulled on his cloak and jumped into the water, swimming toward the stranger on shore. Wading out of the water, his waterlogged clothes dragging him down, Simon's excitement suddenly gave way to shame. He was the one who had boasted he would never deny Jesus, yet that is exactly what he had done. Three times. He had failed to live up to the name Jesus had given him. *Peter; so-called "Rocky." More like lake mud than a rock,* he thought as he emerged from the water and the shoreline sucked at his sandals.

Awkwardly, Simon turned and waited for the others who were rowing the boat to shore, towing the bulging net full of fish behind them. By this time, they could smell the charcoal fire Jesus had built on the beach. "Bring some of the fish that you have just caught," Jesus said, "Come and have breakfast." Simon pulled the boat ashore and then helped them haul the massive catch onto the beach. It turned out to be 153 large fish, a record haul rivaling the last time Jesus gave them fishing advice!

As they sat around the fire, no one knew what to say, and Jesus sat silently, watching the fish cook. Simon avoided making eye contact and tried in vain to shut out the memories. *"Come follow me and I will make you fish for people." How could a screw-up like me ever catch people?* It wasn't just the miraculous catch that gave him déjà vu. It was the smell of that charcoal fire, just like the one in the courtyard of the High Priest's house. Now the memories came crashing back like a rockslide. *"You will all fall away because of me this night." "Though they all fall away because of you, I will never fall away." "Truly, I tell you, this very night, before the rooster crows, you will deny me three times." "This man was with Jesus of Nazareth." "I do not know the man."* Simon looked down and blinked back the tears. This is why he went back to fishing for fish. He knew he had forfeited the right to fish for people. He knew he had become a stumbling stone and was no longer worthy to be a building block in Jesus' new family.

They ate without speaking, until Jesus finally broke the silence. "Simon, son of John, do you love me more than these?" Simon replied haltingly, "Yes, Lord; you know that I love you." Jesus said, "Feed my lambs." Simon could hardly believe his ears. *Feed my lambs?! What is he saying?* Jesus repeated the question looking him straight in the eye, "Simon, son of John, do you love me?" He returned the stare and said to him more forcefully, "Yes, Lord; you know that I love you." Jesus said to him, "Tend my sheep." *Tend my sheep? Does he mean what I think he means?* A third time Jesus looked at him and repeated the question, "Simon, son of John, do you love me?" A pang of guilt shot through him like a Roman spear. Three questions for three denials. He cried out, "Lord, you know everything; you know that I love you!" Jesus said to him, "Feed my sheep."

Looking around the fire, Simon could see smiles growing on the faces of his friends. James slapped him on the back. They all understood what Jesus was saying. Peter was being restored as the leader of their family. *How is it possible? Shouldn't it be John? I am not worthy.* Now Peter could see the smile on Jesus' face, and he knew it was true. *I am Peter. It is not just a name, it is a calling. This is who God created me to be. To lead. To love. To lay down my life, just as my Master did.* Peter felt the shame melting away and faith taking its place. It was as if Jesus' words were ringing in his ears, giving him the confidence that he could do what he was being called to do. Now Peter knew his failure was behind him and a whole new life was stretching out ahead of him.

When Jesus got up from the fire, Peter jumped up feeling a thousand pounds lighter. As he walked along with his Rabbi in that familiar way, Jesus' tone turned serious. *"Truly, truly, I say to you, when you were young, you used to dress yourself and walk wherever you wanted, but when you are old, you will stretch out your hands, and another will dress you and carry you where you do not want to go."* Instantly Peter knew what Jesus' was referring to. He remembered his words to them on their final retreat up in Caesarea Philippi, *"If anyone would come after me, let him deny himself and take up his cross and follow me."* Peter understood what Jesus was saying. His cross would be a literal one.

Suddenly he was taken back to that moment in the upper room a few weeks earlier when the risen Jesus had said to them, *"Peace be with you. As the Father has sent me, even so I am sending you."* And then he leaned over, breathed on them and said, *"Receive the Holy Spirit."* Peter realized this was the sending. They were to continue to do the things Jesus had trained them to do no matter what, even if it meant their fate would be the same as Jesus' fate. The Holy Spirit would give them the faith and courage they needed to face this challenge and complete this calling. When Jesus had breathed on them, Peter felt a tingling run through his whole body. He felt that same tingling now up his spine. Jesus stopped, turned to Peter, looked him in the eye and said, "Follow me." In that moment Peter knew he would never deny his Lord again. He would never look back. In the authority of Jesus' name and by the power of his Spirit, he would fish for people.

He would make disciples. He would be a building block in God's new family. He would shepherd the sheep entrusted to him. No. Matter. What.

THE SENT ONES

For forty incredible days, the risen Jesus appeared to his twelve closest disciples and the wider community of his followers outside Jerusalem, in the upper room, along the road to Emmaus, on the shores of the Sea of Galilee, and on the Mount of Olives. Through these encounters they became absolutely convinced of the truth of the resurrection, and that changed everything. They came to understand Jesus' full humanity and full divinity, as evidenced by their worship of him and his acceptance of that worship. The risen Jesus continued to teach them from the Scriptures and talk to them about the Kingdom of God. The Gospel writers only give us brief accounts of their time with the risen Jesus, but if Luke's description of the encounter on the road to Emmaus is any indication, we can be sure Jesus gave them a powerful post-resurrection perspective on their identity and mission. As Cleopas and the other disciple said afterward, *"Did not our hearts burn within us while he talked to us on the road, while he opened to us the Scriptures?"* (Luke 24:32)

The risen Jesus made it clear to the disciples that his time with them was limited because he was returning to his Father. Jesus told Mary Magdalene outside the empty tomb, *"Do not cling to me, for I have not yet ascended to the Father; but go to my brothers and say to them, 'I am ascending to my Father and your Father, to my God and your God.'"* (John 20:17). But he also gave them the assurance, as he had on that last night before his arrest, that he would not abandon them. In a dramatic prophetic act, *he breathed on them and said to them, "Receive the Holy Spirit"* (John 20:22). He was giving them a foretaste of the empowering outpouring of the Spirit that was soon to come on the day of Pentecost. Just before his ascension, he made this promise explicit: *"But you will receive power when the Holy Spirit has come upon you, and you will be my witnesses in Jerusalem and in all Judea and Samaria, and to the end of the earth."* (Acts 1:8)

Ultimately the risen Jesus was giving his disciples confirmation of the way forward which he had taught them during the three years they spent together:

• **Vision**: Jesus described his compelling vision again and again through his teaching of *the kingdom of God,* which is nothing less than heaven breaking in and transforming this earth! Jesus demonstrated this vision by offering *good news to the poor...*

liberty to the captives and recovering of sight to the blind, to set at liberty those who are oppressed, to proclaim the year of the Lord's favor (Luke 4:18-19).

• **Mission**: Jesus articulated his simple mission statement in Zacchaeus' house which was *to seek and to save the lost* (Luke 19:10). He carried this out by his gracious welcome of outcasts and so-called "sinners," as well as the wealthy and powerful who were willing to let go and submit to him.

• **Values**: Jesus' core values are summed up in his simple challenge to *love the Lord your God with all your heart and with all your soul and with all your mind and with all your strength* and to *love your neighbor as yourself* (Mark 12:30-31). Jesus' Beatitudes from the Sermon on the Mount give us a picture of those values in action; those who mourn are comforted, those who are persecuted are blessed, and those who are meek inherit the earth (Matthew 5:2-12).

• **Strategy**: Every day Jesus modeled his strategy which was simply discipling men and women into his way of life, so that they could do the same with others. He made disciples in the context of an extended spiritual family that was living on mission together, seeking and saving the lost. He did all of this in the authority given to him as a Son of the Father and by the power that flowed from the exercise of that authority.

The risen Jesus went on to confirm this vision, mission, values, and strategy when he commissioned his disciples in Galilee: *"All authority in heaven and on earth has been given to me. Go therefore and make disciples of all nations, baptizing them in the name of the Father and of the Son and of the Holy Spirit, teaching them to observe all that I have commanded you. And behold, I am with you always, to the end of the age."* (Matthew 28:18-20) This Great Commission is nothing less than the disciples' marching orders to continue doing everything they saw Jesus doing which he had trained them to do! And all of it is made possible by the authority and power that flows from Jesus' continued presence in and among his followers through the Holy Spirit.

The disciples' certainty about the resurrection of Jesus, their understanding of his identity as God who became flesh, their clarity about the commission he gave them, and above all, the empowering presence of his Spirit within transformed these ordinary men and women from cowardly deserters into bold witnesses willing to lay down their lives for the truth of their testimony. This is what happened to Peter, the failure, at that charcoal fire. He was a sheep who was becoming a shepherd! A "disciple" is a follower. An "apostle" is a sent one. Jesus began by inviting men and women to "come follow" as disciples. Now he was commissioning them to "go and make disciples" as apostles who offer that same invitation to others. And that is exactly what they did. The disciples became the disciplers. The sheep became shepherds.

Luke's account in the Acts of the Apostles gives us a vivid picture of the powerful movement Jesus launched through ordinary men and women filled with the Spirit who were following the Way of Jesus, proclaiming the Truth of Jesus, and living the Life of Jesus. They were *followers* who became *the sent ones*. The result was not only the multiplication of disciples living like Jesus, but the formation of extended spiritual families on mission who continued to seek the lost, make disciples, and birth new families across the Mediterranean world. This is how Jesus fulfilled his promise to build his church. As we have seen, historians tell us by the time Constantine adopted Christianity in the early fourth century, over 50% of people in the Roman Empire had become followers of Jesus! The movement Jesus began literally transformed the most powerful empire in the world. This is what changed the world then. This is what is changing our world today. Making disciples by inviting them into a relationship with God through baptism and training them to live in the Way and Truth of Jesus as part of an extended spiritual family on mission is our primary calling until he returns. We are to become disciples who make disciples who make disciples. We are to live as both sheep and shepherds at the same time.

OUR MARCHING ORDERS

Traveling to the places where Jesus lived and carried out his mission is a vivid reminder that the followers of Jesus who changed the world were ordinary, everyday men and women just like us. When you walk the narrow streets of Jerusalem and climb the dusty hills of Galilee, you are confronted with the fact that the Gospels are not just fairy tales or epic hero myths, but eyewitness accounts of real events in actual places that transformed flesh and blood people to live extraordinary lives.

Many years ago, I was giving a slide show (with actual slides of film in a carousel projector!) to a classroom of third graders. It was the week before Easter, and I was showing them the places where the events of Holy Week took place. The room was dark and the students seemed transfixed, when suddenly a little boy cried out, "So it's not just a story!" As he saw photos of the actual places where these events occurred, he suddenly realized the biblical narratives his parents read to him at bedtime were not like the fictitious stories he got from other children's books. These were real events happening in real places to real people!

We all need to come to that same realization if we are going to learn to follow Jesus, live as part of his family, and extend his Kingdom to others. As we have seen, that does not mean you need to travel to the Holy Land and visit the ancient sites, but it does mean you have to recognize the characters in the Gospels are real, everyday people, just like you and me. As we see that the men and women who first followed Jesus are just like us, we will be inspired to follow the *Way* of Jesus as they did, trust the *Truth* of Jesus as they did, and live the *Life* of Jesus as they did by the power of his Spirit!

Are you ready to make disciples, build spiritual family, and live out the mission of God in the world? If so, embrace your identity as a *follower* and respond to your call as a *sent one*, knowing the very power that changed history 2,000 years ago is at work in and through you to do the same today!

About the Author

Bob Rognlien is a pastor, speaker, author, and consultant who teaches and writes extensively on how biblical culture informs contemporary mission. For the past twenty-five years he has led unique spiritual pilgrimages in the historical footsteps of Jesus and Paul. Author of five books, Bob currently serves as a North American Director for 3DMovements and Founder/Director of Footsteps Experience Ministries. He earned a master's degree from Princeton Theological Seminary and has conducted post-graduate studies at Hebrew University and the Ecole Biblique et Archeologique in Jerusalem. He and his wife Pam live in Los Angeles where they love sharing life and mission with their children and grandchildren. For more information visit bobrognlien.com.